The First Imperial Age

The First Imperial Age

European Overseas Expansion c. 1400–1715

G. V. Scammell

London and New York

First published 1989 by HarperCollins *Academic*
Second impression 1991

Reprinted 1992, 1997, 2002 by
Routledge
11 New Fetter Lane, London EC4P 4EE

Simultaneously published in the USA and Canada
by Routledge
a division of Routledge, Chapman and Hall, Inc.
29 West 35th Street, New York, NY 10001

Routledge is an imprint of the Taylor & Francis Group

Printed in Great Britain by Bookcraft, Bath

ISBN 0–415–09085–7

Contents

Acknowledgements

I have incurred many more debts in writing this book than can be adequately recorded here. My thanks are due in particular to Professor K. R. Andrews, Dr John Appleby, Professor Sinnappah Arasaratnam, Dr Geneviève Bouchon, Dr Wendy Childs, Professor J. S. Cummins, Dr A. R. Disney, Professor Peter Marshall, Professor Michel Mollat du Jourdin, the late Admiral Avelino Teixeira da Mota, the late Professor Virginia Rau and the Rev. Dr Teotonio de Souza SJ. They are of course in no way responsible for the use I have made of the ideas and information they have so generously provided.

I am especially grateful for the kindness and encouragement of the late Professor John Bromley, for the goodwill of Professor Denys Hay, and for the unfailing wisdom, scholarship and friendship of Professor Charles Boxer. Claire L'Enfant, at whose suggestion the book was undertaken, has been of exemplary kindness and patience in ensuring its completion. But my greatest debt is to the stimulus and support of my wife, companion in golden years of sailing and in travels by land and sea in many parts of the world here discussed.

Cambridge   G. V. S.
31 March 1988

Introduction

The last remnants of Europe's overseas empires have now all but gone, but their legacy remains. There are acute and world-wide problems of relationships between peoples of different coloured skins. There is a conviction that Europe's prosperity in the expansive years of the nineteenth and twentieth centuries was founded on the exploitation of the rest of the globe, thereby condemning much of it to underdevelopment and dependency.

This book is concerned with those centuries before roughly 1715 which saw the beginnings of Europe's rise to world hegemony, with Europeans firmly established in distant lands, most of them previously largely or totally unknown. Earlier empires there had been in plenty, but none which unshakably spanned the great oceans. Nor is there any parallel before or since to the scale on which European knowledge of the outside world was enlarged, or the pace at which this transformation was effected.

The start, *c.* 1400, was slow and tentative, with (mainly) Portuguese assaults on North Africa and searches in the eastern Atlantic. But between roughly 1500 and 1700, and with a breath-taking surge in the opening decades of the sixteenth century, Europeans in pursuit of Asia and the opportunities encountered *en route*, had determined the outlines of the gigantic African landmass, discovered and in part subjugated the Americas, opened a sea route to the Far East and established themselves in the great and ancient maritime economy of Asia. They marched across the Andes, reached the Rocky Mountains, were marooned in the Seychelles, froze to death in the Arctic, trekked through the jungles of Africa and Brazil, gazed with wonder on the jewels of the Mughal emperors of India and the great cities of China, now identified as the Cathay of Marco Polo. After the circumnavigation (1519–22) commenced by Magellan the intimidating size of the earth and the even more intimidating size of its seas and oceans were understood, but in voyages of unprecedented extent and duration the Atlantic, Pacific and the Indian Ocean were regularly crossed and recrossed. Europeans traded along the maritime routes of the Far East. American silver was carried to Asia and Europe by the shipload, tobacco and sugar from the monoculture plantations of the western Atlantic – their labour provided by African slaves – were imported into the continent. A network of European trading posts, soon seeking to expand, was created along the coasts of the Far East. White settlements took root in the West. Indigenous peoples the world over were converted to Christianity. Colonies became matters of dispute between European states and new strategies were devised for their acquisition or defence. And though Europeans knew the coasts of the worlds they have revealed better than what lay behind them, they had achieved enough to assure themselves that they had at last surpassed the deeds of the revered heroes of Antiquity.

The first imperial age of the centuries between roughly 1400 and 1715 has a unity beyond mere historical convenience. After the spectacular expansion of the era of Magellan and Cortés there was a lull – but not a halt – before the renewed exploration and conquests of the era of Clive, Cook and their successors. By the early 1700s the oceanic maritime economy established by the Iberians had largely passed into the hands of the Dutch, French and English. The foundations of British hegemony in India and of Anglo-French conflict in North America and the West Indies had been laid. The first Protestant colonies were, after a lengthy prelude of failure, growing at a prodigious rate around 1700, while the economies of the Iberian Americas, in trouble in the seventeenth century, were reviving, as were the surviving indigenous populations of the Spanish Indies. Some structure of imperial government had been established everywhere – even eventually in English Puritan America – and its reform, which was to have such unexpected consequences, was much in the air with the dawn of the Enlightenment. Colonies and metropolitan states hardly dwelt in harmony together, but there were as yet no such movements for independence as emerged in the late 1700s. And by the end of the first imperial age the wider world had begun to make some mark on the culture of Europe.

I have not attempted a detailed narrative of exploration, conquest and settlement. Instead, after an outline of the salient features of the story, the ensuing chapters investigate a number of general themes – the reasons for Europe's expansion, how it was that Europeans could establish themselves in some parts of the world but not in others, the means they employed to exploit their new possessions and opportunities, the nature of colonial societies and economies, and the influence on Europe of empire and imperial experience.

Notes and references have been kept to a minimum, but it will appear – or so at least I hope – that the book is based on more than the works cited. It reflects years of wartime service and subsequent travel in many of the lands and across many of the seas discussed, and it employs evidence derived from archives in Europe and elsewhere.

Place-names are given in what I have thought the most easily recognizable forms. Books mentioned are published in London unless otherwise stated.

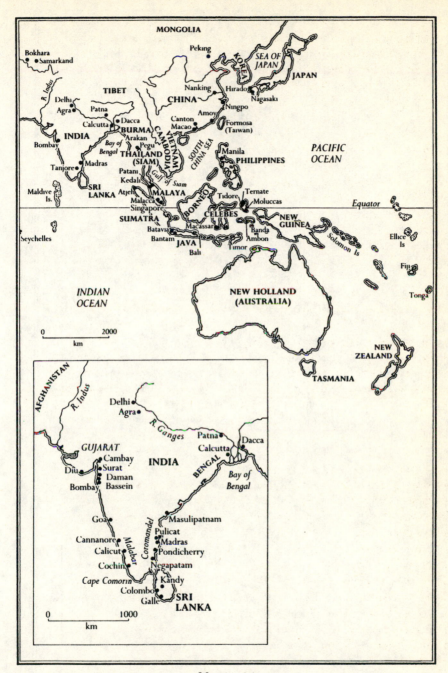

Map 1 *Asia*

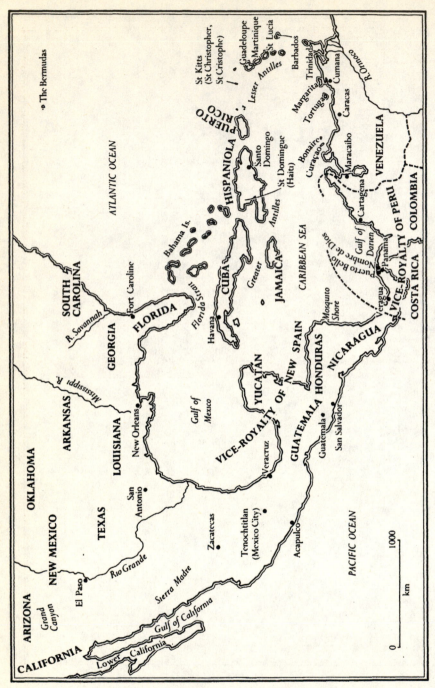

Map 2 *Mexico and West Indies*

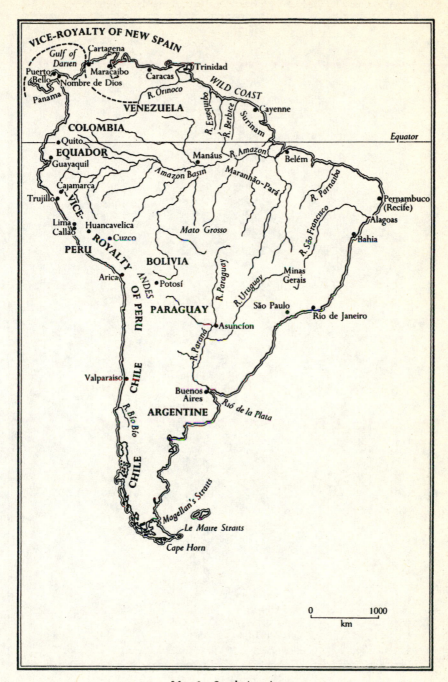

VICE-ROYALTY OF NEW SPAIN

Gulf of Darien • Cartagena

Puerto
Bello • Maracaibo • Trinidad
Nombre de Dios • Caracas

Panama

R. Orinoco

WILD COAST

VENEZUELA

Cayenne

COLOMBIA

R. Essequibo

R. Berbice

Surinam

Equator

• Quito

EQUADOR

Manáus

R. Amazon

Belém

Guayaquil

Amazon Basin

Maranhão-Pará

R. Parnaiba

• Cajamarca

Pernambuco
(Recife)

Trujillo

VICE-

Mato Grosso

R. São Francisco

Alagoas

Lima
Callao • Huancavelica

ROYALTY

Cuzco

Bahia

PERU

OF

BOLIVIA

Minas
Gerais

ANDES

Arica

PERU

• Potosí

R. Paraguay

R. Uruguay

São Paulo

PARAGUAY

Asuncfon

Rio de Janeiro

R. Paraná

CHILE

Valparaiso

Buenos
Aires

Rió de la Plata

ARGENTINE

R. Bío Bío

CHILE

Magellan's Straits

Le Maire Straits

Cape Horn

0   1000
km

Map 3   *South America*

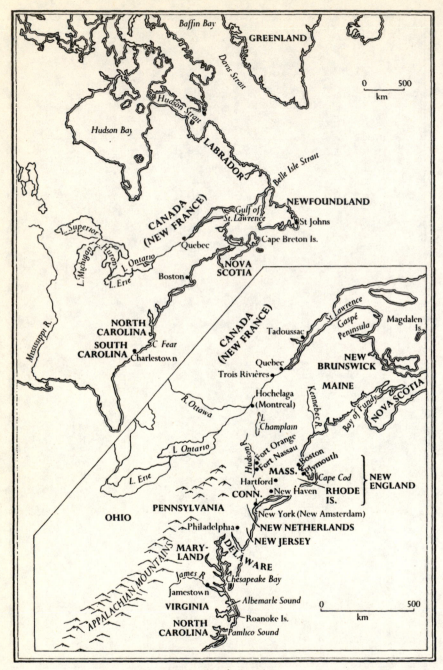

Map 4 *North America*

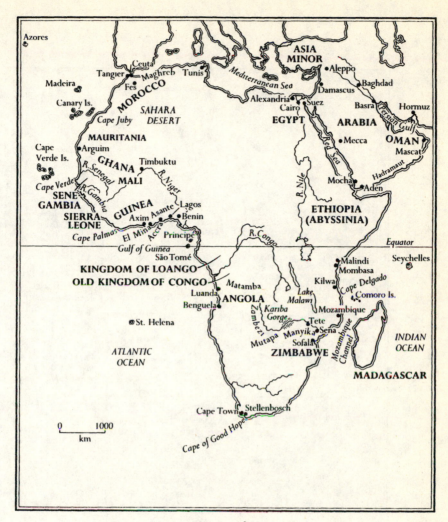

Map 5 *Africa*

Map

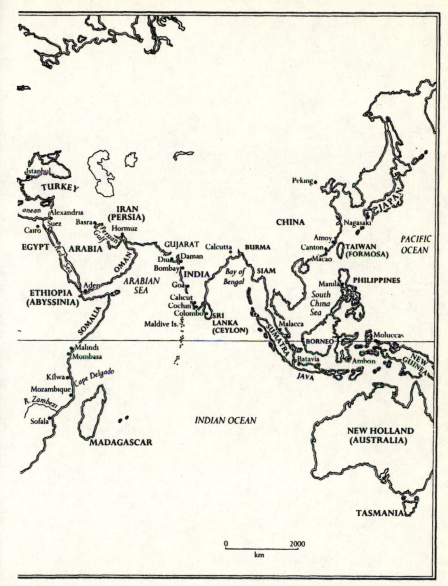

Istanbul
TURKEY
anean
Alexandria
Cairo
Suez
EGYPT
ARABIA
Red Sea
ETHIOPIA
(ABYSSINIA)
SOMALIA
Basra
IRAN
(PERSIA)
Hormuz
Persian Gulf
OMAN
Aden
ARABIAN
SEA
GUJARAT
Diu
Daman
Bombay
INDIA
Goa
Calicut
Cochin
Colombo
Maldive Is.
SRI
LANKA
(CEYLON)
Calcutta
Bay of
Bengal
BURMA
SIAM
CHINA
Peking
Nagasaki
Amoy
Canton
Macao
TAIWAN
(FORMOSA)
JAPAN
PACIFIC
OCEAN
Manila
PHILIPPINES
South
China
Sea
Malacca
SUMATRA
BORNEO
Moluccas
NEW
GUINEA
Batavia
Ambon
JAVA
INDIAN OCEAN
Malindi
Mombasa
Kilwa
Cape Delgado
Mozambique
R. Zambezi
Sofala
MADAGASCAR
NEW HOLLAND
(AUSTRALIA)
TASMANIA

0   2000
km

6

1 Imperial beginnings

Successful crossings of great oceans were nothing new to mankind long before Europe's first imperial age. There had been epic migrations by sea, such as those of the Polynesians, in the prehistoric era. The empires of classical Antiquity in the West had traded to Asia. Arab seamen were sailing the hazardous route to China by about AD 700. Indonesians reached East Africa in the ninth and tenth centuries, just as the Scandinavians, after enduring the far more formidable North Atlantic, colonized Iceland, Greenland and even – briefly – an inhospitable strip of the coast of north-east America. In the high Middle Ages (roughly 1200–1300) citizens of the precocious maritime states of Italy, most notably Venice and Genoa, penetrated to the Far East – some by land and sea from the Levant, others along the great transcontinental caravan routes – while Catalan and Genoese sailors explored the shores and waters of West Africa and Genoese vessels appeared in the Indian Ocean. Yet only occasionally did such European enterprise have any enduring consequences. Overseas settlements were overthrown (as was the Latin kingdom momentarily established around the holy city of Jerusalem) or collapsed (as did Norse Greenland) and, though western trade with Asia and Africa continued to flow, it did so along age-old channels and largely under non-European control.

Very different, however, was the outcome of the voyages undertaken from Europe after 1400 – the foundations of a hegemony ultimately binding so many of the peoples of the world to the white man's will and benefit. Even so, the beginnings were unimpressive enough. At the very time that Chinese ships were sailing the Arabian Sea and the Indian Ocean, and perhaps reaching as far as South America, the Portuguese were engaged in the laborious exploration of the west coast of Africa, which was to occupy them almost till 1500, and the English were renewing Europe's contact with Iceland, insignificant and on the point of extinction. Indeed in the early modern centuries (c. 1400–1600) the realms of Christendom hardly looked the predestined conquerors of the world, of which their knowledge was, to put it charitably, skimpy. Scholars had long understood that the earth was spherical and some, with the invincible optimism of their calling, held its circumnavigation to be quite possible. However, the legacy of Christianity decreed Jerusalem to be its centre, obliging the Venetian Fra

1

Mauro to apologize for showing otherwise in his celebrated world map of the mid 1400s. The Americas and the southern hemisphere were unknown, but as a result of trade, travel and exploration in the thirteenth and fourteenth centuries, cartographers were able to record, with some degree of accuracy, the geography of North Africa, the Middle East and even parts of Asia. Nevertheless, serious misunderstandings remained and were aggravated by the recovery of the works of classical authorities, received with adulatory deference. Hence some believed the Indian Ocean to be a lake and the extent of the seas that cover so much of the world's surface was in general grossly underestimated.

Nor, apparently, was Europe any better equipped for an imperial destiny in other ways. Its technology was of a modest order, perhaps at its best in the construction of imposing ecclesiastical and military edifices and in the building of a variety of seagoing ships. As the Vikings had long since shown, the continent had vessels capable of regularly crossing oceans and seamen capable of navigating them out of sight of land. But such voyages were rare by 1400, whereas Arab and Chinese sailors continued to make far longer oceanic passages. Furthermore Europe had nothing like the population and probably nothing like the wealth of India or China, whose cities, so it seemed to a fourteenth-century missionary, made those of his native Italy look like mere villages. The political organization of the West was scarcely more imposing. No state before the Spain of Philip II (1556–98) or the France of Louis XIV (1661–1715) possessed a bureaucracy comparable to that which administered China. Rarely could rulers exercise effective authority over more than a few hundred kilometres of their realms unless, like the celebrated Catholic Spanish monarchs, Ferdinand of Aragon (1479–1516) and Isabella of Castile (1474–1504), they were prepared to travel almost incessantly through them. Rarely, too, could they tax their subjects – and least of all the aristocracy – to anything like their real potential without provoking resistance or worse. Wars old and new were ubiquitous. The Christian monarchs of Spain were engaged until 1492 in the subjugation of the Moorish Islamic kingdoms long-established in the peninsula. Well into the fifteenth century France and England were locked in a struggle whose most likely outcome had at one time seemed the destruction of the nebulous French state. Italy and Germany were bywords for internecine warfare and in eastern Europe German power, which had once expanded so dramatically, was in retreat before that of the Slavs. Against external enemies Europe made a consistently poor showing. The crusades to destroy Muslim control of the Holy Land had ignominiously failed by the end of the twelfth century and subsequent godly ventures in North Africa were for long to do no better. Mongol invaders from Asia in the thirteenth century were deflected only by accident and Christian arms were rarely a match for the Muslim Turks who pushed westwards out of Asia Minor from the late 1300s. In the Middle East, Asia and Africa, Islam, a religion of precise and clear precepts and unencumbered by any such priestly hierarchy as western Catholicism supported, was in full and triumphant expansion. In Europe the spiritual authority of the papacy, barely recovered from the damage inflicted by decades in which rival popes had vilified and excommunicated one another (1378–1430), was challenged by a series of powerfully backed reformers such as the Czech John Huss (1369–1415) and the German Martin Luther (1483–1546). From roughly 1350 to 1450 the whole continent was affected in greater or lesser degree by economic depression marked by popular risings, epidemics of plague, depopulation, the contraction of trade and bitter struggles to control such commerce as survived. The hundred years after 1500, a golden age indeed for some, saw renewed crisis, with rising prices, food in short supply and economic, political and religious discontent merging with dynastic ambitions to provoke wars increasingly bitter and destructive which, like the prolonged Anglo-Dutch and Franco-British conflicts, continued through or beyond the latter part of the period with which this book is concerned.

However, famine (as in India), mutual mayhem (as in Japan), disease and revolt (as in China) were the common lot of mankind, and Europe was consequently less at a disadvantage than might at first appear. Furthermore, in many parts of the world where climates were hard, terrain and environment hostile, yields of indigenous crops feeble and communications difficult, societies had developed whose energies were largely or entirely devoted to endeavouring to keep their members alive. Their peoples were hunters, fishers and gatherers of food, occupations prodigiously expensive in time and energy. They had no means of sustaining leisured classes. They were unable to engage in anything which might be described as trade and which might have drawn them into larger political groupings, and their isolation denied them the stimulus that comes from the interaction of cultures. This pattern of nomadic hunting and gathering, of tiny political units and of a bewildering galaxy of languages, occurred among many African peoples south of the Sahara and throughout much of the Americas outside the Andean valleys and Mexican highlands. So, for example, the Amerindians of the Atlantic seaboard of eastern Canada and north-eastern America fished the streams in spring, the sea in summer and retreated to the forests in winter to hunt and shelter from the fury of the elements. Their skills and their knowledge of nature Europeans early admitted, and their style of life has come to be admired, not to say idealized, by a world increasingly divorced from such ways. They cleared the shores where they fished, just as they cleared forest undergrowth to facilitate hunting, yet were careful not to drive to extinction species on which they depended. They lived, chiefly united by bonds of kinship, in small and largely self-contained and self-sustaining communities, with the Micmac of Nova Scotia perhaps numbering no more than 2000 in all in 1500, when indeed the total population of North America may only have been 10 million.

Such peoples were, however, a minority, certainly in numbers, and like as not in terms of the amount of the globe they occupied. Everywhere, other than in Australasia, there existed a rich variety of states and civilizations. In North Africa the descendants of a succession of invaders had settled the coasts and fertile plains of Tunis and Morocco, where a powerful Muslim dynasty scotched European expansionist urges in the sixteenth century. A more or less independent indigenous Berber population survived in the Atlas mountains, while from opulent towns and cities – some pre-classical, some, like Tunis, Arab in origin – a cosmopolitan Jewish and Islamic merchant class traded to Europe, the Far East and across the Sahara. Elsewhere in northern Africa ancient centres of wealth and culture were in decay or difficulty. None was more remarkable than the venerable non-Negro and Christian empire of Ethiopia, briefly and mistakenly idealized by Europeans as the realm of their putative ally, the great and godly Prester John. In the late Middle Ages it was under an able royal house, enjoying reasonable prosperity and supporting a vigorous cultural and religious life.But to the dismay of the first western visitors in the early 1500s it had no identifiable towns, its economy was primarily pastoral and its inhabitants perversely addicted to cow-dung sauce. The emperor was a peripatetic authoritarian chief living on tribute levied from an unfree peasantry, and though the country was certainly Christian it was Coptic, not Catholic. It had strong ties with Egypt and so powerful was the influence of African and Islamic neighbours that its Christian lord had at least three official wives and the greatest in the land appeared before him naked to the waist.

Ethiopia was, however, increasingly at the mercy of formidable Islamic states, notably Mamluk Egypt. Here, in one of the most ancient centres of world civilization, 6 million or so Egyptians were subject to a governing class a few thousand strong recruited from among the warlike Turkish tribes of the south Russian steppe – a legacy from Saladin, the conqueror of the Latin kingdom of Jerusalem. From these peoples, imported as slaves, there was raised the redoubtable and for long invincible cavalry army to whose existence and upkeep the entire regime was dedicated, with state and army ruled by sovereigns themselves drawn from the various regiments. The incessant financial demands of war, reckless fiscal policies and friction with European merchants eventually weakened the country and facilitated the Turkish conquest of 1517. Nevertheless in the late 1400s Egypt was still the major entrepôt for the immensely valuable commerce between Europe and the Orient, with its subjects controlling some of the great luxury trades and doing business as far afield as India and southern China. It was, furthermore, an illustrious centre of religion and the arts, and in Cairo, the veritable seminary of Islam, sultans presided over a court where incense burned, wine flowed, musicians played and poets declaimed to perfumed and silk-clad audiences.

Hardly less remarkable was Negro Mali, controlling, or aspiring to control, the lands lying between the eastern arm of the Niger bend and the Atlantic coast from Senegal to Gambia. It, too, was ruled by Muslim lords, several of whom, like many of their leading subjects, knew the holy city of Mecca and something of the great Islamic world. Aliens were welcome, the royal court cosmopolitan and the country's trade reached from Benin in the south to the shores of the Mediterranean in the north. But, like Ethiopia, Mali was in trouble, threatened by Songhay, which was rich on Niger gold and strong in the possession of the cavalry army such wealth permitted. Elsewhere, whether in Congo in the west or Mutapa in the east, Europeans had no difficulty in identifying – though they might have great troubles in naming – states and empires. And on the east coast of Africa they were to encounter a sequence of great Arab and Islamic cities, trading to Asia, the Red Sea and Iran, and backed by a Negro hinterland where copper and precious metals were mined, farming flourished and imposing architectural remains testified to past glories.

In the Americas, similarly fragmented by natural and climatic obstacles, but unlike Africa and Asia isolated from the rest of the world before the arrival of Christopher Columbus – an insignificant Norse incursion apart – there was an equally rich diversity of cultures. Hunters, of that same remote Asian ancestry as all Amerindian peoples, roamed the Great Plains of what are now western Canada and the USA. There were farmers, like the Iroquois of the present-day New York State and the Huron of southern Ontario, who grew maize in sufficient quantities to produce a surplus for storage or to be traded to non-agricultural neighbours. Such were their skills and those of their fellows that early white colonists could entertain the happy thought of living off the fruits of their labours. Though they dwelt for the most part in villages they also possessed what Europeans recognized as townships, some housing as many as 6000 inhabitants, and were subject to a complex political organization. Groups were under leaders, who might well be women, governing with the advice and consent of councils, and at times recognizing the authority of some paramount chief. Further south, where there had flourished a succession of societies and cultures of often imposing achievement – the Maya, for example, of Yucatán and Honduras (c. AD 300–900), builders on a massive scale and consummate experts in astronomical observation – there had emerged on the eve of the European invasion regimes which were to excite the cupidity, loathing, wonder and even grudging admiration of their despoilers. From a base in the Valley of Mexico the Aztecs had created, in the century before 1500, an empire reaching from the Caribbean to the Pacific. Like that of their Turkish contemporaries in the Old World it was dedicated to war, and primarily devoted to exacting tribute and manpower from subject peoples otherwise largely left to their own devices. Though ruled by an emperor – seen as the representative of the deity on earth – it was still in the process of evolving from a collection of tribes into something of a unitary state. A land-owning aristocracy provided the major governmental officers, most of the priesthood and the military commanders who controlled troops whose many and effective weapons did not, any more than those of other pre-conquest Amerindians, include firearms. Freeborn young males were educated in establishments inculcating the virtues of martial valour and public service. A peasantry paid taxes, provided soldiers and, together with slaves, supplied goods and labour. Trade was largely local, but the Aztecs nevertheless had a merchant class, some of whose members travelled in armed convoy throughout the empire. The Spaniards, on their arrival, remarked on the teeming population they found – which modern estimates put at between 11 and 25 million – the prosperous villages, flourishing markets and great and fastidiously kept cities. With life and leisure sustained by quick-growing maize, there had developed a culture outstanding in engineering, architecture, mathematics and astronomy, yet without any writing other than the painting of records on paper or their inscription on stone. And as many Europeans were to testify, Aztec craftsmen possessed 'amazing skills', particularly in the working of precious metals. The state enforced a stern morality while a numerous priesthood expounded a religion of utter pessimism which saw puny man pitted against gods only to be appeased by frequent and abundant human sacrifice.

Meanwhile, high in the Andes – some 4000 metres above sea-level – there had evolved the Inca empire, which by the end of the fifteenth century controlled most of modern Peru, Chile, Bolivia and Ecuador together with much of the present-day Argentine, and contained in all between 7 and 9 million people. It, too, comprised subjugated ethnic communities, had imposing buildings and cities, and was subject to an emperor held to be divine. But ruling as he did as a benign and paternalistic despot over a tough but obedient populace his powers were more extensive than those of his Aztec counterpart. Much land was state-owned. A peasantry from village clan communities laboured in the public service, not only in agriculture but in such occupations as the making of cloth; in addition it supplied manpower for the army. The empire was unified and controlled by adept imperial policies. Whole peoples were forcibly resettled; a state religion was imposed; provincial aristocrats were obliged to spend some time in the Inca capital; and, as the Spaniards remarked, 'the most punished vice was leisure'. The state could put into the field a well-equipped army, fed and supplied from special estates and depots. An impressive network of roads, designed only for runners and infantry – for no Amerindian people knew the horse or wheeled transport – made the remotest corners of the empire readily accessible, and the realm was defended by a series of powerful and strategically sited fortresses. It was governed, under the emperor, by the 'natural lords' of incorporated ethnic groups and by members of the imperial household and the aristocracy. Inca will was implemented through a bureaucracy which included young men recruited from the ablest of their region, working together for a master who rewarded their loyalty by granting them, among other things, especially delectable wives.

Like Mexico the Inca empire had great temples served by a large, influential and predominantly hereditary priesthood. Andean religion, reflecting a threatening environment of awesome mountains and unpredictable earthquakes, was yet another creed of undiluted pessimism. All disasters were attributed to the ill-will of neglected or offended deities who thus had to be placated by human sacrifice before the Incas engaged in anything of so uncertain an outcome as war. The state insisted on the universal acceptance of its own beliefs – a hierarchy of nature deities headed by a creator god – but was sensibly prepared to tolerate those of subjugated peoples, providing there was no clash with imperial ideals and values. Hence individual households continued to worship their own gods – mummified ancestors among them – with a devotion the Christian missions were to find hard to shake. Inca civilization was the richest in the Americas, despite lack of knowledge of the wheel and writing. A caste of professional historians handed down traditions by word of mouth. Bureaucrats were capable, with the aid of a simple calculating device, of assembling and interpreting statistics. The various peoples of the empire possessed outstanding skills in ceramics, the making of textiles, the working of precious metals and in medicine and engineering – witness the elaborate irrigation schemes and the great stone buildings able to withstand earthquakes. Even the *conquistadores*, not noted for their enthusiasm for indigenous merit, admitted the magnitude of the Incas' achievements.

Nothing, however, could rival the great states and ancient civilizations of Asia. But between them and Europe there lay the swiftly growing possessions of the Muslim Ottoman Turks who, emerging from the obscurity of Asia Minor in the late Middle Ages had, by the early sixteenth century, carved out an empire stretching from Hungary, through the Middle East and into North Africa, with its capital at Istanbul, the former Byzantine Constantinople. Ottoman strength sprang in part, paradoxically enough, from Ottoman weakness. The Turks were few in number and lacking the governmental and technical skills of most of the peoples they subdued. Their regime was consequently one, like that of the Mughals in India, of pragmatic tolerance and one in which ability, not birth, brought promotion. And as Muslims they had to heed the injunction of the Prophet to protect 'people of the book'; adherents, that is, of monotheistic religions with written scriptures. A vital element of their huge, well-organized and highly disciplined army was a corps of infantry raised from Christians of the occupied lands. The Turkish artillery which breached, as no previous attacker had managed, the walls of Constantinople, was largely manufactured and handled by European renegades. Others, many of them Jews from Iberia – the hotbed of anti-semitism – held key posts in the imperial administration, while some of the most celebrated commanders by land and sea were erstwhile Mediterranean peasants or fishermen. Faced as a rule only by indifferent and disunited Christian forces under patricians of meagre ability, a succession of outstanding Ottoman sultans led their armies to the conquest of ever more lands to provide themselves and their followers with loot and tribute. Istanbul housed one of Islam's most renowned mosques and was the capital of rulers who were now both defenders of the faith and, as they saw it, the heirs of Alexander the Great. And in the fifteenth century, having absorbed some of the ancient centres of Mediterranean seafaring, the Turks, like the Arabs before them, took to the sea to become for a time a naval power second to none.

With the Ottomans, as with the Egyptian Mamluks, Europeans intrigued, fought and traded as opportunity offered. Few, however, were able to penetrate overland to the Far East, as had been the case in the thirteenth century when the Mongol empire, stretching from the borders of Hungary to the Sea of Japan, had allowed westerners – none more celebrated than Marco Polo – to reach, trade and live in the Orient. There the Indian subcontinent, once known to the warriors and merchants of Antiquity, was inhabited by a huge population – perhaps reaching 150 million c. 1600 – periodically reduced by famines of a severity which shocked even Europeans accustomed to the grinding poverty of the masses in their homeland. Some Indians were Muslims, but the majority were Hindus, adherents of a religion which inculcated non-violence, taught that the divine assumed human form and maintained the agreeable doctrine that one soul enjoyed many incarnations. Hinduism was ancient and eclectic, reinvigorated over the centuries by such offshoots as Buddhism, and sanctioning and reflecting a society organized in rigidly defined castes.

Travellers marvelled at the priceless precious stones found in the subcontinent and equally at its flourishing agriculture, characterized by elaborate irrigation works and, as along the Indus, the 'great fertility of the land . . . abounding in foodstuffs of all kinds'. Even so India was probably more highly urbanized c. 1600 than was Britain two centuries later and likely as not possessed more big cities – 200,000 inhabitants or above – than did the contemporary West. Many, by their size and splendour, were to elicit the admiration of Europeans, as did the network of roads linking them and the provision made for the comfort of travellers. Other visitors, however, condemned the ubiquity of robbers, the depredations of indigenous pirates and the general squalor, as it seemed, of much of the land. Throughout the subcontinent there were many considerable pockets of industry, employing a work-force whose range of skills and manual dexterity were, then as now, much admired. Indian swords and leatherware were widely known. Textiles were produced almost everywhere, with the output of cottons on a scale, and of a quality, unequalled in any other continent. There was an important internal and long-distance trade, with India not only handling its own products and serving its own needs, but acting as an entrepôt between the

Far and Middle East. Slaves, gold and ivory were imported from East Africa, horses from Iran and silk from China. Cottons were sent to Africa and Indonesia alike, whose spices, together with those of local origin, were exported to the Levant and Iran. This commerce – some carried in Hindu-owned ships, but more in Muslim and often Arab vessels – sustained, as Europeans were quick to appreciate, a rich and resourceful merchant class. Yet these were the least indications that India, quite unlike pre-European America or much of contemporary Africa, was firmly integrated into a wider world whose civilizations her arts, science and religions had influenced for centuries.

The subcontinent's flourishing economy and vast population were subject, when the first Portuguese seamen arrived (1498), to no single authority. Since the eleventh century India, once the seat of great and resplendent Hindu empires, had experienced a succession of Islamic invasions from Central Asia and Afghanistan, so that by the late 1400s virtually all that remained of Hindu power was a string of trading princi-palities on the south-west coast and the state of Vijayanagar in the south, and this too shortly to be overwhelmed by Islam. Hence throughout much of the subcontinent an alien and martial aristocracy had been imposed, or was in the process of being imposed on Hindu society, living, like its counterparts elsewhere, on what it could exact from the subject populace. And the influence of Islam was soon spread further with the emergence, in the sixteenth century, from the remnants of earlier Muslim regimes, of the Mughal empire. This brought to India a culture deriving from Iran, whose language was that of the ruling house, the aristocracy and the cosmopolitan body of soldiers – many of them European, Central Asian or Iranian in origin – who held the major administrative and military posts. Revenues exacted – extorted some would say – from merchants and peasants were lavished on a huge cavalry army or squandered, in envious European eyes, on bizarre whims and luxuries. The tusks of favourite elephants were encrusted with gold; cavalry mounts were bathed in perfume by specially appointed attendants; amidst the opulent refinement of the imperial court every attempt was made to 'stimulate the most jaded appetites to gluttony'. But there was more to the empire than this. Mughal justice, it was generally acknowledged, was swift. Those same officials who collected taxes were also charged with the encouragement of agriculture, the development of irrigation and the fostering of cash crops for export. The empire had ocean-going ships and what, by pre-industrial standards, were good internal communications. And most remarkably, from the long interaction of Hindu and Muslim civilizations, it came to possess a rich and distinguished culture, outstanding in its art and architecture.

Further east the handsome islands of Japan, bristling with vast but elegantly built fortresses, housed a formidably martial people, many of them schooled in the rigorous self-discipline imposed by Zen Buddhism.

They were nominally ruled by a divine emperor and his generalissimo (*shogun*), but were in fact at the mercy of the warlike aristocrats in whose fiefs they lived. Feared by their neighbours, the Japanese nevertheless initially appeared to Europeans, after their rebuffs elsewhere, as affable, hospitable and 'courteous beyond all measure'. On the adjoining mainland lay the huge and ancient empire of China, ruled from 1368–1644 by the Ming dynasty. Its precise territorial extent was uncertain, but in size, population – perhaps 200 million c. 1500 – and most other ways it had no equal. It saw itself as the centre of the world and the cradle of civilization, entitled to receive tribute from barbarians far and near – and thus conveniently able to engage in a trade otherwise supposedly prohibited. The emperor, 'the son of heaven', was virtually absolute, claimed universal sovereignty and lived in the splendid isolation of a vast walled palace in the imperial city of Peking, where only the influential court eunuchs were permitted to dwell. This immense agglomeration of lands was linked, uniquely, by a postal system covering the entire country and run, equally uniquely, by a salaried bureaucracy some 100,000 strong, whose upper echelons were recruited by competitive examination from (basically) the gentry. Hence the government could devise and exact a multiplicity of taxes, or quickly and efficiently muster a huge body of manpower. And hence, too, the empire was more united politically and culturally – and felt itself to be so – than any comparable state of the time. But by the late 1500s China had serious, if far from insoluble, problems. It was weakened by epidemics of disease and frequent harvest failures. Its great civilization had retreated into characteristic introspection and xenophobia. Imperial authority and the unity of the state were undermined by the growing concentration of land in fewer hands, by Mongol pressure from the north and by piratical attacks – allegedly Japanese, but most in fact indigenous – along the coast.

The assumptions of Chinese government and society reflected the traditions of an age-old civilization and the teachings of equally ancient religions. Punishments, incentives, obedience and consensus were of paramount importance. The widely influential Buddhism and Taoism taught the blessings of harmony with nature. Upper-class Confucianism held that rulers should, by their character and education, be able to set an example to their subjects. The reality no doubt left much to be desired. Even so, China had already sustained, for a span of time unequalled elsewhere, a civilization of the greatest distinction in every field. It had made astonishing technical and technological advances and by the fourteenth century possessed the world's largest mechanized industry. It produced commodities as different as cottons, silks, porcelain and firearms. Visitors, when not overwhelmed by the sight of great cities, thriving ports, people beyond number and a government that so clearly governed, remarked on China's hard-working population and its agricultural skills. Such things mattered little to the intellectual patrician ruling class, but farming was fundamental to the empire's well-being and Chinese technological virtuosity nowhere better shown than in irrigation works employing both wind and water power. China, moreover, had maritime skills and experience of an outstanding order – the still-flourishing junk, at first sight the most improbable of vessels, is for example one of the most ingenious and efficient sailing craft ever devised. Chinese ships had perhaps reached the Cape of Good Hope by the fourteenth century, and by the early 1400s they were in the Persian Gulf and off western India and East Africa.

Nevertheless it was not for centuries after Europeans had sailed to America and Asia that seamen from the East were to bring their vessels into European waters. That they might well have done so earlier is suggested by the voyages, already noticed, undertaken (1405–33) in the time of the Emperor Yung-lo, when huge fleets (allegedly sixty ships carrying nearly 30,000 men) reached alike the shores of Indonesia and the western littorals of the Indian Ocean and the Arabian Sea, exacting tribute and collecting curiosities and information. But these expeditions were undertaken when Muslim influence was powerful at the imperial court. Once this dwindled there was no further backing for such ventures, particularly since they were so expensive to mount, and traditional xenophobic and anti-commercial views prevailed. Nor was there any pressing reason for further Chinese exploration since neither in myth or reality did the West offer anything that the empire could not obtain more easily elsewhere, least of all riches comparable to those of the East.

Meanwhile, as the voyages of the Norse to their desolate and decaying Atlantic settlements petered out – Greenland was extinct by about 1500, Iceland only rescued by the arrival of the English in the early 1400s – other European seamen had been pushing into waters hardly less formidable. A Genoese expedition bound 'for the parts of India' disappeared into the blazing heat of West Africa in 1291. The Catalans, unsurpassed as slavers, traders and warriors by land and sea, were seeking direct maritime access to the gold of the Niger basin in the early 1300s. In the fourteenth and early fifteenth centuries Spaniards, Normans, Portuguese and Genoese (from their powerful communities in Iberia), reached the Canary Islands, once known to Antiquity, and set about their slow and bloodthirsty subjugation. Madeira and the Azores were perhaps found. There were raids on the north-west African coast, occasional talk of a search for fellow Christians, 'the increase of our holy faith', and a sustained and ruthless pursuit of gold, slaves and spices. Of all those engaged in this archetypal imperial endeavour none were more persistent and none ultimately better rewarded than the Portuguese.

In 1415, in the venerable tradition of Christian assaults on Islamic Africa, a Portuguese army, with more success than had usually been the case,

captured Ceuta in Morocco. Shortly after this victory, Portuguese seamen
– some in the service of the royal Prince Henry, their achievements consequently better recorded – resumed that reconnaissance of the West African
coast begun by Italian and Iberian sailors. Islands in the Atlantic were
discovered or rediscovered when ships were forced out to sea by prevailing
winds or as they searched for the idyllic realms sited in these waters by
medieval flights of fancy. So there once again came to light the uninhabited
Madeira group (c. 1420) and the Azores (1427). The Cape Verdes (1456–60)
and other clusters further south were found and all soon populated and
brought into profitable cultivation, especially as producers of sugar. And
the dogged investigation of the West African littoral was vindicated with
the discovery that gold and slaves were to be had on the Saharan and
Senegambian coasts, albeit by commerce with Muslim merchants rather
than as the fruits of godly war against the infidel. The pace and scale of
Portuguese endeavour accordingly increased. By the 1460s they had reached
those latitudes which from the roar of tropical thunder they named the
Mountains of the Lions – Sierra Leone. They were across the equator a
decade later and in 1483 entered the Congo. Now, however, they were
seeking not only the gold, slaves, ivory and spices of Africa – impressive
and acceptable though these were – but a way to Asia round or through
the continent.

Accounts of the wonders of the Orient were increasingly known and
popular in late medieval Europe. The rediscovered works of classical geographers suggested the apparent and inviting proximity of the East, and
rumours which had long circulated in the West of the existence of a great
Christian potentate in the uncertainly defined 'Indies' (thought by some to
extend as far as the Nile) were seemingly confirmed by stories picked up
by the Portuguese in West Africa. Moreover, as they shipped the sugar of
their Atlantic colonies into the Mediterranean they could see for themselves
in the magnificence of Venice – the effective monopolist of the importation
of Asian spices through the Levant – the rewards of such a commerce.
Spice was a vast, ill-defined generic, then embracing many commodities
now considered dyes and perfumes. But in essence it meant the pepper,
ginger, mace, cloves and nutmeg of India and Indonesia, used to make
salted-down meat palatable for the rich and to put life into the preserves
and wines they consumed, as indeed into the consumers themselves. The
trade was minute in volume but of prodigious value, with pepper selling in
northern Europe at over £200 a ton in the mid 1400s when a brand new
ship cost only £2 to £3 a ton. After some false starts an overland reconnaissance was sent, under royal direction, through the Middle East (1487) to
identify the Christian sovereign, Prester John, to discover 'whether he
bordered on the sea' and to find the origin of those spices reaching Venice
from the Levant. One of its members apparently learned that the Indian
Ocean was accessible from the Atlantic, but the information probably failed

to reach the king. A similar task was presumably entrusted to Bartolomeu Dias, who, after sailing the length of West Africa – the first in a series of Portuguese voyages of unprecedented audacity – rounded (1488) the southernmost tip of the continent, where the Cape of Good Hope was so named 'for the promise it gave of the finding of India'.

Thus in roughly a hundred years the Portuguese had explored most of Africa's immense Atlantic littoral. They had bases from Arguim (Mauritania) in the north, to Angola (1520) in the south. Where great rivers permitted, or where, as in Morocco, there were trade routes to be followed, they knew something of the interior. More important still, they understood the pattern of Atlantic winds which obliged seamen seeking a fair wind – as all found it prudent to do in an age when ships performed poorly with any other – to make a sweep westward to clear the Cape of Good Hope. Hence in 1497, in one of the greatest passages ever made under sail, a squadron commanded by the prickly aristocrat Vasco da Gama rounded the Cape, turned up the East African coast and eventually reached the flourishing but squabbling Arab and Islamic trading centres north of the Zambezi. From Malindi (Kenya), guided by a local pilot, the expedition sailed to western India along the route normally followed by native shipping. Thus the Portuguese had opened a new way into that vast Asian maritime economy extending from China and the islands of Indonesia to the eastern shores of Africa and the Middle East. They were now in waters crossed and recrossed by vessels belonging to merchants and seamen of an infinity of races and religions, carrying spices from the Far East to the Red Sea and the Persian Gulf, the products of Africa to Asia, European textiles (from the Levant) to the East, Chinese silks and porcelains to India and Indian textiles to Africa, the Middle East and Indonesia. Because of the monsoons of the eastern seas – whose seasonal winds dictated that ships could only sail in a particular direction at a particular time – and because of the enormous distances involved, the greater part of this rich commerce was trans-shipped at a handful of wealthy, easily accessible and consequently vulnerable entrepôts. Of these none were more celebrated than Hormuz, at the mouth of the Persian Gulf, and Malacca, in the south of the Malay peninsula, 'the mine of spices', so it seemed to the Portuguese pioneers, and 'the richest place in all the world'.

With a speed surpassing even that of Spain's whirlwind conquest of the Americas, the Portuguese spread along the ancient trade routes of the East and within little more than a decade of rounding the Cape – reached only after so long and arduous a struggle – they were in China. Their voyages of these years were intelligently and purposefully directed by a succession of able kings. Modest resources, entrusted to talented commanders, were concentrated on carefully identified and defined objectives, though inevitably there were difficulties with forceful individuals operating well beyond the reach of their royal master. And to their great good fortune the Portu-

guese met no united indigenous opposition – and indeed benefited enormously from local co-operation – while their depredations by sea were of
little concern to the rulers of the major land-based empires. On royal
instructions Afonso de Albuquerque – tireless, brutal, splenetic – took the
vital Malacca (1511) and Hormuz (1515), but failed against Aden, the key
to the Red Sea. On his own initiative he secured the one-time Muslim
stronghold of Goa (1510) in western India, soon to be the capital of the
grandiosely named State of India (*Estado da India*). By the 1520s the
Portuguese had acquired, by a combination of luck, force and diplomacy,
bases along the coasts of the subcontinent and in Sri Lanka. They had
footholds reaching from East Africa – where, among other places, they
held Kilwa and Mozambique – to the Moluccas, and were strenuously
endeavouring to divert the westward flow of spices away from the venerable
routes through the Red Sea and Persian Gulf to that route they had opened
round southern Africa. Thus would they acquire 'infinite riches', gained,
as befitted Christian gentlemen, not by demeaning toil but by martial valour
while, as was only proper, the Muslim merchants who had previously
dominated this commerce would be ruined.

A royal monopoly of the import of spices to Europe was established
(1505–6). Attempts were made to regulate and tax indigenous shipping in
the Arabian Sea and Indian Ocean – scuffles with Chinese patrols and the
countless routes among the islands of Malaysia and Indonesia having shown
such aspirations to be impracticable further east. For a time these remarkable
ambitions came near to success, an astonishing achievement for a tiny
country short of ships and men, and with such forces as it possessed thinly
scattered through dozens of forts and posts in East and West alike. But by
the 1560s so vigorous was the commerce along the old Red Sea route that
the Portuguese crown had hopes of being allowed to participate, as indeed
some of its subjects were, by a variety of subterfuges, already doing. Yet
the golden days were far from over. In attempts to assert their pretensions,
in the search for further riches, and eventually in the endeavour to escape
from enemies local and European, the Portuguese spread further still. By
the end of the century they were pushing into Africa in Mozambique. A
base was obtained at Macao (southern China) and another in Japan (reached
by accident in 1543) and for the best part of a hundred years the Portuguese
grew rich as middlemen and monopolists in a trade, otherwise forbidden
by the Ming emperors, in which the gold and silks of China were exchanged
for the silver of Japan. Enterprising individuals made a good living among
the islands of Indonesia. Merchants and adventurers reached Burma, Indo-
China, Manila, New Guinea and the Seychelles. In India traders settled in
Muslim Cambay, in Bengal and on the Coromandel coast. Portuguese
pirates roamed the Bay of Bengal and footloose captains served warring
princelings in Mesopotamia. Catholic missions were soon at work in Japan,
East Africa, China, India and Indonesia, with some of their members

making their way to Vietnam and even to Tibet.

But whatever the grandiloquent styles adopted by its rulers – who called themselves 'Lord of Guinea and of the Conquest of the Navigation and Commerce of Ethiopia, Arabia, Persia, and India' – and notwithstanding the bellicose language of some of their servants, the *Estado* never became a body of lands and peoples effectively controlled by a metropolitan authority. It was a network of trading posts, linked by sea and with the influence of the mother country spread less by glorious feats of arms than by the zeal of missionaries and the enterprise of traders commonly living and working far beyond even the most tenuous jurisidiction of the Portuguese crown. Faced by the organized and densely-populated states of Asia, and with their own feeble resources in manpower – 1½ million inhabitants at best – further eroded by the ravages of climate and disease, the Portuguese were never in a position to subdue and colonize more than a few minuscule territories. The country had no military strength to speak of, while her seapower was soon destroyed by the sheer extent of the demands imposed on it. But in any case it was early appreciated that wealth came from maritime commerce. It might be acquired from the trades – particularly those within Asia – in which the Portuguese themselves engaged, or it might come from taxing or looting indigenous merchants. Hence among the so-called 'conquests' which made up the State of India the only appreciable territories were the pockets of settlement in the west of the subcontinent and those in Sri Lanka – and all of them, as events were rapidly to show, at the mercy of enemies.

Ever since the arrival of Vasco da Gama in the East the Portuguese had faced opposition, though never sustained and only rarely concerted. The hostility of the Mamluks of Egypt, soldiers not seamen, was scotched when their fleet, and that of their co-religionaries from north-west India, was destroyed off Diu (1509). The Ottoman Turks, who by the mid sixteenth century controlled most of the Middle East – and thus had direct access to the Red Sea and the Persian Gulf – were, with their satellites, more formidable. But eastern waters were of little concern to the sultans in the age of their country's massive expansion in and around the Mediterranean. All the same incursions into the Indian Ocean alarmed the *Estado* and humiliatingly demonstrated the fatuity of its pretensions, most notoriously when in 1585–6 Mir Ali Bey, with a single ship, swept the Portuguese from the entire Swahili coast of Africa, except Malindi. And even if these possessions were eventually regained, the prestige of Portugal was, like its ailing imperial finances, shaken. Meanwhile piracy was on the increase, vessels from Atjeh (Sumatra) were sailing directly to the Red Sea by routes avoiding Portuguese bases (and taxes) in the Arabian Sea, and were attacking, like their fellows from Malaysia, Portuguese shipping and laying siege to Malacca. Worse was to come with the appearance, in the seventeenth century, of the Omani Arabs, working from the mouth of the Persian Gulf. They took Mascat, the last remaining Portuguese base of any consequence in the area in 1650, harried Portuguese shipping in the Indian Ocean and Arabian Sea, attacked western India (as in 1668), paralysing Portuguese local trade, and eventually expelled the Portuguese from the East African littoral north of Cape Delgado.

But if the isolated footholds of the *Estado*, scattered along coasts, were conveniently at the mercy of enemies with ships, they were equally at the mercy of those with troops. They were small, widely dispersed and inadequately defended. The loyalty of their indigenous inhabitants was uncertain, they were commonly dependent on local goodwill for all their needs and they required for their relief a volume of manpower and shipping the Portuguese were increasingly unable to muster. In the 1570s the State of India triumphantly withstood the sole concerted Muslim attack launched against it, losing only Ternate in the Moluccas. But such successes were rarely repeated. Iran, aided by the English, took Hormuz in 1622. The Japanese, alarmed by the spread of western religion, suspicious of the motives of the Portuguese, and no longer requiring them as intermediaries with China following the arrival of other Europeans, expelled merchants and missionaries alike and brutally suppressed Christianity (1614–39). In India spasmodic scufflings with various minor powers were eclipsed in the seventeenth century by the threat, first from the Mughals and then from the formidable Hindu Marathas, whose conquest of Goa itself (1683) was only averted by luck.

Serious enough though these blows were they were nothing to those inflicted by other European powers, some, like Spain and France, fellow Catholics, others, like Holland and England, Protestants. In the century after 1600 they seized most of Portugal's territorial possessions and annexed the best part of her one-time trades. There was trouble with Spain from the very beginning. Fierce clashes off West Africa in the 1400s were soon followed by struggles in Asia. The Spanish crown, rumoured to be interested in Malacca as early as 1506, was persuaded that the Spice Islands lay within that part of the world assigned to it by papal arbitration and diplomatic fencing with Portugal following the discovery of America.[1]* Hence it was that in 1521 the remnants of a Spanish expedition which had sailed under the command of Ferdinand Magellan (a disgruntled former Portuguese officer) arrived in the Moluccas, having found a way to the East round the southern tip of America and across the seemingly endless waters of the Pacific. A single vessel, though not Magellan himself, eventually reached home by way of the Cape of Good Hope, thus completing, in an unequalled epic of seamanship, the first circumnavigation of the globe. Then, no sooner had the Spaniards subjugated Mexico than further forays were launched towards Asia from the west coast of the Americas. But the

* Superior figures refer to the Notes and references sections following each chapter.

route, like that round the world, was considered impossible for regular commercial use, particularly since prevailing winds apparently precluded a return passage. And in any case the Spaniards had more than enough irons in the fire. Claims on the Moluccas were sold to Portugal (1529) and eventually, after some wild talk of the subjugation of China and neighbouring realms and some searches for the rumoured great southern continent, the Spaniards settled for the conquest (1542–65), colonization and conversion of the islands thereafter known as the Philippines. The happy discovery (1565) that in latitudes 37°–39°N it was possible to find a fair wind for America subsequently allowed the Philippine capital, Manila, to become the base to which New World silver was shipped, and the focus of an impressively valuable trade linking China, Japan (for a time) and much of south-east Asia with Spanish Mexico and Peru.

These, however, were the least of Portugal's troubles. From 1580 to 1640 the country and its colonies were under Spanish rule and the victims, as patriots saw it, of Spanish neglect or worse. The French, already notorious poachers in supposed Lusitanian preserves elsewhere, appeared in the Indian Ocean as early as 1518. Yet, notwithstanding the backing of Italian commercial skills and capital and the services of Portuguese renegades, this threat was slow to materialize. In the first half of the sixteenth century France was fully occupied in challenging the power of the Habsburgs, rulers, in the time of the Emperor Charles V (1519–58) of Spain, the Low Countries, Germany and much of Italy. In the later 1500s the country was paralysed by civil war. Thereafter its monarchs were chiefly concerned with asserting their pre-eminence in Europe. Nor did kings and courtiers in land-locked Paris have many interests in common with merchants – frequently Protestants until the grudging tolerance they enjoyed was revoked in 1685 – from the Atlantic seaports. And if French monarchs thought of the sea at all it was like as not of the Mediterranean, a traditional theatre for their ambitions. Nevertheless from the mid 1600s some attention was given to the East, inspired in part by the success enjoyed there by others, in part by that long-held belief that nowhere could France be seen to be second to any. There were plans (1642) to colonize Madagascar and eventually (1664) a monopoly trading company was set up. But it faced formidable Dutch and English competition and it lacked money, not least since merchant capital could find a lucrative outlet in Spain's American possessions which France aspired to control at the end of the seventeenth century. Even so the French successfully penetrated what had once been Portugal's Asian commercial empire. In India they acquired trading rights at Surat (1668) and a base at Pondicherry (1672). French Indiamen sailed for the East – admittedly no more than thirty-nine in all between 1679 and 1695 – and in 1698 companies were established to handle commerce with China and the Pacific. Some French vessels made the long passage to the Orient via Cape Horn, traded in Chile and Peru *en route* and returned home by the Cape of Good Hope. But such voyages were too long and too costly to be more than spasmodic, and France, fully committed to the struggle for supremacy in Europe under Louis XIV, was not to be a major force in Asia until the following century.

With Protestant England and Holland it was a very different story. Both, for much of the sixteenth and seventeenth centuries, considered Catholic Iberia their mortal enemy, and both were redoubtable maritime powers – England pre-eminent in piracy and privateering, Holland owning Europe's largest and most efficient merchant fleet. For much of the hundred years after roughly 1550 the English persisted with more fortitude than success in attempts to reach Asia one way or another – to the north-west past America, eastwards round or across Russia, along the ancient Mediterranean route through the Middle East. But not until relatively late did they penetrate to the Spice Islands when in 1579 Francis Drake, returning by a circumnavigation of the world from his depredations in the Spanish Pacific, made a landfall in Ternate. For a time little came of this. So arduous a voyage had no attractions for English merchants, then profitably shipping home from the eastern Mediterranean oriental goods which arrived there by the traditional routes. Besides which there was the prospect of vast gains to be had in the privateering war against Iberia – at its peak from the 1570s till the end of the century – conducted in waters nearer to home. When, however, it seemed that the Dutch, now in Asia, were likely to seal off the flow of goods to the Levant, and when it was plain to even the most sanguine that nothing could be expected from negotiations with the joint Hispano-Portuguese monarchy, Elizabeth I issued a charter incorporating the English East India Company (1600) and granting it the monopoly of the country's trade with Asia.

Much of the EIC's initial capital came from London and from city plutocrats enriched by the war at sea and by dealings in the Levant. Many of its first ships were powerful vessels designed for privateering and many of their commanders were men long experienced in such ventures. Hence, though England was nominally at peace with the Iberians after 1604, it was to the accompaniment of skirmishes, pitched battles and the capture of Portuguese prizes anywhere from East Africa to South China that the Company pushed into Asia. By the second decade of the seventeenth century it had posts alike in Iran and Japan and was established on both coasts of the Indian subcontinent and in Indonesia. But not for long. The Dutch, erstwhile allies of their fellow Protestants, became England's most resolute opponents and soon drove the Company from its footholds east of India. Such setbacks and a timely appreciation of the opportunities of western Asia diverted English efforts to waters where there was as yet little Dutch activity and where the only opposition was that of the relatively feeble Portuguese. Off north-west India Portuguese ships (and with them Portuguese prestige) were sunk in the full and admiring view of Mughal pro-consuls and the Iranians aided in the capture of Hormuz. The message was well marked by local potentates and thus the English acquired bases in western India, most notably at Surat, established posts well inland and were able to open trades to – among other places – Iran and Indonesia. Reconciliation with Portugal (1635) gave access to the ports of the *Estado* and the subsequent marriage of Charles II to a Portuguese princess brought the Company the then obscure island of Bombay with its magnificent natural harbour (1668). The site was fortified and developed and, to the disgust of the Portuguese, indigenous merchants were attracted. At the same time the rich potential of the south and east of the subcontinent was exploited. The absence of any dominant political power gave room for manoeuvre, while Coromandel provided cotton textiles commanding an enormous market. A post was secured at Madras (1639) and shortly after the English were in Bengal – renowned for its cloths and agricultural wealth and the centre of a network of commercial routes – where in 1691 they obtained Calcutta. So were laid the foundations of British rule in the subcontinent, with the Company's now numerous possessions divided (1700) into the presidencies of Bombay, Madras and Calcutta. So, too, there had been established the trades which were, for the time being, to generate the bulk of EIC profits. And the shape of still better things to come was foreshadowed with the penetration of China. The imperial government's opening of the country's ports (1685) regularized the position the Company already occupied in Amoy, while in 1710 it gained access to Canton, from where the English shipped silks, tea and porcelain in exchange for silver in a commerce soon immensely lucrative.

Nevertheless the position of the EIC long remained precarious. It was dismissed (1664) by Louis XIV's minister, Colbert, as constituting no threat to his plans and even the Portuguese – admittedly more addicted than most to wishful thinking – believed it to be 'living in our shadow'. In the East it had to face the sustained hostility of the Dutch. At home political conflict and governmental financial needs threatened its monopoly, not to say its existence, its misfortunes culminating in the foundation (1698) of a rival body. Not until 1709 were the two reconciled and the United Company launched. All the same by the late 1600s, and notwithstanding a misguided clash with the Mughals (1688–90), English trade in Asia was going from strength to strength. The Company now had behind it a state which commercially and financially was fast matching Holland and which in naval strength had already overhauled it. The EIC accounted for something like 14 per cent of the value of England's imports (chiefly bringing in cloth, like its European competitors, and no longer spices).[2] Before the upsets following the overthrow of James II – with whose dynasty it had, to its cost, long been closely associated – it was paying investors dividends of an order more commonly rumoured than received, reaching even 50 per cent in 1682. Meanwhile in Asia, after the usual slow start, the English were reaping the rich rewards of local commerce with a determination, and on a scale, unequalled by any other European people.[3]

For long, however, it seemed that the Dutch would dominate Europe's trade with Asia, just as they dominated that of the continent itself. Yet they arrived in the East relatively late – the first ships in 1596 – earlier schemes allegedly having been set aside as a result of the outbreak of the revolt against the Spanish Habsburgs, of whose patrimony the Low Countries were then a part. But it was this war, eventually ending with Spain's recognition of Holland's independence (1648) that brought the Dutch to Asia. Until the end of the sixteenth century they had been able to obtain the products of the Spanish and Portuguese overseas empires in Lisbon and Seville, much of whose European commerce was handled by their ships. But when, in the course of the war against England and Holland, the Spaniards closed Lisbon (1595–6) and took to arresting alien vessels in Iberian ports, the Dutch were driven to seek exotic commodities at source. But there was more to this radical shift than economic calculation. An attack on Iberian overseas possessions would, as Protestant zealots – especially those refugees from Spanish occupied Flanders – urged, divert Habsburg energies and forces away from the war in the Low Countries. Nevertheless the Dutch, members of a loose confederation of provinces rather than a recognizable state, made heavy going to begin with. Expeditions were despatched, without any overall direction, by every route actual or potential, and since so many ports had the resources to mount them the Hollanders were for a time their own worst enemies. The price of spices was driven up in Asia by their competition among themselves and in danger of being lowered in Europe. Not until the establishment, through government intervention, of the United East India Company (VOC, from the initials of its name in Dutch) in 1602 did Holland's expansion in Asia begin in earnest.

Like its English rival the Dutch company was a joint-stock monopoly corporation.[4] But its powers were more extensive, and while the EIC was largely controlled by London merchants and was politically independent, the VOC drew on far greater resources, including those of several other major seaports besides the dominant Amsterdam. Moreover, since it was run by members of that same urban merchant class so influential in affairs of state, it was to all intents an instrument of the Dutch government. To oppose it there was only the failing power of Portugal and the as yet faltering hostility of the English. Holland's impressive seapower could be deployed to fullest effect in the Asian maritime economy. The Company had no need to confront any major indigenous state and it could find, at least to start with, allies among those happy to welcome an opponent of the Portuguese. Nor was the East unknown to the Dutch. Many of their seamen had served the Portuguese there or were familiar, from long residence in Iberian ports, with the supposed secrets of the *Carreira da India* (the round voyage between Portugal and India). Indeed Jan Huyghen van Linschoten, once a clerk to the Archbishop of Goa, produced on his return home (1592) that celebrated *Itinerary* which described to his compatriots the whole pattern of Asian trade and urged the importance and opportunities of Indonesia. Hence initial Dutch endeavour was concentrated on penetrating to the very heart of spice production – to Java, Sumatra, the Bandas and the Moluccas – where crops commanding the highest prices were grown, and where Holland would be conveniently clear of the centres of Portuguese power in the Arabian Sea and of the Spaniards in the Pacific. Characteristically, too, Dutch sailors soon opened a new route round the Cape of Good Hope and then eastwards in the latitudes of the 'roaring forties' giving direct and quicker access to Indonesia and, for the unwary, to the western shores of Australia.

Meanwhile the VOC had set about its opponents. The English were for a time worsted and Spanish Manila was blockaded to divert Chinese trade and Mexican silver into Company hands. The commerce of the *Estado* was ruined and the conquest of its major bases begun, which was to prove far more difficult than expected. Malacca was eventually taken in 1641, most of Sri Lanka by 1658 and the footholds on the pepper-producing Malabar coast of India in the 1660s. Dutch trading stations were established in Coromandel and Bengal. Despite Spanish prohibition commerce was opened (after the peace of 1648) with Manila. The Iberians were driven out of the trade of eastern Indonesia and the Dutch became the only Europeans allowed in Japan, with a base first at Hirado and then, after 1641, at Deshima. Above all the Company established a monopoly of the purchase of spices for shipment to the West which, whatever its shortcomings, was stricter and more effective than anything previously attempted. Rigorous control was exercised over the cinnamon of the conquered Sri Lanka. Local rulers in India and Indonesia were persuaded, usually by force, to supply their produce only to the Dutch. Any infringement of Holland's interests brought violent retaliation, as with the sinking of eighty Chinese junks in 1622. Where such tactics were unacceptable, the Company, backed by the economic skills and resources of the Netherlands, could usually succeed by offering indigenous peoples goods or services on a scale and at prices their competitors could rarely match. And from the very start it was understood, not only by the VOC's many redoubtable servants in the East, but by the government at home, that trade would be supported by dominion, whatever the fears of prudent investors. A beginning was made with Amboina, taken in 1605, and by the end of the century most of Indonesia was, though far from securely, in Dutch hands, ruled from the patriotically named capital of Batavia (Djakarta) in Java. Little energy was wasted on anything else. Australia was discovered by accident (1605, 1616) and its coasts mapped. Periodic searches were launched for the legendary great Southland. New Zealand, Tasmania, Tonga and Fiji were found (1642–4), but, offering nothing to excite the acquisitive urges of businessmen, abandoned. Such policies brought familiar results. The prosperity of much of Indonesia was destroyed and many of its peoples driven to piracy. The imposition of Dutch rule was accompanied, as in Java, by massacres, rebellions and prolonged fighting. The attempted conquest and government of such territories laid a massive financial burden on the VOC whose troubles were aggravated by corrupt and inept management – of which there was no more notable instance than the failure to grasp the importance of Chinese tea – and by the early 1700s the Company was in serious financial difficulties.

Thus, roughly two centuries after Vasco da Gama's epic voyage, little remained of what the Portuguese still resolutely called their 'Conquests'. The country now accounted for only a tiny but still important fraction of the trade between Asia and Europe and, though some of the ports of the *Estado* remained active in local commerce, much of this was financed and conducted by indigenous merchants. The imperial government was usually penniless – though the fortunes of some of its subjects was another matter – and by 1700 there was even talk of quitting Goa. Yet like so much and so many of the chronically decrepit the empire showed amazing resilience. Following the ending of the war with Holland (1663) and the prolonged and successful struggle to secure independence from Spain (1640–68), the old trades from Portuguese India to China and East Africa revived and the *Estado*, under competent management, briefly made a profit in 1680.

Nevertheless by *c*. 1700 the rich commerce between Asia and the West was virtually monopolized by England and Holland, apart from what was left to the French and to a number of other minor European East India companies, usually the progeny of Dutch opponents of the VOC. It was a trade no longer principally in spices, but – other than such 'gruff goods' as the saltpetre and sugar used to ballast ships – largely in cotton textiles, precious stones, silks and the opulent artefacts of China. And just beginning, with enormous consequences for the future, was the import of coffee and tea. Underlying these shifts in fashion lay a radical change in the pattern of commerce. Eastern goods, which had once moved westwards through the Middle East and the Mediterranean in a series of short voyages between entrepôts, were now carried directly to Europe via the Cape in western vessels. European intervention in Asia, intensifying trades such as that of Japan with China or the export of Indian textiles to Indonesia, stimulated closer economic relations between India, China and South-East Asia. Throughout much of the maritime economy of the East there were now scattered Europeans, or those of some degree of European ancestry, engaged in extensive and frequently highly lucrative 'country' trades, as often as not at the expense of the parent state or company.[5] Asian ships continued to sail and Asian commerce continued to flow, though not necessarily along traditional routes and no longer with the freedom of pre-European days.

But Asian vessels, like Asian armies, were increasingly equipped with western weapons, and Europeans, though they might trade inland (as in Bengal) were in general confined to the coasts of the great Asian landmass. Outside the islands of Indonesia and Sri Lanka they controlled no significant amounts of territory and despite the often prodigious journeys of traders and missionaries – many recorded in highly perceptive and eminently readable accounts – European knowledge of the East amounted to little more than knowledge of maritime Asia. And even so the true nature of whole immense areas, such as Australasia, remained uncertain.

In the West, unlike the Orient, European seamen faced oceans and climates unknown and unpredictable, with no native pilots to guide them and with no indigenous trade routes for them to follow. Progress was slower and the rewards initially more elusive; but the ultimate outcome, the finding of a new continent, was an achievement of unparallelled magnitude. The Portuguese, as we have seen, recommenced the exploration of the Atlantic in the early fifteenth century, and the English, seeking new fishing grounds and those delectable islands in which the ocean was alleged to abound, may have reached the modern Newfoundland c. 1480. But such endeavours were eclipsed when in 1492 Christopher Columbus, in one of the most celebrated of all voyages, made a landfall in the Bahamas, bound as he thought for China. He was Genoese, a magnificent sailor, but a man of strange visionary impulses and singularly unhappy in dealings with his fellows. He was in Spanish service (but not Spanish royal pay), supported in the euphoric aftermath of the fall of the last Moorish stronghold in the country (1492) by the goodwill of the pious Queen Isabella of Castile. His plan for a westward passage to Asia had previously been rejected by the King of Portugal and other monarchs, though some contemporaries accepted such a voyage was possible, even if they grossly underestimated the distance involved.[6] Columbus' discovery of gold, of primitive peoples ideally suited in his view to enslavement, and of naked women, ensured that the search, now backed by the Spanish crown, continued. In three subsequent expeditions he explored much of the Caribbean and its shores, long convinced, notwithstanding the absence of any signs of high civilizations, that he was in or on the threshold of Cathay. So he named his discoveries 'The Indies', as they remained to the Spaniards, though in northern Europe the great continent became America, after Amerigo Vespucci, a persuasive Florentine who claimed to have got there first.

It was quickly understood that this previously unknown 'New World' offered riches for the taking. Thoughts of trade with China evaporated, slaving and looting intensified and the conquest and exploitation of the Caribbean islands were ruthlessly pursued. But it was equally clear that the Indies were a barrier obstructing the way to Asia, through or round which, as with Africa, a way had to be found. Columbus and others searched along the Panama Isthmus and the northern coast of South America. The

English, under the Venetian John Cabot, tried (1497) to the north-west, in those waters beyond Canada which were to lead them to the frozen seas of the Arctic. The Portuguese discovered Brazil by accident and in expeditions mounted from both the mother country and the Atlantic islands reached Greenland, Newfoundland and Labrador *c.* 1500, even briefly establishing a colony in the Gulf of St Lawrence, where the Spaniards also appeared (1525). The French, under yet another Italian, searched the eastern shores of the present USA northwards from Cape Fear (1524), while Iberian ships pushed further and further down the coasts of Brazil and South America until Magellan eventually discovered (1520) the passage to the Pacific which still bears his name.

This, however, was little consolation to the Spanish monarchy. Whereas the 'grocer king' of Portugal prospered on the gold and slaves of Africa and the spices of Asia, Spain was engaged in costly wars and had apparently gained nothing from her new overseas possessions. The Canaries, acquired from Portugal in 1479 were not, in the face of the tenacious resistance of their Guanche inhabitants, subdued till 1496. The islands of the New World produced some precious metals and brought sovereignty over a few primitive peoples, spared, however, on Isabella's insistence, from enslavement and in any case rapidly dwindling in numbers as a result of contact with Europeans. Nevertheless the crown's title to this disappointing heritage was carefully established with characteristic prudence. The privileges obtained (1493) from a Spanish pope were too generous for Portuguese liking.[7] Subsequent negotiations resulted in an agreement (1497) dividing the world between the two Iberian powers by a meridian to be drawn north/south 370 leagues west of the Cape Verde Islands, and which Spain at least assumed would be projected into Asia.

And now Spanish fortunes changed dramatically. The islands of the Caribbean failed to come up to the expectations of the settlers who flocked in by the thousand. European numbers increased, pressure on land intensified, precious metals became scarcer and the rapid decline of the indigenous population meant a shortage of labour to discharge those many menial tasks colonists had no intention of performing themselves. Expeditions were accordingly sent out to find slaves, while ambitious Spaniards, or those worsted in the feuds which raged in the islands, tried their luck elsewhere. These ventures were mounted with royal licence, but were privately financed. They included, like a ship's company, men with a wide range of skills, which endowed them with remarkable powers of adaptability, endurance and survival. The penetration of the mainland began with the settlement of Darien, in the modern Colombia (1509) and with raids on the shores of the Gulf of Mexico. Here, before long, noses finely attuned to scenting plunder got wind of the existence inland of great and wealthy empires. In 1519 an expedition from Cuba, commissioned by the royal governor, landed in Mexico. Its leader was Hernán Cortés, an adept publicist, consummate manager of men and practised charmer of women. Now in his mid thirties he was to reveal, like many before and since, superlative and unsuspected qualities as a soldier and statesman. He disavowed his master's authority and by 1522, in a campaign of staggering audacity, his tiny force (about 400 infantry and sixteen horsemen to start with) had overthrown the Aztec empire, eclipsing, as his troops were well aware, even the improbable achievements of the heroes of contemporary romance.[8] Success was primarily due to the qualities of Cortés himself. It was aided by massive indigenous assistance from enemies and disaffected subjects of the Aztecs, and by the ingenuity and superiority of Spanish tactics. Aztec armies were huge but unwieldy, chiefly concerned with taking prisoners for sacrifice. The Spaniards fought to win, and with their use of dogs and horses – unknown in the Americas – enjoyed all those classic advantages of mobility, speed and surprise. Unchallenged control of the sea allowed them to bring in men and materials at will from neighbouring bases. And whereas Aztec religion was pessimistic, and Aztec morale eroded by the ravages of European-borne diseases, the Spaniards were impelled by an unquenchable thirst for riches, precious metals in particular, now encountered on a scale beyond their wildest imaginings.

From Mexico conquerors moved on in similar hopes to the surrounding lands. They made epic marches through Central America, pushed up the Pacific coast, penetrated inland to what is now Arizona and reached as far as the Grand Canyon. But all in vain. Then, in an unsurpassed feat of arms, Francisco Pizarro and Diego Almagro overthrew the Incas.[9] The expedition was mounted initially and unsuccessfully from Panama, followed by a renewed attempt (1531) from Spain. Its commanders were of even obscurer origins than Cortés – both were illiterate and Pizarro a chronically bad horseman – but from that same great reservoir of unprivileged and normally neglected ability. The war was fought in the Andes, among mountains dwarfing the greatest in Europe, where the valleys were deeper, the deserts more arid and the distances involved greater than in any campaign previously undertaken by Europeans. The Spaniards succeeded for the same reasons as in Mexico and from the fact that a civil war between two contenders to the imperial throne was raging when they arrived. But the subjugation of the Incas was to be a longer and more arduous undertaking than that of the Aztecs. The potential loot – gold and silver in amounts 'never before seen anywhere in the world' – was greater. The terrain was more difficult. The Spanish commanders, whatever their individual talents, lacked the political dexterity of Cortés and their personal rivalries shortly developed into savage fighting between rival bands of followers. Nor had Inca rule ended in the same summary fashion as that of the Aztecs. In Mexico the power of the imperial house was extinguished with the death of Montezuma, but in Peru attempts to establish a puppet regime allowed the re-emergence of an Inca state, encouraging resistance to the invaders

and not destroyed till 1572. At the same time the replacement of the ancient
Andean city of Cuzco as capital by the new coastal Lima (1535) weakened
Spanish control of the highlands. But in the end Spain prevailed, while for
the same reasons and with the same outcome as in Mexico, expeditions
were launched into neighbouring lands. Marches down the eastern flanks
of the Andes revealed only the great rivers and fearsome jungles of
Amazonia, or routes leading to Spanish footholds now established in the
scarcely more appealing hinterland of the Río de la Plata and its confluents.
In Chile the *conquistadores* came up against the Araucanians, the least
amenable of any indigenous people to subjugation and exploitation. Their
unrelenting opposition forced the first Spanish retreat in the New World
in the 1550s, and the southern frontier remained the scene of constant
fighting, raiding and slave-trading.

In the century and a half after *c.* 1550 Spanish government was established, not without difficulty, in Central and South America. A revolt by
disgruntled conquerors was suppressed in Peru (1548) and a rising by the
discontented heirs of the vanquishers of Mexico nipped in the bud (1566).
Exercised by the threat to its authority and economic interests and encouraged by the increasingly vociferous denunciations of the behaviour of the
colonists by the missionaries – the most celebrated the Dominican Bartolomé de las Casas (1474–1566) – the crown repeatedly intervened on behalf
of its new Indian subjects. In 1549, in a move unparalleled in any other
empire, expansion was halted while their unhappy lot was considered and
debated.[10] Thereafter it recommenced, under stricter royal control and into
less promising regions, while Spanish hold on the Indies was consolidated
and extended. After a cursory survey it was accepted that the North American landmass had nothing to offer. The west coast of the continent was
explored up to 43°N to eradicate any threat to commerce with the
Philippines. Posts were maintained and the missions persisted among the
hostile peoples of Florida to safeguard the maritime route leading out of
the Caribbean past the tip of the peninsula. There was spasmodic advance,
sustained by a blend of force and persuasion, into the unsubdued silver-
producing lands of northern Mexico and, with the missions to the fore, to
the upper reaches of the Río Grande – where New Mexico succumbed to
the last of the *conquistadores* in 1593 – and to Lower California. Venezuela
was settled, from where, as also via the Amazon, vain attempts were launched to find yet more riches in the realms of El Dorado, the gold-painted
ruler of the alleged city of Manoa. In the south the great hinterland of the
Río de la Plata was settled, trade illicitly flowed across the Andes between
Peru and the new city of Buenos Aires, and Spain and Portugal disputed
an uncertain boundary.

The white population of the Indies increased. The fortunate secured
lands, titles and legendary wealth. A richly endowed Catholic church was
firmly established and through the labours of the missionary Orders,

whether old (like the Franciscans and Dominicans) or new (like the Jesuits) the surviving Indian peoples became in some measure Christian. Throughout the empire there sprang up handsome towns and cities – the best part of 200 by 1570 – testimony to Spanish victory and the instruments of Spanish hegemony. The weaknesses of Spain's American empire, the first and most enduring of this initial wave of Europe's expansion, were clear enough. Settlements were widely dispersed. The non-Indian population was outnumbered by the surviving indigenous peoples and, in some areas, by imported African slaves. It was, furthermore, heavily concentrated in a few (chiefly administrative) centres, linked only by poor communications stretching across a continent about forty times the size of the mother country. All the same Spain put down deep and fruitful roots. Sited on the best lands, Spanish-owned estates produced crops on a commercial scale, some indigenous – cotton, maize, tobacco, chocolate, *coca* (cocaine) – others of European or alien origin, notably wheat, sugar and ginger. In the one-time Aztec and Inca realms there was freely to hand a large and skilled labour force, soon ruthlessly geared to supposed Spanish needs. Where Indians were unsuitable, or where through royal policy and the massive fall in the indigenous population they were not available, African slaves were shipped in. European livestock, happily acclimatized in virgin pastures that previously knew neither horse, cow, ox, sheep or pig, multiplied at a prodigious rate, providing easy wealth for ranchers, frequently destroying native agriculture and supporting the colourful and quintessentially Iberian way of life of the gaucho (cowboy). By about 1700 the greatest centres of ranching were in such sparsely populated regions as northern Mexico and the vast plains of the Argentine and Venezuela. Elsewhere industries developed and some, for a time, flourished, particularly the manufacture of textiles. Many regions, where the vine was introduced, became, like Chile, celebrated for their wines, while shipbuilding and its various associated trades were major enterprises in several parts of the empire.[11]

Nothing, however, attracted more attention than the extraction, on a scale beyond all previous European experience, of precious metals; first, gold from the Caribbean islands, then silver from Mexico (where the mines of Zacatecas were in production from 1548) and Peru (where Potosí was opened in 1545, followed by lesser finds into the mid 1600s). In the late 1500s, with better mining techniques and a reorganized supply of native labour, output soared. It reached a peak in the early decades of the seventeenth century, first at Potosí and then in Mexico – where miners and high grade ore were more easily available – followed by contraction until the later seventeenth century. Bullion (some gold, but mostly silver) was shipped to Europe via Seville (and, after 1679, Cadiz) through an elaborately organized monopoly. Publicists remarked upon its widespread penetration of the continent from the mid 1500s, and the arrival of silver by the shipload seemed to Spain's many enemies the obvious explanation of the country's ubiquitous and evil power. At the same time another flow was directed through Acapulco, in a similarly organized monopoly, to Manila and the Far East. The true scale of the trade is unknown, except that precious metals accounted for the best part of the value – 80 per cent at least – of cargoes from the Indies to Europe. For the Atlantic official statistics indicate a dramatic collapse in amounts reaching Spain after c. 1600. Other sources suggest a recovery from the mid 1600s, with the flow into Europe surpassing the earlier peak in each and every decade of the rest of the century.[12] The discrepancies have yet to be adequately explained – a tempting solution is vigorous clandestine production and exports – but are hardly surprising. The royal monopoly was almost from the start riddled with the fraud and corruption inseparable from dealings in such a form of wealth. Ships in the treasure fleets commonly carried far more than they declared and at the same time illicit routes flourished. By 1600 something like 25 per cent of Potosí's output was disappearing across the Andes to the Río de la Plata and thence to Brazil, Lisbon and markets beyond – a haemorrhage momentarily staunched following Portugal's revolt from Spain in 1640, but soon reopened. At the same date perhaps ten times the supposed permitted maximum was being carried across the Pacific.

With purchasing power of this order, and from the proceeds of the sale of such other commodities as tobacco, hides and sugar, the Indies became an important market for European products. In the years of the conquests pioneers demanded the wheat, wine and olives essential to the Spanish way of life. As this heroic age passed wealthy colonists expected African slaves, fashionable garments, furniture and books and the many luxuries they could easily afford. Some part of this trade was handled through the channels decreed by the state, most by a variety of clandestine ventures and the rest by affluent South American born Spaniards or their agents visiting Europe. Meanwhile, to the displeasure of the imperial government, the colonies developed flourishing commercial relations among themselves, exchanging their various specialities and entered into dealings with the neighbouring European settlements now established in the New World. They also traded across the Pacific, so allowing Chinese silks, shipped through Manila and Mexico, to be marketed in the mother country.

The accumulation of such wealth, lands and powers swiftly aroused alarm and hostility in Europe, the more so when Spain's annexation (1580) of Portugal and her empire threatened to add Habsburg global hegemony to Habsburg mastery of the continent, entailing, as it seemed to ardent Protestants, the speedy destruction of their religion. But if Spain was enriched by sea she was also vulnerable by sea. Starting with Francis Drake's circumnavigation of the world (1577–80) enemies pushed into the Pacific, damaging Habsburg prestige and pretensions, though before 1700 rarely inflicting any serious damage. But in the Caribbean this was not so: here the destruction of the indigenous peoples, the exhaustion of many of the islands' resources and the overwhelming attractions of the mainland had left the Spanish possessions underpopulated, impoverished and consequently indifferently governed and inadequately defended. This, it seemed to bold strategists, was Spain's Achilles' heel. There were secluded bases galore, secure anchorages and magnificent beaches for the repair and refitting of ships. At the least there was the chance of trading with colonists who, through the feebleness of the Spanish economy and the inadequacies of Spanish commercial policy, were short of everything; and above all there was the prospect of capturing the whole or part of the treasure fleet.

The French were the first on the scene in strength, attacking Havana itself in 1555, but they were soon eclipsed by the English. The brazen attempts of John Hawkins to trade in the 1560s were followed by Drake's triumphant raid (1573) on Nombre de Dios, where bullion was loaded for Europe. Other settlements were subsequently attacked or threatened and plans for colonization aired in a war which continued until 1604. Spanish prestige was again damaged, the movements of the treasure fleets disrupted and Spain's Atlantic commerce dislocated. Then, in the course of a devastating war which paralysed Spanish seaborne trade in the Caribbean, the Dutch took the treasure fleet (1628). Nor were things much better when these comparatively regular naval operations – evidence of the widening scope of European warfare – died down. Spain's enemies and rivals were now established in the New World. Piracy was endemic in waters which long remained beyond the effective control of any state, culminating in the depredations of the buccaneers who, living off the flesh of wild cattle to begin with, took their name from the Indian word for the preparation of smoked meat. They operated from sparsely populated islands, pushing further and further into the Caribbean – Hispaniola, Tortuga, Jamaica – using tiny but well-equipped vessels and enjoying indigenous support. Their main forces were chiefly French (based in St Domingue) or English (based in Jamaica), recruited from assorted desperadoes, deserters from ships and armies, failed colonists, escaped African slaves and runaway unfree European labourers or servants – of whom none was better known than Henry Morgan. From modest beginnings in piracy and bartering hides and flesh to settlers in exchange for supplies, drink and women, they went on to such feats as Morgan's surprise of Puerto Bello (1668) and subsequent sackings of Maracaibo (1669) and Panama (1670–1). Others crossed the Isthmus and launched out into the Pacific, and a handful circumnavigated the globe.

If it suited their purpose, buccaneers might serve their mother country in time of war, but their prime devotion was to booty. Like the Spanish *conquistadores* before them some were highly literate, some were men of pathological violence and some were to prove themselves accomplished commanders and seamen. And whatever the damage they inflicted on Spain, their impact was more than merely destructive. Their forces aided the new colonies founded by their compatriots, just as their demand for supplies and disbursement of loot stimulated the economies of the nascent settlements. Indeed some erstwhile buccaneers, like prudent businessmen, eventually invested their takings in plantations in Jamaica and St Domingue and some turned to a profitable living from contraband trade. By the end of the seventeenth century the heyday of Caribbean piracy had passed. Violence provoked reprisals, or the threat of reprisals, against the colonies of fellow countrymen. It also ensured the united opposition of those, of whatsoever nationality, whose burgeoning and valuable trade, legal or otherwise, it disrupted. Buccaneers who persisted in their accustomed ways were driven out, some to the Bahamas from where they continued to cause trouble, some to the Indian Ocean.

But the most obvious erosion of the power of Spain came with the steady encroachment of other European states on those areas to which its rulers claimed exclusive title. The French tried and failed in Florida (as also in Brazil) in the mid 1500s. The next and more cautious move was into North America, well out of Spanish reach and, in the early decades of the seventeenth century, into the outer islands of the Caribbean, either neglected or abandoned by Spain, and on to the equally remote coasts north of Brazil. There was much talk of greater schemes – of English seizure of Mexico and Peru in the 1620s and, on and off from the days of Oliver Cromwell, of intervention in Chile. The Dutch, with hopes of securing Peru, invaded and were ejected from Brazil (1624–54). And other than in the Caribbean and along its southern littoral this was to be the usual outcome wherever Spain was prepared to defend her claims. Hence by the early 1600s English, French and Dutch New World colonies were confined – North America apart, where Spanish interest had early cooled – to the Bermudas, the Lesser Antilles, the islands off the Venezuelan coast and the wild lands between the deltas of the Orinoco and the Amazon.[13] From these apparently unpromising footholds it was initially hoped to secure, in one way or another, products such as tobacco, which had become increasingly difficult to acquire from smugglers as a result of Spanish policies. Then came penetration to the very heart of the Caribbean. In 1655, following an ignominious repulse from Hispaniola, the English captured Jamaica in pursuit of a grand strategy to ruin Spain and control the riches of the Indies. In 1670, following lengthy endeavours, they eventually secured a base off the Nicaraguan coast and shortly after set up semi-piratical logging settlements on the neighbouring mainland. St Domingue (Hispaniola) became the centre of French buccaneering while the Dutch conducted a vital (and illicit) commerce throughout the West Indies. Spain was at length forced to acknowledge the existence of such colonies, as in the agreement (1670) with England. Thus by the end of the seventeenth century an area once claimed as an exclusive Hispanic imperial domain had become yet another theatre of conflict between European powers, and what had for long been the most depressed part of the Spanish American empire now contained, as we shall see, some of the richest colonial lands, all the possessions of Spain's opponents past and present. And at the beginning of the eighteenth century the English, having secured the monopoly of the provision of African slaves to the Indies, obtained a foothold in the south at Buenos Aires and soon rapidly expanded it.[14]

On the mainland Spain had problems of another sort. The disastrous decline in the indigenous populations meant a drop in the amount of work, payments and goods that could be exacted from them. Silver production fell from the early 1600s, not recovering till after mid century. Many of the most accessible veins of ore had been exploited and Spanish technology was unequal to working the more difficult – or, indeed, according to critics, to minting presentable coins. The mercury essential for refining was everywhere in short supply. In northern Mexico, where there was ore in abundance, the terrain was wild and the land barely subdued. In Peru, where by the end of the sixteenth century most of the work-force were unfree Indians, there was a lack of miners – eventually overcome, as already in Mexico, by the use of paid labour – as the native population shrank and as the survivors fled to escape service or found ways to avoid it. Furthermore, of the silver produced, greater amounts were retained in the New World for conspicuous consumption (public and private), and to meet rising defence costs. Still more, in all probability, was smuggled out. Hence to the government's embarrassment there was less bullion – on official reckoning, hardly a sixth in 1650 of what there had been in 1600 – at the very time when, chiefly through the burden of incessant war, its needs were desperately urgent.

The difficulties in the mining industry had widespread repercussions. As output fell the currency was devalued in Peru and sound coin hoarded in Mexico, while a lack of bullion damaged Manila's Asian trade in the mid 1600s. Landowners who supplied the mines with food, livestock, leather and other goods lost valuable markets. And indeed the whole Atlantic economy, as officially defined, contracted, with annual sailings of the fleets between Spain and America down from the 300 of the heyday to a mere fifty in the mid 1600s. Nor did imperial policy help. In the hope of stemming the illicit outflow of bullion, trade between Mexico and Peru was banned in 1634, provoking riots in Manila (now starved of silver) and aggravating depression in Mexico. The Inquisition's pursuit of heresy and deviance drove Jews from colonies such as Venezuela (1620–50), depriving the economy of some of its ablest entrepreneurs. The prolonged struggle against the Dutch meant that till the peace of 1648 the Republic's naval campaigns in the Atlantic disrupted the influx and forced up the price of African slaves. Some undertakings were crippled by natural disaster, as was Venezuelan cacao-growing in the mid 1600s. Others foundered, or had already foundered, in the face of foreign competition, like Caribbean sugar, undercut by that of Portuguese Brazil in the late 1500s. Yet though economic contraction, war and piracy meant that intercolonial commerce was virtually defunct in many areas by the mid seventeenth century, the gloom was not so unrelieved as officially depicted. Nor, of course, was what was bad for Spain necessarily bad for her colonies. True, they experienced no such economic growth as those of other powers in North America and the West Indies. Equally true, many of their economies were of a primitive subsistence nature, insulated from external influences. Yet some enterprises, like shipbuilding, flourished under the demands of war. Primary producers found outlets within the continent itself and industries such as the manufacture of sugar and textiles flourished for much of the seventeenth century in Mexico. Even more significantly illegal intercolonial trades (as with the Philippines) continued and there was a roaring business with European smugglers.

Meanwhile Spain had to face the insoluble problem, which eventually confronts all imperial powers, of reconciling the wishes and interests of influential colonial subjects with those of the mother country. The empire became richer and the Spanish kingdoms poorer. Wealthy urban centres like Mexico City, controlling great hinterlands were, rather than Seville, the veritable centres of power in the Indies. Colonists of European descent rapidly developed a consciousness of their own identity and superiority, and already in the mid 1500s royal officials were complaining of the emergence of a generation born in the Indies who neither knew their king nor wished to know him.[15] They equally rapidly developed a keen sense of the contempt in which they were generally held in metropolitan society. To their disgust it was Spaniards from the peninsula, not creoles (American-born Spaniards) who monopolized the most lucrative and prestigious posts in church and state in the Indies, while the colonies were now expected, as never before, to contribute to the massive burden of imperial defence. A delicate situation was made worse by the declining quality of the once-celebrated imperial bureaucracy and by the general bankruptcy of Spanish statecraft and the mediocrity of Spanish statesmen after the early 1600s.[16] The outcome was friction, conflict and political disorder on a scale not seen since the Peruvian civil wars of the mid 1500s. Creole monks in Lima denounced their Spanish superiors as 'tyrants and enemies'. The Viceroy of Mexico was driven from office in 1624 when, in the course of a hamfisted attempt to exact a larger contribution to defence, he simultaneously fell foul of both church and well-entrenched creole merchants and oligarchs. A successor feared an uprising in 1640 and there was renewed revolt in 1692. In the Philippines, governors clashed with the church and one was arrested (1671) by the Inquisition. Not surprisingly there was widespread suspicion of colonial loyalties in seventeenth-century Spain. Furthermore, underlying these outbursts there was a general weakening of Spanish control, allowing local officials, in that familiar style of early medieval Europe, to turn themselves into local potentates. Even so, compared with the disorders in contemporary Europe, or the persistent turbulence of the colonies of English North America, the record of Spain's rule in the Indies was creditable enough.

Over and above these problems was that of the surviving indigenous peoples, soon identified by Spain's European enemies as potential allies. Some of the so-called 'wild Indians', like the man-eating Caribs, of the Lesser Antilles, the Spaniards prudently left to their own devices. Others, however, had to be contained or controlled in the interests of profit or security. Christian kindness, 'cruel war', the settlement of 'pacified Indians' and the erection of fortified posts were all tried in attempts to ensure access to the silver-producing areas of northern Mexico. The heartlands of the one-time Amerindian empires were eventually secure enough, notwithstanding Inca survival in Peru into the 1570s, a large-scale anti-Christian millenarian movement in the preceding decade and the discovery, in the seventeenth century, of the fragility of the supposed conversion of the Andean peoples. But outside the ancient Aztec and Inca boundaries the going was hard. There was more or less continuous warfare against the Araucanians in Chile. Nearly as bad were relations with the Chiriguanos of Paraguay, old enemies of the Incas, who in the 1560s almost reached Potosí, and who remained unsubdued in the eastern foothills of the Andes. Revolt in New Mexico in 1680 – one of a series of uncoordinated Amerindian risings running the length of the Americas as European pressures increased – pushed the Spaniards back to El Paso and authority was only slowly reimposed from the end of the century by a combination of missionary endeavour and military conquest. In the wild lands of the Caribbean, on the Isthmus of Panama and in difficult country elsewhere there flourished virtually independent communities of escaped African slaves (*cimarrones*), willing allies of Spain's enemies; while the so-called Sambos and Mosquitos of the eastern coasts of Honduras and Nicaragua, an improbable blend of Amerindians, whites and former black slaves, threatened Guatemala.

But the most fundamental weakness of the Spanish empire was the feeble economy of the mother country itself, increasingly unable to meet the demands, or benefit from the products, of the colonies, and in ruins by the early 1600s. The Spanish state was a federation of kingdoms and principalities united only in their allegiance to a common ruler. Of these realms Castile alone could be taxed to, and indeed far beyond, its full potential. Yet Castile was a land with an overwhelmingly agrarian economy, burdened wih the impossible volume of demands for men, money and goods generated by the European ambitions of the Habsburgs and further weakened by their unfortunate economic policies. Spain's supposed monopoly of the commerce of the Indies was hence either ignored by those able and willing to trade there, or operated as the means whereby the goods of others flowed out across the Atlantic and colonial products in turn flowed back to non-Spanish hands. Nearly 70 per cent of the bullion imported into Spain in 1608 was, according to official figures, in return for foreign goods. Roughly a century later about 90 per cent of imports from America were for non-Spaniards, while New World markets were allegedly clogged with commodities brought in by the Dutch and French.

Much French business was transacted through the official monopoly, with merchants using local partners or taking Spanish nationality to qualify. Much more trade was conducted illicitly and with brazen effrontery, the Dutch transhipping silver even in Cadiz itself (1651) 'out of the command of any of the forts or castles'. English Jamaica, Dutch Curaçao, and French St Domingue were flourishing entrepôts for dealings with mainland Spanish America. With the encouragement of their government French Atlantic ports (St Malo and Nantes in particular) and French colonies in the Antilles entered the same market and a company was set up in 1698 with the express purpose of pursuing such opportunities. France secured (1701) the monopoly of supplying African slaves, and French ships (especially those of St Malo) worked to Chile and Peru. Indeed, for a time it appeared that French hegemony might become absolute. With the failure of the Habsburg dynasty the grandson of Louis XIV of France was, despite the opposition of Holland and England, established as ruler of Spain and its overseas empire. But by armed force the English secured for themselves (1713) the monopoly of the slave trade – in anticipation of which the South Sea Company had been established (1711) – and the right to send an annual shipload of merchandise to the Caribbean, which in fact allowed them to funnel in as much as they could manage.

By this date, and partly as a result of such stimuli, the Spanish Indies were reviving. The supply of African slaves improved. Bullion output recovered, helped among other things by the consolidation of workings into larger units and the belated introduction of such technical advances as blasting and improved drainage. Silver exports had increased in the later 1600s and agriculture looked up, with sugar planting re-established in the Caribbean islands. Despite the many and obvious shortcomings of the imperial government, the Spanish Americas remained essentially territorially intact, losing no inland urban centre of any importance until the USA took Mexico City in 1847. The major areas of settlement and prosperity were remote, or sited in the interior and so inaccessible as to be beyond the reach of casual incursions. And from a convenient combination of policy and apathy the few overland routes there were remained unimproved. Nevertheless even isolated outposts could, if need be, defend themselves resolutely. But this became less necessary as, with the passage of time, the Indies came to be seen in Europe more as a market of huge potential than as a suitable victim for pillage.

The only equivalent to Spanish America was Portuguese Brazil. It too was of immense size and indeterminate frontiers, supporting a slave-based economy of planting, ranching and mining and inhabited by settlers conscious of their country's individual identity. And it too had been discovered by accident when, in 1500, an expedition to Asia, making a wide sweep westwards to clear the Cape of Good Hope, sighted what was briefly known as the 'Land of the Holy Cross'. The speedy realization that the country was rich in Brazil wood – producing a dye much in demand in the manufacture of textiles in Europe – gave it its present name and first aroused Portugal's imperial urge, with the crown licensing the trade in timber. The royal house, however, preoccupied with the opportunities of Asia and the gold and slaves of West Africa, had little time and less resources to attempt the colonization of this huge and largely impenetrable land. It contained millions of acres of tropical forest, either uninhabited or sparsely populated merely by primitive and often nomadic peoples who, unlike those of the Aztec and Inca realms, could only with the greatest difficulty be harnessed to European needs.

A livelier concern was awakened by rumours of precious metals and the incursions of rivals. The French, who had been taking dyewood on the coast since almost the beginning of the sixteenth century, showed an interest in the area to the north of the Río de la Plata in the mid 1500s and in 1555 colonized an island in the Bay of Rio de Janeiro. They were eventually driven off, but their clandestine trade continued, as did that of the English and Dutch, while the Spaniards, in an undertaking desperate even by their standards, crossed the Andes to reach the Atlantic by descending the Amazon. So in 1534 the Portuguese crown parcelled the country out into captaincies which, at their own expense, were to be subjugated, colonized and exploited by entrepreneurs who were rewarded with hereditary and virtually sovereign powers to encourage them in this costly and daunting task. The ensuing settlement of Brazil was recorded by the Portuguese in characteristically bellicose terms. But though there was certainly no lack of fighting with the indigenous inhabitants there was no brisk conquest, as in the Spanish Indies, and many reverses. Some of the first settlements were wiped out; in tropical swamps, deltas and forests European cavalry proved as useless as in densely wooded North America; expeditions bigger than any launched by Cortés and his contemporaries came to grief; Indians withdrew to the interior to keep their independence and fight again another day. Nor did the Portuguese make much headway as settlers until the introduction of sugar planting, in which they were already experienced in the Atlantic islands. On the rich virgin lands of the north-eastern littoral the crop prospered and soon became, as it was to remain almost till 1700, the basis of the Brazilian economy and the vital prop of the finances of the Portuguese state. In its heyday it employed the largest volume of tonnage (mostly foreign and mainly Dutch) of any trans-oceanic trade, with fleets commonly over one hundred strong, carrying to Europe a commodity which, chiefly through Portuguese enterprise, had been converted from a luxury enjoyed by an affluent minority to one of mass consumption. With sugar came big plantations and, inevitably, the African slaves to work them – 500,000 by 1700 – in such numbers as to leave modern Brazil with the largest black population outside Africa.

Such riches speedily attracted predators. As in most of Portugal's empire, wealth and settlement were concentrated on an oceanic littoral, easily vulnerable to attack by sea. Brazil's few towns and cities, separated by enormous distances and sited in regions producing much the same commodities, were in closer touch with Portugal than with one another. Most of the country's trade was, unlike that of the Spanish Indies, external and consequently at risk, while Portugal was notoriously weak by sea and commonly regarded as too feeble to defend her possessions. Nevertheless would-be French and English settlers were, for the most part, eventually driven from posts in the Amazon delta and Belém was founded (1616) to strengthen Portuguese control of the region. The Dutch were, in the end, confined to the future and unpromising Guyana and Surinam, but not before they had invaded Brazil itself in the course of their wars against the Hispano-Portuguese empires. After some inept fumblings they established a foothold (1630) and soon controlled the north-east, where the best sugar-producing lands lay. After a struggle they were, like other intruders, finally expelled (1654) through a combination of their own incompetence, the deflection of their energies elsewhere and the dogged opposition of the Brazilians.

These pressures, together with the needs and problems of the sugar industry, stimulated Portuguese territorial expansion and changes in the economy of Brazil. The state of Maranhão was founded (1621) in the north, from where a handful of Europeans, living lives almost as Indian as those of the indigenous peoples, fought, traded – especially for slaves – and fornicated with the locals. In the south there were attempts, destined to failure, to control the Río de la Plata, and thus enjoy the fruits of the silver trade with Peru. Settlement was pushed further inland, with Manáus founded (1674) 1200 kilometres up the Amazon. Expeditions from São Paulo, in pursuit of silver and slaves, penetrated, in epics of endurance as remarkable as any by sea, to the foothills of the Andes in the west, the tributaries of the Amazon in the north and the Uruguay River in the south, where they were embroiled with the Jesuit missionary enclaves in Spanish Paraguay. Fighting with Amerindian tribes was ubiquitous and as fierce and prolonged as anywhere, culminating in the suppression of a great rising in the north in 1712.

To meet the demands of colonists for livestock, meat and leather there developed, as in Spanish America, ranching on a vast scale – with some holdings bigger than entire Portuguese provinces – while both European crops (notably wheat) and those of indigenous origin (tobacco and cotton especially) were successfully cultivated, allowing the export of the surplus together with dyewood, hides and the all-important sugar and its by-products, most notoriously a fearsome rum. But by the late seventeenth century Brazilian sugar was in difficulties. Prices were falling, the soil in the pioneer producing areas was exhausted, the industry was afflicted by disease and hampered by heavy taxation. Brazilian technology was poor and there was a shortage of capital and as a result of the feckless and expensive way of life of the planters, many of whom, so it was alleged in 1717, being Jewish were also in trouble with the Inquisition.[17] Worst of all the industry now had to face the competition of imports from Asia and of the output – more easily accessible – of the Caribbean islands.[18] But the gloom was short-lived. Sugar markets recovered by the early 1700s and better still the long search for some new Potosí was at last rewarded when *c.* 1695 gold was found in the region still known by the unalluring name of 'The General Mines'. It was, furthermore, mostly alluvial gold, needing none of the equipment and capital demanded by deep mining. The glad tidings set off the first of the great gold rushes of modern times, attracting, despite royal injunctions, peoples of many races and of all ages and social classes. Their frenetic pursuit of wealth degenerated into open war (1708–9) between the Brazilian backwoodsmen who had made the find and newcomers from Europe. It ended with victory for the so-called 'tenderfeet' from the mother country, so leaving the fields in the hands of a population of basically Portuguese origins.

The impact of the discovery was far-reaching. It dealt a further blow to sugar as labour fled or was directed to the mines. It forced up the price of slaves, similarly in demand for mining, to levels too high for planters. It stimulated penetration inland – where towns were founded to consolidate Portuguese authority – and it hastened the southward shift of population and consequently of political power within the country. Brazil's wealth, further increased by the finding of diamonds in the same region, redressed Portugal's loss of revenues and prestige in Asia. The royal finances were restored. Lisbon once again became one of the richest cities. The country enjoyed a gold currency of renowned purity and its affluence enabled it to become once again integrated into a wider economy, with the resources to buy such manufactures as English textiles or raw materials like North American naval stores. This happy outcome was achieved to the usual accompaniment of the decimation of the indigenous population of the colony, the conversion of some of the survivors to Christianity, and the massive import of luckless African slaves. For the fortunate white minority it was a different but equally familiar story. Planters lived in grand style in palatial houses. Brazil now had towns and cities, even if fewer and less elegant than the best in Spanish America, and it had churches and cathedrals of an ornate and distinctive Baroque. After a lengthy period of relatively free trade its seaborne commerce with Europe was conducted (at least in theory), like that of the Spanish Indies, in organized convoys under armed escort, provided between 1649 and 1720 by the Brazil Company. And despite renewed enemy assaults, like that of the French on Rio de Janeiro in 1711, the country lived in reasonable stability under metropolitan control.

The Iberian hold on Central and South America, combined with the accidents of European politics – such as the desire of the English crown for an accommodation with Spain well into the sixteenth century and again under the early Stuarts – were sufficient to deflect the endeavours of other potential colonial powers to higher latitudes. Under Protestant (Huguenot) inspiration the French were indeed momentarily established in Florida (1562–5) and Brazil (1555) and their illicit trade with Portuguese and Spanish possessions continued after their expulsion. But their main endeavour to find a passage leading to the riches of Asia was directed further north, with the Florentine Giovanni Verrazzano reconnoitring (1524) the American coast above Cape Fear (North Carolina) and Jacques Cartier the St Lawrence (1534). Hopes of gold, spices and great cities sprang eternal, but French energies were soon profitably directed to the acquisition of furs – those of the beaver in particular – which could be obtained by barter from the Amerindian tribes and for which there was an excellent market in Europe. So while French fishermen worked the rich waters of Newfoundland and its environs, French traders, from posts on the St Lawrence, received furs from the indigenous peoples in a commerce resembling that of the Portuguese in Asia in that the sources of production were outside European control.

Ambitious schemes for colonization, however, came to little. A modest settlement in Acadia (New Brunswick, Maine, Nova Scotia) had by the mid 1600s been reduced to a few footholds by the English and Scots. Along the banks of the St Lawrence the effort was greater and the outcome enduring. Even so the position was long precarious, and as late as 1683 the total European population of what was now known as Canada[19] was no more than 10,000. Neither the climate nor the opportunities were particularly attractive, not least since the fur trade was the monopoly of a series of commercial and colonizing companies. There were no precious metals. There was no subjugation of indigenous peoples by French power, no mass conversions of docile natives by Catholic missions and no rich lands for the taking, while some Frenchmen (*coureurs des bois*) were drawn as hunters and traders into an existence more Indian than European in that style already familiar on other colonial frontiers. But in the late seventeenth century there was a dramatic change when as part of an imperial grand strategy there commenced a southward drive from Canada designed to secure French control of the interior and to isolate the flourishing settlements of the English enemy on the eastern seaboard. La Salle descended the mighty Mississippi from the Great Lakes to the Gulf of Mexico (1682), Louisiana was occupied (1699), and in the course of the long and bitter Anglo-French struggles of 1689–97 and 1702–13 the English colonies in New York and New England were threatened and the English fur trade through Hudson Bay crippled.

Elsewhere French power and influence were similarly growing. Slave-trading stations were acquired in West Africa (as at Goree) during the wars against the Dutch. France's already strong economic influence in the Spanish Indies was confirmed by the acquisition of the monopoly of supplying African slaves.[20] The French, moreover, like other one-time opponents of Spain, had eventually established colonies in the Indies, starting on the fringes of Iberian power, as at Cayenne (1604), north of the Amazon delta, and in the remoter West Indian islands, notably St Christophe (1625), which they shared with the English, Martinique and Guadeloupe and ending with deeper penetration of the Caribbean with the acquisition (1697) of the old buccaneering stronghold of St Domingue. The islands became centres of French maritime and military ambitions and also, after some troubles, producers of considerable wealth. They were bases for buccaneering or for illicit dealings with Spanish possessions. They grew tobacco to start with, using unfree white labour. Then, as over-production brought prices down, they turned, like their English neighbours, to sugar, increasingly produced on large plantations worked by black slaves. Further ambitions were for a time curbed when, through military defeat and financial exhaustion France was worsted in the War of the Spanish Succession. By the Treaty of Utrecht (1713) she surrendered to the English her part of St Christophe, Nova Scotia, claims on Newfoundland, gains made around Hudson Bay and lost the monopoly of the Indies slave trade.[21]

Dutch expansion in the West was of much the same pattern, though briefly the achievement was more extensive and spectacular. A colony, the future New York, was founded in North America (1614) as an outcome of Henry Hudson's attempt to find a passage to Asia. Notwithstanding the failure, despite much experiment, to devise an effective way of encouraging settlement, the colony was soon contesting the Canadian fur trade with the French, drawing it away from the St Lawrence to the more accessible outlet of the Hudson River. But neither here – nor as a rule elsewhere – did the Dutch succeed as colonists. The New Netherlands, as the territory was then known, failed to attract settlers from a homeland which, by contemporary standards, was prosperous and tolerant, and to which, rather than from which, people fled. Nor was Holland prepared to allow colonists any part in the lucrative fur trade, or indeed consider them engaging in anything other than the most rudimentary agriculture. Under-populated – with 5000 Europeans at best by the mid 1600s – its inhabitants a rich and unassimilated diversity of nations and religions, and restive under military rule, the New Netherlands succumbed to the English (1664) and became New York.

For much the same reasons Dutch attempts to hold Brazil also collapsed. This ambitious venture was entrusted to the West India Company, founded in 1621, but soon hamstrung by the political, military and economic disputes within the Republic as to Dutch objectives. And any likelihood of success was further diminished by the dissipation of Dutch resources on projects throughout the southern Atlantic and the irreconcilable differences between Catholic Brazilians and their Protestant would-be masters. Thus by the mid seventeenth century all that remained of Holland's colonies in mainland America were some tenuous posts on the coast between the deltas of the Amazon and the Orinoco, recognized by Spain in 1648. In the Caribbean, however, the Dutch went from strength to strength. As in Asia they first appeared to obtain commodities no longer available to them in Europe as a result of their supposed exclusion from Iberian ports.[22] They established themselves in such tiny islands as Curaçao, Bonaire, Aruba and Tortuga and with an economy more highly developed than that of any other pioneer colonial power they were soon engaged in a massive clandestine trade. The creation of the West India Company brought the vigorous implementation of venerable Protestant schemes to cut off Spain's life-blood by the capture of the bullion fleet, triumphantly accomplished in 1628. Dutch influence was further strengthened when, following their expulsion from Brazil, they disseminated throughout the islands now colonized by other European powers skills they had learned from the Portuguese in the production of sugar. Dutch capital backed the nascent industry. Dutch ships carried sugar to Europe, where much was refined for resale in the very states claiming sovereignty over the islands, and Dutch vessels returned with whatever goods colonists required. Above all, in the second half of the seventeenth century, and in defiance of Spanish policy the Dutch (ostensibly the West India Company) supplied, largely through their base in Curaçao, many of the African slaves needed for the plantations.[23]

Of a very different order were the doings of the English in the Americas. Attempts, from the late fifteenth century, to find a north-west passage to the East brought them to the inhospitable coasts of north-east America and Canada. Persistence in this desperate undertaking throughout the best part of the first imperial age led, with little profit and at enormous cost in endurance and sacrifice, to the discovery of a multitude of islands, bays and straits among the frozen seas of the Pole, named after the magnates who backed the voyages, or the seamen, like Martin Frobisher and John Davis, who undertook them. In the late sixteenth century energies were turned to attempts to found settlements further south, as at Roanoke (North Carolina), largely inspired by hopes, particularly dear to a nation addicted to piracy and privateering, of establishing bases from which to attack the Spanish treasure fleets. In these and most subsequent ventures the crown took no other part than selling privileges – often the same one to different entrepreneurs – to individuals or companies willing to undertake some

particular scheme. After shaky beginnings Virginia (1607) eventually prospered, following the introduction of tobacco growing, and since its initial
support speedily collapsed it was brought under royal control to become
(1624) the first crown colony.

On the coast of New England, as it had been known since 1614, there
subsequently appeared settlements of a fundamentally different nature.
They were founded in lands in which, as in Virginia, indigenous opposition
was weakened by the ravages of European disease. But they were founded
by groups of ardent biblical Protestants whose tenets were affronted by the
doctrines and policies of the Anglican church, making England unique in
permitting colonization by those whose views were unacceptable in the
mother country. The first was at Plymouth (1620), a tiny community in a
harsh environment which, aided by local inter-tribal rivalries and by the
hard work and tenacious faith of its members, survived to become an
agrarian settlement of small family-worked farms. Relations with neighbouring Indians were, as such things went, reasonably good, even if
professions of Christian love were at times reinforced by the use of firearms.
Far larger and more prosperous was the influentially backed Massachusetts
(1630) remarkable among other things in that its foundation involved the
emigration of whole families and communities, and where there quickly
grew up a thriving settlement of farms and small towns, with a highly
literate gentry and a superabundant and learned clergy influential in its
government. Other settlements soon followed. Theological dispute in
Massachusetts in the 1630s scattered the oppressed to Providence, Connecticut, Rhode Island and New Haven. Colonies were founded for the benefit
of those persecuted at home, like Maryland (1632) for Catholics, and Penn's
later haven in the former New Netherlands for Quakers. Of prime importance in this activity was the willingness, not to say eagerness, of the later
Stuart monarchs to grant charters as a means of rewarding their followers
or raising funds. Furthermore, there was after 1660 an influential group in
politics – among its members the future James II – advocating colonization
and better able to implement their views than their Elizabethan precursors.
A major objective was to oppose first Holland and then France. Hence
settlements were acquired (like New York) or established (like New Jersey,
Delaware and Pennsylvania) to close the gap between Virginia and New
England. Thus would the commercially triumphant Dutch, ubiquitous in
colonial trades, be bridled, just as they were to be driven out of Atlantic
slave-trading, while the furs of North America were to be diverted into
English hands by the opening of a new route through Hudson Bay.

So, by 1700 there were along the east coast of America eleven separate,
not to say independent, English colonies running from Maine in the north
to Carolina in the south. Unlike the Iberian Americas, settlement was
confined to a narrow coastal strip, commonly no more than a day or
so's march away from untouched and untamed Indian country, and often

concentrated along the banks of a river, so permitting travel and transport. The colonial economies ranged from farming, smuggling and maritime communities in the north to the plantations of Virginia and the sprawling, sparsely inhabited lands of South Carolina. Political organization was even more diverse, embracing the remnants of theocracy in Massachusetts and neo-feudalism in Carolina with its landgraves and caciques. Until the French and Indian attacks in the wars of the late 1600s the colonies in general flourished. Settlers, though never in sufficient numbers, were drawn in from near and far – from Barbados to South Carolina; from English fishing fleets to Massachusetts; from among the oppressed of Ireland, Scotland and Europe to Pennsylvania. And where there were insufficient hands, as was widely the case, unfree white labour and eventually black slaves were shipped in. Within a dozen years of its foundation Philadelphia was among the six biggest towns of North America and by 1740 the region had a white population of well over a million and one far less footloose than those of the French and Iberian Americas.

But settlement meant pressure on land and hence on the luckless indigenous survivors. Those of Virginia rose against their oppressors in the first half of the seventeenth century. Similar happenings in New England culminated in the so-called King Philip's War of the 1670s when concerted Indian attack rendered only the major seaports safe. Twelve out of the territory's ninety towns were destroyed and the damage was on such a scale that not until the mid eighteenth century were the losses made good. Eventually the rising collapsed through disease, shortage of food and weapons and in the face of the onslaughts of the colonial forces, among them Indian allies and Caribbean buccaneers. Nor were things all that much better in Pennsylvania, despite the founder's laudable desire to live with the local peoples as 'neighbours and friends'; while in the south slaving raids from Carolina provoked revolts by the Tuscaroras (1711) and Yama-sees (1715). With indigenous aid both were finally suppressed and the survivors obliged to move on.

The political life of the colonies was equally turbulent. Some were private (proprietary) foundations, some crown colonies and none effectively subject to any overall authority. Many had populations embracing an improbable diversity of ethnic groups and religious persuasions – like South Carolina's mixture of Anglicans, royalists, French Protestants and Scottish dissenters. In societies in the process of formation there was the usual acrimonious competition for such few offices as there were among those eager to ratify their pretensions to superiority. There was trouble in Virginia in the later 1600s when new immigrants found the best land already in the hands of established planters, while the latter were in difficulties through falling tobacco prices. Discontent, intensified by the governor's allegedly soft policy on natives and his resolute restriction of power and profit to his own intimates, brought an attack on the Indians (1675–6) which soon turned into open rebellion, only ended by the death of its leader. There were further riots (1682) over depressed tobacco prices, while in Maryland friction was engendered by the exclusion from office of prosperous but non-Catholic settlers and a rising sparked off in North Carolina (1677) by the attempted imposition of a tobacco duty. New England, the haven for persecuted sects in its day, faced the problem of containing the repercussions of their proliferation as ardent biblical study and individual interpretation of Holy Writ multiplied warring factions. The stern Congregationalists of Rhode Island had no time for any discipline, civil or ecclesiastical. In Massachusetts, aggressive, expansionist and generally on bad terms with its neighbours, the heirs of the founding fathers found themselves a minority in a prosperous world of ungodly merchants, sailors and sea captains who were not prepared to be denied political rights by a theocratic constitution which long restricted the vote to church members, so disenfranchising the majority of the population.

Troubles, already serious, were exacerbated when, through the pressures of war and the ambitions of the post-Restoration monarchy, attempts were made to set up some effective form of English colonial administration. The bold project of James II for a Dominion of New England brought to the New World such vigorous military men as governors Dongan (New York) and Andros (New England) whose brusque proceedings – attempts at taxation, support for the Anglican church, government without consultation – were not to the liking of representative assemblies accustomed to having their own way. The fall of James (1688) further fuelled the flames and only in the early decades of the eighteenth century was comparative stability established under some general degree of metropolitan supervision.[24] The American colonies, not surprisingly, never became the apple of the English government's eye. At a time when resources in manpower were believed to be dwindling, and demand on such as there were was certainly growing (notably for crews for merchant and fighting ships), they required settlers. Unlike the colonies of all the other European powers, for a long time they produced little of use to the mother country, other than the tobacco of the southern plantations and the Canadian furs shipped from New York. To add insult to injury some set up industries of their own, competing with those of the mother country, and others, in defiance of her policies, employed Dutch shipping and supported pirates, privateers and smugglers. Worse still, New England and especially Boston were neither able – through lack of natural resources – nor willing to live as the parent state demanded by exchanging colonial raw materials for English manufactures. Instead they developed an important shipping industry handling valuable trades. New England vessels sold American agricultural produce in the West Indies (English and French alike), re-exported Caribbean sugar and its by-products (again both English and French) to Europe and returned with European commodities. In so doing they violated the fiscal and commercial system devised by the English government, damaged the interests of English merchants and deprived the crown of customs revenues. Unabashed they demanded aid against native and European attack and naval protection for their seaborne commerce, much of it with the mother country's greatest enemy, France.[25]

But England's chief concern in the West was not with mainland America but with the islands of the West Indies which, after exiguous beginnings became its most treasured possessions, accounting by 1700 for 12 per cent of the value of the country's recorded imports.[26] Like the Dutch and the French, and for the same reasons, the English had acquired footholds on islands unoccupied or abandoned by Spain, settling in Barbados, St Kitts (shared with the French who knew it as St Christophe) and elsewhere in the Lesser Antilles, together with the Bermudas and, after 1655, Jamaica. The islands in the Caribbean were quickly, and as a rule densely, populated – none more so than Barbados – and before long were exporting some dyes, cocoa and ginger and substantial amounts of tobacco and cotton mostly grown by unfree white labour. The future, however, lay with sugar, increasingly produced in the course of time on large plantations worked by African slaves, as was the case elsewhere. Primacy passed from Barbados to the Leeward Islands and Jamaica. Nor was this the only source of the wealth and importance of this Cromwellian legacy, ruled by a planter aristocracy in part descended from officers of the Republic's army. It was a major privateering and buccaneering base in its early days. It developed valuable dealings with Spanish possessions as its predatory urges cooled and as Spain recognized the legitimacy of the English colonies. It illicitly traded rum and sugar to the Yucatán (Mexico) in exchange for its celebrated dyewood. In return for 'great quantities of bullion' it provided, also illicitly, the Spanish islands and mainland with anything from English woollens to African slaves, and on a scale sufficient to bring about a decline in English trade with the Indies by the old official route through Seville/Cadiz. Such was the wealth and influence of its merchants that at the very height of the War of the Spanish Succession they could demand naval protection for their goods going to Spanish territories and immunity from naval attack for the Spanish bases where they carried on their business.

English hegemony in the West was confirmed by the peace of 1713. The country guaranteed the integrity of Spain's possessions while Spain undertook not to alienate any territory to other nations or to allow France (a branch of whose royal house ruled the country and its empire) any special privileges. In the meanwhile the Dutch had effectively been excluded by English naval strength and commercial policies from the trade of England's New World colonies. And there was no more emphatic indication of this supremacy than when in 1715 the French, having scraped together sufficient shipping for the renewed sailing of the treasure fleet, saw the vessels overwhelmed by a hurricane and a good part of the bullion looted by an erstwhile Jamaican pirate.

Even so, the English West Indies had their problems. Widely dispersed throughout waters where the prevailing winds made communications slow and difficult the islands were particularly vulnerable to attack. Among their inhabitants in the early years were substantial numbers of unfree and often restive, not to say desperate, whites. Later they had large and potentially rebellious slave populations. Their political history was often as wayward and turbulent as that of the mainland colonies.[27] Nevertheless they were, by contemporary criteria, ideal imperial possessions. They stimulated the long distance trade of the mother country, offered no competition to its industries and indeed provided a useful market for their products. They were no drain on England's population once they employed black slaves, and the provision of these was yet another business to enrich English merchants and give work to English ships. Sugar from the islands was a commodity which contributed notably to the affluence of men of substance (planters, merchants, shipowners) and above all generated substantial revenues for the metropolitan state. Such virtue could not be left undefended and the Caribbean colonies were speedily brought under direct royal control.[28]

Thus by the beginning of the eighteenth century, in the New World as in Asia, power, wealth and influence had passed from the Iberian states to those of northern Europe. In the East the European impact was modest, primarily commercial and showing few signs of that massive extension it was shortly to undergo. In the West, despite Indian risings everywhere from New England to Brazil, white dominance was growing and white exploitation intensifying. Indigenous populations were destroyed or weakened and the whole ethnic balance radically and irrevocably altered by European settlement and the influx of African slaves. The Americas, their inhabitants previously the most isolated of all mankind, were linked for the first time to the economy of a wider world of which Asia, on the other hand, had for centuries been a fundamental part, but linked, unlike the East, in a subordinate role. All the most profitable European New World enterprises, whether the acquisition of sugar, fish or silver, were, unlike those in Asia, the fruits of the introduction of new forms of exploitation. They reflected, as was not the case in the East, the subjugation and settlement of vast tracts of land, eventually brought under some measure of metropolitan control. This in itself was a remarkable achievement given the distances involved, the dispersed nature of white settlement and the uncertain communications – a round trip of at least fourteen months between Spain and the Indies; two months either way between England and Barbados.

Pursuit of profit in the West and the defence of colonial possessions affected the economies and policies of parent states, brought clashes between colonists and their mother countries and geographically extended the field of conflict between European powers. In the Americas, Spain and Portugal successfully defended the territorial integrity of their empires and ensured by a missionary effort more rewarding than that in the East that their new subjects were nominally Catholic and certainly not Protestant. They drew some economic benefit from their overseas possessions, but eventually ended as their poor relatives and although they were able to retain sovereignty over territories more extensive than those of fellow European powers (Holland and France in particular) imperial profits were increasingly reaped by others and nowhere in the New World did there develop economies as vigorous as those of the quarrelsome and variegated English settlements in North America.

Finally there was Africa, the first continent to experience and the last to reject white ambitions in the modern age. But before the nineteenth century, from its sheer size, its resources in manpower, its difficult terrain, hostile climates and lethal diseases, it endured only minimal colonization. The most persistent were the Portuguese, many of them convinced that this was their land of destiny. Following the capture of Ceuta (1415) they established some tenuous footholds in Morocco and spent the best part of the next two hundred years in the time-honoured aristocratic pursuits of raiding, pillaging, slaving and exacting tribute. This predatory regime ended when a crushing defeat (1578) at the hands of a resurgent local dynasty, enriched and strengthened by control of the gold of the upper Niger and supplied by Portugal's many European opponents, led to their virtual expulsion from North Africa. Even so, they had managed to occupy non-European Muslim territory for a longer period than any other western power.

In the course of their prolonged push down the west coast of the continent the Portuguese established a series of bases – Arguim (1443) and on the Gold Coast at Mina (1482) and Axim (1503). From these, after rebuffs by indigenous military strength and the ravages of tropical disease had disabused them of visions of conquest and colonization, they settled down to trade with local peoples, Muslims included, chiefly for ivory, gold and slaves. Meanwhile the islands of the eastern Atlantic were colonized. Those, like Madeira and the Azores, in non-tropical waters, eventually became peasant-worked white settlements producing wine or wheat. But those to the south (the Cape Verdes, São Tomé, Príncipe), where heat and endemic sickness speedily disposed of most Europeans, developed into non-white – basically mulatto – slave-based societies displaying many of the unlovable features of much future tropical colonialism.[29] There were spasmodic incursions into the African interior – with some hardy individuals perhaps even reaching Timbuktu from Senegambia. Here, too, where the Portuguese faced by organized African societies could do no more than carry on a commerce from creeks and rivers, outcasts (the so-called lançados) settled inland in African villages, lived as Africans, and while evading any pretended Portuguese jurisdiction, served, like fellow frontiersmen elsewhere, as valuable intermediaries in trade.

South of the equator the pattern was different. The Portuguese reached the Bantu kingdom of the Congo in 1483. Here, as a result of their initial respect for a state they admitted to be governed 'by reason', because of the ruling house's eagerness for European tools, weapons, skills and military support, and not least from its genuine interest in Christianity, there emerged a remarkable Lusified and Catholic African monarchy which survived until the mid seventeenth century and in which vestiges of Christianity lasted longer still. But if the Portuguese rapidly and destructively drew the Congo into the Atlantic slave trade, unhappier still was the lot of Angola which they knew from about 1520. Inspired by hopes of silver and now convinced by the general failure of their Catholic missions in Africa that the faith could only be spread by force, they attempted (1571) the country's conquest and colonization. The outcome was some settlement, largely Luso-African, the reduction of Angola to the role of prime supplier of African slaves, the foundation of Luanda (1576) – Portugal's only major urban creation in the continent – the exacerbation of tribal wars and the ultimate ruin of the indigenous political organization.

From such activities Portugal long drew substantial wealth. The gold of Arguim allowed the minting of the renowned golden coin the *cruzado* (1457). In the early 1500s the Portuguese were reputedly exporting 400 kilograms of gold annually from Mina and Axim, in part paid for with metal goods improbably ranging from shaving mugs to chamber pots, and enjoying profits of 500 per cent. Africa was firmly linked to the slave trade of the wider world, while in the luckless Angola, entrepreneurs in the traffic were housed in 'costly and sumptuous buildings'. Such a commerce, and Portugal's growing inability to exploit and defend it, rapidly brought other Europeans to West Africa. After a bloodthirsty war the Spaniards had to admit – at least on paper – the pretended Lusitanian dominion in the region (1479). There were trading and slaving incursions by the English and French from the early 1500s. The formidable Dutch, then in the process of destroying the Portuguese empire in Asia, eventually took Mina (1638) though not without trouble and by 1663 controlled the entire Gold Coast and its trade. They also attempted, as part of their ambitious South Atlantic strategy against the joint Iberian monarchies, to hold Angola but failed, though securing in the end (1663) a post at Loango. By the second half of the seventeenth century Portugal's erstwhile monopoly of the African slave trade was disputed among the Dutch, French and English, together with various lesser contenders. Most now had factories on the coast and traded both in Angola and Guinea, whose former importance as a supplier revived towards 1700.

Equally promising were the prospects of East Africa where, as part of the rich and ancient maritime economy of Asia, gold and ivory from the Negro interior were brought to the coast to be exchanged for imports from the East and Middle East in a cluster of independent Arab and Muslim cities. To the Portuguese, in the euphoria of their triumphs of the early 1500s, it seemed no great matter to drive the disunited infidels of the littoral from such a commerce, take it into their own hands and then, benefiting from African tribal rivalries, to penetrate inland to the sources of production. They acquired a series of bases, such as Sofala (1505), on the East African coast. In pursuit of copper, ivory and gold they pushed into the interior, before long reaching Zimbabwe and, until defeated by the climate and Arab opposition, the southern shores of Lake Malawi. They settled on the Zambezi and in 1568–72 attempted, though in vain, the conquest of Manyika. In the following century, successfully exploiting the troubles of the crumbling Mutapa empire by offering aid to the various aspirants to power, they obtained privileges (such as the promise of tribute in gold) and land. More remarkably still, with the failure of the Makalanga confederacy adventurers – white, mulatto, Goan – were able to set themselves up as virtually independent sovereigns ruling over vast territories in the Zambezian hinterland, discharging the ritual functions of chiefs and ruling with an authority, observers remarked, as absolute as any German prince. Thus the Portuguese were able to destroy or disrupt much former Arab trade. They tightened their grip on ivory, established themselves in the gold-producing regions of the Mutapa empire for most of the seventeenth century and so effectively monopolized the commerce in gold that, in its heyday in the mid 1500s, their stronghold at Mozambique was annually exporting as much as eight tonnes to Asia. But though the Portuguese successfully rebuffed the incursions of other Europeans their hegemony was of the usual precarious nature. They were, as everywhere, chronically short of manpower and the more vulnerable since they were at the mercy of a hostile climate. They were expelled from the gold fields of the interior in the late 1600s just as they were driven from all their coastal posts north of Cape Delgado by the Omanis. Their remaining commerce was of a familiar pattern, heavily dependent on the goodwill and co-operation of local potentates and merchants, some of them converts to Christianity but the majority Muslims, and with principle sacrificed to profit and indeed to survival.

The only other African colony, and one of the few European settlements outside the Americas, was that of the Dutch at the Cape of Good Hope. It was founded (1652) in lands of idyllic climate, free (unlike their abortive ventures in Brazil and the New Netherlands) from the dangerous proximity of any other white power, and with the native Khoikhoi few and far between and living in a primitive state of endemic if not particularly sanguinary war. It was intended as a port of call for ships of the Dutch East India Company to refresh and reprovision. After some initial difficulties, largely stemming from the cost-conscious VOC's hostility to the expense of settlement and its well-founded suspicions that crews would desert or engage in smuggling, it began to grow. Colonists, most notably French Huguenots exiled after the revocation of the Edict of Nantes (1685) were brought in, and by the end of the century the Cape supported both arable and pastoral farming, though with livestock endangered by fierce native predators the ranching of the semi-nomadic *Trekboers* was never on the scale of their counterparts in the Americas. This transformation was accomplished to the usual accompaniment of the introduction of European-controlled slavery and the disorganization of the way of life of the indigenous peoples.

The chronicler of Magellan's great voyage of circumnavigation doubted that such a feat could ever be repeated. In fact, by the end of the sixteenth century an enterprising Italian merchant was able, despite some upsets, to go round the world almost entirely in a series of Iberian merchant ships working established routes, while a hundred years later pirates and priva- teers embarked on circumnavigations more or less as a matter of course. Yet much of the world and its seas were still unknown. It remained to be seen whether the Pacific was, like the Indian Ocean, land-locked to the north, what lay between Chile and New Zealand and whether there was some great continent in the South. And of such lands as were known outside Europe knowledge was largely confined, as with Africa, and much of North America, to coasts and their immediate hinterlands. What, however, Europeans knew by 1700, as they had not known 300 years earlier, was the nature and pattern of the major wind systems of the world, allowing them to move comparatively freely across so much of its seas and oceans; and what they had revealed was the will and ability, which most non-Europeans had either never possessed or were in the process of losing, to arrive at and remain in such lands, however distant, as they thought might offer them some reward.

NOTES AND REFERENCES

1 See p. 24.
2 D. C. Coleman, *The Economy of England 1450–1750* (Oxford University Press, 1977), p. 138.
3 See pp. 99–100, 103, 106–7.
4 See pp. 101, 236.
5 See pp. 99, 104, 106–7.
6 See pp. 57–58.
7 Two papal bulls were issued in 1493 enunciating Spanish sovereignty in the Columban discoveries and in other non-Christian lands yet to be found in the West. A third privilege defined the donation as lying beyond a meridian drawn north/south 100 leagues out from the Azores and the Cape Verde Islands. This destroyed any Portuguese claims in the West, while leaving Spain free to reach the East by circumnavigating the globe. Portuguese protest resulted in even more generous concessions to Spain, allowing her to explore to the West and the South, and leaving India open to her. Only the actual possessions of Christian princes were excluded from her reach.
8 See pp. 74–7.

9 See pp. 6–7, 74–7.
10 See pp. 219–20.
11 See pp. 124–38.
12 Michel Morineau, *Incroyables Gazettes et Fabuleux Métaux: Les Retours des Trésors Americains d'après les Gazettes Hollandaises (XVIᵉ–XVIIIᵉ Siècles* (Cambridge, 1985). See also pp. 31, 34, 133–4.
13 See pp. 39–40, 44–5.
14 See pp. 39, 44.
15 See the valuable essay of Bernard Lavallé in *Esprit Créole et Conscience Nationale*, ed. Joseph Perez (Paris, 1980).
16 See pp. 95, 150.
17 *Descriptive List of the State Papers Portugal 1661–1780 in the Public Record Office London*, vol. I, 1661–1723 (Lisbon, 1979), p. 399, no. 175.
18 See pp. 39, 44, 130–2.
19 From the Iroquois *caignetdaze* (metals other than gold).
20 See pp. 34, 121.
21 See pp. 44, 121, 129–32.
22 See p. 20.
23 See pp. 119–20.
24 See pp. 162–6.
25 See pp. 136, 243.
26 David W. Galenson, *Traders, Planters and Slaves. Market Behavior in early English America* (Cambridge, 1986), pp. 3–4.
27 See pp. 113–5, 165–6, 184.
28 See pp. 162–3.
29 See pp. 117, 184–7. Mulatto: of mixed negroid and European parentage.

2   Motives, ideals and ambitions

No single or simple reason explains what set in motion and sustained the staggering sequence of European exploration, conquest and colonization which commenced around 1400, though the whole gamut of human motives from economic necessity to idealistic fervour have at various times, and in various combinations, been invoked. It was once plausibly argued that the Turkish advance in the Middle East,[1] blocking the ancient westward flow of oriental spices through the Red Sea and the Levant, obliged Europeans to seek direct access to the source of these luxuries. But when the Portuguese voyages began in earnest towards the mid 1400s, spice imports from the Middle East were rising and prices were falling, as they were in Venice, Europe's main supplier.[2] Nor did the Ottomans conquer the Levant until the opening decades of the sixteenth century, by which date the Portuguese were regularly sailing to Asia, and Turkish rule, imposing order and reducing taxes, facilitated rather than impeded the trade.

Older views gave all the credit to Prince Henry of Portugal (d. 1460), who did indeed inspire some of the first voyages into the Atlantic and down the African coast and who, though never taking to the sea himself, was dubbed 'the Navigator' by an admiring nineteenth-century English scholar. This was in a well-established tradition, for in Renaissance Portugal, as European learned fashion dictated, laudatory histories extolled the achievements of rulers and depicted Henry as one impelled by rational curiosity. Yet important though the prince undoubtedly was, especially in ensuring that the voyages continued even though they brought no return, his motives are unclear, just as they were probably far from constant. His geographical learning was apparently modest and his intellectual interests limited, with his mind much occupied with thoughts of religion, honour and chastity. He apparently saw himself, like some hero of chivalric literature, as obliged to reward his faithful retainers – which, since he was in effect excluded from high politics, meant from sources outside Portugal – convert pagans, chastise infidels and seek out fellow Christians. Even so he was responsible for no more than a quarter of the expeditions known to have been sent down the African coast before his death.

Less satisfactory still are the arguments drawn from the analysis of Europe's subsequent imperial activities and applied to the radically different

circumstances of an earlier age. Thus it has been suggested that only by
about 1400 had the continent reached a sufficient level of economic development to enable it to sustain the costs and burdens of expansion. But great
concentrations of wealth, reflecting and controlled by remarkable commercial and financial skills, had long existed in such cities as Florence, Genoa
and Venice. For centuries maritime republics had been able to raise fleets
– like the 250 vessels provided by Venice for the crusade of 1204 – and
rulers had embarked on wars demanding infinitely greater resources and
capital than any of the first overseas expeditions. Mediterranean wealth and
skills were certainly soon drawn into oceanic ventures. But the majority of
the pioneer voyages were from the relatively backward Portugal and Spain,
undertaken not on the scale of Columbus' second expedition, but in tiny
vessels set out at negligible cost and financed locally. And even as late as
1499–1505 there was an almost entire absence of money from great international financiers in ventures launched from Andalusia.[3] Again, much
subsequent endeavour in Asia was backed by capital borrowed from
indigenous money-lenders, or, in the Americas, from the vast wealth
accumulated there by fellow Europeans. And that there was more to empire
building than ready capital and good credit was shown by the misfortunes
of the Dutch as colonists, while almost everywhere empire became a financial burden which states, whatever their level of economic development,
sooner or later found it difficult, if not impossible, to bear.

Another explanation, reflecting current concern with demography, is that
c. 1400 Europe's population was far greater than the continent was capable
of supporting. Overseas ventures were thus the outcome of an urgent search
for land and food, with the matter particularly pressing as the Ottoman
Turks, advancing westwards, denied Christian Europe access to the space
and resources of the eastern Mediterranean.[4] But the first voyages, in the
opening decades of the fifteenth century, were made at the very time that
Europe's population was static, or still declining, after a massive fall in the
late Middle Ages.[5] A visitor to Portugal in the mid 1400s, far from finding
it teeming with eager would-be emigrants, remarked that much of the
country was plague-stricken and 'quite deserted'.[6] Not surprisingly it
proved difficult, if not impossible, to recruit settlers for possessions which
reputedly offered little. As King Afonso V said (1466) of the Cape Verde
Islands, they were 'so far from our realms that nobody wishes to go and
live [there] unless they are granted exceptional liberties and privileges'.[7]
And not necessarily then, so that some of Portugal's Atlantic islands had
to be settled with foreigners, convicts, lepers, forced converts to Catholicism and any others who could be rounded up. Nor was the problem
peculiarly Portuguese. Almost everywhere outside the bullion-rich Spanish
Indies, emigrants, particularly those destined for any manual occupation,
remained in short supply. Whatever the demographic pressures in Europe,
where population was rising from the late 1400s to the early 1600s, and

where subsistence and other crises were endemic throughout, England, Holland and France could rarely raise anything like the numbers they required for America or the West Indies, without recourse, by the French and English – as by the Portuguese in Brazil – to various forms of compulsion.[8] Even in the Philippines the office of governor was conferred (1580) on 'a man of parts able to provide 600 settlers'.

Nor are there many signs of an urgent search for food, notwithstanding that in the sixteenth century the Iberian monarchies were already regularly obliged to seek supplies from European neighbours. Certainly North Africa, Portugal's first victim, was a grain producer. But in Morocco the Portuguese were more concerned with loot than food, which indeed they were often forced to provide from home to their garrisons cut off from local supplies. Where fisheries were discovered, as off Newfoundland, they were worked by fleets from the majority of Europe's Atlantic maritime states, and came to supply important markets in the continent. But with the possible exception of England, seeking a substitute for Iceland in the fifteenth century, there is nothing to suggest that the initial voyages were undertaken with the intention of finding new grounds. Overseas possessions, furthermore, rarely became the suppliers of basic foodstuffs. Some wheat was produced in the Portuguese Atlantic islands, but the majority rapidly turned to sugar and wine, just as Brazil and the Caribbean became sugar producers and parts of the Americas large-scale tobacco growers. The intention was to meet the demands of the affluent and increasing European minority who could afford such luxuries, not to cater for the undernourished or starving masses. Only Protestant North America eventually exported basic produce, but less to feed Europe than to sustain the monoculture islands of the Caribbean, unable to provide for themselves.

Alternatively, it has been argued, with the present addiction to economic modelling, that the driving force behind the beginnings of Europe's expansion was a search for the gold and silver needed to redress the chronic bullion shortage that afflicted the continent in the late Middle Ages. True, the pressure on Europe's stock of precious metals is well attested in its trade with the Levant, with specie accounting for as much as 60 per cent of the value of Venetian eastward exports, to pay for oriental and local luxuries in the later decades of the fifteenth century.[9] And certainly the Genoese and the Catalans, also involved in the Levant, had already attempted, both overland and by sea, to reach the gold-producing regions of the Niger basin. These, however, were problems confronting highly developed commercial communities involved in trades in which the Portuguese were not engaged. And they were problems which, by and large, had been solved before Portugal's overseas ventures were very far advanced. Venice linked her commerce more firmly to North Africa, where gold was available, from 1440. After prolonged contraction European silver production began to expand in the mid fifteenth century, reducing the need for arduous and distant searches, such as the Genoese, still hard-pressed for bullion for their dealings with south Spain, continued to make in the Sahara.[10] The Portuguese were indeed as glad as any – like those Normans who raided the Saharan coast from the Canaries in 1405 – to encounter gold, representing as it did wealth in its most acceptable and indestructible form, but there is little in their behaviour to suggest it was their initial objective. Only in the 1430s did Prince Henry attempt to secure the Canary Islands, perhaps intended to be an offshore base for African gold. Only thirty years after the capture of Ceuta did his fellow countrymen try to move into the Sahara from where, as others had long understood, bullion flowed to the northern shores of Africa – a very different pattern of behaviour from their vigorous and almost immediate endeavour to dominate the maritime economy they encountered on rounding the Cape of Good Hope. Whether any such economic determinants affected the genesis of Portugal's expansion is doubtful. Taken together they leave the improbable picture of a country overpopulated, underfed and economically depressed, yet allegedly seeking slaves (whose competition would worsen the lot of the free labour force) and endeavouring to step up the production of luxuries (like sugar) and increase the import of others, like spices, which were to compete in an already well-served and stagnant market.[11]

Scarcely more attractive is the contention that Europe's expansion commenced when it did because only then, with the appearance around 1400 of the Portuguese carvel – multi-masted, lateen-rigged[12] – could ships beat against a headwind, so allowing seamen to go where they wished, and not, as previously, where the elements dictated. Meanwhile improvements in navigational techniques, notably the observation of the sun and the stars, now permitted sailors to fix their position when out of sight of land, thereby opening the oceans of the world to explorers. But already in the early Middle Ages Scandinavian vessels had been able, with trouble, to go to windward and had regularly crossed and recrossed singularly difficult and inhospitable waters on their way to and from Iceland, Greenland and North America. Later medieval craft could, if need be, work (admittedly reluctantly) against headwinds, while in the early 1400s the English, in vessels which, whatever else they may have been, were certainly not carvels, opened a regular commerce with Iceland. Nor indeed were carvels themselves necessarily capable of contending with prolonged headwinds, as contemporary accounts graphically reveal. The first oceanic voyages were not, therefore, the outcome of some convenient revolution in the design, construction and navigation of ships. The pioneer Portuguese ventures were undertaken in whatever craft happened to be available, and only as the voyages progressed were the build and rig of vessels – carvels included – modified to meet the conditions encountered.

So, too, Portuguese exploration was well advanced before there is any unambiguous evidence (1455, 1462) that Iberian seamen were navigating by celestial observation. The general practice was to sail by 'dead reckoning'. Good pilots, like their fellows elsewhere in southern Europe, set the compass course their chart indicated and estimated their progress by calculations of speed and drift. But to start with these skills were not employed. Vessels exploring the West African coast kept in sight of land, sailed by day and anchored by night, with their crews, so it was alleged, ignorant alike of compass and chart. But as voyages became longer, as winds dictated passages in the open sea, and as it became necessary to be able to return to newly-discovered territories, something better was needed. For the development of such techniques Portugal, like the rest of western Europe, was able to draw on a considerable body of scientific learning, and more particularly on Iberia's rich Judeo-Arabic heritage of mathematics and cosmography. That a position on land could be fixed by observation of the heavens had been known since the 1100s. That such methods might be used at sea was appreciated in the thirteenth century, and already in 1429 a Florentine galley commander on passage to the English Channel was taking the height of the Pole Star – which would give him his latitude – by astrolabe. Hence, too, in the 1480s, Portuguese astronomers quickly and effectively settled the question of determining latitude in the southern hemisphere (where the Pole Star was not visible) by devising a method using the sun, whose behaviour had long been the subject of close scrutiny. Even so, as late as 1500, with the Cape route to Asia open, there was no general conviction that the latest was best. Some Portuguese pilots scanned the heavens, but others sailed by dead reckoning alone. The passage of time brought refinements in methods and instruments – though the determination of longitude was not satisfactorily solved – but no fundamental change of technique. As with ships themselves navigation showed the adaptation of a very considerable body of existing skill and knowledge to the solution of new problems.[13]

That Iberia was geographically well placed to pioneer Europe's overseas expansion is clear enough. No part of the continent is physically closer to Africa. Given the sensible reluctance of seamen to incur the fatigue and dangers of beating to windward, Portugal had the enormous advantage of being served by fair winds. Off its south-western littoral their prevailing direction is down the West African coast, towards the Atlantic islands and to the shoulder of Brazil. For the return westerlies could be picked up around 35°N off America. But so it had been since time immemorial without any consequent opening of the oceans. What set the whole process in train, with such unforeseen consequences, was Portuguese intervention in Africa, an intervention which stemmed from two well-established European traditions. The first, and the least important, was the continent's ancient interest in trading to North Africa, where the Venetians and Genoese, among others, had long done business. From the thirteenth century onwards there had been a growing interest in seeking direct access to the sources of that Nigerian gold available in the markets of Africa's Mediterranean coast. Occasional travellers penetrated the great Saharan caravan routes and voyages were undertaken down the continent's north-west littoral. In the early 1300s the Catalans were looking for the 'River of Gold', while the Genoese rediscovered the Canary Islands where, in 1341, they were optimistically inquiring for spices, no doubt with the hope of undermining the position of their mortal enemies, the Venetians, in the Levant.

Equally venerable was the tradition of Christian attacks on Muslim Africa, either to deal the infidel a godly blow or to acquire plunder – not, of course, that the two were mutually exclusive. A French expedition from the Canaries raided (1405) the Saharan coast in search of slaves, gold and Christians. The Genoese attacked the great ports of what are now Libya and Tunisia in the late 1300s, and were behind similar ventures launched into the Atlantic from Portugal. They were increasingly entrenched as merchants and financiers in the economy of Iberia, while as Europe's leading naval *condotierri*, renowned (or reviled) for bold acts of war by sea, they entered Portuguese royal service in the early fourteenth century. Before long they were engaged in military expeditions to the Canaries, culminating (1370) in a long and fierce struggle to conquer and colonize one of the islands. Continuing the good work, as the Genoese looked for profits less arduously earned, the Portuguese took Ceuta in 1415. Such a foray allowed royal and aristocratic warriors to perform those glorious deeds against the enemies of Christendom the ideals of contemporary chivalry demanded of them. With access to other possible theatres debarred by peace with Castile (1411) Portugal could only turn south, with the assault providing an outlet for energies otherwise all too likely to be directed into internecine strife. It enabled the aristocracy and gentry, like their English counterparts then fighting in France, to obtain loot and to seize prisoners suitable for ransom – always congenial occupations, but particularly attractive when, through economic recession, rentals and agricultural prices were depressed. And once established in Morocco, the Portuguese went on as they had begun.

Similar motives probably explain the voyages into the Atlantic that commenced soon after the fall of Ceuta, or at least those undertaken at the instigation of Prince Henry. His wish for a godly stroke against the infidel has near contemporary authority. Soon in financial difficulties and ultimately in debt, he may well have regarded the prospect of further finds like the Canaries – and other groups perhaps known or rumoured through Genoese enterprise – as a potentially inexpensive way of rewarding, in the style they expected, the members of his household. And once the riches of the West African coast were revealed, with its gold and slaves, the prince quickly joined in the commerce that sprang up. Indeed the papal privileges secured on his initiative are as much concerned with trading monopolies and business dealings with infidels as with the advancement of Christendom. At some later stage, at an age when pious thoughts commonly begin to stir, Henry had hopes 'of the Indies and of Prester John' and of the discovery of a way to those regions whose inhabitants were said 'to worship the name of Christ'. This may well have meant the Indian subcontinent rather than lands nearer home known or rumoured to contain Christian communities. Stories of a great Christian potentate ruling the Orient had circulated in Europe since the twelfth century. Following the arrival of an Ethiopian embassy in the West (1306), some now believed this realm to be on the Upper Nile. But that this was not Henry's objective is suggested by the fact that an expedition of 1456 or 1458 carried interpreters said to be fluent in 'Indian', and that a contemporary map shows ships sailing eastwards off South Africa.

From about this date the desire to reach Asia was paramount in the Portuguese voyages. Its wealth and wonders, tantalizingly depicted in classical writings, were familiar to Europeans of the late Middle Ages, even if from nothing better than the amiable fables of the mythical Sir John Mandeville. The Mongol conquests had allowed missions to preach in the East and merchants to trade there, with Marco Polo leaving an account (in which Christians appear) which enjoyed – albeit chiefly as a work of fiction – enormous popularity. Some idea of the nearer East was gained from those Nestorian Christians who came to Europe in the fourteenth and fifteenth centuries, while in the early 1400s Asia was visited by the Venetian, Niccolo Conti, whose close and perceptive account circulated widely in the West, encouraging the pope to despatch a letter addressed to the 'Emperor Thomas of the Indians' in 1439. The Orient was mapped by Catalan cosmographers in a recognizable form as early as 1375. That it might be accessible by sea was admitted, the voyages of Polo himself suggesting this must be so. Men of learning had long known the world to be round, and some had concluded that Asia might be reached by sailing westwards.

These views were powerfully reinforced with the rediscovery in the fifteenth century of the works of some of the great geographers of Antiquity, whose opinions were received with that veneration the Renaissance accorded to all things classical. Ptolemy's *Geography* (known from 1410), though it had the Indian Ocean land-locked, drastically shrank the world and temptingly brought Asia near to Europe. The massive authority of Aristotle supported the feasibility of a brief oceanic passage westward to Asia, while Strabo had India projecting into the Atlantic. Ancient learning was supported by contemporary wisdom. Theologians, constrained by biblical authority to deny the existence of lands in which humans other than the descendants of Adam could live, postulated either a world land mass so large as to encompass the entire globe, or so small as to be confined to its northern hemisphere, leaving the rest water and islands. Hence, one way or another, there was nothing to stop the intrepid. In the early 1400s the erudite Cardinal d'Ailly maintained that Asia was accessible by a lengthy eastward voyage just as Morocco was separated from the Orient by an 'ocean of no great width'. Similar assumptions explain various world maps drawn from 1415 onwards, while in 1474 the Italian cosmographer Toscanelli informed the Portuguese that a great Chinese city lay some 9000 kilometres due west from Lisbon and on the same latitude. So, too, Christopher Columbus, fortified by his own idiosyncratic reading of Marco Polo, the Bible, Mandeville and much else, together with his observation of the flotsam washed ashore in Madeira, became convinced of the practicability of a westward passage to Asia.

When and how such ideas reached Portugal and at what stage they had any impact in the entourage of Prince Henry is far from clear. In the course of their raiding and skirmishing in Morocco the Portuguese appear to have learned nothing of North Africa's relations with the East through the Levant, only later reported with astonishment from the Red Sea. The writings of Marco Polo were known from the early 1400s, while various recensions of the doings of Niccolo Conti circulated among the influential group of Florentine merchants in Lisbon at the same date. This vital source may have been known to Henry and was later brought directly to the attention of King John II (1481–95) by the celebrated Castilian traveller, Pero Tafur. The Portuguese were in touch with Toscanelli, the arch-advocate of a maritime route as early as 1459, and by the 1480s some of their savants apparently knew from Arabic sources that East Africa was accessible by sea from the West. There is, however, nothing to suggest that when the Portuguese voyages began Prince Henry was aware of the works of d'Ailly, let alone those of Ptolemy or the great Arab geographers. What may well have directed Portuguese ambitions to Asia was, as already suggested, the realization, when they commenced to ship Atlantic sugar into the Mediterranean, that oriental spices, imported through the Middle East, were the basis of a Venetian wealth and splendour unparalleled in Europe. But if Portugal was to enter this commerce and enjoy such riches it could hardly be, in view of her geographical location and feeble resources, by challenging Venice in her home waters. Be this as it may, from roughly the mid 1400s the Portuguese search for a direct maritime route to the East was on in earnest, and following their success the attempt to find an easier or shorter alternative remained for centuries a major objective of explorers. It was for China that Columbus sailed westwards, just as it was in the hope of reaching Asia that English and Dutch seamen vainly sought to cross the formidable waters of the North Pole, while advocates of the colonization of North America and Canada urged that such settlements would become bases for eastward exploration.

Following the discovery of lands in the West and the opening of an oceanic route to Asia the motives of subsequent generations of explorers, settlers and imperial entrepreneurs became as varied as the horizons now encountered. Least important, probably, was intellectual curiosity and the dedicated pursuit of knowledge. King Manuel of Portugal (1495–1521) indeed demanded of his officers 'where you come upon something new, send it to me', though their zeal had to be sustained by specific instructions to report such phenomena. There were also those of a different order, occasionally merchants, more usually gentry or sprigs of the aristocracy, who joined expeditions – as from France in 1503 - more or less as sightseers, sometimes as they themselves put it, for pleasure, sometimes to see the world, and sometimes, they claimed, 'from curiosity'. Nevertheless there are spasmodic suggestions of a serious and deliberate quest for knowledge. A venture financed by Philip II of Spain himself (1570) was to 'study the history of living things of the Indies, to sketch the plants and describe the land'. Among those interested in English projects for Hudson Bay in the following century was the scientist Robert Boyle, then investigating heat, frost and polar conditions. Hans Sloane accepted appointment as physician to the governor of Jamaica in 1687 to allow him to look for new plants to be used as drugs or food, like, as he significantly admitted, 'many of the Antient and best Physicians' had done. And of course officials, scholars, missionaries and even *conquistadores* were to examine and report in detail on much they encountered, but less in the cause of the advancement of learning than to see how some problem might be solved or some profit extracted. Nor was it to assemble such information that they had left Europe in the first place.

More potent, especially in the early years of expansion, was the ardent search for those assorted marvels with which the imagination of medieval and early-modern Europe had endowed the unknown world. The sixteenth century was the heyday of the romance of chivalry in Iberia, read alike by princes, scholars, soldiers and even future saints such as Teresa of Avila and Ignatius Loyola. Explorers, as besotted with these fantasies as was the hapless Don Quixote himself, and consciously modelling their behaviour on that of the improbable paladins of fiction, sought in the Americas for the land of the Amazons and searched the coast of Florida for that fountain whose waters brought the joys of everlasting youth and virility. They named California after a favourite romance and looked by land and sea – Cortés himself among them – for the Seven Cities of Cibola. And as one myth faded others rose to replace it. Spaniards searched (1539) the modern Arkansas and Oklahoma for further wonders. They later attempted to find the realms of the gold-painted monarch to which the Orinoco and Amazon were thought to lead, and later still they were scouring the Pacific, though with less enthusiasm, for the Great Southern Continent of Inca legend.

Of more profound and enduring consequence was the desire of pious Christians, usually but not exclusively Catholics, to convert pagans and infidels to the true faith. Admittedly, the aims and methods of the missions varied and were often enough inextricably entangled with less elevated motives. Converts, it was found, made useful allies and were usually more amenable to European rule. Nor was Christian zeal particularly prominent in the earliest phase of expansion, though Prince Henry had some hopes of the conversion of alien peoples and Columbus, on his second voyage, was directed to secure the Christianization of the inhabitants of the Caribbean. But by the mid 1500s the missionary impulse was of prime importance, and nowhere more so than in Spain, then swept by an extraordinary religious fervour. In part this reflected the very success of the Castilian monarchy in the world, paladin against Turk, heretic and pagan alike. In part it reflected too the impact in Iberia of, on the one hand, the messianic and millenarian traditions of the Middle Ages and, on the other, of the cultured ideals of the Christian humanism of the Dutch scholar Erasmus.[14] Impelled by such forces, elderly and decrepit clerics thought to embark on crusades. The infant St Teresa dreamed of early martyrdom; the aged Bartolomé de las Casas set out to convert the redoubtable indigenous inhabitants of Guatemala; the friars, believing the end of the world to be imminent, made frenetic attempts to bring all mankind to Christianity in the little time that remained. The missions penetrated to regions like China, Japan or Vietnam far beyond the bounds of European rule, however tenuous, and where, like the French Jesuits in Canada, their members were often to endure fearful martyrdom. Ideals, hardly surprisingly, were frequently not realized and equally frequently tarnished by anything from brutality to blatant material greed. In Africa, in the face of a growing slave trade, indigenous resistance, an overwhelming variety of languages and a lethal climate, effort dwindled to the point of extinction. Elsewhere, as in Japan, missions collapsed or pristine optimism evaporated. But rarely was the work abandoned. In the seventeenth century Anglican missionaries were attempting to spread their faith among the Amerindians of Carolina, and a Portuguese viceroy of India proposed to make good from his own pocket any loss which might arise from the expulsion of Hindus – the rich and indispensable intermediaries in most economic activities – from the vicinity of Goa. Even at the end of the first imperial age the enfeebled Portuguese monarchy was still pressing indigenous rulers anywhere from Africa to Burma to favour the missions, while in the Americas the Spanish Orders pursued their task on and beyond the fringes of European settlement in Texas and California. But perhaps there is no more eloquent testimony to the intensity and sincerity of this great proselytizing urge than the survival in the archives of the Jesuit Order in Rome of some 15,000 letters (1550–1771) from its members all over Europe seeking to serve in the overseas missions, with 2000 specifically invoking St Francis Xavier, the Apostle of Japan, as their exemplar.[15]

Fundamental to the foundation and growth of empires was the hope, cherished in most societies at most times, that somewhere there were lands abounding in all those things and opportunities currently denied to mankind. Legend or rumour might sustain such dreams, as with the stories of the 'hot . . . lascivious' and sexually insatiable women allegedly common in Asia. Others learned of what they might expect of distant lands from relatives or former neighbours who had settled there. One-time citizens of Braga (Portugal) established in Macao wrote home to compatriots letters which still survive. English Puritans in Massachusetts sent money and advice to their kin and co-religionaries in the mother country, their epistles, it was reported, received like 'a sacred script'. Hence in emigration, as in so much of the rest of life, ties of blood and friendship were of especial importance. Nieces, nephews, cousins and others were summoned to join successful pioneers in the Spanish Indies and almost everywhere particular regions and localities were settled from particular areas of the Old World. East Anglians were prominent in New England; Basques in the Philippines; the inhabitants of the northern Portuguese province of Minho in Pernambuco (Brazil). Still others were persuaded to emigrate by an intensive propaganda extolling the attractions of colonies, such as the laudatory ballads, broadsheets, sermons and various erudite discourses and publications urging the merits of North America to the English in the early 1600s.

The motives of those leaving or seeking to leave Europe, in as far as such things can ever be known, spanned the whole range of human ambition and frustration. Many sought to escape from grinding poverty, and there were few more prolific providers of emigrants than the hard and barren lands of northern Portugal. Others endeavoured to get away from some hopeless misery, like those Andalusian and Extramaduran families who in the 1640s tried to find refuge in the Americas from a homeland ravaged by war. Some sought to throw off the pointless drudgery of their present existence, to be free from the shackles of marriages long since gone sour, or to get away from the oppressions of parents, neighbours or society. Hence Spanish insistence in the early sixteenth century that married men going to the Indies were to be joined by their wives, and hence, too, the subsequent denial by an English colonial propagandist that it was his intention to separate children from their parents, servants from their masters or men from their wives.[16] Nevertheless this was commonly the case, with it being remarked of the Portuguese in Asia (c. 1580) that they 'abandon their wives and children and die there without wishing to see them again'. Some departed from their mother country on what appears to have been no more than a petulant whim, like that English youth who in the seventeenth century went to America since his puritanical father was enraged at his having taken dancing lessons from 'a dansing Scott', while a contemporary followed the same route 'being in displeasure of my friends'. For many, however, then as now, speedy and secret departure to distant parts was inspired by the urgent need to avoid creditors. It was for this reason that the redoubtable Balboa, the *conquistador* of Darien, arrived there concealed in a barrel, just as among the pioneers of English Virginia were those fleeing the liabilities of their 'decayed estate'. And with luck such a move could bring a second and highly rewarding chance. One of the most distinguished servants of the Dutch VOC in Asia in these centuries was the erstwhile undischarged bankrupt, Antony van Diemen.

Empire, however, was much more than a refuge. To Europeans highly conscious of the lack of correspondence between merit and reward it brought the prospect, otherwise denied, of advancement, improvement and above all land and riches. In colonies in which white females were almost invariably, to start with, in short supply, ordinary women found unparalleled opportunities. In sixteenth-century Spanish America many achieved affluence and rank by a series of marriages as through violence or excess spouse after spouse died rich but prematurely. By 1700 in one region of Guatemala alone about 25 per cent of the land was in female hands. Of the English Atlantic settlements it was said that girls who arrived as unfree servants could eventually 'pick and chuse' husbands of 'the better sort', or, as it was put in the characteristically vigorous language of Barbados, 'a whore, if handsome, makes a wife for some rich planter'.[17] From every part of the world penetrated by Europeans come stories in abundance of hopes of social advancement, better wages, a better way of life, and in particular the chance to enjoy that affluent and leisured life of gentility to which so many aspire and for which the opportunities are in general so few. Thus it was remarked (1572) that 'poore young men' left Spain for Mexico, where if all else failed they might at least bask in the deference accorded to those born in the peninsula.[18] There were subsequent complaints in England that craftsmen, seamen and fishermen were lured to Massachusetts where, like the skilled and professional men who figure so largely among emigrants to most colonies, they would enjoy higher wages – which in seventeenth-century English Atlantic possessions could be anything from 30 to 300 per cent above the rates at home.

For long, however, the particular attraction of the wider world was that it offered that abundant class of the gentry, or those who wished to be considered such, the opportunity to engage in an appropriate way of life and the chance to secure vast tracts of land on which they might live, as the Spaniards said, 'nobly', sustained by rents, surrounded by servants and freed from the need to work. 'Even the most miserable and unfortunate Spaniards', it was alleged, though they might not share the immortal Sancho Panza's dream of ruling an island, nevertheless aspired to become lords, beholden to none. Portuguese of similar mind gave themselves titles the moment they rounded the Cape on their way to India, while in Lima, so it was said, any whites bold enough to 'call themselves gentlemen can get away with it'. Such pretensions and such an existence, agreeable at any time, appeared all the more attractive as in the sixteenth century members, actual and potential, of the European gentry class seemingly became more numerous while finding themselves pinched by rising prices and the absence in the homeland of adequate outlets for their bellicose and acquisitive urges. Hence French gentry, unemployed after the Franco-Spanish peace of 1559 and again during a brief lull in the ensuing civil war, were ready for colonial ventures in the mid 1500s. In Elizabethan and early-Stuart England there was much talk, following the ending of the long struggle with Spain, of the problem of the 'men of war by sea and land now left destitute of all hopes of employment' and of the unhappy lot of upper-class younger sons.

The salvation of the gentry, and in particular of its many illegitimate members, lay, it was widely agreed, and as events seemed so convincingly to demonstrate, in empire. In the Indies some of the Spanish conquerors – only a handful in fact – their claims to gentility often as bold and improbable as their military tactics, had established themselves as lords over thousands of servile subjects, acquired estates and titles, and lived like the heroes of chivalry. Naturally enough subsequent New World settlements, whether English, French or Dutch, were planned to reflect, almost at times to the point of parody, the familiar European society of lords and peasants. Between 1580 and 1582 a single English entrepreneur, Humphrey Gilbert, then busy in identical projects in Ireland, distributed over 8 million acres of North America, unseen let alone unconquered, to aspirants to rank and affluence.[19] Nor were such dreams in vain. Throughout much of the colonial world there eventually emerged, often from the obscurest origins, and sometimes (as in English Barbados) in part recruited from emigrant younger sons, a landed aristocracy.[20] And wherever such a class developed its members soon settled down to a seigneurial way of life, living as grandly as they could in the colonial equivalents of the great town and country houses of the Old World.

Some entertained, or were alleged to entertain, even wilder ambitions. It was perhaps in the mind of Gonzalo Pizarro, brother of Francisco, to set himself up as King of Peru after the *conquistador*'s murder. That singularly luckless Elizabethan navigator, Edward Fenton, supposedly harboured similar aspirations for St Helena, while in the early seventeenth century it was thought that the colourful Captain John Smith would make himself king in Virginia with the equally colourful Indian princess Pocahontas as his consort. And there were those who achieved such power. Through trade, piracy and judicious marriage a Portuguese adventurer became sovereign of a base in the Bay of Bengal in the early 1600s, just as compatriots became chiefs of vast territories in East Africa.

The great majority of those who left Europe for the wider world thus did so, as the King of Portugal succinctly put it in 1499, 'for profit'. Many pioneers in the Spanish Indies thought only of getting rich and returning home, their favourite expletive, it was alleged, being 'May God get me back to Spain'. It was commonly the ambition of subsequent English and French planters in the Caribbean to make a fortune as soon as possible and then retire to their mother country. Men deserted commanders who failed to find loot. Gold was almost everywhere one of the first things expeditions inquired for. In pursuit of precious metals the Spaniards endured all things

from the freezing heights of the Andes to the fearsome tropical forests of
Amazonia, while the Portuguese trekked across the vastness of Brazil. At
the news of the plunder to be had in Mexico Spanish settlers left the
Caribbean islands in droves in the early 1500s – 'not a single citizen will
be left unless they are tied down', it was gloomily reported – just as those
disappointed in their expectations were soon on the move again. English
dedication to Arctic exploration was never more wholehearted than when
(1576) gold was reported there, just as the Portuguese flocked to Brazil
once it was found to have gold and diamonds. By and large, and despite
some notable exceptions, where there was no prospect of such wealth there
was, until the discovery of the opportunities for plantation monocultures,
little or no empire.

So, too, European merchants, at first indifferent to colonies and oceanic
ventures, warmed to their merits once the potential rewards were apparent.
They were already engaged in West Africa, with its gold and slaves, by the
mid 1400s, and thereafter in anything that showed a likelihood of profit.
The great Italian mercantile houses established in Iberia swiftly came to
dominate the exploitation of the new Portuguese colonies in the Atlantic.
Consortia of international plutocrats controlled Portugal's Asian spice trade
in the later sixteenth century. Meanwhile Genoese bankers in Seville
financed would-be *conquistadores* – though prudently not too many –
provided capital for the nascent sugar industry and for shipping, and
engaged in the slave trade. Even the Fuggers themselves, Europe's greatest
financiers, planned an establishment in Chile in the early 1500s to tap the
pockets of Peru's rich and wild spenders. Merchants excluded from lucrative
markets launched undertakings like the English and Dutch East India
companies to secure their admission to them, or urged imperial expansion
in the interests of better business, with those of London arguing (1690) that
England should annex Nova Scotia and enjoy 'the sole trade of beavers and
all furs'. Other classes underwent similar conversion. Iberian aristocrats, to
whom colonies had initially been a matter of indifference, became, once it
was clear what they could offer, eager contenders for the highest and most
lucrative posts in the imperial administration.

However, to many in Europe the ambitions of emigrants and their alleged
expectation of riches without effort or sacrifice demonstrated that empire
brought out the worst in mankind and that colonials were the very dregs
of humanity. Monarchs, companies and projectors, Catholic and Protestant
alike, were unanimous on the need to ensure that only 'industrious and
willing people', which meant well-regulated and married skilled men of
'small means', should reach overseas settlements.[21] Meanwhile publicists,
especially those demonstrating how empire purged the body politic of
impurities, waxed eloquent on the shortcomings and base motives of
emigrants to the colonies. English Barbados was described in 1654 as a
dunghill 'whereon (the country) doth cast forth its rubbish'. The short-

lived Dutch settlement in Brazil was characterized in like fashion as a 'close stool for voiding the dregs of society' and the employees of the East and West India companies as 'the scum of the United Provinces'. French Martinique, it was bewailed in the late seventeenth century, was full of idle and thieving vagabonds.

Such denigration, common enough at all times, is not of course to be taken at its face value. Nevertheless, in the sixteenth and early seventeenth centuries, when many European statesmen were convinced that the continent was dangerously overburdened with people, it was the common practice to dump allegedly surplus and undesirable population in lands beyond the seas. Many imperial pioneers thus left for distant parts for no better reason than that they were forced to do so. From the late 1400s the Portuguese crown commuted death sentences to transportation for life and the Inquisition imposed sentences of banishment on some of its victims. Thereafter the bulk of emigrants to Portugal's African territories were convicts, as were, in the early stages, many of those going to Brazil and the Atlantic islands, and, from the late 1600s, to Goa. But not even crime, however broadly defined, could produce a sufficient flow, so that for the beginnings of the settlement of Brazil beggars were rounded up off the streets in the mother country, lepers sent to the Cape Verdes and forcibly converted Jews to São Tomé.

Similar policies were enthusiastically pursued by most other colonial powers with the exception of Spain. In the late 1500s the French sent convicts to the Gulf of St Lawrence and in the course of the following century orphans to Martinique and Parisian vagabonds and beggars to the West Indies. The English, already convinced in the sixteenth century that North America was particularly suited to receive those of its citizens who would otherwise drift into riot and rebellion to 'the great disquiet of the better sort', subsequently shipped out to the Caribbean those variously classified as rogues, agitators, rebels, thieves, whores, convicts, military prisoners, waifs and orphans, together with a contingent of the poor, criminal and rebellious rounded up in Scotland by Oliver Cromwell's lieutenants for the settlement of Jamaica. Such indeed was English dedication to policies of this order that it was alleged they would have had 'their own fathers' transported, given the chance. And when in the early seventeenth century France and England found it impossible to raise sufficient labour for their North American and West Indian possessions, they resorted to the use of indentured white servants, some of them kidnapped, and who commonly lived a life tantamount to slavery.[22]

Expansion and empire, however, involved more than the interplay of material forces and ambitions. In early modern Europe, where religious conformity was in general rigorously enforced, the oppressed and persecuted quickly appreciated that lands beyond the seas could offer them a heaven-sent chance to live and worship as they wished. Large numbers of Iberian Jews, on whom Christianity had been forcibly imposed in the 1490s, soon appeared in the Americas. With distances great and ecclesiastical organization still rudimentary there was the opportunity for them to prac- tise their faith, especially in Brazil, laxly ruled until the union of the Spanish and Portuguese empires (1580), and again after their separation in the seventeenth century. Others found sanctuary in Goa (though the Inquisition was speedily introduced to seek them out) or as *lançados* in West Africa.[23] French Protestants attempted to settle in Brazil in the sixteenth century, just as their English co-religionaries, finding Elizabeth's Anglican church too Catholic, thought of taking refuge in the Gulf of St Lawrence. In the intolerant England of the Stuarts such schemes proliferated. New England, from the tiny Plymouth (1620) to the soon affluent Massachusetts (1630) became the home of Puritans of many shades of belief. Maryland was subsequently intended for Catholics and Pennsylvania for Quakers.[24] Para- doxically enough settlements of this sort, convinced of their monopoly of divine truth and frequently unwilling to extend to others the freedoms they craved for themselves, could cause further colonial expansion, with, as we have seen, acrimonious theological dispute driving Massachusetts dissidents to found new refuges.

Expansion was indeed to a very considerable degree self-generated and self-sustained. It could be a matter of strategic necessity. According to Albuquerque the Portuguese, once they had arrived in India, were obliged to undertake conquests as evidence of their intention to remain and in order to impress local potentates. New horizons were opened, as in New England, by ideological disagreement or new lands came to light purely by chance and accident, as when Portuguese traders in Asia were blown off course to Japan. Expansion might also result from political discord, with Spaniards from the faction-torn islands of the Caribbean undertaking the subjugation of much of the American mainland, and those disappointed at their lack of rewards from the conquest of the Amerindian empires moving on to try their luck elsewhere. It could similarly be the outcome of a settlement's overpopulation, of its economic troubles, or of stories of the attractions, real or imagined, of neighbouring territories. Portugal's Azores and Madeira, soon burdened with more people than they could support, supplied immigrants to Brazil. English colonists, finding life hard and opportunities few in the Lesser Antilles, moved to the newly-acquired Jamaica (1655). Later in the century others left the economically depressed Barbados and Virginia for the recently founded South Carolina, and by the early 1700s some of the richest inhabitants of booming Philadelphia were originally from Barbados and Jamaica. The opening of Brazil, involving epic marches of thousands of kilometres and lasting for years, was pioneered by Luso-Brazilians and their mixed race and indigenous associates, just as the expansion of Spain in America was the work of American-born Span- iards and *mestizos*,[25] without whom, as one royal official admitted, 'all the land would be lost'.

Equally potent were the rivalries between European states. Once a country acquired an empire it was only a matter of time before others would seek to attack, reduce or annex it, or to establish colonies of their own. The incentive might be national prestige. It was alleged that the French persisted for so long in Florida in the sixteenth century to revenge earlier setbacks and to 'repair the honour of [the] nation'. Colonies, Louis XIV of France later declared, were chiefly founded to advance 'the greatness of the mother country'. Such notable sentiments were, however, usually underpinned by material and strategic considerations. It was long an article of Protestant faith that the power of Spain could be broken and the sufferings of her victims ended by stopping the flow of the American bullion which sustained it to Seville, for which purpose bases were needed in the Atlantic, the Caribbean and thereabouts.[26] Dutch assaults on Iberian possessions the world over from Brazil to Macao, and the establishment of a Dutch colonial empire in the first half of the seventeenth century in part reflected an attempt to divert Spanish manpower and resources away from the war of independence in the Low Countries. In the later 1600s an influential faction in England secured the country's intervention in West Africa and further settlement on the eastern seaboard of America to bridle Holland, while by the end of the century bold English measures were believed to be essential in North America to counter the southward push of the French from Canada.[27]

Colonial powers similarly attempted to secure what they considered to be their vital interests by occupying territories otherwise thought likely to fall into hostile hands. The Portuguese took Malacca (1511) since the Spaniards were rumoured to have an eye on it, contemplated colonizing the important way station of St Helena to deter intruders and began the settlement of Brazil for the same reason. The Spaniards similarly held on to the hostile and unrewarding Florida to safeguard the route by which treasure fleets left the Caribbean. They moved northwards up the Pacific coast of America to remove any potential threat to the Manila galleons, and they tried to settle the southern extremity of the continent in part to debar hostile shipping from the Pacific. The bounds of empire might also be extended, or existing settlements expanded or reshaped as colonists or merchants sought to escape the attentions of rivals and enemies, or as states, companies or individuals endeavoured to re-route and maintain valuable trades. Dutch maritime and economic superiority directed English activity in the Orient away from South-East Asia and towards the Indian subcontinent and western Asia in the early seventeenth century. So, too, Dutch hostility forced Portuguese commerce in the East into ever remoter areas – Macassar for spices, Solor for copper – and in Brazil encouraged penetration inland.

The beginnings and continuance of Europe's overseas expansion were thus the outcome of an assortment of motives and causes as diverse and often as impenetrable as those governing human conduct itself. Voyages could stem from the determination of an individual, whether Prince Henry of Portugal or Christopher Columbus, to pursue some objective, improbable though it may have seemed. Discoveries could be accidental, as when Columbus, in pursuit of the brilliant civilizations of Marco Polo's Asia, stumbled on the American continent. Once established, colonies begat colonies. With communications slow and metropolitan authority tentative, conquest and settlement could result from the untrammelled initiative of some forceful pioneer, as with Albuquerque's capture of Goa or Cortés' assault on Mexico. As colonies grew dissidents were expelled, the unwanted or unsuccessful fled, the ambitious pursued new opportunities, and the enclaves they founded (like Portuguese Macao) or the lands they subjugated (such as in the Spanish Indies) were eventually added to those under royal control. Meanwhile European states annexed places or territories of potential value or importance since, as a King of Portugal appositely observed, 'possession gives good title'. There is, however, little or nothing in such events to suggest that the creation of the first oceanic empires was inspired by any combination of economic determinants, or that the achievements of Europe's first imperial age were a monument to the level of the continent's economic and technological development. Indeed Holland, the wonder of the times in all things commercial, financial and maritime, was a singularly luckless colonizer, whereas the backward and impoverished Portugal and the scarcely more advanced Spain were astonishingly successful. The initial Portuguese voyages stemmed from well-established European traditions. Their apparently futile continuance owed much to the will of Prince Henry and eventually brought, quite fortuitously, the opening of opportunities for wealth of an order which ensured not only that they would go on but that others would emulate them. In this they differed fundamentally from the ventures of the medieval Norse, whose settlements in Iceland, Greenland and the bleaker parts of North America, though regularly accessible to their seamen, were not of a nature to encourage their development or to attract substantial settlement. Following the initial Portuguese success long-established European skills – notably the astronomical determination of latitude – were adapted to maritime use, while traditional erudition on such matters as the size of the globe and the accessibility of Asia by sea, supported further ambitions. The subsequent endeavours of the Catholic powers in general, and those of Iberia in particular, were in considerable degree governed by the desire to spread the Christian faith, and the bounds of Christendom, as of imperial Spain and Portugal, were enlarged by the efforts of the missionary Orders, especially in the Spanish Indies and Brazil, where much of their work was on and beyond the frontiers of white settlement. But what above all else ensured the survival and growth of the first overseas footholds was the revelation, by Portugal in Asia and by

Spain in the Americas, of riches on an unprecedented scale, often to be had simply for the taking. Thereafter hope sprang eternal of similar finds elsewhere, while the new lands, including those seemingly less favoured, came to be seen, as indeed they frequently were, as the providers of rewards, freedoms and opportunities denied by Europe.

NOTES AND REFERENCES

1 See pp. 4, 7–8.
2 Eliyahu Ashtor, *Levant Trade in the Later Middle Ages* (Princeton, 1983), especially pp. 469–70.
3 Louis-André Vigneras, *The Discovery of South America and the Andalusian Voyages* (Chicago, 1976).
4 Immanuel Wallerstein, *The Modern World System*. I, *Capitalist Agriculture and the Origins of the European World-Economy in the Sixteenth Century* (New York, 1974), 42ff.
5 See p. 3.
6 *The Travels of Leo of Rozmital through Germany, Flanders, England, France, Spain, Portugal and Italy, 1465–1467*, translated and edited by Malcolm Letts, Hakluyt Society (Cambridge, 1957), p. 110.
7 See also Felipe Fernández-Armesto, *Before Columbus. Exploration and Colonisation from the Mediterranean to the Atlantic, 1229–1492* (1987), p. 197.
8 See pp. 65, 113–6.
9 G. V. Scammell, *The World Encompassed: The First European Maritime Empires, c. 800–1650* (1981), p. 110; Artur Attman, *The Bullion Flow between Europe and the East, 1000–1750* (Göteborg, 1981), p. 17.
10 Patrick O'Brien, 'European economic development: The contribution of the periphery', *Economic History Review*, xxxv, 1, (1982), 1ff; Boaz Shoshan, 'Money supply and grain prices in fifteenth-century Egypt', *Economic History Review*, xxxvi, 1, (1983), 47ff.
11 Wallerstein, *The Modern World System*, I, 38ff.
12 Carrying, instead of square sails, those of triangular shape, Arab-oriental in origin, the leading edge held firm by a spar which gave a better set against a headwind.
13 Scammell, *World Encompassed*, pp. 263–4.
14 See pp. 194–5, 221–2.
15 See pp. 191–201.
16 Gillian T. Cell (ed.), *Newfoundland Discovered. English Attempts at Colonisation 1610–1630*, Hakluyt Society (1982), p. 168.
17 David W. Galenson, *White Servitude in Colonial America. An Economic Analysis* (Cambridge, 1981), p. 25; Miles L. Wortman, *Government and Society in Central America 1680–1840* (New York, 1982), p. 84.
18 Antonio Domínguez Ortiz, *La Sociedad Española en el Siglo XVII*, 1 (Madrid, 1963), p. 48.
19 Kenneth R. Andrews, *Trade, Plunder and Settlement. Maritime Enterprise and the Genesis of the British Empire, 1480–1630* (Cambridge, 1984), p. 191.
20 See pp. 179–80.
21 Cell, *Newfoundland*, p. 172.
22 See pp. 113–6.
23 See pp. 37, 46.
24 See p. 41.

25 Of European and Indian parentage. See pp. 187–90.
26 G. V. Scammell, 'The English in the Atlantic Islands *c.* 1450–1650', *The Mariner's Mirror*, 72, 3 (1986), 295ff.
27 See pp. 38–9, 41, 247–9.

3   The roots of empire

The triumphs of Europeans and the establishment of their first oceanic empires have been explained, like the onset of their imperial urges, according to the predilections of the times. To most contemporaries it seemed only natural that pagans, infidels, non-whites and those lacking, as was said, 'civility', should succumb to the paladins of Christendom. Now subtler arguments are generally favoured. Europeans won because of superior morale, greater determination, better political organization, more advanced technology – the mere sound of their guns sufficient to convert unbelievers to 'the worship of Jesus Christ' – more nutritive diet, greater capital resources. It is, however, worth recalling how little of the world was subjugated in this age, remarkable though its achievements were, how few Europeans left for lands overseas – slightly more than 500,000 from Portugal and Spain in the sixteenth century – and how few of these arrived at or survived in the presumed paradise they had chosen.

In Africa nothing more than toeholds were obtained. The Portuguese came up against peoples well able to look after themselves in Morocco and Senegambia. Elsewhere as a rule neither they nor their rivals penetrated to the cool highlands of the interior, later to provide the white man with an existence as imperial as any. Hence Europeans remained pinned to the coasts, where they could indeed get most of the slaves, ivory and gold they were after from local peoples, one way or another, but where tropical heat and disease killed them as inexorably as African and European disease killed the Amerindians of the New World. Rarely did the Portuguese, the only Europeans present in any significant number, survive long enough to engender from indigenous women any such mixed blood population as explains the tenacity of their hold on Brazil.

Nor did Europeans make any conquests to speak of in Asia. The pioneers were the tiny Portugal and Holland, both with populations of under two million, and both with many other calls on their resources. Campaigns in the Cortés style were certainly talked of in sixteenth-century Iberia, including an attack on Mecca itself. But even if feasible such heroics were soon found pointless. The Portuguese, on their arrival in Asia, lighted on a maritime economy attractive in its wealth and vulnerability. Their energies were accordingly primarily devoted to penetrating, redirecting, taxing or

71

simply plundering it. In this way, and with comparatively little effort –
unlike toiling through the backlands of Brazil or marching over the Andes
– they could become exceedingly rich and able to live, as was proper for
Christian gentlemen, without working. True, the Spaniards, having
subdued the Philippines, briefly entertained, but prudently put aside,
ambitions to conquer China, Japan and Taiwan. But thereafter, until the
eighteenth century, other Europeans were chiefly concerned to overthrow
Portugal's privileged position, to insert themselves in a similar or better
role by monopolizing Asia's commerce with the West, and to tap the wealth
offered by the rich local trades. Meanwhile the great indigenous powers
went their own ways, much of the ancient indigenous commerce continued
to flow, and a shrewd observer remarked in 1673 that not all the European
merchants in Asia put together could equal the capital of the Indian
magnates.[1]

More remarkable still, considering the fate of the Aztecs and Incas, was
the modest extent of European conquests in the Americas as a whole. The
French, notwithstanding the astonishing itineraries of individual adventurers, traders and missionaries, remained confined to Canada, or more
strictly speaking, the banks of the St Lawrence, until the late 1600s. The
English and Dutch colonized merely a narrow strip of North America's
Atlantic seaboard. The Portuguese were slow to get away from the eastern
coast of Brazil. Even in the Spanish Indies footholds outside the former
Amerindian empires were widely dispersed and often sparsely populated,
and much of the continent the white man never saw, let alone conquered.
Sometimes Europeans were defeated by the climate. They might with luck
survive the Arctic winter, but their wooden sailing ships were unable to
make their way through frozen polar seas. They were equally at the mercy
of the tropics, without resistance to, or remedies against their endemic
diseases, and usually lethally overclad. They might be halted, or at least
impeded by difficult terrain, though not indefinitely if there was the slightest
prospect of riches. The sheer size of Brazil, its lack of routes, its dense
forests and vast rivers – almost all flowing eastwards and hence not easily
ascended from the Atlantic littoral – were obstacles, though not insur-
mountable ones, to the Portuguese. Occasionally Europeans had little
interest in conquest and subjugation. The extreme English Protestant sects
settled in North America, who could indeed turn on indigenous peoples if
so inclined, had in general little wish to have any dealings with them.
And their very desire to remain together for mutual edification and moral
supervision was in itself a restraint on the territorial expansion of their
colonies.

There were, however, few more effective barriers to would-be conquerors
than nomadic or semi-nomadic peoples living, as they commonly do, in
difficult lands. European successes there certainly were, particularly when
opponents were fatally weakened by newly imported diseases. They might

also succeed, as the Dutch eventually did on the uplands of southern Africa, when in open country and an agreeable climate, they could use mounted men and European weapons against a thinly scattered population. And they could succeed too, where, as in northern Mexico, their resolution was sustained by the prospect of wealth, in this case silver. But these were exceptions. Where there were no commodities that attracted them, where they encountered no political units, whether tribes or states, which could be turned to their own use by the substitution of Europeans for rulers and ruling classes, and where they met unfamiliar ways of fighting, their advance was slow and defeats common. Peoples wholly or partially nomadic, whose possessions were few, melted away at their approach, while the capture of the leader of one small group, or its total destruction, still left others to do battle another day. Over regions such as the pampas of the southern Argentine, northern Mexico (which included much of what is now the southwest of the USA), the hinterland of the Río de la Plata and most of North America European control was imposed slowly, with difficulty, and in many cases not effectively before the nineteenth century.

In the Spanish Americas it was the Chichimeca of northern Mexico, their Apache and Comanche neighours, and the Araucanians of southern Chile who proved most difficult to subdue. The latter were of particularly impressive martial skills and soon found how to handle any would-be conqueror. They murdered most of the Catholic missions that were sent among them. They destroyed pastures which might feed Spanish cavalry mounts. They exhausted the enemy by using reserves to sustain resistance and they quickly took over Spanish weapons, including firearms, the horse and the celebrated Spanish pike. In 1586 their forces were said to be deployed 'in manner like the Christians: for putting their Pikemen in rankes they place Bowmen amongst them'.[2] So equipped and organized they carried the war into enemy territory, and if things went wrong they scattered into country in which it was hard to pursue them to bases which could easily be replaced if destroyed, and whose loss in any case did them little damage. But as in so many other frontier wars the Spaniards neither attempted, nor perhaps envisaged, their opponents' annihilation. This could well invite disaster, whereas raiding and fighting provided a useful outlet for the restive and ambitious of the empire and the slaves they rounded up were a welcome addition to the labour force of northern Chile.

Advances so prolonged and intermittent meant not only that indigenous peoples acquired the white man's weapons and understood his tactics, but that Europeans lost that classic military advantage of surprise which elsewhere stood them in such good stead. In Canada in the sixteenth and seventeenth centuries the French faced, among other tribes, the Iroquois who remained particularly formidable, notwithstanding the ravages of European disease. They were fighters of consummate skill, swift and elusive – like their fellows in Virginia who escaped from the English 'by the

nimblenesse of their heeles' – few in number and not hampered by vast and
unmanoeuvrable forces as were the Aztecs and Incas. Indeed in war there
was much in their favour. They moved easily through a terrain of forests
and rivers. They could withstand the rigours of the Canadian winter and
even benefit from them, crossing the frozen countryside on snow shoes.
In such conditions cavalry, employed so decisively elsewhere by Europeans,
was generally useless. Furthermore the resources which these North American peoples controlled were either, like maize, of little interest to the white
man, or, like furs, acquired in ways largely beyond his supervision. And
the Indian tribes of the north drew considerable benefit from the more or
less simultaneous establishment of French, English and Dutch settlements
whose rivalries they adeptly exploited. Further south English Virginia
nearly came to a speedy end (1608) when the local Algonkian chief was
given time to appreciate that the intruders, who displayed few signs of
either pushing further inland or taking serious steps to feed themselves,
could be starved out.

Europeans succeeded dramatically, however, where the climate was
benign (as in upland Mexico and Peru), where the land was unoccupied or
virtually so (as in the Portuguese Atlantic islands), where they had some
powerful incentive to sustain them (like the flight from religious oppression
in New England or the pursuit of silver in Peru), and where (as in so much
of the New World) local peoples were weakened or destroyed by the
ravages, physical or psychological, of imported and unfamiliar diseases.[3]
Societies which, like those of the Americas, had evolved in isolation were
without natural resistance to illnesses transmitted alike by Europeans and
their African slaves. There was an ominous indication of things to come
when the Canarian Guanches were virtually wiped out by sickness in the
closing stages of the Spanish conquest (1478–96). English settlement in
North America was facilitated by the widespread depopulation, on which
the pioneers themselves frequently remarked, both in Virginia and New
England. In Canada the Hurons lamented (1616) that since the coming of
the French their people 'die and their population is decreasing', and
throughout the Iberian Americas indigenous populations were either totally
destroyed or cripplingly reduced. It was here, against the empires of the
Aztecs and the Incas that Europeans achieved their most overwhelming
success before the British conquest of India in the eighteenth and nineteenth
centuries. With precious metals superabundant the Spaniards had the prospect of untold riches for the taking, and in highly organized states the
opportunity to harness to their needs a huge, skilled and docile labour
force. And the inspiration they drew from the chivalric and Christian ideals
of contemporary Europe was reinforced with a boldness and tenacity born
of the clear understanding that the alternative to success was a fearful death
at the hands of their opponents. True, there was much in their favour.
The Amerindians were already weakened by European diseases before the

conquests began in earnest, with smallpox rampant in much of the continent by the early 1500s. The Maya, at their first encounter with the Spaniards were afflicted by some unidentified epidemic, and the Inca emperor and a large part of his army were destroyed by malaria or smallpox *c*. 1525.

Nevertheless European success was not the inevitable corollary of similar indigenous disasters elsewhere. The Spanish conquests, whatever the many imperfections in their organization – like the divided command in Peru – were daringly conceived and even more daringly executed by a handful of commanders outstanding by the standards of any age. The force of their personalities is barely dimmed by the centuries that now separate us from them: Cortés, who could beguile would-be opponents to join him; Pizarro, who to the consternation of even his compatriots, seized the Inca emperor; Pedro de Alvarado, whose mere presence was sufficient to subdue the Indians of Guatemala to whom he was known as 'The Sun'. Such men were citizens of Europe's leading military power, where martial virtues were admired and where feats of improbable chivalric heroism were the commonplace of popular culture. More important they were, like their followers, of obscure origins – a smattering of alleged minor gentry, the majority artisans and peasants – with few prospects in a mother country even more obsessed with birth, rank, blood and connection than the rest of Europe. Many (Cortés, the Pizarros, Orellana) were from Extramadura, whose huge mountains, vast plains, blazing summers and freezing winters prepared men for most things, and whose inhabitants were, like Don Quixote, great huntsmen, well able to direct skills perfected in the slaughter of game to other ends. They were not professional soldiers. They rose to command by their own wits and exertions, their natural aptitudes further sharpened by years of violent factional strife in the Caribbean or the Central American Isthmus where many were already settled. They were restive for new opportunities as increasing numbers pressed on decreasing resources, skilled in fighting and exploiting the local peoples and untrammelled by the conventions of contemporary warfare. So from a country renowned for its infantry they mounted campaigns whose success, as with those in the closing stages of the subjugation of the Canary Islands, commonly turned on the ingenious use of cavalry. Spanish skills and qualities are all the more apparent from a comparison with the mishaps of other would-be conquerors. In the early 1500s the Portuguese attempted to subdue the scattered semi-nomadic tribes of the forests of Maranhão (north-east Brazil). To this end, in an unhappily conceived undertaking against such peoples in such terrain, they launched two expeditions, the first including the biggest force of cavalry as yet seen in the New World, both of which were engulfed in total disaster.[4] Later in the century came a number of abortive English ventures to North America – to Newfoundland and to Roanoke (North Carolina). Among the commanders were professional soldiers, trained in the style of war practised in the Hispano-Dutch conflict in the Low Countries, where campaigning

was largely a matter of siege and counter-siege and rarely a question of
lightning advances. Many of the leaders were, moreover, gentlemen, reluctant to accept hardship and much concerned with their standing at court,
or at least at home. There was no bold march into the heart of North
America; instead the prime concern was with setting up beach-heads and
maintaining communications with the mother country.

In war, however, speed and surprise are vital to success, as the Spaniards
in the Indies well understood. Controlling the sea they could attack when
and where they wished states without the maritime resources to resist them,
so isolated as to be unable to offer one another support, and in the absence
of other European powers deprived of any opportunity of finding an ally.
The Spaniards had admirable bases near to hand in and around the Caribbean, from which they could bring in reinforcements and supplies. And
already in the islands, and in Panama and Nicaragua, Europeans had
accumulated the wealth to back such ventures, with Cortés financed from
Cuba and Pizarro and Almagro initially, so it was alleged, from the revenues
of the bishopric of Panama. The unheralded appearance of intruders from
lands unheard of was in itself a shock to the Amerindians, who may have
briefly thought them to be of divine origin. More unnerving still was the
Spanish use of the horse in a continent where it was previously unknown
and against peoples with no equivalent, without wheeled transport and
obliged to rely on human muscle, reinforced in the Andes by the sturdy
but tiny llama and alpaca. The horse, already acclimatized and flourishing
in the Caribbean islands, and therefore readily available, allowed the Spaniards to deploy cavalry, which with its speed and mobility could easily
outstrip and outmanoeuvre infantry, and which enjoyed enormous tactical
advantages against opponents on foot. Standing in his stirrups a horseman
could hack at densely-packed infantry with devastating effect, and once
they broke and ran he could, in open country, pursue and spear them at
will. And to strengthen the impact the Spaniards trained their mounts to
rear up on their hind legs and launched them into battle festooned with
rattles to add to the terror of the charge. Time and again handfuls of Spanish
horsemen defeated and scattered numerically overwhelming bodies of
indigenous foot-soldiers. Commanders and contemporary chroniclers
repeatedly refer to the indispensable role of cavalry, while Amerindian
peoples sought to obtain horses for themselves and found how to cripple
or bring down those of the invaders, having discovered that their numbers
could tell and that they might well win if they could oblige the enemy to
fight on foot.

Much the same happened, or was proposed, elsewhere. In Portuguese
Angola, where once again the horse was a stranger, it was reckoned that
one mounted man 'is of more worth than a hundred Negroes, because the
Horsemen doe afright them greatly'.[5] In western India cavalry played an
important part in the Portuguese capture and subsequent defence of Goa.

The horse was, of course, well-known in the subcontinent, but was supplied to the south, where it failed to breed satisfactorily, from Iran and Arabia. With Goa in their hands the Portuguese aspired to control and monopolize this traffic, thereby ensuring that they alone had cavalry and their opponents did not. When in the late 1500s there was talk of disbanding Goa's mounted forces, such as they were, a reformer wrote, in terms reminiscent of those used by the Spanish *conquistadores*, of the cavalry 'without which we are of no account to our neighbours'. So, too, when in 1635 ambitious projects were aired for Portuguese colonization of East Africa an integral part of the scheme was provision for the breeding and raising of horses.

The horse was not the white man's only ally. Against societies which possessed no large native dogs European varieties were loosed, as had already been done in the conquest of the Canary Islands, with formidable effect. Amerindian art and European chronicles both bear witness to the terror they inspired and to their ferocity in the pursuit and destruction of their victims. They were used by Columbus and then by the *conquistadores*, being found especially effective against peoples without organized military forces – as in the Caribbean islands or Venezuela – who could be hunted down like animals. The dogs were set on their prey wearing armour made from hides to protect them against arrows, and their value and importance were such as to ensure that their names were recorded for posterity – Amigo, Calisto and, inevitably, Amadis after the hero of chivalry. Their use persisted and spread. In 1603 the English in North America reported that 'when we would be rid of the Savages company wee would let loose the Mastives', and dogs were subsequently considered particularly suitable to be employed against the indigenous inhabitants of New England who, since they ungallantly refused to fight according to European conventions, were dismissed as no better than 'thieves and murderers'.[6]

Brutality, ingenuity, surprise, heroism and all those many other vices and virtues that ensure military victory certainly brought Europeans rich rewards, but their greatest success came when they encountered highly organized societies whose internal divisions, rivalries and conflicts they could exploit. In the Aztec and Inca empires the Spaniards were able to substitute themselves for the existing ruling classes and redirect the native economies to their own benefit. In Mexico, whose condition put Cortés in mind of that fundamental truth 'that every kingdom divided against itself is brought to ruin', the Spaniards won the support of tribes opposed to, or imperfectly subdued by, the Aztecs. Better still were the opportunities in Peru where similar weaknesses were aggravated by a war of succession in progress at their arrival. Once again they had from the very start the support of many tribes restive under Inca rule, most notably the Huancas in whose lands, strategically sited between the old imperial capital of Cuzco and the new Spanish foundation of Lima, the majority of the decisive battles of the conquest were fought.

Comparable opportunities were expected, discovered and exploited else-where. Europeans enjoyed the goodwill of those seeking allies. They were accepted as possible purchasers of local products, as suppliers of useful skills, tools and weapons, as distributors of honours, pensions and bribes and eventually as protectors from the oppressions of fellow white men. Dutch pioneers at the Cape of Good Hope found local herdsmen willing to supply beef and mutton in exchange for tobacco, copper (for ornament) and iron (for weapons). In Portuguese royal correspondence dealing with North Africa in the early 1500s there is much concern to identify potentially friendly Muslim potentates and many references to those in both the north and east of the African continent who were doing the king 'good service'. In the vast hinterland of the Río de la Plata Spaniards and Portuguese alike were able to ally themselves with semi-sedentary tribes against their nomadic neighbours. Portuguese success in the Congo was partly due to the ruler's need for aid against opponents, while their subsequent penetration of Angola was said to have been supported by chiefs who wished 'to avoid the yoke' of the indigenous ruler. English plans for intervention in Guyana (1608) assumed local tribes would welcome assistance against the incursions of the Caribs, which would 'in time . . . much availe us'. In North America, where before long rival European powers were supported by rival Amerindian peoples in their wars, an English governor enunciated a classic precept of imperial strategy when he wrote (1717), 'If we cannot destroy one nation of Indians by another our country must be lost'. And throughout the whole white colonial world African slave rebellions failed time and again since masters were forewarned by slaves themselves, perhaps from loyalty, but more often because of those bitter inter-tribal jealousies which made such risings so difficult to mount.

In Asia a willingness to accept intruders and the lack of any united opposition allowed Europe's feeblest imperial state to establish itself amongst great and ancient powers and civilizations. When they first reached the East the Portuguese met no concerted resistance from a world so immense, and inhabited by peoples of such a diversity of races, religions and cultures as to preclude the emergence of any single dominant authority, and in particular of any single dominant maritime authority. Long-distance seaborne commerce flowed through great entrepôts accustomed to the presence of merchants and sailors of differing races and beliefs. Portuguese preoccupation with maritime trades kept them clear of the major land-locked states of the Indian subcontinent. Other great eastern powers had other interests. The Ottoman Turks were engaged in conquests in the Levant and Europe while China was little concerned with the doings of 'barbarians'. The Portuguese quickly appreciated that in India they could profit from friction between Hindus and Muslims. Discovering that Islam itself was divided between the Sunni Ottomans and the Shia Persians they had hopes of aid from the 'Grand Sophy' of Iran against their mutual

Turkish enemy. Indeed to Albuquerque, in the days when his compatriots appeared able to carry all before them, the recipe for imperial success was vigorous fishing in such troubled waters so that 'some [king] will take you as protector and give you part of his lands'.[7]

Furthermore, though few of the Hindu and Muslim princelings of the western coast of India had anything of a commercial or maritime policy, and none the means to enforce one effectively, they were nevertheless well aware of the fiscal benefits deriving from trade. The governor of Diu accordingly abandoned (1508) the 'league of all Muslims' which was to have overthrown the Portuguese and hastened to secure the best commercial terms he could from them, while the King of Cochin was happy to welcome strangers rejected by his fellow Hindu, but age-old rival, the Samorin of Calicut. Thereafter Portuguese penetration of Asia owed much, and in some cases everything, to indigenous disunity and consequent indigenous approval or support. Their first attempts on Malacca were aided by allies (Muslims among them) within the city. Their colony at Macao grew with local consent, if not encouragement, whatever the xenophobic policies of the Chinese imperial government. They were later invited to settle in Bengal by the Mughal pro-consul himself, 'the natives', it was reported, not objecting.

When other Europeans subsequently arrived in the East they benefited from similar circumstances together with the goodwill – at least for a time – of those whose enmity the Portuguese had incurred. The Dutch attacked Malacca in 1606 in alliance with the erstwhile ruling house and eleven other local princes. They intervened in Sri Lanka in opposition to the Portuguese, and against Cochin they were assisted (1662) by Portugal's old enemy the Samorin of Calicut. In the early 1600s both the Dutch and the English East India companies were granted liberal concessions, as on the Coromandel coast of India, by local potentates or officials. Whatever the implicit threat of the European presence they hoped to ensure that the commercial and fiscal benefits it was expected that the companies would bring would flow into their own and not their neighbours' coffers.

Naturally enough, too, once Europeans had shown they could succeed they were joined by those eager to share the benefits of being on the winning side. In the early 1500s the ruler of a minuscule Indonesian island, hearing that the Portuguese aided those who favoured them, 'so that their realms increase', prudently made contact with Lisbon. In the Americas Spanish pioneers gained not only willing and agreeable bedmates, but invaluable purveyors of intelligence and information, in those Amerindian women attracted to ruthless and masterful *conquistadores*. Following their suppression of a Khoikhoi rising at the Cape of Good Hope in 1673 the Dutch soon had many tribes seeking their friendship, chiefly in expectation of the booty which might come their way. Furthermore, 'pacified natives', accepting in some measure Christianity and the norms of European behaviour, could usefully be turned against their unsubdued fellows. In the Canaries in the late 1400s the conquered Guanches of one island were often enough the conquerors of another. The Spaniards moved 'friendly natives' to northern Mexico to help against the Chichimeca. Christian Indians were staunch allies of the Portuguese in Brazil, fighting alike 'their owne kindred' and the Dutch invaders in the seventeenth century. In South Africa in the mid 1600s whites could use Khoikhoi associates to round up escaped Angolan slaves.

There was, however, no more eloquent testimony to the eternal validity of the ancient adage 'divide and rule' than the benefit Europeans drew from the friction or worse which developed between the African slaves they introduced into so much of the world and local peoples. For blacks, or indeed any other race, irrevocably torn from their homeland, the best prospect of a tolerable life was to accept the whims and wishes of their masters. So Africans served the Spaniards as formidable overseers and oppressors of Amerindians, despised by both, in the Americas, or could be used by the Dutch to hunt down troublesome Asians in Indonesia. For the same reason Asian slaves could be employed against Africans in the Dutch Cape, while in English South Carolina in the early 1700s Amerindians were loosed in pursuit of runaway Africans and were settled in areas where large number of black slaves were held in the hope of overawing them. And in these same years the businesslike government of Jamaica brought in mixed race fighting men (Mosquitos) from the Central American mainland to round up escaped Africans on the island.[8]

Hence with the consent, and very commonly with the encouragement of indigenous peoples, European rule or a European presence was established in the wider world. In particular intruders could almost invariably count on, or easily organize, military assistance. Small bodies of European troops were thus rapidly converted into impressive armies, their indigenous allies supplying them with expert knowledge of the local terrain, tactics and political situation, and more often than not bearing the brunt of the fighting 'to save', as many white commanders freely admitted, 'our men'. When Cortés first entered the Aztec lands he had with him 4000 of what he refers to as 'our native allies', soon allegedly swelled to over 150,000. Some were simply labourers and porters, without whom no white colonial force would take the field, but many were fighting men who proved their worth in such actions as the capture of the Aztec capital. Other indigenous warriors were used throughout the rest of the empire. They might be mercenaries or the troops of friendly local potentates, and they might fight under their own commanders using traditional weapons, or as an integral part of a European force, using European arms. 'Pascac, captain general of the Indians', was engaged in the Peruvian civil wars of the 1540s. On one occasion a Spanish contingent in Paraguay is described as comprising Indians and non-Indians mixed in the ratio of one white harquebusier to two Indians without firearms. Spain's enemies in the Caribbean regularly came up against her redoubtable local allies, especially archers 'with their arrowes most villanously empoisened'. The pattern was the same in the East where Japanese mercenaries fought in the Catholic cause in Cambodia (1595), where the invasion of China by 10,000 Europeans and the same number of Filippinos was once projected, and where the Spaniards hired warriors from the Christian province of Pampanga in the Philippines on such a scale that Pampangueno became virtually synonymous with mercenary in their oriental empire.

More lavish still was Portugal's use of native allies and mercenaries – no radical innovation since mercenaries were the backbone of armies in Europe – to reduce, if not eradicate, what at first sight was a crippling numerical inferiority. In the East Portuguese troops were raised, when occasion demanded, from unmarried Europeans (*soldados*), of whom, despite the thousands of names on the official muster rolls, there were never more than a few hundred available. But the ranks were filled with indigenous peoples of an astonishing assortment of races and religions. Already in 1509 armed Malabar seamen were serving in Portuguese ships in the Indian Ocean. To take and hold Goa (1510) Albuquerque had the help of at least forty Hindu captains and their troops. Over the ensuing decades, under their own officers, Goan and Malabar infantry and archers in their thousands served the *Estado* anywhere from Indonesia to Aden. Before, in the mid sixteenth century, religious bigotry checked their employment, Hindu mercenary captains were, like the commanders of the auxiliaries used by Spain, well-known, well-regarded and well-rewarded figures. It was the pirate and general military entrepreneur Timoja who suggested to Albuquerque, in furtherance of schemes of his own, the desirability of taking Muslim Goa, served in the campaign that led to its capture with about 2000 men, and thereafter briefly garrisoned the territory and farmed its revenues.

This dependence on alien and non-Christian arms had obvious disadvantages. It outraged pious Catholics and it raised the ominous possibility of the Portuguese ending as little better than the clients of their own employees, particularly the formidable Japanese. The collapse of Portugal's authority in Sri Lanka was blamed on the defection of erstwhile local allies and there was a general feeling, as disaster after disaster befell the *Estado* in the seventeenth century, that Asians were militarily useless. Yet in the absence of any obvious alternative necessity was an irrefutable argument for their continued use. Moreover, since Africans and Amerindians made so vital a contribution to the defeat of the Dutch in Brazil there was always the chance that Asians might do as well in the East. And in any case, it was pointed out, it would be impolitic for the Portuguese not to use them when they were employed on such a scale by the VOC. Furthermore they had the overwhelming attraction of coming cheap. Indians would accept half of what Portuguese fighting men allegedly received. Indeed they very often served at their own cost, 'without pay and only for victuals' or 'without pay or goods' in the expectation of rewards and booty. Hence forces as polyglot as ever in composition, including alike Japanese and Ethiopians, Indians and Malays, continued to go into action, with varying degrees of enthusiasm, in the Lusitanian cause. Sometimes there were no Europeans whatsoever with them, and even when there were they were almost invariably in a minority. In the seventeenth century 2000 Portuguese, 1000 Muslim Indians and an unspecified number of Iranians took part in the final and abortive defence of Hormuz and Arabs served against the Omanis in Mascat. In the last stages of the battle against the Dutch for Sri Lanka there are repeated mentions of bodies of up to 5000 so called 'Blacks', without whom, it was frequently conceded, the war could not have gone on.

Similar policies were pursued elsewhere. Muslim Arabs fought their co-religionaries in the Portuguese cause in North Africa in the early 1500s. Lusitanian forces in Mozambique commonly comprised a handful of whites accompanied by hundreds and often thousands of Africans. Local head hunters helped to expel Dutch invaders from West Africa in 1625, and in Angola – where subject chiefs were expected to provide their overlords with fighting men and bearers – the bulk of Christian Portugal's indigenous auxiliaries were nomadic and reputedly cannibal warriors. Would-be intruders in Brazil encountered, as in the Spanish Caribbean, Amerindians fighting in strength and to great effect in the white man's service. Indeed, at the height of the struggle to expel the Dutch, the Portuguese government was much concerned with ensuring the loyalty of its indigenous supporters and with depriving the enemy of the services of those currently aiding him. To which end it was proposed, in the best imperial style, to distribute gifts and to bestow upon the most notable leader ('a good Christian'), a pension, a coat of arms and the title of 'Chief Captain of all the Indians'.

Other European powers followed suit as opportunity offered. In North America both the English and the French used Amerindian braves to defend and extend their footholds, and even settlers of the most pacific persuasions saw fit to employ local warriors. In 1637 Puritan Connecticut paid the Mohegans to scalp the restive Pequots, while a century later liberal Pennsylvania got the Iroquois to drive out unwanted natives. In India the French, when they intervened in Coromandel in the late seventeenth century, did so with the aid of Hindu troops 'very clever in the use of arms and indefatigable in war' whom they had trained in European fashion. The better part of the English garrison at Madras in 1673 similarly consisted of Hindus. The Dutch, never given to half measures, were by the mid 1600s using Sri Lankan, Ambonese, Bandanese and Indian fighting men, sometimes reinforced by Japanese mercenaries or the forces of local rulers, like the thousand cavalry obtained from an Indian ranee in 1659. As in other empires the leaders of these troops occasionally emerge as identifiable persons. The VOC's Ambonese in Indonesia were commanded from 1665 by a Muslim known as Captain Jonker whose many years of loyal service against the Company's European and indigenous enemies came to a sudden and characteristic end when in 1689 he was executed for planning the massacre of his white masters in Batavia.[9]

Finally, and with the cruelest irony, the establishment and defence of European dominion often enough depended on the collaboration, whether from hopeless resignation or desperate optimism, of slaves. They were used by all European colonial powers in the exploitation of land and on a lavish scale by the Iberians in particular as military auxiliaries. Manacled Amerindian porters accompanied the Spaniards in some of their most arduous expeditions in the early sixteenth century. In Asia the Portuguese employed alike Africans, Chinese, Japanese, Sri Lankans, Indians – many sold into servitude by their own peoples or families. Women carried their masters' weapons in war, men built fortresses – as did their fellows in Dutch hands – cleared jungles and manufactured gunpowder. They served at sea to ensure Europeans did not 'die from overwork' and they fought in impressive numbers as soldiers. Two thousand 'of many nations' helped to defend Malacca in the early 1600s. But the majority used by the Portuguese, in East and West alike, were Africans, especially the redoubtable warriors of Guinea. Their courage and loyalty, a chronicler admitted in 1539, had enabled his compatriots to conquer 'those regions which we hold', just as their desperate and often drunken valour was subsequently to save the day for their masters on many occasions. They were provided, none too willingly, by their owners, were equipped with what are described in the mid 1600s as bows, arrows and assegais, and served under leaders of their own race. It even briefly appeared to some Portuguese, as the struggle in Sri Lanka went from bad to worse, that the only possible military solution was to free the Africans, grant them land in the island and thus create a readily available and effective fighting force.[10]

Such proceedings reflect a general European willingness and ability to profit from rivalries among the peoples and within the societies they encountered and an equally keen indigenous willingness to extract whatever advantage they could from the presence of white intruders. In Africa black and mulatto intermediaries gladly provided Europeans with slaves, as did some of the tribes of North America, while others fought for the chance to supply them with furs. Highly developed states and civilizations might, as in Asia, pragmatically accept Europeans, or could be, as in Spanish America, geared by conquest to European demands. Even in Muslim North Africa a 'valiant Moor' could be sworn in 'according to his law' in 1514 to rule his fellows as a pro-consul of Portugal. In the Spanish Indies tribal chiefs, to their own considerable benefit, collected revenues for, and generally enforced the will of their new masters.[11]

In the East the Portuguese, their pragmatism fostered by their feebleness, employed local peoples whenever they could, ranging from the peasants who tilled the soil in India to the Hindu secretaries and Parsee businessmen who advised viceroys and the Hindu physicians who tended the ailments of the opulent. From the very beginning they entered into commercial partnerships with eastern, including Muslim merchants, of whose wealth, skills and acumen they were soon keenly aware. Trading ventures from Malacca were, until its loss, in part financed by Coromandel Hindus, while in the sixteenth century there were close, if not always cordial relations with a number of Muslim plutocrats in the subcontinent who took the opportunity to transmit news of Portuguese intentions to the sultans in Istanbul. In Goa the Portuguese employed the indigenous labour system they found and the whole machinery of revenue collection and administration, anticipating on a minuscule scale what the Spaniards were in essence to do in the Americas. Around the capital of the *Estado*, a traveller recorded, local merchants 'hired and farmed out the customs and rents of the Portugals and the king's revenues'. As indeed they profitably did, with Timoja, the instigator of Portugal's capture of the city, departing with all he had gathered and leaving his supposed masters unpaid. By the seventeenth century a tight-knit group of high caste Hindus accounted for the best part of the taxes collected, while the bulk of the capital invested in Goa's trade was non-Christian. Rich Asians owned vessels in partnership with Europeans and in India acted as their factors, lent money to individuals, the government and to the viceroys themselves. With the passage of time local wealth was of even greater importance to the Portuguese, so that when in the late 1600s there was talk of expelling non-Christians from the Indian lands of the *Estado*, royal officials warned that without their capital and business skills the empire would be ruined. Ironically, too, Portugal, whose eastern footholds were linked and sustained by sea, became increasingly dependent on local maritime resources. Indigenous shipwrights, especially in India, constructed vessels for the use of merchants, the *Estado* and its servants. Local craft with local crews profitably carried anything from the provisions to feed the empire's inhabitants to the troops to defend its possessions. Local seamen, among them Arabs, Gujarati Indians, Turks, Ethiopians and Filippinos, manned Portuguese ships, it being admitted in the seventeenth century that without those of western India 'we cannot live or sustain ourselves'. Even more ironically, while Church and Crown urged the godly task of spreading the Christian message and denounced the evils of pagans and infidels, the majority of Portugal's sailors in the East were Muslims and most of its ships to all intent Muslim, reflecting the pre-eminence of Islam in so much of the oriental maritime economy.

Portugal's European rivals trod a similar path. The Chinese were indispensable as traders and artisans to the Dutch in Batavia. The English and Dutch raised capital from Indian money-lenders and employed Indian factors. Both Muslims and Hindus went into commercial partnerships with

English merchants in seventeenth-century Madras. In white enclaves of any importance in India (particularly those of the English) there appeared indigenous 'chief merchants', acknowledged as such by compatriots and Europeans alike. They were ubiquitous and influential. They advised whites on native affairs. They were commonly the sole agents for the supply of the commodities Europeans needed, just as they had first call on the goods Europeans imported. They shared the fiscal privileges the western companies obtained and often further improved their lot by enrolling European support against indigenous authorities or joining whites in harrying and oppressing undesirable native competition.[12]

European experiences of the past century, whether of the havoc wrought by modern weapons on peoples with no equivalents, or of the wounds inflicted on white self-esteem by crushing defeats at the hands of Japan and Vietnam, have suggested to fertile minds other and seemingly persuasive explanations of the continent's triumphs in the wider world. Europeans, it has been urged, were sustained by superior morale and impelled by a greater will to win than were their opponents, or, as it has been more portentously put, the dynamic, restless and utilitarian civilization of Europe subdued realms culturally and economically static.[13] Admittedly Europeans, and the pioneers in particular, frequently displayed purposeful violence. The Spaniards employed what they themselves described as 'cruel war' in the Americas, which entailed burning Indians alive or torturing, mutilating and throwing their victims to the dogs, while the Portuguese behaved in much the same fashion to start with in the East. Undeniably, too, Europeans might pursue victory with greater tenacity than their opponents. Aztec armies fought bravely, but to secure victims for sacrifice rather than the destruction of the enemy. The regimented Incas, who could struggle long and desperately on occasion, might equally well give up if their leaders fell, while the resistance of both peoples was undermined by their intensely pessimistic religions and their morale sapped as defeat and disease seemingly showed their gods to be fallible. The following century the Amerindian allies of the New Englanders, though greatly impressed by 'the manner of the English men's fight', found it 'too furious' and resulting in the death of 'too many'.[14]

Yet bearing in mind the brutalities inflicted on their victims (such as missionaries) by Amerindians, or on outlawed Christians by the Japanese, it must be a matter of doubt as to whether whites shocked and demoralized their opponents by violence and cruelty of an unprecedented order. Nor is the morale of a whole society an easy thing to gauge, and where, furthermore, we have some indications of that of Europeans they frequently reflect a spirit far removed from easy expectations of divinely appointed victory. In the Americas a whole succession of Dutch and French attempts at colonization withered as would-be settlers discovered that the winters of Canada or the overwhelming heat and scant opportunities of the Wild

Coast[15] were more than a match for their resolve. On the north-eastern seaboard of America English colonies failed under Elizabeth, while in the ensuing century even the Puritans initially quailed at the nature of the land – 'a hideous and desolate wilderness' – to which they had committed themselves. The extent of European conquest was, as we have seen, closely circumscribed, and far from surrendering at the first appearance of Europeans Amerindian peoples fought hard and sometimes successfully against the intruders, while white penetration of Asia was no sequence of bloodless triumphs. The Portuguese were defeated at sea, failed against Aden, were initially rebuffed from Goa and Malacca and subsequently endured crushing reverses at the hands of the Omanis. The Dutch eventually succeeded against Mataram (1678) then, however, already in 'a natural process of disintegration', but failed to subjugate the kingdom of Kandy (Sri Lanka) and were expelled from Taiwan (1661) by the Chinese. The English came to grief against the Mughals later in the century and throughout this period most Europeans trod carefully with China and more carefully still with Japan.

European success, it has also been argued, stemmed from the continent's superior technology – which at various times has been taken to mean anything from nautical charts to guns and ships – and the 'utilitarian' approach of Europeans to such matters as opposed to the 'dilettante' attitude of other peoples, especially those of the Orient. However, as many have learned to their cost in recent wars, there is more to military victory than a command of high technology. Nor in the early modern period did European technology, whose superiority to that of China is in any case open to debate, bring substantial conquests in Asia or Africa. It did not lead to the subjugation of North America or of the determined and elusive nomads of the south of the continent. Admittedly European tactics were often wrong. Most Amerindians refused pitched battles, relying instead on surprise and ambush, which thus allowed them to pick off 'disorderly stragglers' in pioneer Virginia. But European success frequently came, particularly in the early and crucial decades in which they established themselves in the wider world, in campaigns fought (as in Mexico) by choice or necessity very largely without the firearms usually considered the most decisive manifestation of white technical superiority. In Asia in the first half of the sixteenth century Portuguese authority was commonly demonstrated by raids on enemy villages accompanied by the destruction of palm groves and the burning of crops. Engagements at sea were often a matter of boarding and hand to hand fighting with swords, in part to ensure no loot was lost through the premature destruction of prizes, in part as a brash demonstration of Christian valour. Moreover Europeans readily admitted, especially after defeat, the efficacy of indigenous tactics and weapons. Stones hurled from the mountain tops by Canarian Guanches shattered Spanish shields and limbs. Inca slings, the Spaniards conceded, were 'not much less effective than an arquebus', and the 'wild Indians' of Mexico, it was discovered, had arrows that 'will pierce any coat of mail'. War elephants intimidated the Portuguese in sixteenth-century India and European sailing ships, inopportunely becalmed in Asian waters, could find themselves at the mercy of local oar-propelled craft. Even as late as 1735 the Marathas could take an English East Indiaman fresh out from home using such vessels. Not surprisingly Europeans adopted indigenous armour (as in the Spanish Indies), indigenous styles of fighting (as in Brazil) and in Asia regularly employed every type of oriental ship from the smallest to the great junks of the Chinese.

Certainly European firearms might, for a time, disperse or intimidate peoples unaccustomed to them. Artillery could batter walls and undoubtedly helped to save Portuguese possessions in western India in the late sixteenth century, while at a crucial moment in the conquest of Mexico Cortés urged his desperate need of 'horses, arms, crossbows and powder' – the very order of the demand is significant. By about 1600 the records of European military operations in the East are full of references to guns, bombs, mines and grenades. Weapons of this nature had indeed long been known in Asia – firearms were for example employed in Hindu Vijayanagar as early as the fourteenth century and in China earlier still. But other than that of the Chinese and some pieces (probably of Turkish origin) in western India, there was no artillery of any size in the East when the first Europeans arrived. Nor, since the planking of eastern vessels – apart from those of the Chinese – was sewn together, and not, as in Europe, nailed, could they have fired such guns without disintegrating. And even in the seventeenth century some Asians accepted that Europeans were the 'most expert' in anything to do with firearms.

The imbalance was, however, more apparent than real. Already in 1508 the Portuguese reported vessels 'equivalent to our own' being constructed in the East. Asian peoples soon acquired firearms by purchase or capture and in such amounts that it became a prime objective of Portuguese negotiations with indigenous rulers to secure the return of any artillery they had obtained. Nor was there any shortage of Christian renegades, well rewarded by their new employers, happy to teach Muslims, Hindus or any others how to manufacture and use such weapons. Albuquerque himself talks in 1513 of an Indian craftsman who could 'make guns as good as those of Bohemia'. Western travellers, merchants and diplomats subsequently remarked on the quantity and quality of the artillery belonging to rulers such as the King of Pegu and the Mughal emperor and on the proficiency of their gunners. Soon after their arrival in the East the English learned that even the tiniest pirate vessel of the Malabar coast of India could carry 'many fireworks', while Portugal's old enemy Atjeh had ships mounting a full range of western-style pieces at a time when many of the Estado's own craft were still unarmed. Much the same happened in the West. Though few

Amerindians were able to make European firearms for themselves many
were using them by the second half of the sixteenth century. Some they
obtained from white traders, some were provided by renegades, and some
they captured which, as with the Araucanians, reflects rather than explains
their military prowess. Nor should we overestimate the importance of guns
in establishing and sustaining the European presence in the non-European
world. Crude, cumbersome and uncertain in aim and operation, they often
allowed their users to be overwhelmed by the scale and speed of an enemy's
advance. In hot and humid climates they were all too likely to be defective,
and with their powder wet and the match to ignite it extinguished by some
downpour, they were totally useless, failing Europeans and non-Europeans
alike time and again and obliging them to fight with other arms.

Nevertheless in the two centuries after roughly 1500 Europeans clearly
achieved spectacular and decisive successes in some parts of the world. They
penetrated the maritime economy of Asia, and in Central and southern
America the Spaniards overthrew the Aztec and Inca empires, exploiting
the political weaknesses of highly organized societies whose resistance was
undermined by the shock of unfamiliar tactics and the impact of hitherto
unknown diseases. In the West opposition was further weakened by the
invaders' disruption of an agrarian economy which had ensured, especially
in Mexico, the cultivation of the quick-growing maize whose rapid
succession of harvests allowed the land to support so huge a population.
But these very numbers were in themselves a liability. Without cavalry and
wheeled transport Aztec and Inca armies had none of the mobility and
manoeuvrability of the forces of their white opponents. Their operations
were difficult to co-ordinate, while by reason of their heavy demands for
food and the need to release manpower to provide it, they were unable to
keep the field more than briefly.

Before such victories could be achieved Europeans had to identify and
reach what one *conquistador* described as these 'vineyards of the Lord'. It
could be by accident, as with Columbus' revelation of a hitherto unknown
continent, or it might be, as was notably the case with Portugal, the result
of the persistent pursuit of specific objectives. In very large measure the
astonishing successes of this minuscule state are to be attributed to the
policies of the royal house which, unlike any other in Europe initially
concentrated its efforts and resources on the wider world. The influence of
the royal princes, Henry in particular, ensured the continuance of the
pioneering voyages. Manuel I (1495–1521) decided that the enterprise of
Asia should not, as some wished, be abandoned. Sovereigns despatched
expeditions in the crucial early decades of the sixteenth century whose
commanders were given full and explicit instructions as to where they were
to go, what they were to do and how they were to do it. The information
they gathered was carefully sifted and formed the basis for orders to
succeeding ventures. In the same way the Spanish monarchy, once it

appreciated what Columbus and his successors had stumbled on, made a determined effort to bring the whole process of empire building under its control.

Where such support and direction either failed to develop or were not sustained colonial beginnings were generally modest, negligible or slow in coming to fruition. The Spanish defeat and imprisonment of Francis I (1525–6) meant that France failed to follow up the discoveries made by his protégé Giovanni Verrazzano on the Atlantic coast of North America. Subsequent plans to bridle the Spaniards from a base in Florida languished because of the outbreak of the Wars of Religion in the mother country, while Flemish projects to search for the north-west passage to Asia allegedly came to nothing because of the revolt against Habsburg rule (1568).[16] England's promising start in oceanic ventures c. 1500 had little immediate outcome since the early Tudors had no wish to clash with Spain, and under Elizabeth and the first Stuarts the plethora of conflicting and generally abortive schemes – to reach Asia by every conceivable route, to colonize North America, to cripple Spain by privateering wars – reflected the crown's reluctance to commit itself to any, and the consequent squandering, through lack of direction, of resources and opportunities. Dutch beginnings in Asia were similarly a poor indication of the maritime and commercial pre-eminence of the Low Countries until the incorporation of the VOC, a *de facto* expression of the power of the Dutch state.

Once, for any reason, Europeans secured footholds outside their own continent they were rarely ejected, despite local and individual setbacks. They had ships capable of crossing and recrossing oceans to bring them settlers, reinforcements, supplies and commodities to trade. The Vikings, however, had earlier possessed craft able to endure such voyages, and those of the Arabs and Chinese were, at the very time of the first great European expeditions, perfectly capable of similar undertakings. Yet this had no such imperial consequences as the achievements of Columbus and Vasco da Gama. Europeans were from a civilization then powerfully affected by religious convictions, not noted for their tolerance or willingness to compromise. Many, like the English Puritans, abandoned their parent society to live according to their own tenaciously held beliefs. Others, like the *conquistadores*, were in pursuit of rewards they had no prospect of obtaining in their mother country. There were indeed perhaps stronger reasons for leaving Europe for distant lands than for departing from any comparable civilization. The indigenous economies of the pre-conquest Americas were self-contained. Their inhabitants neither knew of or were in any position to seek the products of other cultures. Contemporary Africa had trading links with Asia from its east coast and with Europe and Asia through its northern and north-eastern states. Asia could satisfy all its needs from its own and its neighbours' resources. Not so Europe, which from time immemorial had sought those choice luxuries for which the East was renowned and for which it had little to offer in exchange. Nor unlike China or India could it provide from within its own borders rewards sufficiently rich – like those accumulated by Mughal emperors – to quell expansionist urges. Once it was clear to Europeans that empire could mean wealth and profit its survival was ensured and there was no difficulty in raising the capital to support further ventures: the bigger the likelihood of gain the more affluent the backers attracted, as with the Dutch and English East India companies. With climates in many parts of the world similar to those of Europe settlers could flourish, sustained by the familiar crops and livestock they had introduced and opposed only by indigenous populations weakened by European-transmitted diseases. Elusive nomads living in wild country might defeat the military skills and governmental techniques of the whites, but otherwise they could count on some measure of indigenous co-operation. In the East they could use the troops of mercenary captains, to whom they were but another employer and do business with local merchants, to whom they were yet another customer. Almost everywhere they could secure the support, for any number of reasons, of local chiefs, princes, monarchs and indeed whole peoples. Europe's success in this first imperial age was less a measure of its own strength than of the weaknesses and opportunism of the states and societies it encountered, unable or unwilling to mount a united or sustained opposition and suffering in consequence the same fate as befell Spanish-dominated Italy or Turkish-occupied eastern Europe in these very years.

NOTES AND REFERENCES

1   Goa (India), Historical Archives, *Monções do Reino*, 37, folios 274ff.
2   Samuel Purchas, *Hakluyt Posthumus, or Purchas His Pilgrimes*, MacLehose edition, 20 vols (Glasgow, 1905–7), **XVII**, 276–7.
3   See p. 182.
4   C. R. Boxer, *João de Barros, Portuguese Humanist and Historian of Asia* (New Delhi, 1981), p. 30.
5   Purchas, *Pilgrimes*, **VI**, 440.
6   David B. Quinn and Alison M. Quinn (eds), *The English New England Voyages, 1602–1608*, Hakluyt Society (1983), p. 221; James Axtell, *The European and the Indian. Essays in the Ethnohistory of Colonial North America* (Oxford, 1981), p. 142.
7   *Cartas de Affonso de Albuquerque, seguidas de documentos que as elucidam*, ed. Raymundo Antonio de Bulhão Pato, 7 vols, (Lisbon, 1884–1935), *Carta* no. xli, p. 204.
8   Captain Alfred Dewar (ed.), *The Voyages and Travels of Captain Nathaniel Uring* (1928), pp. 160–1.
9   M. C. Ricklefs, *A History of Modern Indonesia c. 1300 to the Present* (1981), p. 81.
10 G. V. Scammell, 'The pillars of empire: indigenous assistance and the survival of the *Estado da India c. 1600–1700*', *Modern Asian Studies*, 22, 3 (1988), 473–89.

11 See pp. 148–9, 183.
12 See the magisterial analysis in Sinnappah Arasaratnam, *Merchants, Companies and Commerce on the Coromandel Coast, 1650–1740* (Delhi, 1986).
13 David S. Landes, 'The foundations of European expansion and dominion: an equilibrium model', *Itinerario* V, 1 (1981), 46ff.
14 Axtell, *European and Indian*, p. 140.
15 See pp. 30, 39–40.
16 *The Original Writings and Correspondence of the two Richard Hakluyts*, ed. E. G. R. Taylor, 2 vols, Hakluyt Society (1935), II, 279.

4   *Exploitation*

Empire, St Francis Xavier once splenetically wrote, meant no more than conjugating 'the verb to rob in all its moods and tenses'. Nor is there any lack of evidence to support him. The Spanish conquest of Mexico and Peru was accompanied by a search for loot so brutal and frenetic as to convince many Indians that bullion was their new masters' staple diet. No sooner had Europeans arrived in North America than they fell to ransacking Amerindian graves for whatever treasures they contained – 'pearles, Copper and braceletts' in Virginia, 'robes of beaver skins' in Canada.[1] Western seamen looted indigenous shipping anywhere from the Red Sea to the Pacific. Proconsuls of empire, whether serving the Catholic kings of Spain and Portugal or the trading companies of the Protestant powers, grew rich by fraud and extortion whatever the problems that beset their lords or masters. Travellers reported the 'especially fine booty' conveniently assembled in distant realms and ready for the taking. It was generally accepted that the natural resources God has so generously provided man might improvidently consume. The life of a sugar plantation in seventeenth-century English Jamaica could be less than fifty years. Tobacco planters in contemporary Virginia bought land it was said 'as they might buy a waggon – with the expectation of wearing it out'.[2] Fishermen pointlessly destroyed the forests of Newfoundland, while it was alleged of New England and New York in 1702 that 'oaks and pines of the largest dimensions were converted to pipe staves and deal boards'.

Despoliation and exaction could profitably be institutionalized, thereby both enhancing the intruders' revenues and extending their authority. Portugal, ever conscious of her imperial dignity, demanded tribute from subject or client peoples wherever possible – grain from Morocco, cinnamon and elephants from Sri Lanka, pearls from Hormuz, cloves from Tidore, gold from Mombasa and slaves from Angola. But nowhere was the imperial dream of willing natives bearing riches to their European masters more fully realized than in the Spanish New World. Columbus imposed tribute in gold (or whatever else was available) on the indigenous inhabitants of the Caribbean islands. The crown ordered its payment in 1501 and following the overthrow of the Aztec empire it was extended to the mainland, where it was to be rendered in recognition of Spanish sovereignty. Thus there was introduced what was in effect a capitation tax on able-bodied Amerindians between the ages of 18 and 50. Its inception ratified exactions in goods or labour which for a time Spaniards who had secured themselves *encomienda* over Indians – the right to the services and dues provided by a given number of subjugated peoples – enjoyed.[3] It conferred, as we shall see, immense benefit on *encomenderos*, provided the state with a useful revenue – since tribute was split half and half between crown and *encomendero* – and with a tax capable of extension to such other classes as mulattos, free blacks and peoples of mixed Amerindian and African blood.

Proceedings of this order reflect the general view that empire should yield 'every possible profit', as a knowing investor in the conquest of Peru put it. Territories which failed, or seemed unlikely to fulfil such expectations, were commonly farmed out to those willing to take them on at their own cost and risk, as was initially the case with Portugal's Atlantic islands and with Brazil. Between 1629 and 1635 the Dutch West India Company tried a similar policy, entrusting the settlement of the New Netherlands (North America) to 'patroons'. The Stuart rulers of England sold or granted rights to colonize North America to 'proprietors' and left such unrewarding settlements as Massachusetts to their own devices until well into the seventeenth century, while France leased out (1710) the fragile and newly-established Louisiana.

Prospects of wealth, on the other hand, brought strenuous efforts to enforce the authority of the metropolitan state. The silver-bearing lands of the Indies became the heart of Spain's American empire and the government of Mexico and Peru a prime concern of the ruling house. Charles II of England swiftly converted the rich English tobacco and sugar-producing settlements of North America and the Caribbean into royal colonies. Governments endeavoured with varying degrees of alacrity and urgency to ensure their exclusive title and access to regions from which profit and revenue were anticipated. Between 1452 and 1456 the Portuguese crown secured from the papacy three bulls (privileges) granting it, among other things, the monopoly of the trade and navigation with those parts of Africa discovered or yet to be discovered by its subjects as far as the Indies, and forbidding any nation to intervene within these preserves. For the advancement of profit the conduct of rich colonial trades was restricted to carefully defined bodies. Such a commerce might be handled directly by the crown itself, as was that of Portugal with Asia for most of the sixteenth century. It might be entrusted, as was Spain's trade with the Americas, to members of a corporate body (the Seville merchant guild), or it might become, like Dutch and English trade to Asia, the prerogative of a monopoly joint-stock company.[4] Even Portugal's commerce with the immense littoral of Brazil, demanding a volume of tonnage far beyond the mother country's resources, and which until the early 1600s had been open to all Portuguese subjects and friendly foreign nationals, was in 1649 restricted (albeit unsuccessfully) to a monopoly company. It was widely assumed that colonial industries would not compete with those of the mother country which was to be the sole supplier of whatever goods its colonies required and the sole recipient of their valuable products. It might even be the case that a country's entire imperial commerce came to be conducted under strict and potentially lucrative supervision through a single port, with Lisbon handling Portugal's Asian and African trades and Spain's commerce with the Americas supposedly confined to Seville/Cadiz.[5]

From colonial possessions imperial powers exacted revenues old and new alike. In seventeenth-century Java the Dutch were collecting tribute formerly rendered to the Sultan of Mataram and ensuring by armed force the delivery of the crops they desired. The Portuguese converted Brazil and West Africa to substantial contributors to their revenues. In Goa they received the customs, rents and proceeds of various monopolies previously accruing to the Muslim rulers. To these exactions they added others of their own devising. In the Indian Ocean they taxed such local shipping as they could direct into their ports and licenced its movements – as the Protestant trading companies subsequently did – through the sale of passes. On the mainland they seized whenever they could the assets of non-Christian merchants who died in lands under their jurisdiction. The same spirit flourished elsewhere. In the early 1500s the recipient of a tiny island in the Gulf of Guinea promptly demanded a charter detailing the taxes he could collect. A century later the king himself was being urged to introduce into East Africa the sensible practice of Indian rulers of taxing the tusks of dead elephants.

In Spain, once the implications of Columbus' discoveries were plain the crown assumed control of the voyages, and once the mainland empires had fallen, the full panoply of secular and ecclesiastical taxation, as it was understood in the peninsula, and as far as the colonists would permit, was introduced into the Indies. The church took 10 per cent of most agricultural goods produced by non-Indians (and sometimes by Indians too). The transoceanic trades of the Atlantic and Pacific became elaborately administered monopolies, with the state taxing commerce to and from the Americas, in the Americas and in Europe. There were taxes of increasing frequency and severity on non-Indians (and Indians as well at times), levied on pensions, on entry into office, on sales (at 2 per cent), on precious metals and precious stones (at 20 per cent), and (from 1638) at 1 per cent allegedly to meet defence costs. The non-European classes subject to tribute were steadily increased. The Chinese in the Philippines were taxed and there was a poll-tax on African slaves imported into the Americas. The crown or its nominees drew an income from assorted monopolies or licence to breach them, from the sale of papal indulgences and from fees on anything from the purchase of official stationery to the confirmation of title to land. By enterprise, and through the generosity of the faithful – not least indigenous converts – the church grew rich, enabling it to lend money both to colonists and to the crown itself in its many moments of need at a reasonable rate of 5 per cent. The lower, and sometimes the higher ranks of the secular clergy meanwhile laid up such treasure on earth as they could, engaging in straightforward business, simple extortion or charging their flocks for whatever ministrations were bestowed on them. As the burden of empire increased so did the ingenuity of the projects to extract yet more from the Indies. In 1631 it was proposed to sell offices and patents of nobility, to demand 'gracious donations' from merchants and officials, and to force Indian leaders to hand over the funds of their communities. Private shipments of bullion to Europe were confiscated and the Americas were saddled with pensions to old soldiers, faithful bureaucrats and desirable court ladies.

From such rich veins still more could be quarried. At no cost to metropolitan resources royal creditors could be paid off and men of influence rewarded. Iberian aristocrats and gentlemen were granted military, ecclesiastical and administrative offices in the empire – the records of the Portuguese *Casa da India*[6] mentioning over 2500 such grants for the East alone between 1508 and 1633 – from whose proceeds they could in turn reward their relatives and clients. In that time-honoured style which has ruined many a business the directors of the Dutch VOC nominated their talentless friends and relations to Company posts in Asia. Charles II of England granted William Penn that land in America which still bears his name in part satisfaction of a debt owed him by the crown. Monopolies of various colonial trades could be farmed out for cash or for services rendered or expected; permission to ignore them could be granted or sold. And when all else failed fines could be levied or threatened for the alleged breach of some prerogative, with an English official writing enthusiastically to his patron in 1683 of the possibility of selling pardons at up to the princely sum of £10,000 a time in New England.

One simple and remunerative way of exploiting the resources of the wider world was for Europeans to adjust some existing commerce to their needs. Indigenous peoples were usually willing to accept new customers, especially those able to offer them something particularly acceptable in exchange for whatever goods they possessed. Europeans might thus penetrate, redirect or expand trades already well-established. They soon realized that North America, where furs were used by and exchanged among the native inhabitants, could readily provide a commodity much in demand in Europe and currently and expensively supplied from Russia and the Baltic hinterland. And the prospects were all the better since the Amerindians were only too eager to have European trinkets, tools and weapons, together with the white man's liquor for which they speedily developed an unquenchable thirst. Nevertheless Europeans had to acquire their furs through indigenous intermediaries in a trade over which they exercised little control since the Indian population was unsubjugated. The handful of French settlers in Canada were unable, individuals apart, to

penetrate beyond the St Lawrence Valley. By the early 1600s the Montagnais
Indians denied them access to the furs of the river's northern hinterland.
The Algonkians controlled the way westward along the upper Ottawa and
the opportunities of the Great Lakes were firmly in Huron hands. French
trade was hence conducted from posts pushed as far inland as the tribes
would permit, and to which the Indians themselves brought the furs which
they increasingly collected from other peoples further afield. The business
was a considerable one, running at the annual export of up to 15,000 beaver
skins alone by the 1630s, and these selling in Europe at ten times their
purchase price. Soon, to the Indians' great advantage, the trade was disputed
by other white men – the Dutch from the New Netherlands; the English
from their various settlements on the north-east seaboard and subsequently
from their base in Hudson Bay. Some Europeans, most notably the French
coureurs des bois, penetrated inland like frontiersmen elsewhere. They
traded with local peoples, or persuaded them to bring their furs to French
posts. But the Indians remained in control of the sources of supply,
depleting them with the aid of European weapons at such a rate that those
of the banks of the lower St Lawrence were exhausted by 1600 and those
of modern up-state New York shortly after. Further south, commencing
in the late seventeenth century, traders from Carolina similarly acquired
deerskins from Indian hunters, and soon in such numbers that over one
million were exported between 1700 and 1710.

Of much the same pattern, though infinitely more lucrative, were European dealings with Asia. There the Portuguese pioneers found an ancient
and complex maritime economy, comprising a galaxy of long distance and
country trades, most of them concerned with commodities of the highest
value. It was soon appreciated by the bellicose and Catholic royal house
and its aristocratic retainers that in the Indian Ocean and Arabian Sea
much of this commerce was conducted by Muslims. By diverting it into
Portuguese hands and by deflecting its westward flow round the Cape of
Good Hope the trade of 'the Moors' through the Levant would be
destroyed, a mighty blow delivered against Islam and the crown of Portugal
richly and rightly rewarded. After some brief experiment the import of
Asian spices, drugs and dyes was declared a royal monopoly (1505–6), as
was the export of those things needed to pay for them which, since Europe
had little suitable to offer, and since affluent markets in the East were
limited, chiefly meant silver which was being shipped out at the rate of 30
tonnes a year by the late 1500s. The trade was to be conducted along that
intimidating maritime route opened by Vasco da Gama, in vessels provided,
or at least licenced by the crown. The entire commerce was to be the
responsibility of a specially created royal office, the India House (*Casa da
India*), from where, in the early stages, spices were forwarded for resale to
the king's agent in the great international market of Antwerp – dealings it
was found necessary to transfer to Lisbon itself by the mid 1500s.[7]

Monopoly was commonplace in the organization of European commerce, and was for centuries to remain a widely accepted way of handling valuable long distance trades. The Portuguese had already organized their commerce with West Africa in such fashion, and the influential and much-admired model was the Venetian Republic, which had long dominated the import of Asian spices into Europe through the Middle East. What Portugal now proposed, however, was of unprecedented scale and scope, and there were soon hopes of a monopoly even more extensive. Fundamental to the realization of these ambitions was that the Portuguese should be able to obtain all the spices they needed even though, apart from their tenuous footholds in the Spice Islands and Sri Lanka, they had no direct control of the sources of supply. The acquisition of spice was the responsibility of royal factors stationed in the country's various oriental trading posts and possessions. Some, in the early years, was simply taken by force, just as for a time prices were held down by force. Thereafter some was obtained from friendly or intimidated rulers – pepper from western India, cinnamon from Sri Lanka, the more exotic varieties from Indonesia – and some from those bribed to give Portugal preference. The rest was supplied by contractors or purchased on the open market. There was no suggestion that the Portuguese should themselves grow spices. Equally vital was that Muslims should be driven out of the trade and the commerce of other indigenous merchants controlled. A network of bases was established around the Indian Ocean and Arabian Sea – and indeed beyond – and some of the great entrepôts of the Asian maritime economy, such as Hormuz and Malacca, were taken. The Portuguese struggled, as in western India, to block rival outlets for spice and to ensure that competitors and enemies were deprived of supplies. Royal squadrons did their best to patrol the waters of western Asia, destroying Muslim trade and obliging other indigenous craft – which by 1600 had expanded in some minds to embrace those of 'Christians, Moors and Hindus' – to obtain the necessary Portuguese permission to be at sea and to pay their dues.

Portugal's rulers aimed to become the sole suppliers of spice to Europe, taking the highest price they could obtain for their imports, with no thoughts of selling cheaper to widen the market. Policies in the East were of similar inspiration, with Portugal attempting to exact whatever revenues it could from indigenous traffic and to control, whenever it could, the richest trades. For a time all went astonishingly well. The Portuguese became the indispensable commercial intermediaries between China and Japan and, at the expense of the Arabs, pushed into the luxury trade of East Africa. For a time in the early 1500s Venice's ancient commerce in spices was disrupted. Soon after Portugal was accounting for about 75 per cent of Europe's spice imports and its rulers, to the envy of their fellows, reaping profits of 90 per cent net. Even at the beginning of the seventeenth century, when the tide was running strongly against the Portuguese,

Hormuz, from which looters could remove precious stones and the like by the boat load, was still returning profits of 200 per cent as were other posts on the Indian subcontinent.

To enforce such policies rigorously over huge tracts of sea was, however, neither practicable – least of all for a country with few men and fewer ships – nor indeed desirable. Portugal accordingly exempted the Shia Muslims of Iran from the blockade of the Middle Eastern routes as potential allies against the Sunni Ottomans, and similarly favoured the Islamic Gujaratis whose textiles were needed for the *Estado's* own commerce. Furthermore, within a matter of years of their arrival in the East the Portuguese found that old trades were reviving, though usually re-routed to avoid their attentions. Indonesian spice was shipped direct from Atjeh to the Red Sea, or was taken first to south-east India, carried overland and then sent northward in small craft from Malabar. Hence by roughly 1600 only about 20 per cent of the pepper and less than 50 per cent of other spices reaching Europe had come round the Cape in Portuguese ships and the royal spice monopoly was running at a loss.

But this did not necessarily mean any slackening in the Portuguese pursuit of profit. Indigenous shipping caught working prohibited routes could be fined, and trades which could not be suppressed could be tolerated and taxed. Already in the sixteenth century European travellers remarked on the Muslims buying cloves in Amboina and on their co-religionaries and the Hindus conducting a flourishing business in Hormuz. By the early 1600s such was the flow of trade through the supposedly blockaded Red Sea – in which the Portuguese were themselves vigorous participants – and such the revenues produced by the sale of licences, that it was claimed that if the route were to be opened and this income lost Portuguese India would be finished. By this date, too, the nature and pattern of Portugal's Asian trade had changed. Spice had lost its pre-eminence, in part since European and indigenous competition made it difficult to acquire, in part since English and Dutch hostility made it dangerous to carry. Instead cargoes were increasingly made up of cotton textiles – the cheapest for Africa, the best for Europe and the Americas – expensive artefacts and above all precious stones which constituted the maximum value in the most easily (and frequently indelicately) concealable form. Returning clergy and officials are reported laden with 'curious jewels', many of which, in the late 1600s, were sent home in English Indiamen to avoid royal exactions, and so flourishing was the traffic that in 1642 zealous Turkish customs officials in Aleppo were said to assume that 'every one who comes from India has pearls and diamonds sewn into his clothes'.[8]

Thus whatever the misfortunes of the *Estado* and its rulers, many of its inhabitants and officers long continued to prosper. Some bought, or were granted, royal privileges to breach crown monopolies, others simply arrogated such liberties to themselves. Royal officials plundered indigenous commerce, took bribes from wealthy locals, sold licences to indigenous traders to sail to supposedly prohibited ports, participated in local commercial ventures. Till its loss to the Persians the captains of Hormuz carried on their own trade in their own ships to India and the Persian Gulf, while their colleagues in Malacca, before it fell to the Dutch, were dealing in precious stones anywhere from Thailand to Manila. So it was that Portuguese dignitaries, like the servants of the Dutch and English East India companies later, could amass impressive fortunes, with one viceroy of the mid 1600s known to Europeans and Asians alike as the 'King of Gold'. Some took their wealth home, some employed it in ventures elsewhere, and some who remained in the East used it to recruit support for the furtherance of their interests.

Not all such endeavour was in blatant breach of royal injunctions. The crown monopoly did not extend to textiles, porcelain or precious stones and the kings virtually abandoned the entire 'country' trade – that rich flow of goods between eastern ports – to their subjects. This was a commerce, ancient and extensive, which it was quickly appreciated was of far greater value than that with Europe and one in which Portuguese of every class were accordingly soon engaged. Magnates employed Hindu, Jewish and Parsee merchants as their commercial agents and borrowed money from local financiers. In the mid 1500s Catholic merchants were in partnership with rich Muslims in trades, such as that to the Red Sea ports, from which Islam was supposedly excluded. The clergy, secular and regular alike, were universally busy in commerce, and none more so than the Jesuits in Japan till the prohibition of Christianity (1614) and the subsequent expulsion of the Portuguese. Indeed to a visiting fellow Catholic in 1672, marvelling at the riches of the monasteries and convents of Portuguese India, it seemed that 'all the commerce of [this] nation is in their hands'.[9]

Particularly skilled and tenacious in business were those humbler citizens of the *Estado*, white, black and of mixed race who before long were seemingly ubiquitous in the vast Asian maritime economy. Many were clearly men of parts, whose obscure origins denied them, like the Spanish pioneers in the Americas, any worthwhile opportunity in their mother country. Rarely did they aspire to return home since there were such rewarding outlets for their ambitions in Asia. At relatively little risk wealthy communities dedicated to opulent living could be provided with the expensive luxuries they demanded, easily and profitably transported in small amounts, like the pearls, jewelry and porcelain supplied to the Mughal court at Agra in the early 1600s, or the pepper and cinnamon illicitly sent to Bengal. Few in number, such Portuguese posed no threat to indigenous states, nor were their technical and commercial skills of an order to allow them to isolate themselves from local peoples. Hence they emulated indigenous practice, married or lived with local women, joined local commercial ventures and employed local capital and local ships. Virtually

independent, scattered throughout much of maritime Asia and well integrated into local commerce and society, they largely survived Holland's
destruction of Portugal's eastern empire in the seventeenth century. And
when danger threatened they shifted their interests, concentrating for
example in the late 1600s on the infinity of trades among the Indonesian
islands. Such enterprise brought its rewards. Even in so bleak a year of the
Luso-Dutch struggle as 1630 Portuguese country traders could invest in
Goa a sum equal to the initial capital of the VOC. They could afford to
erect elegant and striking buildings in the imperial city and Macao and to
lend money, if they wished, to aristocrats.

   To exploit the opportunities of Asia the Portuguese created a royal
monopoly of dealings in certain goods and secured for themselves bases
through which these could be obtained and from which a thriving
indigenous commerce could be taxed, regulated or pillaged, so that by the
opening decades of the seventeenth century well over half the revenues of
the *Estado* came not from active enterprise but simply from dues collected.
This combination of despoliation and pragmatic involvement in local luxury
trades explains the reputation for easy affluence enjoyed, until the disasters
of the early seventeenth century, by Hormuz, Malacca, Goa and Macao.
From Hormuz (lost in 1622) the Portuguese participated in the rewarding
commerce of the Persian Gulf and Middle East, subsequently continued
from Mascat (lost in 1650) and then on a much reduced scale from lesser
ports. In Malacca (lost in 1641) they held what had once been the focal
point of exchanges between the Orient, western Asia and the Middle East
and where, despite the damage inflicted by their own attacks on native
shipping, the spices of South-East Asia could be bought with Indian rice
and textiles for resale in the West or, at profits of allegedly 400 per cent,
in China. Macao waxed rich as the monopolist of that opulent commerce
reopened by the Portuguese between China and Japan, in which Chinese
gold and silks were exchanged for Japanese silver at profits rumoured to
reach 150 per cent. And following the expulsion of the Portuguese from
Japan (1639) its citizens turned to the new, if less rewarding opportunities
of Macassar, Indo-China and Thailand. Goa, whose fortunes dwindled even
more rapidly after the mid 1600s, was the centre for Portuguese commerce
with Europe and the focus of a number of major trades, some to distant
regions such as East Africa (where textiles were sold for gold and ivory),
others more local, whether to provide food for the imperial city or to
collect goods for shipment home. And here again agreeable windfalls – 60
per cent gain on currency transactions – were to be had for very little effort
in the palmy days.

   The royal monopoly of trade between Europe and Asia, now no longer
profitable, was farmed out in the late sixteenth century, briefly handled
(1628–33) by a specially created company, and then resumed, for lack of
any alternative, by the crown. European and indigenous hostility disrupted,

diminished or destroyed country trades, but the basic structure of Portugal's Asian commerce – a central monopoly supported, if not overshadowed by, participation in the indigenous maritime economy – was subsequently accepted by their Dutch and English rivals, both of whom, however, entrusted their eastern trade to private joint-stock companies. These were under state control to the extent that their charters were issued by their respective governments. But otherwise the companies were, at least in theory, independent commercial associations. Their capital was raised by the sale of shares, a financial technique already widely employed in undertakings in which costs and risks were greater than individuals or small groups of individuals were prepared to accept. In the English and Dutch Asian trades there was no royal or state monopoly supported to some degree by royal or state money, and no provision for protection by state ships and fortresses. All this the companies had to provide at their own considerable cost while investors impatiently awaited returns on capital tied up far longer than was usual in voyages to and from the East. But though shareholders provided the money, the actual trade of the companies was conducted by their agents and both enterprises controlled, much to their own liking, by elected bodies of directors.

The Dutch VOC (1602) originated in the fusion of existing interests and so continued as an organization of six so-called 'Chambers', deriving from the earlier companies.[10] It had an initial monopoly of twenty-one years, could make treaties with local rulers in the name of the Republic, occupy lands, declare war, raise armies and was to start with a far more powerful and effective body than its English rival. Both built their own ships – the Dutch over 700 before 1700 – in their own establishments and to their own specifications. But whereas the English soon gave up and contracted the work out, the VOC's yard in Amsterdam became one of the wonders of Europe – not surprisingly since the Company was an offshoot of the continent's leading commercial and maritime power, supreme in the carrying trades of the Baltic and the North and controlling Europe's largest merchant fleet. England, though formidable enough in bellicose undertakings, long had far fewer merchantmen and for most of the seventeenth century felt herself to be in danger of becoming a mere economic satellite of Holland. The Dutch company also had access, thanks to the parent community's highly developed economy, to greater capital resources. Its shares were available to all on especially attractive terms and money was thus drawn in from the whole range of society and from important investors abroad. The English, to begin with, conducted their trade through a series of short-term 'ventures', each wound up in due course. The Dutch, on the other hand, ploughed back profits in the early years, borrowed money to pay dividends (which rarely fell below 12 per cent after 1630) and in Asia accumulated and deployed a body of capital which gave them obvious advantages in making purchases, raising loans and ensuring a steady flow of trade. Furthermore, unlike the Portuguese or the English, they gained effective control of a number of spice-producing areas and indeed grew some spices themselves. With Banda (1609) and parts of Sri Lanka (1658) subjugated they had a firm grip on the highly priced nutmeg and cinnamon. Seapower allowed them to restrict the production of cloves to Dutch Amboina, with trees elsewhere destroyed in naval sweeps, just as it enabled them to cut off the ancient flow of spices through the Middle East. Monopoly, moreover, was interpreted in the widest sense, embracing not only Holland's commerce with the East, but entailing the VOC's retention of the country trade in its hands and the exclusion of Asians and Europeans alike from areas where it had interests.

Policies elsewhere were of the same order. The Company originally envisaged that land in South Africa would be worked by its own employees. In Europe its commercial monopoly was even tighter than might at first appear since VOC directors were often clandestine partners in the consortia to which Company spices were sold, and which in turn resold them to merchants. Thus by regulating the amounts released on to the market the VOC could manipulate prices, undermine rivals and ensure a steady demand for its goods. Equally characteristically, when in the 1640s war disrupted the pepper market in Europe the Company attempted to make good the loss by stepping up sales of porcelain – offering bounties to encourage retailers – and already in mid century, in a striking anticipation of modern practice, it was testing reactions to new products in northern Europe before making them generally available.

Furthermore the VOC was less an independent trading corporation than a formidable expression of the power of the Dutch state. Its foundation was in part inspired by the policies of Oldenbarneveldt, the then effective head of the nascent republic, who saw expansion in Asia at the expense of Portugal as one more way of attacking the united Iberian empires and thereby diverting Spanish energies and resources away from Holland. More important still, the Company was run by those same powerful urban oligarchs who ran the Dutch state. Indeed so closely did public good and private gain become identified that when the VOC's charter came up for its first renewal the unseasonable views of shareholders seeking a say in its affairs were declared treasonable by the state.

Thus backed and financed, sustained by the wealth of the great city of Amsterdam and the affluent province of Holland, and rarely dissipating its energies, the Dutch East India Company was initially far more successful than its English counterpart. By 1700 it had established control of much of Indonesia, the source of the most expensive spices. It had a colonial capital on the site of the former Djakarta and a chain of trading posts, forts and concessions reaching from Japan, Cambodia and Thailand to Sri Lanka and the Indian subcontinent. These had in general been secured by force from the weak and by diplomacy from the strong, from whom, if need be, the

Dutch were prepared to accept, as in Japan, the most humiliating terms. With trade came settlement, chiefly that of the officials, commercial agents and servants required by a trading corporation, together with small groups of colonists, the 'free burghers', characteristically allowed only the most narrowly circumscribed privileges in places under the Company's eye and permission to trade where it was unwilling or unable to do so. A corollary of Dutch expansion in the East was the establishment of a colony of a very different nature at the Cape of Good Hope, originally intended to provide victuals for VOC ships, and where by the early 1700s a white population of no more than two thousand was engaged, with the help of slave labour, in growing wheat and vines and herding sheep and cattle.

The VOC's policies in many ways resembled, and at times were consciously based on those of the Portuguese. To start with the Company imported, as they had done, predominantly spices and then similarly changed to a wider range of goods, notably Indian textiles. In the same way the trade was conducted as a monopoly, carried in convoys sailing at predetermined times, and with Djakarta (Batavia) functioning, as did Goa, as the central entrepôt. Like the Portuguese before them, and those who came after, the Dutch were rapidly involved in a galaxy of profitable country trades, and most of their commerce was – at least officially – carried on, as was that of the Portuguese, through a network of factories and trading posts. As the Portuguese had already done they endeavoured to reduce the need for large bullion imports from Europe, finding they could pay for most of their purchases in western India in the mid 1600s with copper and cloves, or that they could exchange spice for silver in Iran. Like the Portuguese they employed indigenous factors and agents (sometimes the same ones), borrowed money from indigenous financiers, licenced indigenous shipping and eventually became, as did the English later, much devoted to collecting rents, taxes and tribute.

But as with all things Dutch at the time, emulation meant improvement. The assembly of goods and the operation of fleets for their carriage were far better organized than by the Portuguese. Dutch business methods were more rational and ruthless. In Europe they sought to cripple competitors; they attempted to divert Chinese trade from Spanish Manila; in Taiwan they taxed the population together with Chinese agriculture and fisheries; around Batavia they opened up the land (1680–1720) for the production, by Chinese labour, of the highly profitable sugar. Initially, too, they enjoyed the unique and enormous advantage of what was in effect a comprehensive purchasing and marketing policy. The governing body of the VOC in Holland annually instructed its officers in Batavia, precisely and minutely, what goods were to be purchased. This information they in turn passed on to the Company's various posts, adding their own views on what was needed for the local trades. Meanwhile the factories themselves relayed to Batavia intelligence on everything of relevance, all of which was in due course transmitted home in the annual letter or letters reviewing the entire situation in Asia and so enabling the directors to formulate an appropriate strategy.[11]

But the VOC's golden days were to last little longer than those of the *Estado*. The Company slid into the usual and expensive grandiose imperial delusions. The directors talked of the annexation of Taiwan 'near the mighty Chinese empire, from where as many poor laborious people will stream into this colony as can be wished'. The Company became ensnared in cripplingly expensive wars in Java, and soon after 1700 was running at a loss. Nor was its commercial performance much of a tribute to a parent society widely admired for its financial and business skills. Its accounting system was confused and archaic – no doubt in part remaining so to throw dust in prying eyes – producing only simple and misleading calculations of profit and loss. By the late 1600s brutality, incompetence and corruption were widespread in the East, with allegations that under Governor-general Speelman (1681–4) textile sales dropped by 90 per cent, freemen were sold into slavery and payments made to non-existent troops. Nor could the officers appointed by the directors to investigate such matters effect any improvement in the face of powerful vested interests.

More fundamentally, as is all too well-known in life and business, those qualities which had initially ensured success were now conspicuously lacking to sustain it. Holland lapsed into a cosy affluence engendered by the sheer extent of its earlier triumphs. The VOC's shipping was less efficient and more expensive than that of the English by the early eighteenth century. When, in the late 1600s, the importance of Chinese tea was growing, the English made their purchases in China itself for cash whereas the Dutch company continued its cumbersome but traditional practice of obtaining Chinese products through Batavia in exchange for other goods. In Europe VOC directors illegally joined associations that purchased its imports, so putting themselves at the mercy of the plutocrats who dominated such dealings. To pacify shareholders and keep them at arm's length they paid greater dividends – around 20 per cent nominally in the century after 1620 – than earnings justified and were for the same reason unwilling to call on investors for the extra capital urgently needed. The numbers of the Company's employees increased while their quality deteriorated, speeded by the nepotism in which directors so freely indulged. Hence the VOC's administration, which demanded above all things efficient bookkeeping, became overburdened with indifferent staff while in Batavia senior officials devoted themselves, in true imperial style, to high living or the accumulation of private fortunes. The Company's policy of depressing indigenous prices in Indonesia, destroying competition and limiting the output of commodities ensured the decline of local markets and the growth of poverty and piracy. Meanwhile the country trade, vital to the VOC's entire strategy – in that it generated the resources to purchase goods for despatch to Europe – was undermined by the financial speculation, down-right extortion and extensive illicit commerce of its employees. In 1679 it was discovered that the head of the Bengal factory was running, in his wife's name, an impressive business specializing in high value/low bulk commodities (opium in particular), all obtained through the Company's organization and carried in its ships. And, as the crowning blow, Holland had to contend, from the end of the seventeenth century, with the rapidly growing strength and competition of the English.

The attitude of England, the future imperial power *par excellence* in the East, to the riches of Asia was initially the same as that of Portugal or Holland. The country's oriental trade was originally of a similar nature and subsequently underwent similar shifts in pattern. It was, to start with, the exclusive prerogative of the East India Company (1600) whose monopoly, like those of the Portuguese crown and the VOC, was modified in the course of time by accident or design. In the 1660s, for example, bowing to the inevitable, the Company allowed (for a fee) 'all persons' to bring home commodities 'of great value but small bulk'. Like the VOC it operated on a joint-stock, though in the beginning it was far weaker and less efficiently run than its rival and in a chronically parlous financial state. The number of shares was kept to a minimum to enhance dividends and extra capital raised less to expand business than to redress past losses. In its dealings with the East it was hampered by a shortage of the vital silver and for long vehemently criticized by its opponents at home for exporting such as it could find. The more precocious Dutch had few such inhibitions and were, by virtue of their grip on the Iberian economy, able to tap the bullion flowing from the Americas to Spain. The Company's governing body lacked, because of its constitution, the continuity, stability and freedom from the pressure of shareholders enjoyed by the Dutch directors, while among its early backers was a vociferous group of courtiers and gentry demanding speedy and generous returns on their investments.

The EIC was independent of the state even to the extent of conducting an anti-Iberian policy in Asia conflicting directly with the pro-Spanish inclinations of the early Stuart monarchs. They in turn, far from offering any such support as the VOC received from the Dutch Republic, aimed to curb it and to raise money by selling, or threatening to sell, privileges to rival organizations. Not until the beginning of the eighteenth century, with its domestic political problems solved, did the Company resume that growth it had achieved in the late 1600s. It was now backed by burgeoning English naval and commercial power, opposed only by a weakened Holland and able to drawn on the skills and resources of an economy rapidly emerging as the most advanced in Europe, so that knowledgeable foreign observers, such as the Abbé Carré, remarked with enthusiasm on the high quality of both its shipping and its employees.

Like its erstwhile competitors the EIC moved away from spices (pepper especially) to the large-scale import of Indian cotton textiles which in the late 1600s accounted for 80 per cent of the value of its westward trade. These ranged from exquisite muslins and fine calicoes – for which there was allegedly 'an ungovernable female passion' in northern Europe – to the coarser varieties used, as by the Portuguese and Dutch, for the purchase of slaves in West Africa. Then, around 1700, with remarkable prescience, and in response to a demand it had helped to foster, it commenced to ship home increasing amounts of Arabian (Mocha) coffee and China tea. This latter delicacy it purchased directly in China, unlike its competitors, using cottons, silver and (eventually) opium from Bengal, while prudently stimulating the influx of bullion to its Madras factory by encouraging the diamond trade there.

The EIC's commerce between Asia and Europe was conducted, like that of the Dutch, in Company ships – provided, however, after the early years not by the EIC itself but by a body of private shipowners – sailing in seasonal convoy.[12] Like the Portuguese and the Dutch the English came to control various forts and posts, and indeed in the eighteenth century Company servants were to develop an almost insatiable appetite for conquering the provinces of the Indian subcontinent. But before 1700 the ambitions of the EIC were modest. It had no central entrepôt comparable to Batavia or Goa. As a result of Dutch hostility its operations were initially confined to India and western Asia, but subsequent European demand for Indian textiles and Chinese tea and silk inspired renewed and spectacular penetration eastwards and the accumulation, as we have seen, of footholds along both coasts of India.[13]

Thus placed, and exercising a far looser control over its servants than did the VOC, the Company, and far more important the many Englishmen in the East, came to realize the magnificent opportunities of the local trades of Asia to a greater extent than any other Europeans. The Company withdrew its shipping from inter-Asian commerce in 1661 and in 1674 allowed its employees, under certain restrictions, to trade in all eastern products. Not that they required any encouragement. By 1700 one of its Bengal-based agents was selling goods in Dacca, Patna and many other places as well, using both European and Indian associates, while the richest English freeman in Madras, owner of ships and land, was the former head of one of its factories.[14] Fleets of merchantmen belonging to the English communities in Bombay, Calcutta and Madras – some of their members Company servants, many not – flourished. English vessels carried not only the goods of Englishmen but, with their reputation for strength and safety, were favoured by indigenous merchants and travellers. They transported Muslim pilgrims from northern India to Mecca, traded from Surat to Indonesia, were much in evidence in and around the Bay of Bengal, and took Indian textiles to the Persian Gulf from where they returned laden with what were enviously described as 'vast quantities of pearl and treasure'. From roughly 1700 whole areas of the great Asian maritime economy came to be dominated by English private traders whose business was a larger, better-financed and even more lucrative version of that of their Portuguese and Dutch counterparts. Some of these entrepreneurs were Company servants, able to ensure their own commerce prospered even if that of their employer languished and adept at disguising the scale of their activities by conducting them in their wives' names. But most private traders were independent of the Company. Among their many ventures they sold opium and Indian goods in the Indonesian archipelago – thereby raising capital for EIC purchases in China – did business in Canton and traded from Madras to the Philippines in partnership with Asian and Indo-European merchants. The Company wisely acquiesced in their doings and licenced what it had no power to suppress.

By far the most important trade which Europeans entered and adapted, with devastating consequences, to their own needs, was that in slaves. Slavery was endemic in almost every part of the world they reached. It had been widespread in medieval Europe and was flourishing along the continent's Mediterranean littoral at the time of the first voyages, with males used especially in the production of sugar and women in domestic servitude, which meant anything from the discharge of household chores to concubinage. Hence wherever they encountered slavery Europeans speedily redirected or expanded it to their own benefit, developing trades which like those in Asian luxuries or the riches of the Americas were handled by state monopolies, chartered corporations or groups of enterprising desperadoes. It was a commerce destined to succeed. Protagonists of empire might dream of colonies populated by skilled married men, virtuously working for their living, and of a life so ordered that whites and natives were kept well apart. Few emigrants, however, envisaged their new life as one involving hard labour. As the first settlers in Dutch America explained to their masters, had they wished to engage in such things they could have stayed at home. Manual work was degrading to those who were, or wished to be considered, of superior birth, entailing so great a loss of status that it was even thought better to starve than to toil. And in Asia, as a celebrated pro-consul of the VOC tartly observed, it rendered Europeans ridiculous in indigenous eyes. The advantages of slavery were, on the other hand, self-evident. Slaves, once the cost of their purchase had been met, required no wages and only minimal outlay on food and clothing. They were unable to move away, were available for life, and any offspring they might produce came as a bonus to their owners. So, almost universally, the exploitation of imperial resources, and the maintenance of proper imperial style rested to some degree on slavery or unfree labour.

Where missionary influence was weak, where slavery was already widely practised, where exertion was arduous, or where profit or comfort demanded an abundance of manpower, Europeans enslaved whoever they could. In the East the Portuguese employed Africans by the thousand. They bought slaves in India and Madagascar and unwanted Chinese girls from their parents in Macao. They accepted those forced to sell themselves into servitude through poverty, as in Sri Lanka. They enslaved prisoners taken in war, irrespective of sex, and with such zest in western India and Japan as to undermine the work of the missions. In the early 1600s the Portuguese in Bengal regularly launched 'general attacks' throughout the year into the neighbouring countryside, in addition to lesser assaults which, as was said, went on 'most of the time', rounding up 3000 or so slaves annually. Some of these were disposed of locally, some sold to fellow Europeans and some kept to serve in the footholds of the *Estado* as labourers, craftsmen, soldiers and (the women) as maids, mistresses and prostitutes, and to discharge all those many functions held to be too demeaning for Europeans.

What suited Catholic Portugal equally suited Protestant Holland.[15] In 1694 over half the recorded population of Dutch Colombo (Sri Lanka) were slaves and 11 per cent of the households had more than eleven each. As individuals, and in the person of the VOC, Hollanders used slaves to grow nutmeg in Amboina and to mine gold in Sumatra. They were employed, men and women alike, in domestic service and for 'the dirtiest and heaviest work' in South Africa and Sri Lanka and for fortress building everywhere. They were likewise used to demonstrate the status of their owners, with the wives of VOC officials in Batavia escorted in public by slave retinues and their husbands accompanied by 'little black boys'.

Dutch slaving in the East was supposedly the monopoly of the VOC and many slaves were prisoners taken in the course of its wars or the vanquished opponents of its rule. Others were purchased in Madagascar for guns, drink and silver, while in Indonesia, in characteristic service of God and Mammon, indigenous debtors who refused to accept Christianity were enslaved. The Dutch cast their net as wide as any. Chinese were rounded up from the Fukien coast in the 1620s. The VOC's major eastern possessions were initially supplied from India – with 30,000 slaves demanded in 1622 – and Madagascar, then subsequently from Bali, Timor and the neighbouring islands. For South Africa, where the Company (vainly) prohibited the enslavement of local peoples, Indonesia, India, East Africa and Madagascar were the chief suppliers. Before long these rich resources attracted others. English slavers were in Madagascar in the 1660s and were soon carrying cargoes to the Dutch Cape, Barbados and (eventually) to Virginia and Buenos Aires. By 1700 they had been joined by vessels from English North America.[16]

In the West it was the initial intention of most Iberians to enslave the Amerindians who, as the bishop of Darien declared in 1519, were 'hardly men . . . [and] slavery is the most effective and indeed the only means that can be used with them'. These ambitions were checked by the unsuitability of many of the victims for the tasks for which they were intended, by the disastrous drop in the indigenous populations and by royal policy and the vigorous opposition of the missions. In Brazil the Jesuit fathers resettled Amerindians in villages for their better protection and proselytization – as the king had already ordered – and secured (1570) royal prohibition of the enslavement of any except those practising cannibalism or resisting Christian rule and the Christian message. But this was far from the end of the matter. Demand for labour was urgent, not relieved by the import of black Africans till late in the sixteenth century, and the human resources of Brazil seemingly superabundant. In the south expeditions penetrated deep into the interior rounding up Indians. Colonists passed themselves off as missionaries to hunt down alleged candidates for conversion; some raided mission settlements and abducted the Indians conveniently assembled there. In Amazonia the majority of indigenous slaves were those supposedly rescued from the grip of other tribes by frontiersmen and forced into Portuguese service as a token of their gratitude. When the Jesuits objected the Order was, for its pains, twice expelled from Maranhão and eventually obliged to acquiesce in the policies of the colonists (1686). And as the area of Portuguese settlement grew and as the native population dwindled, the searches of the slavers were extended, bringing clashes with the Spaniards in the south and with the Dutch in the backlands of Pará in the course of the seventeenth century.

Enslavement of the Amerindians of the Caribbean was forbidden by the Spanish crown as early as 1500 and that of the inhabitants of the mainland in 1542. Nevertheless, just as in Brazil, slaving continued. It was the fate of cannibals and of those who resisted or rebelled against Spanish rule. More important, without its profits, soldiers and settlers were reluctant to remain in poor or frontier regions. So Indians were taken in northern Mexico, in the Isthmus, in great sweeps in southern Chile and along the borders of Venezuela, and Amerindian slaves played a vital role in the initial white exploitation of the Caribbean islands, were used to mine the first precious metals in Central America, and died in their hundreds as porters with the expeditions that conquered the mainland.

But, uniquely for Spain, there were even better prospects of imperial exploitation. In the reconquest of the homeland from the Moors it had been the practice to reward warriors and entrepreneurs not with land, but with the services and dues of a given number of subjugated peoples. Something the same swiftly appeared in the Spanish-occupied Caribbean islands and shortly after, at the initiative of the conquerors, on the mainland. Thus there emerged the *encomienda* which quickly came to mean, as Cortés tersely put it, that 'the Indians will serve the Spaniards in all they may require'. Holders of *encomiendas* would receive goods, treasure and labour from the indigenous population which would in turn enjoy the alleged benefits of Spanish protection and conversion to Christianity. By no means all *conquistadores* obtained such grants, and some of the largest and most populous areas of the Americas, which could hardly be entrusted to any individual, were retained by the crown. But for the fortunate few there was the unparalleled prospect of a society so organized that they could live in the comfort and security of their town houses – as the crown insisted they should – supported by the tribute and toil of the Indians of the neighbouring countryside.

In those parts of the Americas where comparable services had long been rendered by large, disciplined and skilled labour forces to their native lords, as in the heartlands of the Aztec and Incas empires, the benefit to pioneer *encomenderos* was enormous, sometimes endowing them with the economic potential of thousands of indigenous peoples, like the 115,000 secured by Cortés himself. At the outset *encomienda* commonly meant little more than systematic pillage. Holders ruled their Indians as absolute lords, sending armed bands to strip them of whatever they could, and subsequently dividing up the booty. Before long *encomenderos* established that they collected the tribute in money or goods due to the crown, but retained for themselves that part which could be commuted into personal service. Thus ensconced in towns or cities, surrounded by friends, relatives and retainers and supposedly ready to spring to the defence of the empire, they were housed and lived free. They ate food provided by their Indians and their comforts were attended to by their native servants, maids and mistresses. Tribute paid in bullion brought them instant riches together with a free gift of capital which some invested in productive undertakings. They controlled a mass of labour which they could either use themselves – in building or silver mining for example – or hire out to fellow Spaniards. As a royal official succinctly observed, 'our true wealth is the sweat and toil of the Indians'.

This parasitic idyll, which inspired among some Portuguese vain hopes of similar happenings in Brazil, was not to last. The rapid growth of a white population enjoying no such privilege made *encomienda* a source of dangerous political friction. The massive indigenous demographic decline brought a dramatic fall in its value to holders, exacerbated by the ability of Spaniards enriched through other enterprises to compete, by offering wages, for native labour. Furthermore the crown, after its domestic experiences, had no desire to see a new feudal nobility develop in the Americas. During the course of the sixteenth century it asserted its control over the granting and tenure of *encomiendas* – which holders sought to make hereditary – and urged on by the missions and officials in Spain, restricted the services which could be exacted from the native population. From 1550 Indians were to be allocated, chiefly to mining, agriculture and public works, by royal officials, and though made to provide their own implements, were at least promised a wage. In 1601 they were exempted from working in such arduous undertakings as the production of sugar, and in 1632 from compulsory service in agriculture. By the early 1600s the long-proclaimed principle of direct royal jurisdiction over the Indian populace had been realized in Peru and Central Mexico and large numbers of *encomiendas* had reverted to the crown, to be innocuously regranted as pensions and annuities paid from the tribute of some particular area.

But this brought little comfort to the majority of the surviving Indians. A prime and at times overriding Spanish concern was with the mining of silver and the mercury needed to refine it. In Peru, where there were immense deposits in remote sites high in the Andes, there was great difficulty in securing labour. Such work was hardly for Europeans, while expensive African slaves were unsuited to the climate. *Encomienda* Indians often refused to serve, and there were those in Spain who doubted they could be obliged to do so. Yet even humanitarians accepted that since silver was vital to the well-being of the mother country, then 'for the public good' natives should be put down the mines. This was accomplished by converting, from the 1570s, the labour services formerly exacted by the Inca state from its subjects (the *mita*) into yet another form of servitude in which males from a mass of villages throughout southern Peru and the modern Bolivia were compelled to work in rotation in mining. The indigenous population continued to dwindle, however, while some tribal chiefs were unwilling or unable to supply their quotas. Elsewhere men fled, refused to serve, or bought or secured exemption, obliging the Spaniards to attempt to attract workers through the offer of wages by the early seventeenth century.[17]

Thus over much of Spanish America there came a shift from forced to nominally free labour. This was particularly the case where enterprises of a technical or technological order developed, requiring a permanent and resident work-force, and it occurred most rapidly in regions where, for any reason, the native population was small and the white presence strong. Thus in Central Mexico wage labour predominated by the 1630s, whereas in Peru forced servitude sufficed in general till about 1650. But despite such changes indigenous people remained subject to fearsome oppression. The official allocation of native labour was, where it survived, corruptly and fraudulently administered. Indians supposedly employed for the public benefit were directed into the private enterprises of the influential.[18] Entrepreneurs made a good living buying and selling labour. In the Philippines unsubjugated peoples were provoked into retaliation and then attacked in 'just wars', stripped of their lands and enslaved. Where the native population remained substantial, where the natural resources were of no use to the Spaniards, or where the indigenous inhabitants were unable to pay tribute, forced labour survived and flourished throughout and beyond this period. On such imperial frontiers as Paraguay nomads and semi-nomads were rounded up into settlements from which services could be exacted. Indians near Quito made cloth for one of Spain's greatest grandees (1627), spun thread for a villainous old soldier in Costa Rica (1642) and were widely engaged in providing tortillas for impecunious Europeans to sell. In the Philippines, and notwithstanding a constant flow of royal condemnations of such brutal behaviour, the inhabitants were forced to work in agriculture, shipbuilding and much else besides, well into the eighteenth century. And where tribute was paid in goods the recipients were able to auction what they received to their compatriots, who thus obtained at little cost and less effort saleable commodities, while the Indians were compelled to acquire whatever they needed from their Spanish masters and at prices dictated by their whim. ¹⁸

In the Americas the conquerors also came across various other established forms of indigenous unfree labour which they similarly adapted to their own needs. Hence the abundance of *naborias* (Mexico) and *yanaconas* (Peru), who were neither slave nor free, and who were widely employed as artisans, labourers and domestic servants. Some received wages or were even granted lands and others were bound to white masters by agreements – a form of servitude soon to appear in other Atlantic empires – in which they committed themselves to serve for a given period in return for pay, shelter and exemption from impressment for the mines.

But wages were not to save indigenous workers from conditions often only theologically distinguishable from slavery, particularly in textile work-shops or desert mining camps. Pay was frequently abysmally low since, as a Spaniard declared in the 1590s, it would be absurd for such people to get the same rate as Europeans, and since tribute was deducted from the wages they received. Moreover, many employers ensured, one way or another, that their workers remained permanently in their debt and thereby absolutely subject to their authority. They were given advances in cash or kind they were unable to pay off, and children were held responsible for what their parents owed. At one Peruvian silver mine in the late 1500s the majority of the workforce receiving wages had debts amounting to over 60 per cent of what they earned. The verb 'to owe' significantly entered the Mexican vernacular at this time, and towards the end of our period Jesuit accounts for some of their great estates show no expectation that the workers would ever be able to free themselves from debt.¹⁹

No other contemporary European power encountered, as the Spaniards had done, indigenous societies so apparently predestined to assist their masters in gathering the rewards of imperial success. Nevertheless they did their best with whatever came to hand. English pioneers in North America had some local Indians in *de facto* slavery by the early 1600s and the first settlers in Barbados (1627) managed to secure a number of Amerindian slaves from Surinam. Thereafter it was the familiar story. In Puritan New England, following the Massachusetts attack on the Pequots (1637), the survivors, women and children included, were enslaved. Some the colonists kept for themselves and the rest were sold in the West Indies. The same fate overtook the tribes who rose against the New Englanders in 1675. Worse was to come in the south, where many of the settlers in Carolina were from Barbados, home of an already flourishing slave-based economy. Encouraged by the colonists, who supplied them with arms and plied them with drink, the Indian peoples set about each other in slaving forays reminiscent of those of Portuguese Brazil, and which by 1700 had reached as far as Spanish Florida. Some of the victims were used in Carolina – Charleston alone had 1400 in 1708 – chiefly as artisans and domestic slaves, but the majority were shipped to the West Indies, New York and New England in a trade which continued until the American Revolution. Indians were similarly taken and employed in French Louisiana, while from bases on the Nicaraguan and neighbouring coasts English frontiersmen and their local allies seized Amerindians – mainly women and children – for sale in Jamaica.[20]

Where the indigenous population was unsubdued, insufficient or unsuitable, other sources of unfree labour had to be found. In Batavia the Dutch employed, alongside their various slaves, Chinese coolies provided by Chinese brokers. In the West, and especially in the English and French possessions in North America and the Caribbean, fellow whites were used for much of the first imperial age. The conviction was strong in early modern Europe that colonies were the proper receptacle for the continent's surplus population, while it had long been the practice for young men to be bound to masters by written contracts, usually to learn a skill, or to be committed to serving them by some less formal arrangement. Agreements of this sort were being made in the Spanish Indies by the mid 1500s, both between Indians and Spaniards and between Spaniards and their compatriots.[21] Early in the following century indentured servitude, as it came to be known, was adapted to the needs of the newly-established English and French Atlantic footholds, almost all of them chronically short of settlers and even more desperately short of labour. In exchange for the payment of their passage to the New World, would-be emigrants, male and female alike, agreed in writing to serve a master for a given period – normally from four to seven years. He would feed and clothe them, but they would be at his absolute disposal, sustained by the promise or hope that they would eventually be granted their liberty, together with either land or a lump sum, or that they would live to enjoy the high wages commanded by the free.

The provision of labour to settlements soon aware of the profits to be had from tobacco and sugar rapidly became a considerable industry, centred in such strategically sited ports as La Rochelle (from where 6000 emigrants departed to France's possessions between 1635 and 1715) and Bristol. Entrepreneurs, usually merchants or shipmasters, recruited cargoes by persuasion, propaganda kidnapping, the use (in Paris) of press gangs, or simply by relieving local authorities of their unwanted. They entered into agreements with those so assembled and shipped them across the Atlantic where they were auctioned off and the terms of their indentures passed to their new owners. Some English servants were in origin gentry – so at least they claimed – farmers, craftsmen or shopkeepers down on their luck. Some were prisoners and convicts and some in the 1660s former troopers in Cromwell's once renowned army. Others were children and a fair number were women – about 25 per cent of those leaving Bristol in the late 1600s – many acquired in Ireland where outward-bound English ships topped up their complements. But the majority of both English indentured servants and French *engagés* were poor, unskilled males in their late teens or early twenties, for whom the only alternative was rural unemployment or starvation in some overpopulated town.

These unfortunates, if English, were in the early years sent to Virginia, and then, in the mid seventeenth century, increasingly to the major West Indian islands – with Barbados paramount in the 1650s – which were in turn eventually eclipsed by the American mainland colonies. The limitations of servitude were manifest. Masters were put to the cost and trouble of frequently replacing servants as their indentures expired and saddled with buying labour that was relatively more expensive, as in the later 1600s the price of African slaves dropped through, among other things, the depression of West Indian sugar prices. At the same time a falling population in England meant better opportunities for employment at home, reluctance to leave, a consequent shortage of emigrants and enhanced costs. For servants the Caribbean climate was lethal, the prospect of toiling as field hands unappealing, and the chance of obtaining holdings of their own increasingly remote as large plantations developed, devoted to sugar in the islands and tobacco on the mainland. So the flow of indentured whites to the English Caribbean dwindled from the mid seventeenth century as they were replaced at the humblest level by black slaves, and of those sent out a higher percentage were now skilled men destined to undertake tasks for which there were as yet few suitably trained Africans. Nevertheless white servitude was of fundamental importance in converting islands (one-time Spanish Jamaica apart) either formerly unpopulated or inhabited only by a few intractable indigenous survivors, into profitable producers of cotton, tobacco and sugar. And in the French West Indies, where cash crops were introduced later, *engagés* provided the bulk of the work-force into the late 1600s, and with little competition from the unattractive and insecurely held Canada. Overall, servitude was steadily undermined by black slavery. Africans displaced Europeans first from purely manual jobs and then from skilled occupations, initially in the English islands and eventually in the tobacco-producing colonies of Virginia and Maryland which, by the late 1600s, had become the prime market for indentured whites. Young males were arriving in Virginia at the rate of about a thousand a year between

1625 and 1640 and before 1700 accounted for some 75 per cent of its work-force. But with the influx of Africans the picture changed swiftly and dramatically, with white servants dropping from 80 per cent to 25 per cent of unfree labour in neighbouring Maryland in the early 1700s.

Servitude was for the most part little more than slavery by another name. The majority of servants probably entered into agreements at their own freewill in the innocent expectation of golden opportunities. To what extent they were aware of the life to which they were committing themselves must remain a matter of doubt, and in any case for prisoners or the impoverished with any ambition, there was no other option but to accept what was offered. Once the indentures were signed they were at the mercy of their masters. Since, unlike non-European slaves, they were only short-term investments, of use merely for the relatively brief span of their agreements, they were treated, as one contemporary put it (1681), worse than blacks, horses or dogs. True, skilled craftsmen employed in the manufacture of sugar, might fare better. But most were sold like slaves, denied any sexual life, and flogged senseless, men and women alike, by irate owners. Their period of service could be extended for any supposed misdemeanour. Their movements were restricted, and should they run away there was provision in some colonies for their corporal or even capital punishment. The treat-ment normally accorded them may be gathered from the fact that in the French and English West Indies there was legislation to establish minimum standards of food and clothing, while on the mainland it was in time accepted that masters who killed their servants should be tried for murder.

Such suffering, which sustained the initial exploitation of the non-Spanish Caribbean islands and of much of English North America, brought few who endured it any appreciable reward. There were of course exceptions, like the Dubucqs of Martinique who, starting as *engagés*, ended as rich planters, helped on their way by the sure recipe of judicious marriages and the profits of war and privateering. But overall out of every ten servants perhaps one became a successful craftsman and another a prosperous farmer. And as the years went by opportunities diminished. Land, and particularly good land – neither marginal, inaccessible nor exhausted by the expanding cultivation of tobacco – became scarcer through the growth of big plan-tations just as it became harder to raise the capital to work it. Besides which, when West Indian sugar prices tumbled in the late 1600s the lot of many deteriorated further as masters pressed more heavily still on their workers, reducing some ex-servants into perpetual indebtedness to their employers, like the Indians of Spanish America. From such conditions many fled – as they had done right from the start – to live among local tribes or to become pirates in the Caribbean. The survivors commonly worked reluctantly, like any other slaves, and like them set fire to the houses and crops of their masters (as in Barbados), broke into revolt (as in

Virginia and Martinique) and were in general regarded with that same suspicion and apprehension as were their black counterparts.

Eventually, almost everywhere, it was Africans who provided Europeans with the bulk of the labour to exploit their colonial possessions and to sustain the luxuriant ways of expatriate life. Many Portuguese in Goa each had twenty or so black slaves in the early 1600s. It became nothing unusual for planters to own several hundred in Iberian America, and one estate in tiny Martinique had over 600 in 1718. There were already more Africans than Spaniards in coastal Peru in 1600, while by the early 1700s they accounted for 20 per cent of the population of Maryland and the best part of that of the Caribbean islands. Their attractions were many, making them worth three times as much as local slaves in the Spanish Indies in the mid 1500s. They could endure physical hardship better than Amerindians and withstand tropical climates better than Europeans. Coming from societies accustomed to intensive agriculture they commonly possessed useful agrarian and craft skills. And whereas in the West indigenous peoples died out at an alarming rate, blacks were abundantly and readily available, recruited from a continent long familiar with slavery. Well before the arrival of whites in Africa slaving was in progress on a massive scale, and these internal flows, such as the provision of domestic slaves to Morocco from West Africa, were to continue, probably eclipsing in volume the trades which Europeans established with the wider world. Nor did the acquisition of those wretches, who came to be known as 'pieces', present any problems. Local potentates, modestly rewarded, were all too willing to do business. 'For a coral necklace or a little wine', it was said of the Congolese, 'they will sell their own parents, their own children or their brothers and sisters.'

Thus Africans were rapidly drawn into what soon became an almost universal commerce. It was one little impeded by such qualms as troubled Europeans as to the fate of the Amerindians. Blacks had been employed as slaves in southern Europe since the Middle Ages. In their homelands many were found to be pagan or idolatrous, and most to be living in communities which failed to accord with white preconceptions as to the proper ordering of political life. True, some Europeans enthused over the beauty of African women and more enjoyed their charms, just as there were those who admired the dancing, athletic prowess and resonant voices of the men. But the common view was that blacks closely resembled 'bruite beasts' and were 'nastier than swine' – language, it should be remembered, of the order regularly employed by the European upper classes to describe their own peasantry. Africans differed from whites in appearance, were often scantily and therefore immorally clad and were, worst of all, black, the colour of evil, corruption and ugliness in the popular lore of medieval Europe. Black, moreover, was rarely the pigmentation of any formidable opponent of Europeans, actual or potential, who had to be treated with the respect given to the Japanese or the Ottoman Turks. Some Africans, such as the peoples of Senegambia, who could beat them in war, the whites, or at least the Portuguese, came to accept more or less as fellow Europeans. But these, like the occasional blacks of medieval iconography or those clearly westernized figures in Renaissance paintings, were a minority and it was the divinely ordained lot of Africans to labour as slaves – 'animals to be used for any kind of work' – for white Christian masters. This was only proper since they were allegedly of the race that carried, as the Bible recorded, the burden of Noah's curse on the offspring of his son Ham, and because, as their colour testified, of the enormity of the sins of their ancestors. The very fact that they could be used as slaves established their inferiority and, consequently, according to one contemporary school of thought, their need for subjection to natural superiors. Their well-found reluctance to work whole-heartedly in servitude was similarly taken as proof of their inadequacy. Enslavement would accustom them to the virtues of regular toil and so prepare them to receive the blessings of the Christian message. Nor, in a Europe where vagrants were branded and religious dissidents tortured or burned to death, was there any serious objection to treating supposedly recalcitrant blacks the same way.

African slavery was firmly geared to European needs by the Portuguese, who, as a result of their voyages down the Atlantic littoral of the continent were able, in the fifteenth century, to supply the south-European market with blacks to supplement and eventually replace the slaves of other races long employed there. The discovery and exploitation of such islands as Madeira, the Canaries and São Tomé – substantial producers of sugar on slave-worked plantations by the late 1400s – further enlarged demand. But the trade's future was guaranteed with the colonization of the Americas, urgently demanding labour to mine precious metals or produce such eminently saleable crops as sugar and tobacco. Europeans were reluctant, and in any case too few, to undertake the work themselves. Indigenous peoples were, as in the Caribbean or Brazil, often unsuitable or were destroyed or decimated by disease, while the survivors were protected by the Iberian monarchies and missions. Hence by the end of the seventeenth century Africans were being shipped to almost everywhere Europeans had penetrated, but above all to the plantation economies of the Americas and the Caribbean. And it was a commerce that burgeoned from the mid 1600s, with the cost of slaves falling, largely as a result of the intervention of the Dutch, with their business skills and resources in capital and shipping, and because of the depression of sugar prices.

The precise number of Africans despatched to the New World is impossible to determine in a trade in which three infirm or under-aged humans could be counted as two 'pieces' – a 'piece' being a prime male of between 15 and 25 – and in which smuggling and fraud were universal. In the century after 1600 they may have been transported to Spanish America at the rate of about 3000 a year and to Brazil at the rate of roughly 5000. By

1780 North America had perhaps received 350,000; Brazil 2 million; the
West Indies 3 million; and Spanish America about three-quarters of a
million, besides those held in Africa itself or sent to Asia. It was a seaborne
migration of a scale, nature and consequences unparallelled till modern
times. The majority of black slaves (about 70 per cent) were young males,
the rest children, the middle-aged and young women, all supposedly physically whole and sound. They were supplied by entrepreneurs some of
whom allegedly reaped profits of several hundred per cent and grew 'even
richer' than the plutocrats of the East Indies trades.

Some Africans were used as personal servants and craftsmen, especially
in the Spanish Indies, but most were employed as agricultural labourers
under brutal and arduous conditions. More and more were needed as
empires grew, as indigenous populations dwindled and as exploitation intensified. Many were required merely to replace those who never got to the
New World or who could never be set to work there. Of those shipped in
slavers, disease, overcrowding and sheer misery brought losses anticipated
at between 20 per cent and 40 per cent by contemporaries, and put at from
12 per cent to 20 per cent by modern estimates. Many of the survivors
promptly escaped on arrival. Others died shortly after in unfamiliar climates
and environments – despite rudimentary efforts in Hispanic lands at least
to acclimatize them – or killed themselves in despair. Still more were needed
to maintain a labour force which otherwise fell by up to 5 per cent per
year. Disease, malnutrition and mistreatment brought a high death rate
amongst field hands, particularly in the Caribbean and Brazil, while many
were maimed or crippled by sugar-milling machines. Though marriage and
family life were certainly not unknown, slaves did not in general reproduce
in captivity.[22] Their lives were in ruins, women were few and usually sickly
since they were worked in the same way as males. Infant mortality was
accordingly high and misery such that infanticide and abortion were
common. And for most planters, with prices as they were, it was cheaper
to import adults than encourage procreation.

The first black slaves came very largely from the Saharan coast, and then
from the littoral of the Gulf of Guinea. After the mid 1500s regions further
south were of increasing importance, with Angola eventually the principal
market – its inhabitants, like those of the Congo, considered less volatile
and dangerous than their physically bigger northern compatriots. Then, at
the beginning of the eighteenth century, when this despoliation and the
ravages of European-transmitted disease brought a drastic fall in Angola's
population, Guinea regained its former importance. Besides which, as we
have seen, substantial numbers of blacks were also sent to Asia and the
New World from East Africa. In these trades whites were middlemen,
hauliers and consumers, but rarely producers, since it was unusual for them
to hunt Africans themselves. The Portuguese pioneers soon came to rely
on local (and Muslim) merchants in Mauritania and Senegambia. Their

successors in the Congo and Angola did indeed undertake military sweeps – like those in Brazil – to round up slaves, and often in retaliation against African risings provoked by their own presence and behaviour. Even so, most were obtained from black and mulatto agents and intermediaries, like those Angolan chiefs made to pay their tribute in humans. In exchange Europeans offered horses, cotton cloth, drink, tobacco, metal wares and weapons. The victims so acquired were assembled on the coast, penned, checked for fitness – 'every part of every one to the smallest member, men and women' – and branded. Those obtained by the agents of Catholic powers were supposedly baptized. Most Protestant slavers, however, thought Africans 'too savage and brutal' for this to be worthwhile. They were then shipped across the Atlantic in conditions horrifying and degrading even by the unexacting standards of an age to which physical and mental deformity were matters for mirth. On passage they were kept alive by forced feeding if need be, rechecked on reaching the New World and sold either privately or by auction.

The trade was initially in the hands of the Portuguese, conducted through a royal monopoly, as was the commerce with Asia later, and similarly farmed out. In the sixteenth century it became largely focused on Brazil, served by contractors who, for a fee, agreed with the crown to deliver a given number of blacks there. Spain, with no possessions in Black Africa, and with no transatlantic slaving organization of its own, was early a customer of the Portuguese to meet its American needs, much to the concern of its rulers, exercised not only by the expense but in case blacks should contaminate the Amerindians and perhaps even convert them to Islam. But necessity triumphed. First under licence, and then in a more or less free trade, Africans obtained from the Portuguese by entrepreneurs were brought to Spain for reshipment, and from the 1520s sent directly to the Indies. Following the Hispano-Portuguese union of 1580 the Spanish monarchy was able to employ contractors – monopolists usually belonging to the same circle of plutocrats predominant in Portugal's Asian spice trade – who agreed (in the so-called *Asiento*) to deliver a specified number of slaves at specified prices from Portuguese Africa to the New World. This convenient arrangement was disrupted, but not entirely destroyed, by Portugal's struggle for independence after 1640. This obliged the Spaniards to obtain their slaves in the West Indies from assorted adventurers who in turn had acquired them from the Dutch, French and English who were now, after earlier and generally unsuccessful incursions into West Africa, the main suppliers. Indeed the Dutch, as part of their grand oceanic strategy against the Hispano-Portugese monarchy, envisaged an Atlantic privateering onslaught on the silver fleets combined with the simultaneous conquest of Brazil and those parts of West Africa from which it obtained its slaves. These notable aims were to be realized by a powerful joint-stock corporation, the West India Company (1621). And for a time all went well.

After a slow start the Dutch secured control (1638–48) of vital areas of the Guinea, Angolan and Benguelan coasts, and following their capture of Pernambuco (1630) of about half of Portugese Brazil. Between 1630 and 1650 they shipped in some 26,000 Africans until over-ambitious strategies, internal dissensions and vigorous Brazilian resistance led to their expulsion and the curtailment of Dutch authority in West Africa.[23]

Nevertheless, the Republic, with its economic and maritime strength, remained pre-eminent in Atlantic slaving. Its vessels continued to carry Africans to Brazil, while from their Caribbean base at Curaçao the Dutch supplied not only the Spanish mainland but also the West Indian settlements of other European powers. Not even they, however, could monopolize a trade insatiable in its demands and widely believed to yield immense profits. From the mid 1600s there sprang up an assortment of monopoly companies, based on the Dutch model, and all aspiring to share in the bonanza. Some belonged to well-established slavers, like that set up by the Portuguese in 1675. Others belonged to newcomers such as the Swedes, Danes and Germans. France, an interloper in all pretended Iberian preserves since the early sixteenth century, and now with Caribbean possessions of its own, established an imposing West India Company in 1664, the first of a line of failures. The English, similarly eager to share the profits of slaving since the sixteenth century – witness the voyages of John Hawkins to the Caribbean in the 1560s – and with their own flourishing Atlantic possessions to supply, founded the Royal African Company in 1672, heir to a succession of unfortunate earlier ventures.

The companies operated in the customary ways of the trade, obtaining posts in West Africa – like those of the French at Goree and Arguim – supposedly enjoying extensive monopolies and acquiring their slaves either through agents or through the enterprise of shipmasters haggling with local rulers along coasts where there were no European footholds. But success eluded them. They were in competition with one another. They had considerable overheads – the upkeep, for example, of forts in Africa – their structure was cumbersome and delays in communication, together with their inability to control their employees, were fatal. A typical history was that of the English company, which in the course of its brief and troubled life (effectively over by 1712), shipped about 120,000 blacks westwards, first to the Caribbean and subsequently to North America as well. There were constant complaints from the colonies that it failed to provide the numbers needed, while the company, despite the efforts of its management, rarely made a profit. When (and if) it was paid for its slaves it received cash or promissory notes in the West Indies, since sugar prices were depressed for most of its existence and because of the enormous delay and danger in attempting to assemble full ladings of sugar from plantations scattered around the Caribbean. It secured little support and endured much hostility from the planter-dominated governments of the English islands. It had to face foreign rivals, together with the activities of those who everywhere blatantly ignored its monopoly. It found it virtually impossible to check the misdeeds of its servants or the competition (which it was obliged to license) of the owners and masters of the ships it used.

The pattern was a venerable one. The Portugese monopoly had never been absolute even in its heyday. An illicit direct trade from West Africa to the Indies – cutting out Iberia – had early sprung up, conducted from such islands as São Tomé and the Cape Verdes. Foreign intruders, starting with the Spaniards in the fifteenth century, were soon on the scene. Subsequently contractors, supposedly supplying Brazil, sold their cargoes in Spanish America for a better price. Slaving was thus conducted by a blend of foundering monopoly organizations and vigorous and growing private concerns. Its value and importance were such that by the mid seventeenth century control of the West African sources of supply was a matter of international rivalry, as was, later in the century, receipt of the exclusive contract (*Asiento*) to provide blacks for Spanish America, secured by France (1701) but quickly appropriated by England (1713).[24]

The persistent and ruthless pursuit of labour on such a scale and by such means reflected the widespread European ambition to extract the maximum benefit from whatever might be grown on, harvested from, or dug out of the lands now under white control. Land, a Puritan divine lamented, was 'the idol' colonists worshipped. And not without reason. It could produce riches, and if held in sufficient amounts it could bestow and confirm social and political pre-eminence. Its settlement, pro-consuls and protagonists of empire urged, gave the clearest indication to indigenous peoples that Europeans were there to stay, upheld the claims and reputation of the mother country, and, if properly ordered, provided the parent society with stable, loyal and (best of all) revenue-producing possessions.

Much land Europeans simply seized in military operations under varying degrees of metropolitan control. Royal authority was most successfully asserted in the Spanish Americas, where the crown adroitly confirmed the dispositions made by the conquerors - who in turn distributed holdings to their followers – and made grants of its own, while the councils of the many new towns and cities allotted land to members of their communities. In East Africa, on the other hand, Portugese adventurers, unimpeded by any European superiors, were able to assemble vast and virtually independent domains by skilful fishing in troubled waters.[25] In many places Europeans assumed, with what now seems staggering arrogance, that the land was theirs for the taking. It was accepted, first by the Iberians and then by their rivals, that terrain in the Americas not actually occupied or used by Amerindians was vacant and consequently freely available. In the early sixteenth century the Portugese crown parcelled out – at least on the map – the whole of Brazil to would-be colonizers, just as English sovereigns subsequently allocated by charter vast areas of North America to those who, for grace, favour or cash, they wished to reward. Thus empowered, the Elizabethan colonial pioneer Humphrey Gilbert distributed, as we have seen, millions of acres of the continent to potential settlers, while a later English governor of New York made huge and 'extravagant grants' to his friends.

Once established in the wider world, and once aware of its potential, to what they already had Europeans swiftly added more. Indigenous peoples were forced off coveted lands by violence or by subjecting them to fines and exactions they could only meet by surrendering their property. Sometimes nothing more was needed than to loose European animals on native crops. 'Once the white man has got some ground', it was said of Virginia in 1678, 'then he comes and settles himself . . . and with his cattle and hogs destroys all the corn of the other Indians', who were thus obliged to move on. Sometimes, in the Americas, land was extorted from Indians too drunk to know what they were doing, or collusively purchased from those disposing of what was not theirs to sell. In many parts of the world indigenous rulers made grants to Europeans in the hope of securing their support or goodwill. There were colonists who, like their fellows at home, assembled patrimonies by prudent marriages which, in the old native empires of Spanish America, could include marriages into the higher ranks of Amerindian society, recalled in wills that record 'the land provided by my father-in-law'.[26]

In English America the benefits of 'headright' – the reward for bringing in indentured labour – added to the holdings of the fortunate.[27] In the Spanish Indies there were those who improved their lot by encroaching on the royal demesne, while others prospered as the result, directly or indirectly, of crown policy. It was the practice of Spanish monarchs to reward faithful, distinguished or influential servants with land. This the recipients were often obliged to sell to relieve some urgent shortage of funds, and few were better placed to snap up such bargains than colonials enriched by the spoils of office or other enterprises, like that Gaspar da Rivadeneyra who, having arrived in Mexico in 1555, was in possession of cattle ranches within six years and had become an affluent mine owner by the 1580s. It was a story repeated thereafter often and widely. Merchant families in the Iberian Americas married or bought into land on a large scale. In the seventeenth century creditors foreclosed on indebted West Indian planters, as did those Dieppe merchants who in the mid 1600s thus became owners of estates scattered throughout the French Caribbean. Ex-buccaneers invested their loot in property, like that French veteran of the sack of Cartagena (1697) so transformed into a landowner in St Domingue. But in the accumulation of land not many could match either the capital deployed or the success enjoyed by the Catholic church. It was enriched in Asia by the piety of Europeans and the fruits of the commercial operations of the religious Orders, and in the West by similar business acumen, the generosity of indigenous converts and the spasmodically fervent piety of the colonists. By *c.* 1600 it probably owned one third of the productive lands of the Americas, with latifundia such as those of the Jesuits in both Spanish and Portugese America, or a plantation like that of the Dominicans in Central America in the early 1700s, employing 1000 Indians and 150 black slaves, distinctive features of the Iberian colonial economy.

Thus in one way or another formerly non-European land came into European hands – the bulk of that in Mexico by about 1650, for example. It was now owned and held in ways long familiar in Europe, which for the most part meant that men of wealth and influence lorded it over tenants, serfs and slaves. The first Spanish *encomenderos* were barely restrained from establishing hereditary fiefs with the Indians as their vassals. English pioneers in North America had delusions of becoming lords and governors of vast tracts of the continent. Baronies, countships and marquisates appeared in the French West Indies, and even in Portugese India in the unhappy years of the late seventeenth century, observers remarked on the 'rich and powerful' gentry who lived 'by squandering the revenues they drew from their fine country estates'.[28]

These hierarchical, not to say feudal, ambitions were best realized in regions where the climate suited Europeans (as in highland Mexico and parts of Peru), where a staple crop could be grown (as in Brazil or the Caribbean islands), where labour was, or could be made available, and from where there was easy access to markets. Hence in some of the Portugese Atlantic islands to start with, and subsequently in many of the New World colonies, there developed plantation economies in which large amounts of land were dominated by a handful of whites, worked by some form of unfree labour, and geared to meeting international demand for such products as tobacco and sugar. Most of these estates were lay-owned, but many, as we have seen, in the Iberian empires, belonged to the Catholic church.

The vast latifundia of Spanish and Portugese America stemmed from different roots but evolved in much the same way. By the standards of the time Spain was a bureaucratic state, acutely aware from its own recent history of the dangerous aspirations of landed magnates. The legendary wealth of the former Inca and Aztec empires, and their abundant, docile and industrious populations, ensured that in the triumphant years of the conquest there was no shortage of would-be settlers whose ambitions needed curbing, not encouraging. Brazil, on the other hand, apparently offered no riches, presented dense barriers of forest and jungle and was sparsely inhabited by primitive and often intractable peoples. To colonize even part of this immense land was beyond the resources of the Portuguese crown, more concerned in any case with the gold and slaves of Africa and the spices of Asia, which meant that if the country was to be settled at all, interest had to be stimulated by substantial concessions.

In the Spanish Indies the fortunate among the conquerors and first settlers secured *encomiendas*. Their endeavours to turn these into hereditary fiefs were thwarted by the crown and undermined by the disastrous decline of the indigenous population.[29] At the same time, however, the number of whites in the Americas was growing, with a consequent rise in the demand for familiar foods, drinks, necessities and creature comforts, which neither geographically nor economically was it possible to meet from home. In response, and particularly under the stimulus of the needs of the affluent and characteristically free-spending mining communities, enterprising Spaniards built up impressive holdings (*haciendas*), whose survival, as that of the founder's line, was ensured by entailed primogeniture.[30] Centred on the white master's great house such estates produced, according to location, a variety of cash crops, with a labour force, for the same reason, either African slaves or free mulattos, *mestizos* and Indians working for wages.

In Brazil the fifteen huge and virtually independent captaincies created in 1533–5 set the scene for large-scale landowning. But few of the recipients were able to make much of the opportunity and only with the introduction of sugar did the exploitation of the country begin in earnest. Like tobacco, sugar could well be grown on smallholdings. Requiring, however, as it did, many hands for its speedy harvesting, and expensive crushing and boiling plant to process the cane, it was a crop eminently suited to the great estate. Since the local Amerindians were in some measure protected by the missions, and since as a rule they were unsuitable for agricultural toil – though as late as 1652 they comprised a third of the workers on the lands of the Benedictine monks around Rio de Janeiro – Brazilian planters were increasingly using the ubiquitous African slave by the end of the sixteenth century. Pernambuco alone had some hundred plantations *c.* 1600, the biggest with their own mills and a hundred or so black slaves. Over such estates and their dependent tenants and sharecroppers – obliged to clear an agreed area of virgin land and to pay a percentage of their sugar as rent – there presided the 'lord of the mill', a member of a seigneurial class recruited, like its equivalents elsewhere, from a rich diversity of social origins.[31] Satellite producers, most of them whites, some with land and slaves of their own, and many of them far from poor, had to bring their cane to the lord's crushing plant and allow him part of the sugar produced. Like his Spanish counterparts he was suitably housed in some great mansion from which he exercised more or less absolute authority over his slaves and retainers. And such indeed were the rewards of processing other men's harvests that many mill-owners lived well on them, not bothering to cultivate their lands themselves, but leasing or sharecropping them.

Similar style sugar planting was undertaken on the mainland of tropical Spanish America, collapsed and was re-established in some of the Spanish Caribbean islands. It underwent dramatic expansion following the expulsion of the Dutch from Brazil where, during their brief occupation they had learned the art of its manufacture together with other related skills – like the secrets of making rum and molasses – which they then transmitted to the English and French islands in the West Indies. So, before long, the now familiar picture emerged. Already in 1680 over half the property in Barbados was controlled by less than 6 per cent of the landowners and nineteen planters owned two hundred black slaves each. By the end of the century the best sugar lands in the English islands belonged to a handful of magnates who took the lion's share of the profits and dominated local society and politics, while on the mainland something of the same was happening in Virginia through the production of tobacco and in Carolina with the growing of rice.

Even more extensive were the holdings amassed by pastoral farming. It could be, as in Dutch South Africa, that settlers penetrated to regions already engaged in stock-raising, drove out the indigenous herders and arrogated to themselves ranches of tens of thousands of acres.[32] In the Americas similar results were achieved by different methods. European livestock, introduced into virgin pastures and benign climates and untroubled by any major predators, proliferated, consuming the crops of indigenous farmers, roaming wild beyond the frontiers of empire, or in North America grazing on the rye and white clover brought in by the white man. Settlers needed meat, hides – which, where they could easily be shipped, became a substantial export – and animals for haulage and transport. Hence in Iberian America there developed the herding and ranching or cows, goats, horses, sheep, mules – indispensable for the carriage of goods to and from remote areas – and oxen by the thousand on holdings covering hundreds of thousands of acres, their extent often determined by nothing more than the wanderings of the animals themselves. In many regions, such as northern Mexico, where the religious Orders were among the greatest entrepreneurs, ranching, attracted by the demands of the mining communities, moved on as more intensive undertakings developed, and both here and in the modern Paraguay, tailed off into unsubdued lands.

The industry was, in every sense, rough and ready, lightly touched by thoughts of profit and loss. To Iberians it was a suitable way of life for those who wished to be considered gentlemen but had failed to find the means to support their pretensions, demanding as it did not capital but skill and bravura. With resources so prolific, freely available and seemingly inexhaustible, it was conducted with little heed for the morrow. A Brazilian estate of the early 1700s would have its animals roaming unfenced lands and indeed in danger of reverting to the wild. Milk was not sold and out of a thousand head of cattle perhaps one hundred might be got to some market. In Spanish America meat was so abundant, or available only in such inaccessible places, as to be hardly worth marketing, so that carcasses of slaughtered animals were either left to scavengers or sold to the local Indians.

Things were different in the harder climates of English North America, and where, in Puritan New England, social and religious convictions were initially hostile to such developments. Here the immigrants settled the ·thinly populated coast of a land well able to produce the familiar crops of home. They arrived as self-contained groups – men, women, children – interested not in a life of seigneurial leisure and grandeur, but in conducting their affairs according to their theological tenets and in closely-knit communities. The founding fathers of Plymouth Harbour (1620) expected only hardship from life on earth. Nor were they disappointed. Nevertheless many were countrymen, all were accustomed to arduous toil and most were sustained by an unbending faith. So there emerged a society and economy of small, family-worked farms. Much the same happened in the far larger and more strongly-backed Massachusetts (1630), where, however, the pioneers were predominantly gentry, yeomen, merchants and artisans. Holdings were bigger from the start, with some of the first settlers receiving 200 acres in return for their subscriptions. Estates became larger still through the operation of 'headright', whereby, as in Virginia, the wealthy who could afford to bring in an indentured servant were rewarded with a further fifty acres. Within a short time the colony had progressed from subsistence farming to the export, by conveniently accessible maritime routes, of agricultural and primary produce, accompanied by complaints that too many acres were passing into too few hands.

But if holdings could increase in the North they could equally well decrease or remain small in the South and even in regions where soil and climate were seemingly ideally suited to large-scale undertakings. Many *haciendas* in the densely-populated and urbanized temperate highlands of the Spanish Indies were no more than family farms producing grain. In Brazil whites lacking the will or capital to set up cane crushing mills grew tobacco or sugar on modest plots. In French Guadeloupe in 1670 alongside great sugar plantations were fragments of land raising tobacco and indigo. Many of the holdings in the English Caribbean islands were tiny to the very end of this period, no more than ten to twelve acres, originating in grants to time-expired indentured servants, while in the southern settlements of the English mainland small landowners were numerically predominant until well into the eighteenth century. True, a rough distinction can be drawn between a Spanish and Portuguese colonial world of great latifundia, and a non-Iberian America of small farms. Even so the Spanish and Portuguese colonies, embracing as they did such a variety of climates and terrain and peoples of such diverse social and ethnic origins, produced a richly variegated pattern of exploitation. In Spanish Central America alone there existed side by side c.1700 huge ranches, large slave-worked *haciendas*, small farms and minute subsistence plots belonging to *mestizos* and mulattos.

How and where particular crops were produced depended not only on such factors as the quality of the soil or the nature and availability of labour, but also on the assumptions of the societies from which settlers came and the policies of the parent states. These on the whole welcomed agricultural endeavour as providing food for the population, curbing the peripatetic urges of colonists and depriving would-be intruders of land. They welcomed the cultivation of crops like sugar and tobacco which sold widely in Europe, sustained domestic industries, swelled customs revenues and threatened no existing interests. They equally welcomed such primary products as hides (in Spain) or naval stores (as in England), supplementing local resources always deemed insufficient and freeing the mother country from dependence on unreliable foreign suppliers. Thus colonies came to be cast, as is their usual fate, in the role of providers of raw materials and consumers of the manufactures of the parent state. But this was rarely how they saw it. They could grow acclimatized Old World crops – wheat, grapes, olives, citrus fruits – prolifically and had easy access to indigenous or naturalized raw materials. Hence they could commonly produce commodities similar or superior to those of the mother country and unburdened by expensive transport costs. In the Indies the wines of Peru and Chile undercut those of Andalusia, to the wrath of influential Sevillan landowners. The outcome was a sequence of generally ineffective attempts to stifle such competition, with the Spanish crown prohibiting the planting of new orchards and vineyards in the Americas and forbidding the export of wine and olive oil from Peru and Chile to regions that could be supplied from home.[33]

True, even without the damage inflicted by such measures, much colonial agriculture, as indeed much of that of Europe, remained of the crudest. In Spanish America techniques were often primitive, methods slipshod and debt-ridden and mortgaged *haciendas* no rarity. Nor did this necessarily reflect economic depression, for the amply-endowed heirs of Cortés early settled down to a patrician life sustained by Indian tribute and the profits of money-lending.[34]. In many remote or marginal areas farming never advanced beyond the subsistence level, it being said of western Costa Rica in 1719 that 'even the governor has to grow his own food'. In some places Europeans were content to continue existing indigenous patterns of agriculture, like the Portuguese with their palm and rice plantations on the western coast of India. Elsewhere they merely took away what nature generously provided – emeralds in Colombia, amber washed ashore in East Africa, logwood felled for its dye in Central America.

But this was not the whole story. In many regions land was worked intensively, or at least intelligently, in the vigorous pursuit of profit. A prime incentive was the opportunity to serve some local market. Luso-African planters in the Angolan hinterland grew food for the posts on the Atlantic littoral. In Spanish America, and later in Brazil colonial agriculture responded to the needs of increasing, and in many places immensely rich, white communities, which meant in the Indies a shift from milking the now reduced Indian population to direct exploitation of the soil. In 1586 Drake's men noticed how around Cartagena (Colombia) the land was 'cast into grounds of gardening and orchards'. In Mexico and Peru, particularly in the boom years before the mid 1600s, *haciendas* were purposefully worked, producing, as their location permitted, whatever was most in demand – wheat, barley, sugar, wine, fruit, olives, tobacco – sometimes using irrigation and (in Peru) guano fertilizer. Owners varied their crops to suit the market and some accumulated multiple holdings (vineyards, arable farms, ranches, plantations) to ensure, especially in the vicinity of silver mines, that no opportunity was missed. Nor did recession eradicate such enterprise. The success of Jesuit agriculture in Brazil added to the Order's unpopularity with the colonists, while some of their properties around Quito (Ecuador) were still doing well in the early 1700s from a sensible combination of farming with the manufacture, from their own raw materials, of commodities like soap and textiles.[35]

But nothing more graphically characterized the exploitation of colonial possessions than the extraction from their soil of precious metals and the conversion of their land to the large-scale production of cash crops grown on plantations of a style long familiar in the Mediterranean and the Iberian Atlantic islands. Such undertakings demanded capital. Much came from extortion and loot, whether that amassed by Spanish pioneers in the Americas, transferred from Asia to Brazil by their Portuguese contemporaries or seized from fellow Europeans by Caribbean buccaneers in the seventeenth century. Some came from resources, relatives or financiers in Europe, with the English tycoon Sir Josiah Child putting money into a Jamaican plantation in the 1600s, and the beginnings of the Brazilian sugar industry largely underwritten from the Old World. Much was soon generated locally, particularly by colonial merchants, active and impressively wealthy in the Spanish Indies within years of the conquest. So, too, it was unusual in seventeenth-century Jamaica for planters to have to seek loans outside the island itself. In the Spanish Indies royal resources were used to back the early stages of sugar growing in the Caribbean, as also to finance Peruvian mining in the late 1500s. Much capital represented the rewards of royal favour or the fruits of office and peculation, but some was the product of business or commercial enterprise, with the profits of mining and ranching invested in the nascent textile industry of Spanish America in the sixteenth century. And as we have seen, impressive amounts were provided by the Iberian Catholic church, which both financed its own undertakings and lent to neighbouring colonists.

Some cash crops were of indigenous origin, like the cotton and tobacco found in many parts of the Americas and the Caribbean, the cacao (whence chocolate) whose cultivation was eventually concentrated in Peru and Venezuela, or the fashionable dye, indigo, of which Guatemala reputedly provided the highest quality. Peruvian *coca* (the source of cocaine) was grown for a purely native market. Use of the drug had been controlled by the Incas, but with their authority gone demand rose among the demoralized survivors of the conquest. To profit from their cravings – and to keep the labour force in the silver mines quiescent – the Spaniards grew the crop in plantations on the tropical lower slopes of the Andes, using Indian labour in brutal and arduous conditions.

No indigenous crop, however, was to rival the success, or the far-reaching consequences, of tobacco. It was cultivated from an early date by both Spanish and Portuguese colonists who learned of its debilitating delights from the Amerindians. The Portuguese introduced it into western India *c.*1600 where its popularity was such that it appeared to travellers that the poor 'devoured more smoke than anything else', and where it was soon making a useful contribution to the revenues of the *Estado*.[36] A Brazilian patriot could meanwhile claim that tobacco had rendered his country 'famous in the four corners of the world'. By the early 1600s it was used as a currency in the African slave trade and was praised and execrated in Europe, where smoking was now a well-established habit and fashion among the affluent. They were supplied from the Spanish Indies (Venezuela and Trinidad especially) either legally through Seville, or, in larger measure through the enterprise of the smugglers operating in the Caribbean. Spanish attempts to stamp out this commerce gave islands such as Barbados and St Kitts the chance, soon emulated by their neighbours, to become producers. More important, tobacco from the Spanish Caribbean was introduced into mainland Virginia, then almost on the point of collapse, by John Rolfe, husband of the celebrated Algonkian princess Pocahontas, and by 1639 the colony was exporting 600 tonnes a year.

Though tobacco continued to be shipped from Spanish America, Brazil and (for a time) from the French and English Caribbean islands, it was the leaf of Virginia and nearby Maryland – where it became a medium of exchange – that eventually triumphed. Their harvest, unlike that of their competitors, had to travel only a relatively short distance to Europe along a route favoured by fair winds, and production was not impeded, as in the Spanish Indies, by state imposed restrictions. Furthermore, while to the Habsburg government the crop was an item of small significance in a rich imperial commerce, it was the mainstay of the economy of Virginia which endeavoured to ensure prices maintained a satisfactory level. Hence Virginian tobacco, shipped to the generally prosperous economies of northern Europe, and esteemed alike throughout the vast hinterland of the Baltic and in Ottoman Turkey and Moorish North Africa, became a commodity of almost mass consumption. That of the Spanish colonies, on the other hand, destined to an impoverished homeland, remained a luxury, while the industry of St Domingue, which in its heyday supplied both France and Holland, was eventually destroyed in the late 1600s by war and misguided government policy.

The production of tobacco had a profound effect on the economy and society of those North American settlements in which it was grown. Since it needed only relatively modest processing and storage facilities, no elaborate internal transport network, and nothing like the capital, labour and skills demanded by sugar, it could be satisfactorily cultivated on smallholdings. But as with sugar access to water was vital for its carriage and since it exhausted the soil within four years or so, regular clearing and planting of new land was essential to increase or at least sustain output. Tobacco thus encouraged a riparian, non-urban and dispersed pattern of settlement, and one which was accentuated in Virginia by a farmer's need, in the absence of primogeniture, to provide land for his heirs. By the late seventeenth century the boom had, for the time, collapsed. Over-production had depressed prices, to which misfortune was soon added the damage inflicted by prolonged wars, with a consequent rise in the risks and costs of carrying cargoes to Europe. Both land and labour were more expensive. The crop was burdened with heavy customs charges and its market was distorted by the obligation (imposed by the Navigation Acts) that it must first be shipped to the mother country. As prices lagged and as small producers failed or tried some other crop, tobacco was increasingly grown on large plantations, whether in the Spanish Indies, Brazil or Virginia and Carolina. And on the English mainland, where much of the labour had once been provided by indentured servants, planters turned in the late 1600s, like their Iberian counterparts had already done, to what were seen as more efficient and more economical black slaves.

Other highly successful colonial crops were those introduced from one part of the world into another: Asian ginger and pepper to the Iberian Americas; American maize to Africa; European wheat and vines to the Americas; Asian rice to the southern colonies of North America; and above all sugar, profitably established by the Portuguese pioneers in the Atlantic islands, from where it was taken by Columbus to the Caribbean. There, despite the Spanish obsession with the pursuit of bullion, it enjoyed a brief success, and a more enduring one on the mainland, with Peru soon supplying Chile and what is now the Argentine. But from the late 1500s primacy passed to Brazil. The land of its north-eastern littoral was rich and virgin, the climate ideal, access to the eager markets of Europe not difficult and Africa's massive resources of manpower within easy reach. Vast plantations on which agricultural and industrial undertakings were combined, speedily developed.[37] Production soared, helped by the skills and resources of Portuguese Jews, closely associated with their co-religionaries in the great commercial and financial centre of Amsterdam, and on the eve of the Dutch occupation (1630) Brazil's output was around 20,000 tonnes a year. As the result, as we have seen, of the expulsion of the Hollanders from the country, techniques of cane-growing and sugar refining were disseminated throughout the West Indies – very often by Jews now fleeing the attentions of the Inquisition under the restored regime in Brazil – and a new Caribbean industry developed. Among the islands, as tobacco prices fell, there had already begun a search for new crops (such as indigo) and some enterprising Barbadians had visited Brazil to see what they could learn. True, the price of sugar was also dropping – reaching rock bottom on the Amsterdam market in the late 1680s – but demand was growing. Sugar was the main ingredient in countless delicacies, was used in brewing and distilling, and was increasingly consumed with the chocolate, coffee and tea coming into fashion.

Benefiting from such opportunities and the difficulties of the Brazilian industry, that of the Caribbean colonies grew, as did also the size of the units of production.[38] This was to the ultimate advantage of the bigger islands, such as Jamaica and St Domingue, where there was abundant water and plenty of virgin soil, and hence no need, as in the densely settled Barbados, for expansion to be at the expense of smallholders. Aided by protected home markets and efficient shipping Caribbean sugar overtook that of Brazil, and by 1700 the English plantations alone were exporting 25,000 tonnes annually. Estates were often worked intensively, not to say ruthlessly, with improvements financed from profits and local commercial capital - more than half the 500-odd merchants at Port Royal (Jamaica) had money invested in the island's agriculture between 1664 and 1700. Such a pace was hard to sustain. Much soil became exhausted, and in the early eighteenth century the English colonies were surpassed by those of the French whose more abundant and better land yielded a cheaper and superior product.

Sugar, like tobacco, was thus converted from an erstwhile high-priced luxury to a commodity of widespread consumption, even doled out to patients in French hospitals by 1700, while its potent by-product, rum, became still another currency in the slave trade. The sugar industry, part of an international commerce and, from its expensive processes, thirsty for capital, became intimately linked to the money markets first of Amsterdam and then of London. In the West Indies it stimulated the growth of mono-cultures in which every scrap of land was utilized, and everywhere cane was produced primarily on estates which (as in Brazil) were already large, or which, as in the Caribbean, steadily became so, thus diminishing the importance and prosperity of those small farmers once so vital in the exploitation of islands like Barbados. And everywhere sugar production was eventually dependent on black slave labour, of which it was indeed the main and insatiable consumer, giving rise to societies such as that of Jamaica where, by 1713, there were eight blacks to every white. But while sugar soothed the palates (and rotted the teeth) of Europeans, the Caribbean entered a further phase of its long and unhappy experience of white control. The islands were too small, their economy and society too intensely special-ized, slave labour too widespread to permit them to enjoy anything of the

prosperity of much of the neighbouring Americas. The region was in easy
and regular contact with Europe, for whose wars – which the mainland
escaped - it became yet another cockpit. Its white population was largely
transient and much of whatever wealth planters and their associates accumulated was notoriously not spent locally.

To the many riches extracted from the soils of the New World there
were early added those provided by its seas. Fish was in urgent demand in
a Europe generally short of livestock and hard pressed to find some nutritive
food for those meatless days observed in Catholic countries – a difficulty
further aggravated by the apparent failure of some traditional sources of
supply in the late fifteenth century. European fishermen were hence soon
in pursuit of whatever the newly opened seas yielded. Fresh grounds were
being worked off West Africa in the 1400s. The waters of the Brazilian
coast not only provided fish in great quantities but reputedly of such quality
that it could be eaten without oil or vinegar to no ill effect. In the course
of their early attempts to reach Asia by a north-west passage the English
came across shoals of cod off Newfoundland that could be scooped up by
the bucketful. By the end of the sixteenth century there had grown up there
and in neighbouring waters one of the most celebrated of all fisheries,
already of sufficient importance to invite attack in times of war. It was
worked by vessels from the Atlantic ports of France and from Iberia and
England, which alone sent out some 300 annually. Portuguese and Spanish
activity dwindled in the 1600s, but not that of the French, who mostly
took cod on the Grand Banks and pickled it in salt aboard their ships, or
of the English who worked the Newfoundland coast and landed to dry
their catch. By the mid 1600s there were nearly 200 English and allegedly
400 French craft engaged, and it was said (1702) of St Malo that if anything
happened to its Newfoundland fleet 'it would affect the town as much as
a bombardment'. And to the ships out from Europe there were now added
those belonging to New England. Some of the fish taken was destined for
domestic or local markets – like that sent from Massachusetts to Virginia –
but the bulk was sold, in an international trade of prime importance, in
Italy and Iberia.

There were smaller, but nevertheless important, enterprises elsewhere.
Whales, the source of valuable oil, were hunted in the Arctic, chiefly by
the Dutch, off north-east America by the French and along the Brazilian
coast by the Portuguese. By 1700 New England fishermen were providing
the Portuguese Atlantic islands with salt mackerel and in the West Indies
there had sprung up a considerable fishery devoted to taking turtles, with
those from the Caymen Islands used to feed the poor whites of Jamaica.[39]

But though propagandists might wax eloquent on the economic and
moral benefits arising from such endeavours, and though both individuals
and whole areas might be enriched by them, there was a widely and strongly
held conviction that the best sort of empire was one whose colonies were

replete with precious metals. Bullion meant wealth in its most visible, enduring and generally acceptable form, ensuring that explorers and conquerors were immediately and suitably rewarded and the mother country endowed with a new – and usually urgently needed – source of strength. Only the Iberians made substantial finds. The Portuguese came across producers of silver in Iran and Japan and of gold in Africa, China and Indonesia. They established a momentary foothold in the goldfields of Mutapa (East Africa) in the seventeenth century, but with insufficient labour they were unable to sustain, let alone increase production, and were ultimately expelled. Eventually, in Brazil, they had a colony spectacularly rich in gold.[40] The Spaniards did even better. In Mexico, Peru and to a lesser extent in the Caribbean islands, precious metals had long been extracted and worked by the indigenous populations for use in personal adornment and, in the great mainland cultures, for the embellishment of temples and imperial buildings. Inspired by what they encountered in Mexico and Peru the Spaniards set about the search for whatever else rumour and their own greed convinced them must exist, with such frenetic zeal that in the end few regions that contained or could provide any bullion to speak of escaped subjugation. Using, with disastrous consequences, Amerindian forced labour, alluvial gold was early worked and exhausted in the Caribbean islands. There were subsequently important finds in Peru, Chile, Mexico and various parts of Central America, together with what could be obtained in the Philippines. In lowland Colombia, where the indigenous population was soon virtually extinct, gold was mined by African slaves. But many other deposits lay beyond the reach of Spanish technology or were too distant from any suitable source of labour. In all perhaps some 300 tonnes of gold were sent to Spain from the Americas before 1660.

Silver was a different story. As with gold what had been accumulated over the years by local peoples was quickly skimmed off. Then, however, there began the exploitation of the extensive veins which often lay in, or near the highly organized Aztec and Inca states, as at Zacatecas and Potosí.[41] Between 1500 and 1660 alone 25,000 tonnes were recorded as shipped to Europe – besides whatever was exported illicitly – and anything up to 350 tonnes a year were flowing across the Pacific. As was subsequently the case in Brazil, ore-bearing land belonged to the crown, but the Spanish royal house no more operated mines than the kings of Portugal grew spices. Instead it took a percentage of the output (a fifth to start with, a tenth later) from those – 500 at Potosí in 1585 – to whom it farmed the concession. Initially most mining was of a modest scale and crude nature, financed by affluent *encomenderos* and local merchants and landowners. It was carried on, with the aid of indigenous refining techniques, by *encomienda* Indians working for those fortunate enough to be able to claim or secure their services. Nor did operations of this sort ever entirely disappear. But the pattern of exploitation soon grew more varied and complex. Mercury, more effective than the lead first employed in refining, came into use from the mid 1500s, bringing a surge in output. In Mexico, where the best ore lay in regions inhabited by non-sedentary peoples, and where *encomienda* labour was consequently not easily available, the Spaniards speedily had recourse to wage labour, so producing a cosmopolitan, ethnically mixed (black, Indian, mulatto, *mestizo*) and Hispanized work-force.

For most of our period Spaniards could only drain deep workings with great difficulty, but at Potosí, 5000 metres up in the bleak and inhospitable Andes, where flooding was not a problem, substantial undertakings developed and there sprang up one of the largest cities in Christendom, a forerunner in its crude dedication to wealth, its brothels and gaming saloons, of some of the later unlovable manifestations of industrialization. Andean mining was increasingly financed by merchants who handled the silver trade, and who often ended in control of the workings themselves. Operations involved tunnelling 200 metres or more into the mountainside, with the result that many miners had to remain below ground for days at a time. Thirteen thousand workers were employed in the boom years of the early 1600s from a labour force initially recruited by compulsory Indian servitude and eventually and increasingly from an indigenous proletariat.[42] Processes and equipment were often relatively complex, supervised by technical experts who were commonly aliens. Nevertheless, with resources so lavish, exploitation was in the familiar feckless style. Ore was not hauled to the surface but carried up, at enormous human cost, on the backs of labourers – as indeed it still is in the mines of Bolivia and where also the senses of the workers are similarly still dulled by the use of cocaine. In Brazil, whose gold occurred in regions as remote as any, the extraction of ore was even more primitive. Since it was recovered by panning from the beds of streams and rivers workings were small and scattered. They demanded no such elaborate refining plant as did Spanish silver and gave rise to no such industrial centre as Potosí. Yet mining, even on this scale, had far-reaching repercussions. It stimulated, especially in the Spanish Indies, industries to feed, clothe and supply its workers. It encouraged stock farming to provide animals (notably mules) to carry goods and work machinery, and it led to the opening of routes to permit the export of bullion and the import of the many necessities and luxuries demanded by wealthy mining entrepreneurs.

There were other important pockets of industrialization elsewhere in the colonial world. Their function often amounted to no more than processing the local harvest, which at its simplest could mean the Spaniards making indigo dye in Central America or the English turning Caribbean fruits into preserves. But by methods more complex there were extracted from sugar such by-products as the potent and lethal rums manufactured in Brazil and the West Indies. Indigenous skills and indigenous raw materials were frequently turned to European benefit, as in India and the Spanish Americas, where local artisans were employed in making textiles, weapons, jewellery and more mundane objects. Sometimes from necessity, not to say desperation, colonies developed substantial industries to meet their own needs. Building, whether of houses, churches, fortresses or entire cities, was undertaken on a large scale throughout the European overseas world, commonly using indigenous labour and, in Asia, indigenous contractors. Everywhere there were obvious attractions for settlers to work up local raw materials. With high quality timber widely available, shipbuilding was ubiquitous, flourishing alike in tiny islands such as the Bermudas – home of a celebrated cedar-wood sloop – the Indian subcontinent and the Americas. Using the renowned local teak indigenous shipwrights built Indiamen and smaller craft for the Portuguese in western India almost from the beginning, while by 1700 many of Portugal's best vessels in Asian waters were said to be of Brazilian construction. The Spaniards had fighting ships built in the Canaries. Their Manila galleons came from the Philippines (and occasionally from Cambodia), and in the Indies they developed a major and highly specialized industry, employing chiefly black and mulatto workers and using alike the fine timbers of Central and equatorial America and the copper of Chile. It supported various ancillary undertakings (such as the making of sails, guns and anchors) and produced craft carefully adapted to the demands of the waters in which they operated. Warships were built at Cartagena. Havana (Cuba) provided vessels for the transatlantic trade, its products accounting for about a third of the ships working to Spain by 1650. Craft for the Pacific were constructed at Guayaquil (Ecuador) – 'without the necessity of other materials being imported except for nails and iron' – and Realejo (Nicaragua), with the Peruvian industry much encouraged in the early 1600s by the need to provide ships to resist Dutch incursions. Meanwhile on the north-eastern coast of America there was developing what quickly became one of the world's foremost centres of every sort of maritime endeavour.

Colonial ships thus appeared anywhere from New England to Macao, employed, as opportunity offered, in trade, war, smuggling or piracy. Already in the 1530s, Gaspar de Espinosa, associate of the conquerors of Peru, controlled six craft operating in various parts of the Americas.[43] In the Portuguese *Estado da India*, ships – allegedly as many as 400 in the early 1500s – were commonly owned in association with Asians and used in anything from the lucrative country trades to the provisioning of the imperial possessions. By 1700 there were substantial English-owned fleets based in the major EIC posts in India, profitably working along established routes and pioneering new ones.[44] In the West hundreds of small craft coasted the Pacific shores of the Spanish Americas. By the mid 1500s there were ships in the Atlantic whose home ports were reported to be minuscule islands like the Cape Verdes and São Tomé. Jamaica (which had about 100 vessels in 1689), the Bermudas (with about 500), Barbados and Martinique were all much in evidence in trade, piracy and privateering, while the shipping of English North America was already so abundant and successful in the 1670s as to be considered a threat to that of the mother country.

The settlements on the north-eastern Atlantic seaboard had initially needed tonnage to feed and supply themselves. It was a need made all the more urgent by the metropolitan government's insistence that colonies should remain primary producers, thus obliging those without profitable staple crops to seek for other ways of financing the purchase of the manufactured goods they required. Apart from trading in agricultural surplus (their own and their neighbours) the obvious answer, enterprising North Americans speedily appreciated, was shipowning. Timber for building was easily available, there were fisheries near to hand, and in the neighbouring Caribbean a new and rich maritime economy was emerging. Then there was the potent stimulus provided by the Navigation Acts introduced by the English government in the second half of the seventeenth century, which, by driving the Dutch out of the colonial carrying trade, left it short of tonnage and so presented the northern settlements with a magnificent opening.[45] Locally owned vessels appeared in Massachusetts in the 1640s, and in the Chesapeake colonies soon after. By the end of the century one Salem magnate owned twenty vessels (and much else besides) and roughly one in three adult males in Boston had money in shipping. New York, Philadelphia and Boston became fierce rivals in local and long distance trades, of which none was more important than the provisioning of the Caribbean sugar islands.[46] Such were the skills, energies and acumen of the New Englanders, and such the advantages of cheap building materials and the proximity of the West Indies, that by 1700 they had virtually cleared English vessels out of the commerce between America and the Caribbean islands. Infuriating though this was to those worsted, no laws had been broken. But the North Americans went, in every sense, much further. Their ships traded to French and Spanish possessions (exchanging provisions for bullion in the latter). They exported sugar and tobacco directly to Europe (so contravening the Navigation Acts) and compounded their sins by passing off French sugar as English. They carried Newfoundland fish to Spain, Central American dyewood to Holland, timber to the corsairs of Algiers, Caribbean rum to Africa and African slaves to the West Indies (flouting the pretensions of the Royal African Company) and imported Asian textiles, opium and black slaves from Madagascar to Virginia. They were, in the eyes of the English government, congenital smugglers, notorious traders with the enemy, associates of pirates and outrageous violators of its economic policies. Others, however, had other views. North American timber was cheap (though labour costs were high) and North American ships of excellent quality. Indeed so attractive did they become to British owners that by the outbreak of the American Revolution as much as a third of the kingdom's registered tonnage was colonial-built.

Similar circumstances – abundant raw materials, local markets, a pool of skilled labour – stimulated the emergence of other industries as colonists first sought to satisfy their own needs and then, despite metropolitan opposition, progressed to the exploitation of wider opportunities. At Santo Domingo (Hispaniola) in 1586 Drake's men found drinking glasses 'whereof they make excellent good and faire'. The manufacture of textiles proliferated in the New World where pressing needs (notably for clothing) could hardly be met, over such vast distances and in the face of so many obstacles to communication, by Europe's industry. It was, nevertheless, a development generally discouraged as undermining the proper dependence of colonies on parent states. For economically advanced countries like Holland and England it meant the loss of potentially splendid markets for their own products. Only Spain, with a much feebler industrial base, uncertainly tolerated such a growth. But in English North America, despite the mother country's prohibition of the manufacture of woollens (1699) and hats (1732), by the early 1700s the locals were not only clothing themselves but also supplying the southern plantations and making 'as good druggets . . . as any in England'.

In the Spanish Indies the authorities were torn between the threat, on the one hand, to what remained of the peninsula's industry and the dangers of countenancing anything that might encourage colonial aspirations to self-sufficiency and independence, and the advantage, on the other, of having the needs of the colonists satisfied by local (and taxable) enterprises, and without the attendant difficulties and dangers of transoceanic commerce. Besides which society would benefit from the drafting of recalcitrant or vagabond natives into cloth-making. Hence to the accompaniment of a barrage of advice and instructions textile industries were established. The production of silks in Mexico was soon overwhelmed by the flood of Chinese imports, but the manufacture of more mundane materials – wool, cotton, flax, hemp – was widespread and successful. In 1692 it was reported that Ecuador produced 'coarse fabrics which serve to clothe the people' of Chile and Peru alike. Mexican woollens were of a quality admired by knowledgeable observers, while the Hispanized Indians of the Argentine were said to make 'a thread as fine as the best of Biscay'. Cloth was produced in factories, like the twenty-five woollen mills around Mexico City in 1600 – the largest of which used up to 700 hands – or those in the vicinity of Quito a century later employing some 30,000 Indians. Where indigenous prisoners or forced labour were not available many of the work-force were children or Indians enmeshed in debt, and all toiling in conditions commonly scarcely distinguishable from penal servitude. Near affluent markets, however, owners could afford to employ African slaves. Mills belonged to the crown, to individual Spaniards (usually from the less elevated ranks of society), to religious Orders and (decreasingly) to indigenous communities. Since wealthy colonials insisted on prestigious

European or oriental cloths the industry supplied in general an Indian market of low purchasing power and of a size limited by poor communications, leaving little incentive to investigate improved techniques of manufacture. Even so, despite brutal conditions and crude technology such enterprises, enjoying a *de facto* monopoly could, like so many others elsewhere before and since, prove remarkably profitable.

So were the fruits of empire harvested. To some pious or learned Europeans of the time it seemed that the mission of the Old World was to bring to the inhabitants of other lands the blessings of Christianity and what they were pleased to define as 'civility'. Others knew better. The wider world was there for Europe's benefit, and indeed it could be seriously argued, both in Protestant England and Catholic Venice, that all that was wrong with the richly endowed Americas was that they were full of idle and undesirable natives.[47] European techniques of colonial exploitation – whether downright robbery, the use of monopoly corporations, the development of extensive pastoral farming and intensive arable cultivation, or the large-scale use of slavery and servitude – were naturally enough those of the homeland, however adapted or modified. But only rarely, unlike that of Europe, was imperial wealth the outcome of white manual toil. True, much of what the continent gained represented the profits of proceedings little removed from pillage: the ruthless extraction of silver from the Americas, the feckless pastoral farming of the New World, or the exactions levied on indigenous commerce in the East. But riches of this order were not necessarily the rewards of brute violence or parasitic indolence. Often enough they were accumulated, by country traders in Asia for example, or by shipowners in New England, through the exercise of remarkable skills and ingenuity. The shortcomings of contemporary European economic ideas and organization have often been detailed by scholars. Nevertheless the continent could successfully turn the opportunities of the wider world to its advantage. Individuals and even (briefly) monarchs were enriched to an extent that, through the unquantifiable volume of loot and pillage, can only be guessed. Oriental luxuries and New World sugar and tobacco flowed in at a rate the home market could barely handle. Labour was found, whatever the human cost, to keep transatlantic mines and plantations going. Huge amounts of silver served to sustain Europe's commerce with Asia. New sources of furs and fish were geared to the continent's demand. In the Americas potentially powerful economies were established, soon so successful as to alarm their parent states. By and large what Europeans wanted from the rest of mankind they got.

NOTES AND REFERENCES

1 James Axtell, *European and Indian*, pp. 117–18.
2 Richard S. Dunn, *Sugar and Slaves. The Rise of the Planter Class in the English*

West Indies 1624–1713 (1973), pp. 222–3.

3   See pp. 109–10.

4   See pp. 96–106, 143–4.

5   See pp. 96, 143, 238–9.

6   See pp. 96, 151.

7   See pp. 8–9, 13–14, 150–1.

8   *Travels of Fray Sebastien Manrique 1629–1643*, translated and edited by C. Eckford Luard and Father H. Hosten SJ, 2 vols, Hakluyt Society (Oxford, 1927), II, 368–9.

9   *The Travels of the Abbé Carré in India and the Near East, 1672 to 1674*, translated by Lady Fawcett and edited by Sir Charles Fawcett with the assistance of Sir Richard Burn, 3 vols, Hakluyt Society (1947–8), I, 214.

10 See pp. 20–21.

11 See Om Prakash in *Itinerario*, VII, 2 (1983), 38ff.

12 G. V. Scammell, *The English Chartered Trading Companies and the Sea* (1983).

13 See pp. 18–19.

14 P. J. Marshall, *East Indian Fortunes. The British in Bengal in the Eighteenth Century* (Oxford, 1976), p. 109.

15 Gerrit Knaap, 'Europeans, mestizos and slaves: the population of Colombo at the end of the seventeenth century', *Itinerario*, V, 2 (1981), 84 ff.

16 Richard Elphick and Hermann Giliomee (eds), *The Shaping of South African Society, 1652–1820* (Cape Town, 1979), pp. 76, 81.

17 Steve J. Stern, *Peru's Indian Peoples and the Challenge of the Spanish Conquest: Huamanga to 1640* (Wisconsin, 1982), p. 49.

18 Nicholas P. Cushner, *Farm and Factory. The Jesuits and the Development of Agrarian Capitalism in Colonial Quito 1600–1767* (Albany, 1982), p. 119.

19 Stern, *op.cit.*, p. 86; Cushner, *op.cit.*, p. 128.

20 Gary B. Nash, *Red, White and Black: The Peoples of Early America*, 2nd ed (New Jersey, 1982), pp. 128 ff; Patricia Dillon Woods, *French-Indian Relations on the Southern Frontier, 1699–1762* (Ann Arbor, 1979), pp. 15–16, 46–7; Dewar (ed.), *The Voyages . . . of Captain Uring*, pp. 156–7.

21 William L. Sherman, *Forced Native Labor in Sixteenth-Century Central America* (Lincoln, Nebraska, 1979), p. 209.

22 See pp. 184–5.

23 See pp. 36, 47, 248–50.

24 See pp. 34, 47.

25 See p. 48.

26 Stern, *Peru's Indian Peoples*, p. 171.

27 See p. 126.

28 *The Travels of the Abbé Carré*, ed. Fawcett and Burn, I, 178.

29 See pp. 110–11, 147.

30 The inalienable succession of the estate to the eldest heir.

31 See pp. 179–80.

32 Elphick and Giliomee, *South African Society*, pp. 6, 8–9.

33 See pp. 238–9.

34 John K. Chance, *Race and Class in Colonial Oaxaca* (Stanford, 1978), pp. 38–9.

35 Cushner, *Farm and Factory*, p. 87.

36 *The Travels of the Abbé Carré*, ed. Fawcett and Burn, I, 227.

37 See pp. 35–6, 124.

38 See pp. 39, 44, 124–5.

39 Dunn, *Sugar and Slaves*, p. 276.

40   See pp. 14, 37, 47–8.

41   See pp. 27–8, 111.

42   See p. 111.

43   Guillermo Lohmann Villena, *Les Espinosa, une Famille et Hommes d'affaires
     en Espagne et aux Indes à l'Epoque de la Colonisation* (Paris, 1968), pp. 172,
     190, 230 ff.

44   See pp. 106–7.

45   See pp. 43–4, 166.

46   See the valuable discussion in Ian K. Steele, *The English Atlantic 1675–1740.
     An Exploration of Communication and Community* (Oxford, 1986).

47   The theme is explored in Federica Ambrosini, *Paesi e Mari Ignoti: America e
     Colonialismo Europeo nella Cultura Veneziana (secoli XVI–XVII)*, (Venice,
     1982).

5   *Imperial and colonial government*

The acquisition and exploitation of empire was one thing, its government quite another. Most pioneering voyages and expeditions, apart from those of the Portuguese, were undertaken not at the instance of monarchs or states, largely indifferent to the pursuit of apparently unrewarding fantasies, but on private initiative. The history of imperial government was thus the history of the subsequent attempts of European rulers or states to impose on distant lands – or at least those likely to yield some profit – an authority they had initially been willing to delegate, not to say abandon, to others. Sometimes, as with Spain in America, where the discovery of riches came hard on the heels of the discovery of the continent itself, and where conquest meant the sudden acquisition of millions of new subjects, this was accomplished early and more or less effectively. Elsewhere, as with England's Atlantic colonies, whose true value was long obscured, it was achieved slowly, imperfectly and with much difficulty. And everywhere the extension of state authority – a matter of bitter contention at home – was accompanied by friction or worse between the mother country and its possessions.

In their earliest days in new lands most European peoples established their title, if they could, by some symbolic act of possession, exacted where possible native recognition of their suzerainty, and set up a military or authoritarian regime. What happened next depended on their own and their parent society's beliefs and aspirations and on the nature of indigenous political organization and the degree to which its members were, or could be, subjugated. Nevertheless all potential colonial powers faced a number of common problems. Overseas settlements offering any prospect of riches attracted those members of the parent state, whether footloose desperadoes or the able and ambitious, least amenable to authority. Communications by sailing ship across thousands of kilometres of ocean, though improving in the English Atlantic by the end of this period, were slow and unreliable. It took on average ninety-one days to reach Vera Cruz from Spain; anything up to a year for the passage between Chile and Mexico; two years for the voyage to and from Portuguese Asia, leaving officials and those supposedly subject to them much to their own devices. Metropolitan governments, moreover, knew little of the situations, changing even as they deliberated, with which they attempted to deal. They were in any case disposed to consider them of lesser moment than those closer to hand, and they lacked the administrative resources – already hard pressed at home – adequately to undertake such responsibilities.

The most ambitious and successful attempt at imperial control was that of Spain, the only European power, prior to Britain's conquest of India, to subjugate millions of non-Europeans, and this, uniquely, at the very time it was adding realm to realm in the Old World. Until the seventeenth century the peninsular kingdoms were ruled by a succession of able, ambitious and hard-working monarchs, inspired by lofty ideals. Their authority over far-flung and widely differing possessions came to be asserted through formidable aristocrats, an assortment of councils and a bureaucracy whose expansion was stimulated by the demands of empire. These servants of the state, like other such officials elsewhere later, were powerfully influenced by their education, imbibing in newly founded or reformed universities the positive precepts of Roman law and the current humanist ideals of serious minded endeavour.[1]

Spain's first overseas ventures owed little to the royal house. Expeditions were indeed under crown licence, but privately financed. Their leaders enjoyed virtually sovereign powers and often became the *de facto* rulers of vast tracts of land and great numbers of people. But not for long. Once the enormous wealth of the New World was apparent it was a very different story. The discoveries were assumed to have been made in the royal name, and until the death of Ferdinand of Aragon (1516) were regarded as part of the royal patrimony. The generous grants accorded to Columbus – who became viceroy and governor-general of the lands he found and hereditary Admiral of the Ocean Sea – were speedily undermined. *Conquistadores* as powerful as Cortés were overthrown and by the end of the reign of Charles V (1556) the most important territories were controlled by royal officers, the ambitions of *encomenderos* had been curtailed, and the emperor, when ordering the affairs of the Indies, spoke simply of his will in such matters. The disposal of all offices, lands and rights was brought into the royal hands, the crown often employing in the task those grandees who governed its possessions or commanded its forces in Europe. From 1573 the whole process of further expansion (now called pacification) was under royal direction, with the privileges for leaders the more generous the less the likelihood of any worthwhile discovery. By papal grant, as also happened in Portugal, the monarchy secured the right to nominate to all preferments in the rapidly growing imperial church, thus extending to the wider world powers long sought in Europe by Spanish and other sovereigns. From 1538 it excluded from its territories papal decrees found unacceptable, and it kept the missionary Orders under strict surveillance. The crown determined who was to be allowed into the Indies and who was to be kept out. It was assumed, as practical experience and classical precept taught, that the stability of Spanish rule would best be ensured by encouraging the emigration of farmers, artisans and respectable married men – those who went without their wives were ordered to be speedily reunited in marital bliss and spouses were to be provided for bachelors – and by the liberal founding of towns. Whole sectors of Iberian society were to be excluded from the New World, ranging from the poor (elsewhere considered prime candidates to settle distant lands) to heretics, Jews, Moors and foreigners. And before long edicts and instructions dealing with every aspect of imperial rule were flowing out from the mother country in ever increasing numbers.

The empire was to be exploited for the benefit of the crown, to which end – and to secure the exclusion of undesirables, to protect the interests of privileged Spanish merchants and to ensure the dependence of the Indies on Spain – imperial oceanic commerce was, after some experiment, to be conducted under the closest supervision. Trade to and from the Americas was organized in the manner long employed by Venice in the handling of her richest European commerce and similarly used by Portugal in her dealings with Asia and Africa. But the Spanish monarchs, unlike the kings of Portugal, did not go into business themselves. They had even grander views of their station, many other interests and commitments, and their imperial revenues were relatively less important to them than were those from Portugal's overseas trades and possessions to the Lusitanian royal house. Nevertheless colonial commerce was to be a monopoly of a minutely defined scope and nature. The Indies could trade only with Spain (via Seville and, from 1519, Cadiz), which was soon taken to mean they could deal only with members of the Seville merchant guild.[2] And by the late 1500s, in accordance with common Spanish practice, Seville merchants were supposed to deal only with members of similar bodies in Mexico and Lima. From the mid sixteenth century these oceanic trades were carried on through waters guarded, in some fashion, by Spanish naval forces and handled by convoys sailing, as conditions deteriorated, under armed escort. Every year from 1564 two fleets left, or were supposed to leave Seville for the Indies, one bound for the Antilles, Vera Cruz and Honduras, and the other primarily for Nombre de Dios (Puerto Bello later). Here the precious bullion was loaded, after which the ships moved out to the shelter of Cartagena. The following spring they met other returning flotillas in Havana, together cleared the Caribbean through the treacherous Florida Strait in early summer, picked up a favourable wind for the Azores to the north, and after a halt in the islands to await stragglers, refresh crews, top up cargoes (and engage in illicit trade), set off on the final leg home.

Such a system started with many and obvious shortcomings and quickly acquired more. A greater volume of tonnage was required outward (to carry the goods demanded by a growing colonial population) than could be laden with bullion for the return, while in the late sixteenth and early seventeenth centuries, as fleets came under enemy attack, defence costs soared but naval protection faltered. More fundamentally the monopoly, like most of the others set up in this period, could never be more than partially enforced. Since the economically enfeebled Spain was soon incapable of providing the goods colonists required, foreign merchants were permitted to trade under licence. Others carried on clandestine business through partners in Seville, while with the connivance of corrupt officials shippers embarked illicit cargoes with impunity. The movements of convoys were irregular, with ships delayed by their own and their crews' shortcomings, the vagaries of the weather or the hazards of war. Hence, among other things, merchants were unable to gauge colonial demand, imports to the Indies were either unsuitable or in short supply and expensive, and colonists accordingly encouraged – not that they needed much persuading in any case – to deal with smugglers. Silver, as we have seen, leaked out across the Pacific and across the Andes. In the Caribbean, largely ignored by the Seville convoys, where Spanish control was fragile and access by foreigners easy, there early sprang up a massive clandestine commerce. And by the late seventeenth century this was more vital still as the Seville fleets became smaller and their sailings were frequently disrupted or suspended. Even so, the essential task of transporting unprecedented amounts of treasure over hitherto unequalled distances was long successfully accomplished, and not until the beginning of the seventeenth century was a silver fleet lost to the enemy. In the Pacific a similar monopoly was instituted with, in its heyday, two to four vessels of specified size working between Acapulco and Manila – the direct sailings from Peru to the Philippines briefly permitted in 1579 soon being suppressed when Seville complained of the unfair competition its imports to the Americas were facing from oriental goods. As in the Atlantic every detail of the trade, from the value of cargoes to the proper ordering of shipboard cooking, was carefully regulated, and as in the Atlantic a vital link was, with difficulty, maintained, the flow of trade capricious and fraud endemic.

To implement such policies there was developed an extensive and complex administration, unparalleled in any other contemporary empire. As in Portugal, and as earlier in Genoa and Venice, imperial commerce and maritime affairs were entrusted (1503) to a specially created department, the *Casa de la Contratación*. All vessels and cargoes destined for or arriving from the Indies were to be recorded and checked there, besides which the office, in familiar bureaucratic style, soon engendered or arrogated to itself other important functions, exercising a wide-ranging maritime jurisdiction and supporting a much admired navigational school.

Exceptional circumstances apart, imperial affairs became the responsibility of the Council of the Indies, set up in 1524, and remained so until 1714. This body was one of the many councils which, under the king, governed the rapidly growing collection of Habsburg domains. Such devolution reflected the impracticability of the direct control of so many different and distant possessions and the strength and diversity of their individual characteristics and interests. The members of the Council of the Indies were, like their colleagues on other similar bodies, professional jurists, many of whom, in its golden years, had served overseas and who brought to its deliberations a unique depth of knowledge and width of experience. Under the crown they corporately exercised supreme authority in the empire – though various responsibilities were over the years delegated to specially created organizations – drafting and issuing laws, nominating to offices and investigating the behaviour of their incumbents.

Overseas, after a period of much trial and many errors as rulers endeavoured to understand the problems confronting them, viceroyalties were instituted in Mexico (1535) and Peru (1543). The office was well-known in the homeland and one already used by the Portuguese in Asia. Its holders were usually aristocrats, supposedly serving for no more than six years or so. They were given no specific jurisdictional or administrative powers, but were in fact heads of the civil and military governments, enjoying overall authority and providing a focus for colonial loyalties and a check on colonial ambitions. They lived and governed in considerable style, surrounded by their own staffs and they were, by reason of slow and infrequent communications, very much left to exercise their own discretion and initiative. Many returned home financially ruined and broken in health and reputation. Many others showed themselves to be men of consummate ability. But whatever their qualities, initiative was not independence. Viceroys were bombarded with royal instructions. They could raise no army to speak of, nor could they disburse money on their own authority, while in any matters of difficulty they had to consult the local *audiencia*. This was yet another Spanish institution which, exported to the Americas, flourished in so encouraging an environment. In Castile the *audiencia* was an appeal court. It was early introduced into the Indies to restrain the conquerors and to keep the peace between inchoate jurisdictions, and by 1700 there were eleven in existence. In the viceregal capitals *audiencias* shared, disputed or usurped viceregal powers. As corporate bodies, staffed by long-serving and influential lawyers, mostly recruited from the lesser aristocracy and urban patriciate of the mother country, they were not intimidated by grandees. Even the remaining *audiencias*, subject in some degree to a viceroyalty, were supreme courts of appeal within their jurisdictions. All exercised considerable powers of inquiry, and all, with varying degrees of enthusiasm, ensured the royal dues were collected and royal policies towards the indigenous populations enforced.

Thus, notwithstanding tenuous communications the Spanish crown established and retained its authority in its new possessions. Viceroys, often innovators, were checked by conservative *audiencias*, and *audiencias*, however pertinacious, by viceroys, and both by the state's prudent separation of the imperial treasuries from the rest of the administration. Officials were, moreover, obliged to consult their colleagues and were encouraged to report their shortcomings directly to the crown, which further restrained any untoward outbreaks of energy and enterprise by playing off one social class against another. Besides which kings were able to deploy that formidable instrument of their will, the imperial church, which by 1700 comprised five archdioceses and thirty-one bishoprics. Over these their authority, secured by papal privileges whose generosity reflects the power of the Habsburg dynasty, was absolute. Before 1600 they filled most of the dioceses with friars from the mendicant Orders of whose policies – sympathetic to the Indians, hostile to the colonists – they approved. But at the same time, by freeing the missions from episcopal jurisdiction in the areas in which they were working, and by allowing their members to discharge routine parochial duties, they weakened the authority of bishops and secular priests alike. In later years the royal objective was to ensure, except in the frontier missions, the supremacy of the secular church, and when all else failed the Inquisition (introduced into Peru in 1570 and Mexico the year after) was blatantly used, as at home, for political ends.

This vast governmental edifice rested on an equally complex local administration. Some important – and characteristic – exceptions apart, all the lands and jurisdictions that made up Spain's overseas empires were embraced within the two viceroyalties. Within these in turn there was a carefully graded hierarchy of officials, the upper ranks filled from the peninsular aristocracy, the lowest from, among others, needy or deserving old soldiers and, increasingly, from among American-born Spaniards. Non-specialists were recruited from those whose blood was of that purity which so obsessed Spain from the late 1500s – untainted, that is, by Jewish or Moorish ancestry. They were supposedly of good repute, and either known to the king from their previous services or recommended to him by influential patrons. As a rule they were employed for a brief term and then moved on to some other preferment. But the backbone of the imperial bureaucracy was a body of university graduates, usually lawyers (hence the many hostile jibes at 'two penn'orth of the law of Salamanca'), serving at the royal pleasure – which commonly meant for the whole of their working lives, when they might well be succeeded by their heirs. In Spain's great days of the late 1500s they shared a devotion to noble ideals of just and ethical rule, and recruited as they were from a small group of prestigious colleges within an equally small group of universities they were united – like that caste of Oxford graduates so influential in the British empire in the nineteenth and twentieth centuries – by intense personal, professional and institutional loyalties into a well-informed, experienced and formidable body. Throughout the Indies there were Spanish magistrates with judicial, administrative and even legislative authority. Cities and towns, the very essence of political life in the peninsula, were founded in abundance as focal points of Spanish power from which Spanish authority could be disseminated and upheld in the surrounding countryside. But their wings were soon clipped. The minutest details of their layout were regulated by royal instructions. By the imposition of royal officers, and through the sale of urban posts their councils were turned into compliant oligarchies, and their early attempts to develop municipal assemblies were thwarted by monarchs who had had their fill of restive urban communities at home.

In the immediate post-conquest years it was Spanish policy to control the vast Amerindian population through amenable Hispanized tribal chiefs. But their authority was undermined by the contempt with which they were generally treated by colonists, and their importance diminished as the indigenous population shrank, so rendering them less able to supply the labour their masters demanded. And it was now Spain's intention that the Indians, once converted to Christianity, should live in Spanish style. They were to have lands to support them, were to dwell – as many were indeed accustomed to do – in townships, and were to be subject to municipal councils composed of their own elected officials. Such a well-ordered existence would ensure their adherence to the new faith and at the same time provide the crown with an effective means of controlling its new subjects. The authority of *encomenderos* over Indians was eroded, and from the mid 1500s there was a massive extension of Spanish royal authority into the American countryside. The hinterlands of Spanish cities became districts centred on the largest Indian town they contained, in which, from 1565, there resided a Spanish magistrate, the *corregidor de Indios*. Through the Indian authorities he collected indigenous taxes and controlled indigenous labour. The Indian corporations kept the peace and ran the day-to-day affairs of their communities under the eye of the *corregidor* and the resident Spanish priest. And alongside this secular administration there was established a rough Indian replica of the organization of Christian life as understood by Spaniards. The outcome was no utopian idyll. Native civic dignitaries who failed to come up to Spanish expectations were fined, imprisoned or flogged, with the not unnatural result that reluctance to serve was widespread.

The Spaniards also endeavoured to reduce semi-sedentary and nomadic peoples to some similar pattern of life, with scattered communities forcibly 'congregated' into more compact and manageable settlements. On the frontiers, the better to control and defend their acolytes, the Franciscan missions in Texas and those of the Jesuits in California and Arizona, brought together large numbers of erstwhile nomads under the authority of what often amounted to semi-independent theocratic states. On the borders of northern Mexico and southern Chile the Spanish regime was of that brutal and tenuous nature common in such circumstances: frontier posts and a military force of native allies, Hispanized Indians and a few whites, upholding imperial authority by raiding and skirmishing and making a living by selling into slavery the indigenous peoples they captured.[3]

Restive *conquistadores* were outmanoeuvred by royal officers. Their descendants, real or alleged, lacked the ability and, with the decline of *encomienda*, the means to assert their ambitions. Subsequent discontents of American-born Spaniards were allayed by the extent to which, whatever supposed royal policies, they could in fact conduct their affairs largely as they wished. Beyond this, Spanish authority in the Americas rested, like that of any imperial power, on the acquiescence of the indigenous population, on their inability or unwillingness to rid themselves of their alien masters, and on the co-operation of many with the intruders. In Peru especially, but also in Mexico, the mass of the people were accustomed to uncomplaining obedience to their superiors. With the conquest these were replaced by Spaniards, enjoying the prestige conferred by total success. Spanish power was further strengthened by the decline of the indigenous populations and by the conversion of the survivors to Christianity, leaving them now subject to both secular and ecclesiastical authority. But more was involved than mere submission. Spain sought to ensure that the Indians had neither means nor opportunity to revolt. They were not allowed to possess European arms, own dogs, ride horses or mules or indulge in the inflammatory pleasures of wine. Nor, when in the late sixteenth century there were thought to be dangerous stirrings of ethnic consciousness, were they any longer to be ordained. Maybe, for a time, as the English reported (1572) from Mexico they were kept 'tame and civil' by their faith in the imperial administration's zeal and ability to defend them against the colonists.

Such things were not, however, left to chance. The majority of Indians were bound by law to live in fixed communities, pay tribute and discharge labour services. Opposition was brutally suppressed, with sixteen chiefs, allegedly troublemakers, fed to the dogs in Nicaragua in 1528. The church, as elsewhere, preached to the natives their duty of submission. It attempted to reconcile them to their lot through a Catholicism full of spectacles, fiestas and colourful local music, and it encouraged them to find in their tribal histories indications that their ancestors had once known Christianity. To further Spanish ends inter-tribal rivalries were exploited and indigenous allies employed to control their fellows and to siphon off goods and labour for the benefit of their masters. Following the fall of the great Amerindian empires there was a resurgence of tribalism, with chiefs or self-appointed chiefs, Christian and Hispanized, collaborating with their new overlords who rewarded them by recognizing their succession and confirming their authority. They were aided against rivals, granted coats of arms and resonant Spanish names, allowed to carry weapons, drink wine and ride horses. Their tribal lands escaped from Spanish clutches and their peoples were treated with some favour. In the *encomendero's* name compliant chiefs levied excessive amounts of labour and tribute, retaining a good part of what was raised for themselves. They obtained *encomiendas* and *haciendas*, went into business partnerships with Europeans and one way and another did remarkably well for themselves. In 1587 the English encountered one on an island off Ecuador who had all the local Indians to 'work and . . . drudge for him' in the manufacture of cordage for Spanish shipping and who, by reason of his 'pleasant habitation and great wealth', had even acquired a European wife.[4] In return, as we have seen, such figures provided their masters with troops, labour, tribute and military support.

The authority of chiefs was weakened by the Spanish creation of municipal councils. These were in turn undermined by the white invasion of indigenous townships and by the hostility of powerful colonial interests, objecting, among other things, to the cost of such measures. Nor, before long, was much expected of them. Indians came to be seen as people incapable of rational behaviour and identified (juridically in the 1640s) as *miserables* – those categories of mankind recognized in the Old Testament and by Roman lawyers as deserving compassion and succour and so inadequate that their affairs needed to be supervised by 'protectors'. The alien institutions wished on them nevertheless continued to function in some form, and indeed multiplied with councils springing up in smaller communities, even if in the end they had lost much of their original Spanish character.

For the first century at least Spanish rule in the Americas was, by contemporary standards, efficient and effective. It was exercised by some outstandingly able officials and was carefully directed and supervised by the metropolitan government. To ensure loyalty kings appointed well-tried and faithful servants, many of them veterans of the war against the Dutch in the Low Countries. To inspire honesty and efficiency they forbade (with limited success) officials to accept gifts, marry local women or in any other way lay themselves open to pressures within their jurisdictions. Imperial rule became more and more a matter of surveillance, investigation and report. There were regular inquiries into almost everything – under nearly 400 heads by 1605 – together with urgent probings of anything suspicious, from major scandals to the doings (1621) of the wives of officials in Manila. All those retiring or removed from any post had to give an account of their tenure and misdemeanours were severely punished.

The weaknesses of the system were soon proverbial. Spanish law, endeavouring to give justice in each and every particular instance, led to an obsession with minutiae. The very complexity of the problems encountered produced inconsistent solutions from different bodies, while old laws were left to run concurrently with new ones. Division of responsibility, a plethora of committees, the professional compilation of lengthy written reports and a predominance of lawyers constituted an unbeatable recipe for confusion and inaction. 'If death came from Spain' quipped the wags, 'we should all live for ever.' Added to which were the delays arising from difficulties of communication between America and Europe and within the

Indies themselves. Here the potential for inertia, evasion or worse was
infinite. Authorities could suspend the implementation of royal orders
pending appeal to the crown for reconsideration. Governors of many
outlying provinces were independent. Within the viceroyalties there was no
clear chain of command, and such was the fragmentation of responsibility
that all taxes of any importance had their own staff of collectors. Most
major officials received fees, not salaries, for the discharge of their functions,
inspiring them to impressive ingenuity in fraud and corruption – such as
opening a casino on government premises. Lesser figures had modest salaries
which they augmented by similar skills. Some ran enterprises, or set up in
business, with capital and labour extorted in one way or another. Others
simply fleeced the Indians, pocketing their tribute or seizing their goods.
And it was customary, not to say a point of honour with all, to provide
for their relatives. In remote and poor regions, where pickings were few
and candidates for office accordingly even fewer, governmental functions
had to be handed over, on a part-time basis, to such local Spaniards as
would undertake them.

Things deteriorated further still when the crown, financially desperate,
took to selling offices, and on such a scale that by 1700 almost all, other
than the two viceroyalties, had been auctioned off. The supreme test of
suitability was wealth. Many posts became hereditary possessions, and
many passed to American-born Spaniards, or to those from the peninsula
with strong local connections and important local interests to further. Thus
in practice royal policy was tempered to creole will and its resultant inof-
fensiveness ensured the longevity of Spanish rule. But the peninsular
government was more than a spectator of events outside its control. Its
authority was implemented even as in the sixteenth century experts forecast
its imminent collapse.[5] The Spanish presence in the Americas was
triumphantly proclaimed by the construction of imposing ecclesiastical and
secular buildings. Much of the indigenous population was converted to
some form of Christianity. The wilder ambitions of the settlers – like
Gonzalo Pizarro's momentary hopes of an independent monarchy – were
restrained. The wealth of the Americas was at the disposal of the Spanish
crown and its European rivals were excluded from the mainland of the
Spanish Indies.

Portuguese imperial government, cruder in pattern and even feebler in
authority, evolved in roughly the same way. Where, as in the islands of
the West African littoral or Brazil, the initial prospects were of loss rather
than profit, the burden of empire was left to those willing to shoulder it.
Where, however, as in West Africa and Asia, wealth in abundance was at
stake, royal authority was swiftly asserted and royal monopolies quickly
created, even if only to be farmed out. The rich trades of West Africa were
conducted through a limited number of local Portuguese trading posts and
a specially created royal department in the mother country. More

ambitiously still, the *Casa da India* was empowered in 1505–6 to handle the entire commerce and navigation between Portugal and Asia, just as the *Casa de la Contratacíon* dealt with that between Seville and the Americas.[6] Like its Spanish counterpart the India House developed an important maritime jurisdiction, kept a cartographical record of the geographical discoveries and supervised the preparation of the ships – some royal, some private under royal permit – sailing to and from Asia. These, fewer in number but larger in size than their Spanish equivalents in the Atlantic – the biggest, at 2000 tonnes the leviathans of their time – worked what long remained the most arduous of all oceanic passages in a rhythm determined by the seasonal pattern of the Asian monsoons. They departed annually in flotillas of no more than five or six. By the hard days of the seventeenth century they were down to two or three and in many years there were no sailings at all. As the dangers from enemy attack increased they were escorted, if suitable men-of-war could be found, along the most vulnerable parts of their route. And as with Spain's American trade they covered one leg of the journey part empty, since outward bound they carried mainly bullion, of low bulk but great value. They returned, however – such as survived – grossly overloaded with whatever riches could be crammed into them.

Since Portugal overthrew no vast realms, and since to begin with its prime concern was trade not settlement, the growth of an imperial administration was slower than in Spain's empire and indeed its pattern owed much to Spanish influence during the period (1580–1640) in which the kingdom was under Habsburg rule. There was a secretary for imperial affairs from 1568, councils to deal with economic and ecclesiastical matters and from 1604 a Council of India (later the Council of Overseas Affairs) responsible for the bulk of the empire. Like that of Spain the Portuguese imperial church was under the king's absolute control, committed, not to say abandoned, to his care by the papacy in a series of privileges dating from the mid fifteenth century. By 1550 he could nominate to all bishoprics – extending from Brazil to China – enjoyed the patronage of all livings, and through his officers administered taxes, collected tithes and supervised the missions.

In Asia Portugal's most important possessions were entrusted to patrician captains, aided by a variety of fiscal, administrative and legal officials, while there were royal commercial agents in the many places through which the major trades were conducted. After 1505 supreme authority was delegated to a governor-general and soon to a viceroy, usually aristocrats from the royal entourage, serving for three years – though many did more and several lasted less. They had their own exchequer, judiciary, chancery and council based in the imperial capital at Goa. But their powers, like those of Spanish grandees in Mexico and Peru, were far from absolute. They were engaged in a voluminous correspondence with Lisbon. Officers and captains in Asian posts thousands of kilometres away from Goa behaved, like the commanders of expeditions to distant parts, much as they liked. In the imperial capital the views of the viceregal Council of State, delivered in the lengthy signed depositions of its members, weighed heavily with the royal representative. Like all colonists, Portuguese settlers in the East were resolute in opposing policies they saw as endangering their chances of making money and equally resolute in their unwillingness to see their wealth taken for the alleged good of the state. The viceroy had no obligation to heed the views of his compatriots, but prudence dictated that he should, particularly if he hoped for ever-more urgently needed financial aid. Hence in especially desperate moments he had to consult the querulous Goan *fidalgos* (gentry) and the rich and vociferous Catholic church. He also had to contend with the various municipal councils which were either established with royal permission, or grew up and were licenced by the crown, in most large Portuguese settlements in the East. No more than their counterparts in Brazil or the Spanish Indies were these democratic multi-racial assemblies. They were made up of whites and *mestiços*[7] elected by whites and *mestiços*. Yet though smaller than most of their Spanish equivalents they were commonly more independently minded, if for no better reason than that they were generally accustomed to looking after themselves – they were, for example, responsible for local defence.[8]

In the East the Portuguese made no attempts to reorganize the societies and economies they encountered, but adapted them as best they could to their own needs, accepting, whatever the Church might say, the continued presence of non-Christians within their possessions for the financial and commercial benefit they brought. In Goa and Malacca in the early years, and subsequently elsewhere, they made influential Hindus, Muslims and others responsible for the affairs of their co-religionaries within the area of Portuguese jurisdiction. There were no such measures as those of the Spaniards – or even the English on the subcontinent – to bring local peoples under European forms of government.[9] The indigenous populations were not represented, nor were their opinions formally sought. But as the State of India tottered into impotence and insolvency, attention, even deference, was accorded to the views of Hindu or Parsee tycoons.[10]

Elsewhere the crown's authority was asserted with varying degrees of success. There were white royal officers in the African possessions, but many posts in the continent, both ecclesiastical and secular, were held – as also in the tropical Atlantic islands – by Christian Africans or mulattos, since in climates so lethal they were commonly the only candidates. Brazil, whose attractions at first seemed so few, was early handed over to *donatorios*.[11] They undertook to colonize and exploit their holdings and were in exchange granted hereditary and more or less absolute authority, being empowered among other things to found towns and enslave the indigenous populations. The virtual failure of these measures, the introduction of sugar and the subsequent rapid growth in the country's wealth and importance brought a change of policy. A royal governor-general was appointed in 1548. The arrival of the Jesuits the following year, and of other missionary Orders later, further strengthened the crown's authority. As in the Spanish Indies the fathers opposed the designs of the colonists on the Amerindians, and the Jesuits, who worked closely with the monarchy, provided schools in all the important coastal towns. There was much experiment as to how Brazil's vast and now valuable territory was to be controlled and defended. Maranhão was made a separate state in 1621, reunited with the rest of the country in 1652 and then reseparated. São Paulo largely went its own way until the 1700s. The office of viceroy was briefly introduced in 1640 and re-established in 1663. Central administrations grew up in Bahia and Maranhão and in the old captaincies there were, with their supporting administrations, subordinate governors-general, in practice enjoying a great measure of independence. This fragmentation of authority reflected the economy and society of Brazil, in which the main centres of wealth and population (Bahia, Pernambuco, Rio de Janeiro) were hundreds of kilo-metres apart and, given the means of communication of the times, more easily in contact with Lisbon than with one another. Such a state of affairs in a country so rich and potentially powerful suited the Portuguese crown. It encouraged local governors to deal directly with the royal capital. It prevented, as did the Spanish ruling house, representatives of colonial towns and cities from meeting in a general assembly, and it further damped the growth of a sense of colonial identity by refusing titles to Brazilians and leaving the country without any universities.

The highest posts in the Brazilian colonial government were, as in the Spanish empire, the preserve of the metropolitan aristocracy, though those appointed were, unlike their Spanish counterparts, usually experienced soldiers, reflecting ever-pressing problems of defence. Lesser offices simi-larly passed to local whites, and as in Spanish America and the English Atlantic colonies, the closely interrelated magnates of this class came, through their wealth, to exert an increasing influence on the government, ensuring their interests were well served. Nowhere was this more apparent than in the country's towns and cities. Like those of the Spaniards in the Indies these were founded to defend and disseminate the authority of the colonizing power. For its size Brazil had relatively few – a mere thirty-seven by 1650 – and these, like the captaincies, in closer contact with Lisbon than with each other. A handful of the seaports were, like Bahia, with its fine buildings and government offices, of some grandeur. The rest were riverine or coastal harbours. But almost everywhere their councils were, as in the towns of the Spanish Indies, converted into well-heeled obligarchies. Power was in the hands of rich planters and (later) merchants and cattle barons who dominated their districts and forcibly made their views known, even though in the later 1600s towns were under pressure from Lisbon. These magnates did their best to exclude the middle classes – weaker than those of the Spanish Indies – from the vote and from office, and had no difficulty in shutting out artisans.

Despite its obvious shortcomings this colonial administration secured considerable wealth for the mother country first from Africa and Asia and subsequently from Brazil, and enabled it, in the face of all probability, long to hold on to possessions scattered across the world. A tenuous authority over an empire far more geographically dispersed – chiefly along oceanic littorals – than that of Spain neither permitted nor demanded forms of government as elaborate as those of the Spanish Indies. In so far as there was a pattern it was one of military control, lacking, however, most of the resources for its effective implementation. There was no Portuguese equivalent to the complex legal machinery of the Spanish possessions, though in Brazil there emerged with the passage of time an important group of salaried (and mostly Portuguese) judges. Brazil's commerce with Europe was for long less closely controlled than was that of the Americas with Spain. Portugal's empire had no such provision for regular investigation and inspection as that of Spain, while the mother country, weaker in every way than its neighbour, was unable to produce anything approaching that body of dedicated officials who for a time served the Habsburgs. Able and outstanding individuals there certainly were. But these were few in relation to the country's commitments and became fewer as offices were, as in Spain, freely sold or granted as favours, so that often a queue of would-be occupants was waiting none too patiently for the death of the incumbent. In Asia, with its wealth and infinity of opportunities, it was agreed from the start by reformers and observers that the supposed servants of the crown were engaged in uninhibited self-enrichment at the expense of their royal master. But the very degree to which power was in local hands or riches flowed into private pockets explains the willingness of the colonies to accept a feeble royal authority and their determination, as in Brazil's struggle against the Dutch, to defend themselves.

The urge, furthermore, of a poor people for private gain, the obvious need of a tiny country for assistance and its simultaneous dealings with so many and diverse societies – primitive Amerindians in the West, great states and civilizations in Asia – early developed among many Portuguese the understanding that empire was heavily dependent on local goodwill or support. To the divinely appointed royal mission to ensure the salvation of souls by the spread of Christianity there was added the more mundane consideration that converted natives would know their duty to serve their superiors. Indigenous converts everywhere played an important role in establishing and maintaining Portugal's authority, while in Brazil Portuguese influence was further spread by the missions' resettlement of whole peoples in communities under their supervision. And to an even greater extent that most empire builders the Portuguese had to take such allies as offered, with their authority extended and preserved by the adept manipulation of local disputes and the pragmatic employment of indigenous assistance.[12]

In Holland, despite the radically different nature of its society, matters were ordered in much the same way. The Republic was in the sixteenth and seventeenth centuries Europe's major shipowning and commercial power, and by the early 1600s possessed the continent's most advanced economy.[13] Its merchants initially penetrated to the wider world to obtain goods and exploit opportunities denied them by Spanish policy, and its government saw attacks on the colonial commerce and possessions of the Hispano-Portuguese empire as a profitable way of deflecting Iberian energies away from the war for independence in the Low Countries. All this was to be achieved not by the state itself, nor by individuals or consortia, but by chartered joint-stock companies in which, however, state authority was to all intents paramount.[14] At the time of their foundation neither the East India Company (1602) nor the West India Company (1621) controlled any territory. The mercantile oligarchs who dominated the companies, and who were so influential in the government of the loosely federated United Provinces, were concerned with profit not conquest. The acquisition of colonies was regarded not only as expensive and irrelevant, but as dangerous. Such possessions might offer scope for the house of Orange, the Republic's only major aristocratic family, to acquire power and glory, thereby inflaming its ambitions to rule the Dutch state.

Such doubts, though never stilled, were not to prevail and empire was steadily amassed by the usual mixture of force and the manipulation of native rivalries. Nor was it limited to Asia, where it could at least be justified as the necessary defence of vital commercial interests. By the late seventeenth century the VOC was not only exacting tribute from local peoples in South Africa, but, as their land passed into Dutch hands, exercising sovereignty by regulating the succession of tribal chiefs. Its clients, like those of the Spaniards in the Indies, were invested with symbols of office and given some such grand name as Hercules or Hannibal. Lands directly subject to the companies were ruled in equally familiar ways. The colony in Taiwan, while it lasted, had a governor, a council and a judiciary. Possessions in the East as a whole were subject to a governor-general who lived in opulent viceregal style in the cosmopolitan and bibulous capital at Batavia, aided by a council and a subordinate hierarchy of lesser officials. His rule was authoritarian, not to say absolute, with the city's 'free burghers' denied, on Company orders, any elected representation.[15] The governor-general controlled that army of clerks and book-keepers an empire of commerce demanded and such small groups of colonists as VOC policies permitted. The heads of the various Asian factories, commanders of forts and residents at the courts of local rulers bound to the Company by treaty were all supposedly under his authority. There was a central judiciary in Batavia and some effort was made, particularly in financial matters, to regulate the behaviour of the Company's officers, with specially appointed functionaries, responsible to the VOC directors themselves, sent out from Holland to investigate (without much success) their misdeeds in the late 1600s. The selection and recruitment of the Company's servants destined for Asia left, as we have seen, much to be desired. There was little incentive for the able and ambitious to leave the prosperous and tolerant Netherlands. There was even less to attract them to the East. The Republic cherished no such aspirations to rule and convert the indigenous masses as drew idealists and visionaries to the service of the Iberian crowns. The VOC's policies offered little for those of more mundane inclinations. Like the West India Company in North America it monopolized – at least in theory – the most lucrative opportunities, and given the modest amounts of territory it controlled there was small prospect of land and less of its successful exploitation in the face of vigorous indigenous competition. So the Company had to recruit who it could where it could. Many in its employment were aliens; many were refugees from misfortune or misdemeanour; and many, with the passage of time, were clients or relatives - usually the least able – of influential investors and directors.

No more than other Protestants were the Dutch greatly concerned to spread their faith in the wider world. Nevertheless the despatch of Calvinist ministers to the lands under its jurisdiction was as closely regulated by the VOC as were the doings of the Catholic missions by the Iberian monarchies. But these *predikants*, such few as they were – with only five a year sent out on average – were usually chosen less for their zeal and piety than for their willingness to accept the Company's authority, and were to minister to the spiritual needs of its servants. However, like other Europeans established among unconquered and powerful civilizations, and without the backing of substantial white settlement, the VOC accepted that the imposition and exercise of its authority was in part dependent on the co-operation of local peoples. Hence the Chinese were involved in the government of Taiwan, Java was administered through native 'regents' and in Batavia, whatever the godly might say, Company rule was remarkably tolerant. The Chinese, valued as craftsmen, building contractors and commercial intermediaries were particularly favoured, though needless to say taxed as well. In the early seventeenth century the so-called 'Captain of the Chinese' and another amenable entrepreneur farmed the various revenues exacted from their compatriots. A joint Dutch–Chinese body was set up to handle Chinese testamentary problems and the Chinese were even encouraged to serve on the municipal council.[16] And though the VOC made little effort to bolster its rule with the pious acquiescence of indigenous converts it made extensive use, in the absence of any alternative, of Catholic Portuguese *mestiços* and Portuguese-speaking native Christians, usually former slaves. These, known as *Mardijkers* were rejected by Asian society and turned to the Dutch conquerors of the Portuguese *Estado*, by whom they were employed as wage labourers, artisans, clerks and soldiers in much the same way that American *mestizos* served the Spaniards or that mulattos were in general such fervent supporters of whites. In Batavia they were gradually incorporated into the Dutch Reformed Church, but prudently allowed to have their own clergy and to conduct their services in the Portuguese they continued to speak.[17]

In the short-lived Brazilian colony of the West India Company an aristocratic governor was briefly employed (1637) until his enlightened policies and growing powers led to his dismissal (1644) through the influence of zealous Calvinists and convinced republicans. The Atlantic empire was for a time adequately run by a complex interlocking group of councils, and after the collapse of the Brazilian venture its surviving fragments – most notably the entrepôt of Curaçao – were administered with that same pragmatic tolerance as flourished in Batavia. In regions less appealing, where climate, resources and opportunities were such as to attract few settlers, and where the indigenous inhabitants were difficult to control and exploit, there was experiment in delegating responsibility to entrepreneurs in the well-tried Portuguese style. The settlements on the 'Wild Coast' of South America survived, but not that in the North. Here the initial puny foothold (the future New York) was passed, after the failure of various other schemes, to the newly-founded West India Company. But this had no more success and in 1629 farmed out holdings to 'patroons' who in exchange for the grant of enormous powers were, like Brazilian *donatorios*, to settle and exploit them. They received in effect outright possession of great tracts of land, together with the monopoly of justice over their tenants. Even so, there was no significant flow of settlers and in 1635 the Company had to resume direct responsibility itself. Its policies, however, primarily designed to safeguard its monopoly of the fur trade, offered would-be colonists very little beyond a wealth of advice and instruction. They were to have no dealings in furs and were forbidden to engage in mining or to develop any 'handicrafts upon which trade is dependent'. Nor were they permitted, until outbreaks of discontent, to have any say in the manner in which the colony was ruled by its military governors. Underpopulated, economically and politically feeble, it succumbed to its English neighbours in 1664.[18]

French colonial government followed the familiar pattern of initial delegation of responsibility to entrepreneurs. But then, under the resurgent and ambitious monarchy of the later seventeenth century the country's minuscule empire, territorially insignificant though it may have been, was subject to a control of a minuteness and purposefulness unequalled since the great days of imperial Spain. There were hints of what lay in store even in the generally inauspicious beginnings of French expansion. In the 1620s, as part of a design to make France a major maritime and naval power, an expedition backed by financial associates of the king's chief minister, Richelieu, and commanded by seasoned privateers, was launched against St Kitts

(St Christophe) in the Caribbean. The various French possessions in the West Indies were subsequently turned over (1635) to the Company of the American Islands which, in exchange for providing settlers, was to hold them virtually untrammelled as fiefs of the crown. But troubles soon arose, not least when attempts were made to tax the colonists, and by 1650 the Company had foundered. With remarkable abandon – at a time when the domestic problems of the mother country were pressing – the islands were then sold to their governors who, as in Martinique, set up more or less independent principalities which they ruled as absolutely as they could with the aid of their relatives and to the accompaniment of further discord over taxation. In an area where Dutch and English influence and prosperity were rapidly growing such a spectacle was an affront to the pretensions of the French monarchy. In 1664 the proprietors were bought out and the islands assigned to the newly created West India Company. Based on the influential Dutch model this was one of the great corporations through which Louis XIV's minister of commerce, Colbert, proposed to increase the wealth – mainly at the expense of Holland – and enhance the prestige of his master.

All the colonists, subjects of a Catholic and absolutist king, were to be Catholics and were to be ruled with a firm hand 'like a good father would his children'. Trade was to be conducted only with the Company's agents: 'the exclusion of all commerce with foreigners is to be ensured everywhere' declared Colbert. But despite the attempted emulation of what seemed best in Dutch and Spanish practice the expected profits never materialized. The settlers, finding it hard enough to make a living, refused to contribute to the costs of empire. The Company was unable to raise the necessary capital, and in 1674 the islands reverted to the crown to be subjected to a regime as absolute as the conditions of the time allowed. They were governed, with no concessions to colonial participation, by members of the royal council, or, as their commercial and strategic importance grew, by naval officers. Private merchants were allowed to trade, as in the English possessions, but the Dutch were in similar fashion excluded. Since, in the monarch's view, colonies were further manifestations of his power and glory a consciousness of imperial unity was, to a greater degree than in any other empire, deliberately fostered, with Louis decreeing (1705) that the richer inhabitants of Martinique should be educated in the mother country to allow them to know something of the kingdom of which they were a part.

Much the same happened in Canada where, despite a promising start in the early sixteenth century, little or nothing was subsequently achieved, largely through some fifty years of civil war in France itself and the royal house's more pressing interests in Europe. Finally in 1627 there was established the Company of New France, again emulating Dutch practice. By royal grant it was to exercise, as did the great companies of the Low Countries, enormous powers. Its jurisdiction stretched from Florida to the

Arctic Circle and from Newfoundland to the Great Lakes. Apart from the offshore fisheries it was to have a fifteen-year monopoly of all Canadian trade, during which period it was to settle 4000 French Catholic families in the country. But though, like other governments, the crown might delegate responsibility, it nevertheless laid down in great detail the policies to be pursued. Territorial lordships were to be created for men of suitable wealth and standing. Hence the land along the banks of the St Lawrence was divided into strips running back from the river, and those upon whom the resultant holdings were bestowed had to render homage to the royal representative and settle them with their own tenants. Admirable though such schemes might be in their logic and in their neat and simplified re-creation of the society of the mother coutry in an alien land, they were more or less pointless in an area where wealth came not from agriculture, but from fishing, trapping and trading. Even in 1663 there were still no more than a hundred lordships and most of these without subtenants. Such difficulties and the consequent financial troubles, led, as in the Caribbean, to an interregnum in which opportunities were seized by enterprising individuals and power briefly exercised, as in 1645, by something like representative assemblies.[19]

The colony subsequently came (1664) under the jurisdiction of the West India Company and eventually under that of the crown. But its problems remained. It failed to attract sufficient settlers, and of those that came many of the most enterprising took to living as semi-nomadic and semi-Indian hunters and trappers. The Catholic church, which it was well understood could be a powerful tool to discipline the unruly – inculcating the virtues of obedience, excommunicating restive settlers – remained feeble. Nowhere did the French encounter Amerindian peoples they could conquer and exploit in the way the Spaniards had done in much of the south, though they bolstered their authority by playing on inter-tribal rivalries. Nor, despite the heroic efforts of the Catholic missions – which after 1636 meant the Jesuits – did they manage to convert many of those pithily described as 'savages' into loyal subjects. Equally fundamentally there was no vulnerable indigenous economy for the French to dominate. On the contrary, since furs were the most valuable commodity the land produced, they were in the position of being the clients of the tribes who controlled, to their own benefit, the flow of these precious goods towards the French trading posts.

Nevertheless from the late seventeenth century France's empire attracted the ever closer attention of the metropolitan government. The West Indian islands prospered from plunder and commerce. Grand strategic vistas were revealed in Canada. Imperial success was seen as the necessary adjunct of monarchical glory. From 1678 all colonial possessions were ruled by military governors appointed by the crown and – Canada in particular – were capable of raising armed forces whose discipline and efficiency were in marked contrast to the behaviour of such bodies as the fractious and disorderly militia of New England. Governors were aided, not to say supervised, by civilian colleagues (those *intendants* of such importance in the mother country) who handled financial and economic affairs. Nominated councils, which also served as courts of appeal, were established to assist them. Colonies were not, unlike those of Portugal and England, to be dumping grounds for undesirables, but were to be populated, as the Spaniards had once planned for the Americas, by virtuous and hard-working Catholics and especially, in good classical style, by old soldiers from the mother country. Such things, like the supposed economic subjection of the colonies to the metropolitan state, were more easily planned than achieved. Convicts had to be sent to the West Indies. The French colonial church acquired nothing of the wealth and power of those of the Iberians. The governors' councils were soon, like similar bodies elsewhere, dominated by cliques of rich, influential and interrelated colonial families, regarded with awe by their less fortunate compatriots and with disfavour by the royal *intendants*.

But the most varied and remarkable pattern of colonial government was that which emerged in England's belatedly acquired overseas possessions. True, for a time in the late sixteenth and early seventeenth centuries there were Englishmen who envisaged their sovereigns as overlords of such lands. Francis Drake, in the course of his circumnavigation, made a Californian chieftain a royal vassal. A little later the governor of Virginia attempted to do the same with the Algonkian leader Powhattan, only to have a cape and a pair of old shoes bestowed on him in return. But such charades apart, and notwithstanding much erudite encouragement, English rulers before the civil wars, beset with problems enough at home, generally took little interest in colonies. Most of those so earnestly advocated had few obvious attractions – certainly no precious metals – and were likely to provoke conflict with Spain, with whom both the early Tudors and the first Stuarts aspired to live in amity. Hence, in a well-established tradition, colonization was left to those who, under royal licence, were willing to pursue it. Such indeed was the crown's indifference that, as with no other European state, some of the country's first successful overseas settlements sprang from the desire of a number of its subjects to escape from what they considered an oppressive regime which prevented them from conducting their lives and organizing their worship according to their beliefs. The first New England colonies were licensed either directly, or – as with the Pilgrim Fathers – indirectly by the king. Thereafter, for some half century, they more or less did as they liked, governing themselves in ways unparalleled elsewhere in the colonial world. The settlers came from a country in which representative assemblies were more vociferous and effective than in Iberia or France. They formed initially, unlike the inhabitants of the Dutch New Netherlands, a cohesive society and they were accustomed to regulating their affairs, according to their vehemently held tenets, in regularly convened gatherings.

So in Plymouth the Pilgrims established a self-governing theocracy in which the franchise was confined to church members. Similarly in Massachusetts the adult males of the congregations chose their clergy; the militia proposed to elect its officers; and a body of church members elected a governor who, together with a legislature, behaved as though sovereign.

For a time things were not all that different in Virginia. Originally the responsibility of a company the colony became, when this collapsed (1624), a crown possession. All the same it lead a life much of its own. The first Stuarts were well disposed towards Catholicism and enmeshed in domestic difficulties. The colony had strong Puritan leanings, though no desire to be separated from the Church of England. It was initially ruled by a governor and council, but in 1619 there appeared an assembly representing the interests of the local freemen. Very soon, with the vote restricted to freeholders and power in the hands of the biggest landowners, this body came to regard itself as at the least another House of Commons, enjoying fiscal and legislative authority. Like viceroys in the Spanish Indies, governors injudicious in the discharge of their office came to grief, with one expelled in 1635 for being too sympathetic to the Indians.

In theory such settlements were royal dominions under the supervision of the king and his Privy Council. Among the advisers of Charles I there were some thoughts, during the years of his personal rule (1629–40), that the royal authority should be exerted, particularly over the tiresome New England. But with the onset of the civil wars nothing was done. Charters were granted to new proprietary colonies like Maryland (1632) and Maine (1639), while Virginia and Massachusetts behaved as though independent. The Republic was more purposeful. Commissioners were appointed to investigate the plantations. Colonies, it was declared, 'are and ought to be subordinate to and dependent on' the mother country, and there was talk of bringing 'a more certaine civill and uniforme way of government' to North America, where natural restiveness was aggravated by the arrival of large numbers of political and religious extremists deported by the Cromwellian regime.[20] With the Navigation Act of 1651 the first considerable step was taken towards regulating, as the Iberian monarchies attempted to do, the commercial activities of the overseas dependencies. Barbados and Virginia were compelled to accept the authority of the new government, and Cromwell's will was enforced in Maryland by his pragmatic support of the proprietor against the local Puritans. Jamaica was conquered (1655) as part of a neo-Elizabethan grand strategy, settled with troops and the surplus population of the neighbouring colonies and envisaged as the cornerstone of a Caribbean policy of naval and military onslaughts against the empire of Spain.[21]

The collapse of the Protectorate and the restoration of the Stuarts (1660) brought renewed disruption of metropolitan authority and, eventually, renewed colonial expansion. Some of these settlements were, like New

York, conquests. Some were to check Dutch economic hegemony, some to forestall European rivals, and almost all to reward the dynasty's supporters or creditors. Hence a further wave of proprietary foundations, whose owners, in return for undertaking the colonization and exploitation of their concessions, were endowed with those same vast powers as were delegated to entrepreneurs elsewhere. They were to be 'lords and governors' of their domains. Few, however, other than the Baltimores, cared to visit such outlandish places, and appointed deputies. These ruled with the aid of nominated councils selected from among local notables. They supervised forms of subordinate government modelled, as in other colonies, on those of the mother country, and comprising counties, parishes, sheriffs, constables and so forth. Nevertheless settlers could be granted – as in Carolina, New Jersey and Pennsylvania – freedom of conscience, extensive political rights and the chance to participate more effectively in the conduct of affairs than they had at home. And sooner or later there emerged almost everywhere, in crown and proprietary colonies alike, and on a scale and to a degree unequalled in any other empire, representative assemblies. Their members were elected on franchises restricted either by requirements of wealth, or, as in New Haven and Massachusetts (until 1692) religion. Like comparable institutions elsewhere they came to be dominated by rich oligarchs and, without any equivalent restraints, and consciously emulating the practice and behaviour of the English parliament, arrogated to themselves whatever powers they could and dealt as they saw fit with governors.[22]

Faced with well-intrenched interests the restored monarchy was in no position to assert its authority overseas with that swift efficacy earlier displayed by the Spanish kings. In the Puritan colonies, which, as royal officials claimed, 'took more power than was ever given or intended them', and where there was little prospect of anything beyond fruitless altercation, Charles II left matters as they were for the time being. But the rich Caribbean sugar islands and prosperous Virginia – whose tobacco alone generated sufficient customs revenues to keep the king independent of Parliament – were all brought, in familiar imperial ways and style, under direct royal control. It was established that governors were appointed and dismissed at the monarch's will. Barbados and the Leeward Islands were so effectively handled that they voted the king taxes on the value of sugar exports. After a struggle and the rule of a succession of old Cromwellian soldiers, Jamaica was similarly tamed. The revolt of 1675–6 in Virginia allowed the reassertion of royal authority, aided by fears of Indian attack and the pursuit, by local magnates, of royal preferment.[23] And at the end of his reign Charles, triumphant at home, took equally forceful measures to bring New England – its loyalty suspect, its maritime activities an affront to king and metropolitan merchants alike – to heel. New Hampshire was hived off to weaken it (1679) and in 1684 its charter was declared forfeit. Under James II

(1685–8) the pace quickened. The customs revenues now accruing from sugar and tobacco were a major element in the royal finances. The king was an experienced fighting man, absolutist by inclination, and the defence of the Atlantic possessions pressing. Military dispositions were rationalized. The revocation of all proprietary charters – derogatory to the royal authority – was mooted and formidable disciplinarians were installed as governors (like the Duke of Albemarle in Jamaica), not least to ensure that taxation was increased. Most ambitiously, a Dominion of New England was projected, embracing the ethnically, religiously and socially incompatible Massachusetts, Rhode Island, Plymouth, Connecticut, New Hampshire, New Jersey and New York. Worse still, it was to be ruled, in the hated style of France and Spain, by a royally appointed governor and council, untrammelled by any representative gatherings.

The overthrow of the king put an end to such schemes, but not before the doings of his lieutenants had alienated powerful factions and provoked revolts.[24] His immediate successors, with the fate of James as a warning, had little time or inclination for such projects, whatever the views of some of their advisers. Their energies were directed to the great wars against France in Europe and the New World. Moreover, after 1688 Parliament – an obstacle to plans of this order – loomed large and aspired to loom larger in colonial affairs, while the rise and fall of ministries brought shifts in policy.

In the aftermath of 1688 some proprietary colonies – among them Pennsylvania, Maryland and (later) New Jersey and Carolina – came into royal hands. But Pennsylvania and Maryland were eventually returned to their owners and the representative assembly of Massachusetts was restored by royal charter. But, as this very fact demonstrated, there was by 1700 a recognizable English empire, even if in Asia, West Africa and northern Canada such posts and possessions as had been acquired were the responsibility of private companies.[25] Royal authority had been extended in part, particularly under Charles II, by adept political manoeuvre. Offices and titles were judiciously distributed. Friction between various local groups was dexterously exploited, with opportunities seized by able royal officers – usually soldiers and often veterans of the civil wars experienced in bending the wills of the restive. Nor of course were such initiatives necessarily opposed. Colonies, however ruggedly independent, required some arbiter in their disputes. Thoughts of home rule were tempered, as in Barbados, by awareness of the need for help against the ever-present threat of slave revolt. As elsewhere there were colonists who, seeking official ratification of their pre-eminence, turned to the mother country for titles and honours and sent their offspring there to acquire those skills, graces and connections that would distance them from the vulgar mass at home. As French pressure increased the settlements assumed, like most other colonies, that the parent state would furnish them with arms and spring to their defence. Under

William III (1689–1702) North America accepted the appointment of an overall governor and military commander so strenuously opposed in 1688 and the general drift of colonial policy reflected the wishes of the metropolitan government.

No doubt the imperial regime of the seventeenth century left much to be desired. Other than in the old Cromwellian outpost of Jamaica the overseas empire lacked any effective fighting force, and what troops it had in the West Indies were as much intended to subdue the black slaves as to confront an enemy. It possessed no such comprehensive system of law courts and tribunals as the Spanish government had introduced into the Indies. Lawyers were anathema to devout Puritans – to whom the Old Testament offered all the guidance they needed – and Quakers, while in Virginia untrained clerks simplified English procedures as best they could by reference to a few elementary legal handbooks. There was no equivalent to the Catholic missionary Orders and that elaborate ecclesiastical administration which reinforced secular authority in the Iberian empires. Nor, as in other colonies – apart from those of the Dutch – were settlers and mother country united in a common faith. Many English colonies had been founded with the express intention of avoiding the persecution suffered at home. They came in time, as did the mother country, to house a diversity of religious belief. Some, like Quaker Pennsylvania, were tolerant from the start. Some became so, like the projected Catholic refuge of Maryland, and some had tolerance thrust on them, as did (1692) the formerly theocratic Massachusetts.

Even by the standards of the time the administration of the English colonies was rudimentary. Their governors were occasionally aristocrats, frequently soldiers and sometimes influential locals. They were, on the whole, less professional than their French counterparts and of less elevated social origins than Iberian viceroys. They lived, as the surviving official residence at Williamsburg (Virginia) shows, in far more modest style than their equivalents elsewhere, just as they received far less official correspondence. Other than in the proprietary colonies they were appointed – after the usual interplay of influence and patronage – by the king, from whom they received their commissions and instructions which over the years became increasingly comprehensive. Potentially they could exercise considerable power. They could prorogue, recall and dissolve the local assembly. They had direct control of the nascent judiciary, and they enjoyed a patronage so rich and rewarding that the office was contested by candidates local and metropolitan. Much of their energy, however, was devoted to attempting to secure payment of their salary from their particular territory and to dealing with its representative assembly.

For the discharge of their office governors had the assistance of no more than a skeletal bureaucracy. As elsewhere merit was of decreasing importance in appointment to the principal posts. They were not, nevertheless, openly sold, as in the Iberian empires, but distributed by patronage, with the fortunate recipients taking their reward in fees. Many of those appointed never set foot in the colony in question, let alone discharged the office in person. Instead they leased it to a deputy on a profit-sharing basis, which commonly meant it was occupied by a local politician opposed to the intentions of the government in England, but whose inefficiency or worse was tolerated by compatriots as a safeguard against the troublesome intrusion of some over-zealous stranger. And so, as in other empires, colonial wealth and influence ensured that the impact of distasteful metropolitan policies – either ignored or suitably modified – was lessened. Nor did England have any such machinery as Spain for the regular investigation and general supervision of colonial affairs, and apart from the views of some of Cromwell's intimates and those of a 'colonial interest' under Charles II, was imbued with little sense of imperial mission.[26] Various committees of the Privy Council handled colonial problems under the restored monarchy, and were at times assiduous in collecting information. Eventually, in 1696, with the Commons pressing to deal with such matters themselves, William III set up the Board of Trade and Plantations. Its members were civil servants and royal councillors, given the responsibility of drafting commissions and instructions for governors and submitting opinions on topics of moment. But though the Board elicited, and was responsive to the views of interested parties, its knowledge of colonial affairs was sketchy, and with its authority limited to advising the king in council it was not held in great esteem.

Thus even at the beginning of the eighteenth century the authority of English monarchs in the New World was more fragile than that of their fellow sovereigns overseas. They dealt, through a rudimentary administration which lacked any transatlantic focus, with an assortment of small, cantankerous, independently minded and often impressively rich settlements, all in direct contact with the mother country. At the height of the French wars there were allegations that anarchy prevailed in some of the proprietary colonies on the American mainland. The government's economic polices were reported to be widely disregarded, royal officials were obstructed and most colonies were resolute in their refusal to contribute to the burden of defence, just as many were equally resolute, like settlements elsewhere, in trading with whom they wished, including the enemy. Elected assemblies in the West Indies assiduously undermined the powers of their governors and came to control finances and appointments to local posts. Troops went unpaid, as did unpopular officals who in Jamaica were impeached.[27] Royal authority was openly flouted, whether by colonial breach of the Royal African Company's supposed monopoly of the provision of black slaves or by Antigua's refusal (1710) to participate in an inquiry into the murder of its governor. Massachusetts indeed received a royal charter in 1692, but this restored immense powers to its elected assembly. It was quickly established that governors not to the colony's liking would be recalled, that the office ought to be held by members of influential local families and that no funds would be voted until grievances had been redressed.

Yet England, at this very time moving to economic and maritime hegemony in the Old World, was far from impotent. Its authority was accepted, within bounds, alike by Jamaican oligarchs and the wealthy New England establishment which agreed to liberty of conscience at the insistence of the mother country and was in any case happier to be dealing with monarchs now so manifestly Protestant. The parent state exerted steady pressure to establish the Church of England in its transatlantic dependencies, where Anglicanism became the official faith. London devised, and in some measure enforced, a commercial policy defined in a series of Navigation Acts. That of 1651 restricted colonial imports to English or colonial ships. This was revived and extended in 1660, with the added stipulation that colonial tobacco, sugar and some other products were to be exported only to the mother country or another English colony. Three years later there were attempts to ensure that all European goods destined for the colonies should pass through England.

No more than the ambitious schemes of the Iberian and French monarchies could such measures be fully implemented. Nevertheless by the end of the seventeenth century colonial governors were under oath to enforce the Acts, royal customs officials were established in the colonies and obstructive local legislation had been nullified. Violations, moreover, were dealt with by royal tribunals, with the maritime jurisdiction of the High Court of Admiralty extended to the colonies by the establishment there of vice-admiralty courts.[28] Settlements made, however reluctantly, increasing contributions to defence and a growing volume of tax revenue flowed to the central government. Courts of equitable jurisdiction were established, royal governors were encouraged to assert their prerogative power over developing colonial law courts and were made vice-admirals of their respective territories. More fundamentally still, the crown secured recognition of its supremacy in the enactment of laws. Such indeed was London's role that from the late 1600s colonies retained regular agents there to watch over their interests.

Colonization and empire brought the establishment overseas of replicas – even at times parodies – of the forms of government familiar in the mother country as settlers attempted to organize life in a new setting to their liking, and as metropolitan authorities attempted to regulate anything from oceanic economies to the ecclesiastical affairs of an entire continent. There was in general little concern to introduce indigenous peoples – who could be controlled through client potentates or vassals – to European political institutions. There were important exceptions, most notably in the empire of Spain, where mission influences were so strong, in some tiny enclaves in

North America, and in Asia where Europeans encountered rich, skilled and influential merchants who belonged to powerful states and civilizations. Chinese were encouraged to serve on the municipal council of Dutch Batavia. Hindus became aldermen in English Madras and (after 1688) sat as advisers to the English court which heard indigenous cases.[29] Nevertheless the main concern of metropolitan states was with possessions that generated wealth and with their inhabitants of European descent, just as one of the chief aims of the colonists was to rebut the unwanted attentions of the parent country, particularly its endeavour to levy taxes.

Metropolitan supremacy was accordingly established and maintained only with difficulty. Communications were poor, slow and unreliable. No more than for their needs and aspirations in Europe itself could states recruit, pay and sustain adequate bureaucracies. Hence a growing body of responsibilities was entrusted to unpaid or underpaid officials who frequently discharged them in ways chiefly directed to their own benefit. As in the mother countries – where taxes were farmed to contractors and offices sold – territories and functions were handed over to individuals, consortia and chartered companies. Meanwhile overseas European states found themselves confronted by wealthy, entrenched and often hereditary oligarchies whose grip, direct and indirect, on local office usually ensured that colonies were spared the full impact of the will of the imperial government. And the longer the mother country delayed the assertion of its authority, the more difficult it became, as England found.

Nevertheless empire brought an enlargement of the governmental ambitions of European monarchs and states, and an extension – tentative though it may have been in many cases – of their authority. If the powers of the Iberian rulers weakened in the seventeenth century, those of their French and English counterparts increased and empire brought a growth in the employment of those legally-trained administrators (such as the French *intendants*) whose activities were such a significant feature of government in Europe. Even in the most decrepit empires the will of the parent state was to some degree enforced. Other than in the English possessions no effective representative institutions were allowed to emerge. Movements for independence were few and unsuccessful, albeit for no better reason that there was little more for colonies to gain. A concerted colonial opposition was difficult, if not impossible to mount, in possessions generally more in contact with the mother country than with one another. Common economic interests united monopolists in Lisbon or Seville with their opposite numbers overseas. A common religion helped to hold the Iberian realms together. In the last resort colony and mother country were usually at one in resisting some external threat. Spain's imperial authority was asserted in the early 1500s by a carefully balanced blend of grandees and less patrician lawyers. France and England could subsequently draw on the talents of an expanding class of military and naval officers generated by the prolonged wars of the seventeenth century. Rarely did their rule measure up to the influential and idealized view of how the Romans had once ordered such matters. But as the events of the next century were to show, this was as much as colonists would tolerate.

NOTES AND REFERENCES

1 See pp. 221–2.
2 See pp. 27–8, 93. A substantial exception to Seville's monopoly was the trade allowed between the Canary Islands and the Indies.
3 See pp. 109, 195–6.
4 Richard Hakluyt, *Principal Navigations*, MacLehose edition, 12 vols (Glasgow, 1903–5), XI, 313.
5 Ambrosini, *Paesi e Mari Ignoti* has a useful discussion.
6 See p. 96.
7 See pp. 170–1, 189–90.
8 M.N.Pearson, *Coastal Western India. Studies from the Portuguese Records* (New Delhi, 1981), pp. 52ff.
9 See pp. 147, 167.
10 Scammell, 'The pillars of empire'.
11 See pp. 35, 123–4.
12 See pp. 78–9, 81–4.
13 The independence of the United Provinces was only formally recognized in 1648.
14 See pp. 101–2, 119–20.
15 See p. 103.
16 Leonard Blussé, 'Testament to a Towkay: Jan Coen, Batavia and the Dutch China trade', *Itinerario* IX, 2 (1985), 3ff.
17 Leonard Blussé, 'The Caryatids of Batavia: reproduction, religion and acculturation under the VOC', *Itinerario* VII, 1 (1983), 57ff.
18 See pp. 36, 39–40.
19 John G. Reid, *Acadia, Maine and New Scotland. Marginal Colonies in the Seventeenth Century* (Toronto, 1981), p. 89.
20 Richard R. Johnson, *Adjustment to Empire. The New England Colonies 1675–1715* (Leicester, 1981), p. 22.
21 See pp. 30, 248–50.
22 See pp. 153–4, 160.
23 See pp. 42–3.
24 See pp. 43–4.
25 See pp. 19, 105–7, 120–1.
26 See pp. 41, 246–7.
27 Richard S. Dunn, *Sugar and Slaves*, p. 338.
28 Civil law courts, which sat without juries – and were thus not amenable to local pressures – and dealt especially with violations of the Navigation Acts, prize, piracy, commercial and maritime disputes. Their introduction into proprietary colonies such as Pennsylvania and South Carolina was strenuously resisted.
29 Arasaratnam, *Coromandel Coast*, p. 275.

6 Colonial society

From the early 1400s onwards Europeans in ever increasing numbers penetrated to and settled in the wider world, often in regions well beyond those over which their compatriots could claim jurisdiction. With some – shipwrecked sailors, convicts left to learn what they could of Africa by Portuguese and English East India fleets, prisoners seized by local peoples – it was the outcome of misfortune or miscalculation. But many whites fled from the society of their fellows to avoid the consequences of misdeeds real or alleged, or to seek a better life. Asia, with its fabulous wealth and its demand (in India especially) for western skills, had attracted renegades long before the arrival of Vasco da Gama. By the seventeenth century such were their numbers that they could be found anywhere from Japan to the Arabian Sea, commanding local ships, serving as soldiers or simply living by their wits. And some did remarkably well, like that eclectic Englishman who, in the 1670s, having made 'a great fortune in commerce at Madras', turned Muslim, built himself 'a fine house' in Hindu style in Coromandel and set up as a landed magnate.[1] Portuguese adventurers became pirate chiefs in the Bay of Bengal and independent potentates in East Africa. Buccaneers roamed the Caribbean, on whose coasts, in Honduras and Campeche, there grew up communities of loggers living as Indians did. In the Americas whites went off to dwell among local tribes and northern frontiersmen hunted and traded far afield native fashion. And where European authority petered out, whether around Goa or in North America, a mixture of 'pacified' natives and those described by contemporaries as 'white savages' warred and traded with their neighbours.

Within the uncertain boundaries of European settlement and influence there developed a rich diversity of colonial societies. White colonization was negligible in Africa, where only the Dutch took root in the south and the Portuguese (and these mostly Luso-Africans) in Mozambique, Angola and the Congo. Ottoman, Moroccan and Negro power kept whites out of the north and north-west, though their merchants were active in many coastal entrepôts. Tropical climates and their related diseases killed off most of the few who ventured, or were sent, elsewhere. Apart from Portuguese Luanda the continent had no European towns of any significance and merely, along its littoral, isolated trading posts, slaving stations and fortresses. In the pioneering years whites made some remarkable journeys into the interior, but thereafter rarely moved far from the coasts and their numbers were limited to a few commercial factors, a scattering of Catholic missionaries, occasional governors and military commanders (mostly in Portuguese enclaves) and a handful of troops. With European women virtually unknown there was the usual desperate white pursuit of indigenous females, but, for reasons already noticed, this produced no racially mixed population of any size.[2]

Climate and disease made much of Asia almost as unwelcoming as Africa, and other than footholds on the coasts of the Indian subcontinent, and in Sri Lanka, Indonesia and the Philippines, there was little European colonization. Nor indeed was there much scope for settlement in the densely populated and independent realms of powerful rulers, or much sense to toiling under a blazing sun when great riches could be had far less arduously. The European East was hence another world of forts and factories, but these richer, more numerous and stronger than their equivalents in Africa. A few were inland, the majority, however, on coasts or offshore islands. In some, and in important centres such as Surat or Nagasaki, Europeans enjoyed only those privileges local potentates would allow. Elsewhere, unlike Africa, there were great European-controlled commercial cities. They might, like Hormuz or Malacca, be former indigenous entrepôts. Or they might, like Macao, Manila or Bombay, be western creations. Many were handsome, all were fortified and their polyglot populations were usually overwhelmingly non-European and frequently non-Christian.

In the possessions of the Iberian states splendid Catholic churches, monasteries and nunneries were erected and richly endowed. Some indigenous peoples were converted, the familiar ecclesiastical hierarchy was introduced – all but its humblest offices, however, long the exclusive preserve of Europeans. The clergy, secular and regular alike, were soon impressively active in business – none more so than the Jesuits – and in the late 1600s a pious traveller was shocked by a friar's obsession with getting his hoard of diamonds home. In the Portuguese *Estado* there were those who acquired estates, chiefly in western India, on which their descendants were still living in cosy affluence at the end of the seventeenth century. The most prestigious and potentially lucrative posts in the Portuguese empire were held by aristocrats and those gentry (*fidalgos*) notorious for their brawlings and amorous intrigues. For the rest, the majority of Europeans in the East were merchants, soldiers, missionaries, seamen, artisans and members of that managerial class employed by the English and Dutch trading companies.

With western women in short supply miscegenation was widespread, and in Portuguese, and later in Dutch possessions, popular inclination became state policy.[3] Following the conquest of Goa Lusitanian rank and file – 'trash' according to some of their compatriots – were married off to local females who had been captured and converted, and the happy pair either endowed with land or the man set up in a trade. So, too, Dutch 'free burghers' and some employees of the English East India Company espoused Christianized Asian women (mostly Indo-Portuguese) since eastern families of any wealth and standing refused to associate with such impoverished social inferiors.

For many Europeans the golden promise of the East was never realized. Many died on passage there and more on arrival or soon after. Renegades struggled to return home. Officials alleged themselves ruined. Dutch burghers, their activities closely scrutinized by the VOC, and facing keen indigenous competition, had to settle for such modest enterprises as tavern-keeping and usury. But for others Asia was the apotheosis of the imperial dream. Slaves were abundant, mistresses easily found and fortunes to be amassed by trade, speculation or pillage.

In the West the European grip was firmer. Climates were in general agreeable, some indigenous peoples were destroyed or subjugated, and limitless land was available. States and settlers could attempt, often in conflict, to create their ideal society. Spanish viceroys ruled from palaces. Some Iberian ranchers and planters acquired immense estates and lived in such magnificent dwellings as that which, to the horror of the West India Company, the aristocratic governor of Dutch Brazil proposed to erect so that he could 'give himself over to the country life'. Not all were so fortunate or indeed so inclined. Family-worked farms abounded in English North America and some of the Portuguese Atlantic islands. In impoverished parts of the Spanish Indies – like the backlands of Central America – there were many in the late seventeenth century living, as they said, 'by our own work and industry'. Scattered along the Newfoundland coast were tiny isolated farming and fishing communities. In Maryland, well after the pioneering days, there were still those who dwelt in crude wooden huts where they could be seen, to the disgust of the fastidious, cramming food into their mouths by the handful. Even many of the 'great houses' of the Iberian lands were of modest proportions.

With conquest and settlement came the foundation of towns and cities, very often in regions – Brazil and much of North America for example – where there had previously been none. The majority were in the Spanish Indies, reflecting the ideals of a parent society to which organized political life was essentially urban, and in which magnates kept town houses and were influential in civic affairs. Some never amounted to more than spasmodically occupied collections of wooden huts, but many were of imposing size and elegance. They were built to a common grid-iron pattern of which the focal point, even in the meanest, was the square and the church. And they quickly acquired much else in common, becoming centres of ecclesiastical wealth and influence, and developing ancillary indigenous suburbs, despite all the efforts of the crown and the missions to confine the Indians to their own settlements.

Some Spanish foundations were refurbished native sites, demonstrating the finality of the conquest. Most were not fortified, though there were those, like Havana, with its massive walls, that were key points in the imperial defences. The affluent and handsome Lima and Mexico City, with their sumptuous buildings, fountains and gardens, were vice-regal capitals in which society congregated and where lawyers and officials lived and worked. And uniquely outside Europe the Indies had in the mining centre of Potosí a great industrial city. Much of this urban vigour and opulence dwindled with the economic and political difficulties of the later 1600s. Many Indian towns degenerated into hamlets as their populations fled or died out. Inhabitants drifted away from European towns to escape from oligarchical rule, withdrew from vulnerable coastal areas or departed to live on their estates or off whatever they could exact from the Indians. Even so, towns were still the primary place of residence for whites.

There were other important urban centres of government and trade in Brazil – where the riches generated by sugar kept them wealthy longer than their Spanish counterparts – and in North America, which, however, despite the rapid growth of, for example, Boston, New York and Philadelphia, remained predominantly rural. Nevertheless, such were the limitations of a rustic existence and such the rumoured opportunities and known delights of urban living – not least that luxuriant immorality that flourished among uprooted peoples of assorted race – that, as in the Old World, towns attracted people of all classes. The destruction of Port Royal – the Jamaican stronghold of buccaneering, smuggling and most known vices – by an earthquake in 1692 was interpreted by the pious as divine retribution.

Even so empire meant the arrival in the New World of Christianity, or at least (Holland and England apart) that version accepted by the mother country. Anglicanism took root in Virginia and subsequently elsewhere in English America. In the old Puritan north-east there flourished a galaxy of dissenting sects, their members – increasingly outnumbered by the less godly - much given to sermons, theological debate, psalm-singing and the hysterical persecution of those identified as deviants. In French Canada, with its tiny white Catholic population, a small band of missionaries, enduring all the hardships of indigenous life, struggled to convert the local tribes while their fellows laboured among those of Louisiana. In the Iberian Americas, where ecclesiastical buildings – some of them veritable fortresses – regularly surpassed in size and magnificence the most impressive works of civil architecture, the Catholic church was richly and grandly established, acquiring, as was rarely the case in Asia, immense estates. Its monasteries and convents provided primary education for non-Indian children, and from the late 1500s the Jesuits opened a network of secondary schools. Opulent towns housed fashionable nunneries whose wealthy creole inmates led a giddy and privileged social life interspersed with outbursts of morbid religiosity. On the imperial frontiers paternalistic missions directed the labours and devotions of Amerindian acolytes, while in the heartlands native converts practised a Catholicism ranging from superstitious piety to scarcely veiled paganism or curious combinations of Christian and indigenous usage.

Everywhere colonial society was astonishingly cosmopolitan, sometimes despite, sometimes because of, the policies of metropolitan governments. Whites freely distributed indigenous peoples around the world, miscegenation was common and colonists were often recruited from wherever they could be found. Flemings were among the earliest settlers in the Portuguese Atlantic islands and the Portuguese themselves were soon seemingly ubiquitous throughout the Spanish Indies. There were Jews in Goa and the Iberian Americas from the early 1500s, and important Jewish communities in the Atlantic and Caribbean islands in the following century. Ships owned by Portuguese, Corsicans, Genoese and Venetians and manned by Africans, *mestizos*, Indians and Chinese were sailing the west coast of Spanish America in the early 1600s, while a traveller in Peru met colonists of French, Italian, Portuguese, German, Flemish, Greek, Ragusan, Canary Island, North African and English origin. There were subsequently Irish settlers in the English Caribbean and Germans and Scandinavians – also employed in large numbers in the East by the VOC – in Dutch North America. Gypsies appeared in Brazil, French Huguenots in English North America and Dutch South Africa, various German pietist sects in Pennsylvania, and Greeks and Frenchmen – formerly gunners in Spanish ships – in Manila.

In such a world the footloose abounded and friction was endemic, convincing many in Europe that even by the unexacting standards of the time colonials were congenitally querulous and unruly. There were clashes between rich and poor, between emigrants in hot pursuit of new opportunities and officials seeking to restrain them, between the descendants of the pioneers and those newly arrived, and between the successful and the many who considered themselves deprived of their due rewards. Spaniards in search of better things abandoned the Caribbean islands for the mainland in the early sixteenth century and Azoreans left their overcrowded homeland for Asia and Brazil. *Conquistadores* tried their luck in campaign after campaign, while in the seventeenth century settlers moved from the English West Indian islands to North America, from colony to colony there, or back to the mother country.

Among those who remained – as did the great majority – there developed a pride and sense of achievement, notably manifested in the luxuriant architecture of the Iberian empires. And to a lesser extent there developed a sense of belonging to societies with their own distinctive characters, reflected in the erection in Mexico in 1680, to greet the incoming viceroy, of a triumphal arch embellished, for the first time, with representations of Aztec emperors and gods. That such feelings were not more intense is in part explained – as in Brazil – by metropolitan policies, by the degree to

which, almost everywhere, colonial upper classes blunted the impact of
undesirable imperial ambitions, by the diversity of the cultural and ethnic
origins of much colonial society, and not least by the need for the wealthy
to stress their essentially Old World qualities to differentiate them from
their social inferiors and the neighbouring indigenous populace and black
slaves.[4] Even so, some sense of identity was fostered by the creation of
colonial universities, soon locally staffed. It was heightened, especially in
the Spanish Indies, by competition between colonials and Europeans for
office, and by the contempt in which colonials were almost universally held
in the Old World, where they were regarded as at best imperfectly governed
and living and behaving in curiously archaic ways. But nowhere was colonial
identity more vigorously asserted than among the religious Orders in
Iberian America. In their houses, closely integrated into local society,
articulate and ambitious creole and European-born members disputed, with
that acerbity endemic in enclosed communities, the few preferments available in organizations whose role was increasingly restricted by the expansion
of the secular church.

Of distinctive white colonial cultures, clearly differentiated from that of
Europe, there are few indications. Some colonies produced their own
histories and had, as in the works of the Mexican Sor Juana Inés de la Cruz
(1648–95) their own poetry and music, just as they had their own saints –
Our Lady of Guadalupe and the Virgin of Copocabana. But they were
generally better known for obscurantism and philistinism. Only the bare
majority of white adult male householders in North America were literate
in 1660. Nearly half the planters of St Kitts, petitioning the government in
1706, were unable to sign their names, and it was said of New York in
1713 'that there is hardly anything more wanted . . . than learning'.[5]
Outside Spain's New World possessions, where universities were early
established – that of Mexico in 1553 – institutions of higher education were
few and rarely of much importance in the great intellectual movements of
the times. There was no university (or printing press) in Brazil, no university in the English Caribbean, and neither colleges nor printing presses in
the French islands. There were many schools and a handful of universities
– eventually to reach great eminence – in North America: Harvard (1636),
William and Mary (1693) and Yale (1701). Even so, the latter was founded
to produce clergy untainted by Harvard liberalism and Harvard itself
primarily to supply learned ministers who could confute the dangerous
doctrines of 'lewd fellows' expounding scripture as the spirit moved them.

True, many colonials studied at European universities, like those New
Englanders and West Indians at Padua in the early 1600s or the Brazilians
who came to Coimbra.[6] VOC officials in Asia frequently owned large
collections of pictures (chiefly European) and books were plentiful in the
Atlantic colonies. Householders in English America commonly possessed
substantial numbers of utilitarian, classical, historical and (especially in the

Puritan settlements) devotional works. Some New England towns had public libraries by the end of our period. Under the eye of the Inquisition books sold by the thousand in the Iberian Americas, from which, it would seem, only outright Protestant tracts were debarred, and where again sizeable libraries – albeit generally religious and conservative – were accumulated. But this did not make colonies conspicuous centres of intellectual freedom and endeavour. Catholic powers, no more liberal than at home, excluded as best they could non-Catholic settlers. England and Holland were more tolerant, but the American Puritan colonies long persecuted dissent. Impressive works of learning were indeed produced in the Iberian Americas in the sixteenth and seventeenth centuries, though often by authors who spent much time in Europe, and almost all were conceived and executed according to European precept. A great deal of the investigation of every aspect of the society and natural history of the non-European world was conducted, according to European ideas, by the servants of European governments or commercial enterprises. The majority of the books read and the plays performed by whites living or serving overseas were by European writers. In Mexico clerical bigotry eventually silenced Sor Juana while creole nuns devoted their energies to the manufacture of paper flowers. After 1600 science flagged in the universities of Spanish America and was for long dormant in the English colonies which supplied the Royal Society with only three fellows in the half century after its foundation.[7] The New World produced no Shakespeare, no Bach, no Rembrandt. Nor surprisingly. It offered European artists, musicians and men of letters no such patronage as did the Old. Its upper classes, sustained in easy affluence, pursuing magnificent opportunities for enrichment and confronted by no challenge from local cultures held in high esteem, displayed, for the most part, little of the intellectual and artistic interests of their European counterparts.

Equally characteristic, colonial society was in its early years predominantly male, and in many parts of the world remained so. Some of the grandees of Portuguese Asia had European wives with them, as did some of the major officers of the Dutch and English East India companies. But by and large women were not attracted to such climates – though the Portuguese, Dutch and English all at various times shipped out unfortunates of the 'meaner kind' as potential spouses for those in their service – nor did they survive there any better than they did in tropical Africa or the Caribbean. But women were also for long a minority, though not such a tiny one, in the better conditions of the Americas. In part this reflects the attitudes of parent societies. In Portugal, profoundly influenced by its Islamic past, females were expected to live in sedentary and secluded virtue. To the Dutch the wider world was initially a place to trade, not to settle. Colonies were in general regarded as outposts in which life was too crude for white women. But the imbalance also reflects the fact that many males emigrated with the intention of returning home as soon as they had made their fortune, while in the tobacco and sugar colonies of the Caribbean and North America, prior to the introduction of black slavery, planters wanted not women but men to work the land.

In Asia and some parts of the West the lack of European females was to endure. Seventeenth-century Bridgetown (Barbados) had a remarkably large number of single men, staying for longer or shorter periods, who had left their wives and families in Europe. True, there were some considerable exceptions. The English Puritans emigrated as entire communities of men, women and children to pursue their own way of life. Elsewhere women were present in greater strength than might at first appear. Encouraged by royal policy they were in the Spanish Indies almost from the start – some accompanying Columbus in 1498 – and the subsequent flow to regions of such agreeable climate and immense opportunity was far greater than was recorded in offical statistics. Besides which large numbers of *mestiza* girls were absorbed into white society. Hence when, for example, the 'European' population of Lima was counted (1610) it comprised almost as many women (4359) as men (5527).

Overall the shortage of women was steadily redressed with the passage of time, most notably in the Iberian Americas by the procreative endeavour of European and creole males with indigenous and *mestiza* girls.[8] There was also increased emigration of families to settled lands – as to Virginia in the later seventeenth century – often the outcome of the policies of metropolitan governments. Indeed so successfully were marriageable girls persuaded or compelled to cross the Atlantic that by the 1680s they outran the supply of potential husbands in the French Antilles. And their numbers were reinforced by demographic growth within the western colonies where locally-born women appear to have married earlier and produced more and healthier children than did their immigrant sisters, much troubled by new climates and unfamiliar diseases (like the malaria of North America).

For the rest colonial society bore a marked resemblance to that of the Old World. It had, from the very beginning, its poor. In the Spanish Indies many of the pioneers either never received any reward or soon gambled it away. The ranks of the impecunious were rapidly swelled by young hopefuls who arrived to seek a living, only to find they were unable to compete with cheap and highly skilled Indian labour. As in Europe there were younger sons who got none of the family riches but who refused to engage in any 'vile' occupation lest it denigrated their supposed nobility. To the alarm of the imperial administration there were also the restive and embittered male offspring of European fathers and indigenous mothers. Some survived in penury among the Amerindian population, some gave vent to their frustration in bouts of desperate wildness and many simply died of hunger in a world hard on the unsuccessful, with abundant silver, growing demand and a shortage of goods forcing up prices. As in Europe this 'undisciplined rabble' – rogues, unfortunates, failures, misfits - grew at a formidable rate so that already before the economic reverses of the seventeenth century there was talk of ridding the empire of their troublesome presence by shipping them off to conquer Thailand and Cambodia. Nor were such problems peculiarly Iberian. In the early 1600s Maryland had plenty of farmers who died in debt or who managed to accumulate no more than a mere competence in the course of an arduous life. Later in the century there were whites in the English Caribbean described as 'poor' or 'very poor'. Paupers are recorded as such in New York and – to the disgust of the godly – in Boston c.1700, while beggars transported from France to Martinique were said to die in misery if not first put to death for their misdemeanours. And if European overseas society had, in general, no white equivalents to those peasants and serfs who, toiling on the land, made up the bulk of the population of the Old World – their place being taken by indigenous or black slave labour – there were none the less white colonists who worked the soil themselves and those who endured conditions barely distinguishable from slavery.[9]

Others enjoyed a far happier lot, not least the members of that new merchant class who, based in the East, could penetrate and dominate lucrative routes, or settled in the West could meet the demands of fellow colonists and handle such exports as sugar and silver unimpeded by indigenous competition. True, many major long distance trades were largely in the hands of European-based merchants – Seville's commerce with the Indies, for example, or the continent's various dealings with Asia. In many cases, too, Europeans came out, whether to the Caribbean sugar islands or the inhospitable Canadian posts of the Hudson's Bay Company, to do a spell as agents or factors for firms and organizations in the Old World. Indeed, in the richest trades of the Spanish Indies it was common for merchants from the mother country to spend much of their working lives in the Americas, returning home when their fortunes were made. Many, however, remained in the Indies, often, like their counterparts in Brazil, marrying into local landed families. Hence by the later seventeenth century a very substantial number of merchants in the transatlantic lands, unlike those representing European interests in Asia, or engaged in country trades there, had been born, or were permanently domiciled overseas. Some Spanish creoles operated, from headquarters in Mexico City or Lima, in the interior of the continent, supplying (like country traders in Asia) those engaged in the main long distance exchanges and redistributing their imports. But others participated themselves in this commerce and predominated on routes such as that linking the Americas and the Philippines, just as New Englanders were much in evidence in the traffic from North America to Europe and the Caribbean. Though colonial business techniques and organization on the whole lagged behind the best contemporary European practice there was no shortage of colonial merchants whose skills and success aroused the envy and alarm of competitors from the homeland. Many invested in other undertakings and assets, particularly land, which also attracted some European merchants in Asia who acquired what were described as 'country houses and farms' in India. Many had extensive international associations, with Martinique Jews in touch with relatives in Bordeaux, London and Amsterdam in 1700. And by this date, too, many, whether in New England, Jamaica or Brazil, were wealthy by any standards. Few, however, could equal the plutocrats of the Spanish Indies in their palmiest days. The silver magnates of Mexico dominated the trade, and very often the politics of the viceroyalty from their great houses in the capital. In Peru equally influential commercial grandees, owners of mines, factories and estates, could reckon their fortunes in tens of thousands of *pesos* or more at a time when 600 a year constituted a comfortable income.

There were other classes of considerable, if lesser, substance. The growing complexity of imperial commerce and colonial society demanded, attracted or produced increasing numbers of professional men, whether physicians (whose ministrations were usually of so infelicitous an outcome that in India sensible Europeans employed Hindus) or those with the business skills needed by trading companies. Imperial bureaucracies required clerks and officials. Courts and the congenital litigiousness of colonial subjects gave employment to more and more lawyers, chiefly in the Spanish Indies, but also in Iberian and Protestant Asia and, by 1700, English North America. To cater for the needs and whims of opulent colonists European artisans and craftsmen soon appeared in the Spanish possessions, practising most of the skills known at home, and organized in those guilds and confraternities familiar in Iberia, and which were subsequently established, on a lesser scale, in Brazil. White craftsmen were most numerous in Spanish America in centres of government or affluence, leaving less favoured areas to indigenous artisans. The wealthiest employed black slaves while others used Amerindian labour, both thereby disseminating Spanish skills and attitudes. Already in the early 1500s they constituted a prosperous, conservative and stabilizing force. And since, as almost everywhere overseas, skilled men were in short supply, they could, like their colleagues in other empires, command high wages and attain considerable wealth.

But if lawyers, merchants, bureaucrats and craftsmen were much in evidence in European possessions in the wider world, scions of blue-blooded families, though not unknown, were rare. As Charles I of England characteristically put it, the 'rugged and laborious beginnings' of a colony were no place for men of breeding.[10] Besides which monarchs, and those of Spain in particular, had no wish to see magnates, with whom they had trouble enough at home, carve out new spheres of influence for themselves in distant lands, though the Iberian crowns were happy enough to employ them to govern, under varying degrees of control, important footholds and territories. But in any case, for men of this class influence was exercised in the mother country and rewards and preferments obtained at the royal court. Even so, they were quick to appreciate that impecunious younger sons might conveniently improve their lot by marrying colonial heiresses or serving in the imperial administration.

Colonies, nevertheless, had their aristocracies, quite apart from the generality of Spaniards in America and Portuguese in Asia who considered themselves ennobled by the simple fact of being there. In the Spanish Indies, Portuguese Brazil and East Africa, parts of English North America, throughout much of the Caribbean and in Dutch South Africa there emerged a new, and often imposingly rich, class of landed magnates. They derived from many, and commonly obscure origins. Some were descended from conquerors (like the Cortés dynasty in Mexico). Some were the heirs of pioneers (as were a number of the dominant Massachusetts families). But the majority, whatever the ingenious pedigrees they might concoct, were the scions of merchants, entrepreneurs, bureaucrats, recipients of official favours (such as *encomiendas*) and creditors of kings. Among the sugar grandees of Bahia and the patricians of Virginia there were those descended from gentlemen and squires, but more whose ancestors were – as in New England – sea captains, traders and artisans and who remained active in commerce themselves. In the Caribbean there were dynasties founded by lawyers, soldiers, and even indentured labourers. The great and powerful of Jamaica were allegedly all 'formerly rude and of mean birth', among them those with fortunes stemming from piracy and smuggling. And as in Brazil, where 50 per cent of the planters in Bahia were, in the late seventeenth century, immigrants or the sons of immigrants, their rise could be dramatically swift. Peter Beckford, who arrived in Port Royal in 1661, 'bred a seaman and merchant', died in 1710, owning twenty estates and 1200 slaves, having probably founded the greatest fortune ever made in planting.

Wealth, moreover, bred wealth. Possession of a *hacienda* in the Spanish Indies provided the economic and territorial base for further advance. Rich Virginian planters became middlemen in the tobacco trade for their poor neighbours, and those of the English Caribbean mopped up properties abandoned by smallholders in the hard times of the French wars of the late 1600s. And naturally enough wealth conferred status and ensured deference. 'The esteem accorded to a plantation owner', it was reported from Brazil in the early 1700s, 'can be equated to the honour in which a titled nobleman is held in Portugal.' Indeed those who in Spanish America lived sufficiently 'nobly' (i.e. grandly and ostentatiously) could be rewarded with a title.

Such families dominated politics and society throughout much of the colonial world, with the wealthiest in Barbados providing in 1680, for example, ten out of twelve of the members of the governor's council, twenty out of twenty-two of the elected assembly, four-fifths of the judges and three-quarters of the justices of the peace.[11] A select and interrelated group, they enlarged and preserved their heritage and safeguarded their political influence, as in the Iberian Americas, by carefully arranged marriages. They lived, it was said of Jamaica, 'in the height of splendour', in great residences, surrounded by their slaves, servants and retainers, much preoccupied, as is the wont of their kind, with the finer points of status and etiquette. No more than the landed grandees of Europe did the majority spend too much time in the seclusion of their estates – made even remoter by vast distances and poor communications – but moved instead to their town houses, from which, whether in Bahia, Port Royal or Charleston, they could enjoy the delights of urban life and exercise political influence, sustained by the revenues and prestige of their properties.

Yet rich or poor, Europeans overseas were conscious that they inhabited huge and largely empty lands – Brazil, where journeys could last for years; Mexico, where travellers used compass and astrolabe like navigators at sea – and that they formed only tiny minorities surrounded by large and potentially hostile slave and indigenous populations.[12] In early seventeenth-century Goa a few hundred whites were isolated in a subcontinent whose inhabitants were numbered in tens of millions. At the same date there were at least eight times as many Chinese as Spaniards in Manila, while in the 1640s some 15,000 New Englanders were established on the fringe of a land mass containing approximately 10 million Amerindians. Colonial populations in the West were growing, and growing by natural increase rather than emigration, but they remained nevertheless minuscule by European, let alone oriental standards. Even as late as 1650, after more than a century of indigenous demographic disaster, about three-quarters of a million whites were outnumbered twelve to one by native peoples in the Spanish Indies. Brazil had at best 100,000 Europeans in 1700, North America over one million forty years later – equalling, that is, about one third of the population of the minute Portugal.

Colonists, not surprisingly, were highly apprehensive as to their safety and survival. Slaves were expected to rise and murder their owners, as indeed they did. Indigenous allies were not to be trusted. Blacks and locals were suspected of conspiring against whites. Slaves and Indians were accordingly evacuated from coastal regions of the Spanish Americas threatened with European incursions, and settlers, as in the Portuguese *Estado*, were supposedly ready to deal with any insurgency. It became official policy in South Carolina to make 'Indians and Negros a checque upon each other least by their Vastly Superior Numbers we should be crushed'.[13] Many in North America thought the only way to guarantee safety was to 'root out' the Amerindians. Failing this, it was widely accepted, exemplary violence and brutality were essential to ensure respect for European authority. The behaviour of slaves was closely regulated. They were forbidden to travel without permission, to meet together, to possess European weapons, or to take strong drink. For any misdemeanour, real or imagined, they were punished with hysterical ferocity – tortured, flogged (males and females alike), castrated, mutilated, burned alive. Some colonies attempted to restrain this frenetic brutality by legislation. In South Africa things reached such a pass that mutilation had to be abandoned (1727) since the many disfigured survivors affronted European sensibilities.

These demonstrations of white superiority and the almost universal colonial assumption that anything arduous, unpleasant or demeaning would be undertaken by others, were hardly likely to benefit indigenous peoples, though most Europeans thought otherwise. Sadistic brutality, forced labour and slavery dislocated or destroyed traditional ways of life. In the Spanish Caribbean Amerindians of both sexes were employed in such unaccustomed tasks as panning for gold or harvesting sugar. As a result the native reproductive cycle was disrupted, since in societies without domestic milk-giving animals children were weaned late and so died if, as now happened, they were separated from their mothers. At the same time indigenous agriculture was deprived of essential labour, diverted to other enterprises, and food supplies consequently cut. The introduction and long survival of *encomienda* worsened the already unhappy lot of much of the local population in many parts of the Spanish empire.[14] As their numbers dwindled people from an ever-widening geographical area and an ever-increasing range of social classes had to abandon or neglect traditional and essential pursuits to undertake heavy and unfamiliar work for their new masters. They were compelled not only to render tribute, but to bear the cost of its administration. They had to provide given amounts, not a percentage, of what they produced, which was particularly onerous in lean years and as the population decreased. They might have to supply goods unknown to the native economy, and they were subjected to an infinity of fraud and abuse. They were, moreover, commonly obliged to give up their accustomed existence and work for Europeans, or produce for the white market, for no better reason than to be able to meet exactions demanded of them, and to their further humiliation and demographic ruin, their women could be taken to serve as wet nurses to Spanish children.

Such pressures speeded the decline or disappearance of entire indigenous peoples. But the most devastating blows came from the ravages of diseases transmitted by Europeans and their African slaves and through the impact of defeat and conquest. The overthrow of the Aztec and Inca empires and Spanish treatment of the survivors convinced many Amerindians of their inferiority and insufficiency. The destruction of the indigenous priesthood and the traditional machinery of government, the apparent betrayal of their peoples by the native gods and the imposition of a European way of life brought abject despair and the widespread collapse of morality. The use of cocaine increased in Peru. Adultery, suicide, infanticide, abortion were frequent – the rate of child-bearing was more than halved in some parts of the Andes – drunks and vagabonds became a common sight. Forced labour, abduction, compulsory resettlement intensified feelings of rootlessness and bewilderment. Many Indian women at Lima in 1613 had no knowledge of their origins and most of the younger ones no idea who their parents were. The destruction of the old empires brought the resurgence of tribal authority and then, before long, rival aspirants to chieftainship were pursuing their claims in Spanish courts while their powers were being eroded by the growth of the indigenous municipal councils favoured by the Spaniards. But the Indians were still the losers. Whites took over the centres of their towns and *mestizos* secured – as in Mexico – the offices supposedly reserved for them.

Nor was this all they had to endure. Across huge areas of the Americas the proliferating livestock introduced by Europeans – pigs, cattle, sheep, horses – damaged or destroyed native agriculture. European pests flourished, like those Peruvian rats so fierce and numerous that 'no cat dare look them in the face'. European weeds and crops took powerful root, ousting those of traditional cultivation. In South Africa European farmers blocked the access of indigenous herders to water. White colonists in North America exacted fearsome retribution from Indian hunters who killed their stock. European clothing, imposed in the name of Christian decency on those who normally lived naked and washed frequently, helped destroy the aboriginal populations of Brazil and the Caribbean. Worst of all European- and African-borne disease – smallpox, yellow fever, malaria, influenza, measles, typhus – demoralized, decimated or wiped out New World peoples who had no natural resistance to infections from which they had hitherto been isolated and who now faced them physically weakened by the disruption of their food supplies. The native inhabitants of the Greater Antilles had been entirely destroyed by the 1540s. The Indian population of Mexico dropped from something like 27 million around 1500 to perhaps only 1 million a century later, and that of Peru from about 7 million to little over half a million between 1500 and 1620. The story was the same in Brazil, French Canada and the Dutch New Netherlands. The victims of disease were so numerous in New England that, as one settler put it, Indian 'bones and skulls . . . made such a spectacle . . . that it seemed to mee a new found Golgotha'. As indeed it was, with the coastal tribes of English America in ruins in the older colonies by the 1680s and in the newer by the 1720s.

The impact of Europe was felt far beyond the bounds of white conquest and settlement. Remote peoples succumbed to sicknesses which reached them accidently or indirectly. Unsubdued populations, like the Amerindians of Canada, incomprehendingly saw their numbers melt away and found themselves beholden to strangers they could beat in war, yet whose much desired weapons, tools, utensils and drink they were unable to produce for themselves. Skills and energies once devoted to agriculture or other customary pursuits were in many parts of the world redirected to securing commodities – whether furs in North America or gold and slaves in Africa – which could be exchanged for the white man's goods, and peoples warred with one another to monopolize such trades. North American Indians slaughtered game with European weapons, abandoned traditional ways and beliefs, committed acts of irredeemable folly when stupified with drink, and with their self-confidence eroded, sank into servile dependence on the intruders.

Nevertheless some peoples, as in parts of the Andes, or the wild country of Central America, were saved by the inaccessibility of their homelands, or their lack of anything to arouse white cupidity. Some fled to regions outside European control, or where at least European authority was fragile. Many in Peru were sustained by covert loyalty to ancient ruling families, by folklore and mythology. Some, like the Araucanians, learned how to meet the intruders on their own terms. And eventually, by about the mid 1600s, the indigenous population of Spanish America began to grow again. Moreover, no more than in Africa or Asia was European presence necessarily synonymous with universal native ruin.[15] In the Spanish Indies many acquired, or as apprentices were taught, white skills in lucrative demand. Some Hispanized Indians became merchants, or accumulated one way or another sufficient wealth to enable them to lend not only to their fellows, but to Spaniards as well. Some secured erstwhile tribal territory for themselves, grew rich through land sales, or produced for the creole market to such good effect that in Guatemala they could compete with whites, supplying even sugar and grain.[16] Co-operative tribal chiefs were (for a time) well rewarded, and as long as they controlled labour – until, that is, Spanish policies of resettlement and the creation of indigenous municipalities undermined their powers – were acceptable to Europeans as partners in *coca* and textile ventures, or might well run their own mines. Some enterprising Indians migrated to Spanish towns, prospered, claimed to be of the upper classes and refused, it was said in 1680, to pay tribute or undertake the work expected of them. Other former commoners secured office in Indian townships where some families improved their status by intermarrying with the Spaniards who settled among them.

If one pillar of colonial society and imperial grandeur was the toil of subjugated indigenous peoples, the other was the labour of slaves. These were everywhere predominantly male, and other than in the Americas of an astonishing variety of ethnic origins. In South Africa, for example, the Dutch used, among others, Indonesians, Indians, Africans and Sri Lankans. They were commonly distributed and employed in small, isolated groups, excluded from their masters' culture and deprived of any family life. The only outlets for their sexual urges were in violent competition for local black women, sodomy or bestiality. And their lot was the worse since they spoke no common language, shared no common religion or political organization and were unable to develop any sense of identity.

But most slaves were Africans, employed in such numbers that by the beginning of the eighteenth century there were throughout much of the world where Europeans had settled, or with which they traded, communities of blacks, chiefly males, often several thousand strong and mostly in countries in which they were previously unknown. Such unfortunates were in general far from resigning themselves to their fate, not least since, largely ignored by the churches, and with their numbers regularly reinforced from Africa, their traditional beliefs and sense of cultural identity survived. Revolts were frequent, and no doubt would have been more frequent still had they not been inhibited by tribal differences and antipathies. Even so there were risings in Hispaniola (1522), Mexico (1537), Jamaica (seven between 1669 and 1690), South Carolina (1739) and others expected. Slaves regularly escaped, fleeing, in the Iberian Americas and the Caribbean islands, into wild terrain to live in freedom and follow as best they could African traditions – most successfully so in Brazil, with the country vast and their numbers high. In Martinique some joined the indigenous survivors. Elsewhere they raided native and European neighbours. In sixteenth-century Venezuela and in seventeenth-century Mexico they had their own rulers for a time, and in Brazil they founded a virtual state at Alagoas which survived till almost 1700. Hence wherever there were large concentrations of African slaves Europeans lived in an oppressive atmosphere of impending trouble. Blacks, if they did not escape, revolt or commit suicide, resisted their masters, worked reluctantly and destroyed crops and property with such regularity that by the early eighteenth century most of the English North American colonies had introduced legislation against arson. In return slaves were treated with horrifying brutality, and the fewer the whites, or the more isolated they were, the harsher the regime.

But this was not the whole story. In the Iberian Americas and (after 1685) in the French Caribbean there were some attempts to ensure that slaves became Christians. Many blacks made the best of things, accepting their masters' religion and language. In Spanish and Portuguese lands they formed their own Catholic confraternities, under the patronage of colonial saints such as St Benedict the Moor, gaining a measure of self-respect for themselves, though at the price of providing the government with yet another means for their surveillance. Many became, if only nominally, their owners' staunch adherents, serving as slavers or fighting for them as soldiers anywhere from Portuguese Asia to eighteenth-century English South Carolina. They might be rewarded with plots of land and in some cases they were allowed to marry. The English had originally intended that their slaves in the Caribbean should marry, both to improve their morale and to ensure stability, and to provide, from their offspring, inexpensive additions to the black population. But though this expectation was not realized, slave marriage remained French policy into the eighteenth century and in the Iberian Americas slaves of either sex could marry free or unfree blacks or mulattos – though the children would remain slaves.[17] The position of Africans in the Spanish Indies was improved by the survival of a large and employable indigenous population and by the abundant opportunities for work other than lethal toil on sugar, cotton or tobacco plantations. Sharing their masters' contempt for the docile Indian they were employed to oversee native workers. By force and enterprise they established themselves as intermediaries between white consumers and Amerindian producers and in many parts of the empire came to dominate the provision of mule transport. Employed as domestic slaves in towns and cities they undertook for their owners tasks which elsewhere would normally have been entrusted to friends or relatives, and the bond between black and white could become one of confidence and amity.

Many Africans worked as artisans and craftsmen – whether metalsmiths or confectioners – and among them were those rich enough to wear silk and gold and to live to all intents free. Some indeed became legally free, and more frequently and easily in the Spanish Indies than in colonies where they were chiefly employed as field-hands. In Iberian America they might secure manumission by appeals to that plethora of civil and ecclesiastical jurisdictions – including the Inquisition – which particularly characterized Spanish imperial rule. They might be freed to undertake the numerous skilled jobs for which there were insufficient whites. They might, especially in towns, accumulate enough wealth either by their own endeavours – which in Martinique allegedly included robbery – or through the help of their kinsfolk, to buy their freedom. Many, particularly the old and useless, were freed through the inexpensive charity of those to whom they belonged. But the largest group, as in other slave economies, comprised owners' favourite mistresses and their offspring. The numbers manumitted are uncertain, though in Lima (1524–1650) it was about a third of the slave population and in Mexico City perhaps 40 per cent. Some of those emancipated flourished, like that Jamaican who in 1711 was 'a factor and agent for several planters' and who had two of his children educated in England, while some acquired slaves of their own.[18]

The majority of black slaves were males since the main colonial demand was for manual labour and in Africa women commanded a high price as wives or concubines, especially in Muslim markets. But some females were shipped abroad, and given that men were most likely to escape, or to be put, or worked, to a premature death, there were regions in which there was a rough balance of sexes or possibly a majority of women. They were chiefly employed in domestic service and thus freely accessible to the lusts, but also, in many cases, to the affections of their white masters. Indeed, titillating in those 'lascivious dresses' regularly condemned by moralists and unburdened by the restraints society placed on their white sisters, black girls were clearly irresistible to most European males. To be a white man's mistress brought the chance of a more tolerable existence – and many had the customary largesse of such a relationship lavished on them – and the prospect of eventual manumission. But black mistresses could equally find themselves exposed to the resentful fury of white wives – stories of beatings and worse are legion – or set to work as prostitutes, like other female slaves, for the benefit of their owners.

Black women were most ardently pursued and most readily available in regions such as Brazil, where white females were scarce, or, as in the English Caribbean, where there were few European or indigenous women. Hence there appeared in the wider world societies resembling those long familiar in the Levant and Asia Minor, where European merchants had for centuries lived surrounded by concubines and female slaves of assorted race. Hence, too, there were engendered those numerous mulattos, who by the mid 1600s perhaps accounted for 2 per cent of the population of the Spanish Americas. But such statistics are not particularly helpful since before long the term was used by Iberians to describe any of dark skin and obvious African ancestry, and by the end of our period Spaniards were apt to lump together as 'free blacks' all of mixed blood. But clearly some Afro-Europeans did well. They could be, through the manumission of their mothers, legally free. True, mulatta girls were pursued with the same determination and the same consequences by white males as were their black sisters, but they might become opulently sustained mistresses or (as in Martinique) the wives of planters. In the Spanish Indies some mulattos lived in European style, with their own social and religious confraternities, and married *mestiza* rather than black or Amerindian wives. They could be overseers of slaves – well-known for their brutal efficiency – or obtain positions of influence in Indian communities, or become successful artisans, employing black or Amerindian labour. Those rich enough could even be accepted as whites. In the West Indies English planters regularly freed their mulatto offspring, setting up the males in a craft or as small farmers. And the fewer the whites the better the chances. In the Iberian Americas some Hispano- or Luso-Africans became men of consequence, commanding their own black troops and successfully entrusted with the defence of imperial outposts against European and other enemies. In parts of Portuguese Africa, and in the Portuguese equatorial Atlantic islands, where Europeans rarely settled and even more rarely survived, Afro-Europeans could become, notably in Angola, traders, slavers, and farmers, able in the absence of other candidates, to hold secular and ecclesiastical office.

The unlucky and unsuccessful, however, sank into poverty and, like fellow whites – and even in association with them – eked out a living by robbery and violence. And in any case most mulattos, like most free Africans, remained black, inferior and dangerous in the eyes of the majority of Europeans – so inferior, indeed, that Louis XIV of France refused to accept correspondence from Caribbean planters married to mulattas. They were everywhere discriminated against. Their freedom of movement was restricted, they were denied the right to bear arms and (in the Spanish Indies) were excluded from the universities and the clergy. Those whose mothers were unfree were classed and treated as slaves, and some, as a measure of economy, were deliberately reared as such.

Unfree males, for the most part deprived of the company of women of their own race, meanwhile associated with whatever females they could. In the Dutch Cape Indians and Indonesians took up with local African women and even occasionally with Europeans. In the Iberian Americas blacks formed alliances with indigenous women, apparently appreciative of such vigorous and ebullient lovers and notwithstanding the efforts of the Spanish crown to exclude them, together with mulattos and *mestizos*, from Indian towns. From these relations there sprang the luckless *zambos* who, if they joined their father's people became blacks, the most despised class in colonial society, while if they attempted to establish themselves as the offspring of legally free Indian women, they were then, in Spanish America, liable for tribute and forced labour. In English America Africans fled to tribes near and far, there siring the Afro-Indians derogatively known as *mustees*. To the horror of contemporaries there were even white women so shameless as to voluntarily engage in sex with black slaves, particularly in the English Caribbean islands where, as plantation economies developed and climate and excess took their toll, white males became so scarce that even marriages between European women and blacks were not unknown. Something the same happened on the mainland. But not for long. This 'Disgrace to our Nation' was banned, interracial fornication punished, and by the eighteenth century most of the English American colonies forbade such unions.

Nor were these the only effects of European empire on the ethnic structure of the wider world. Peoples fled before the white invaders, were driven out by their policies, became the victims of frictions provoked by their presence, or were shipped around the globe by their European masters. Some of the inhabitants of the Philippines retreated as far as the Coromandel coast of India following the Spanish conquest. It was reckoned in 1669 that Portuguese intolerance had obliged 30,000 Hindus to leave Goa in the preceding thirty years. Survivors of the North American coastal tribes were pushed, or drifted, westwards in face of English settlement. Amerindians were taken to the Spice Islands by the Spaniards in the early sixteenth century. Filipinos, Indonesians, Japanese and Chinese were brought to America. Some peoples emigrated in pursuit of opportunities revealed by Europeans, like the Goans who appeared in Lusitanian East Africa. Others served white masters in distant lands, with a Tamil force fighting for the Portuguese in Burma in the early 1600s.

But nothing equalled the outcome of the relentless pursuit of indigenous women by European males. The majority of whites overseas were men. Native females, often encouraging in the hope of benefit or favour, were seemingly there for the taking, and without any of the restraints and responsibilities of marriage. Their beauty, desirability and (very often) lack of clothing were frequently and enthusiastically remarked on – North American Indian girls were 'very frisky' and of 'uncommon delicacy of shape'. There were some vain attempts, as by the French church in Canada and the Spanish crown in the Indies, to keep the races apart, just as there were spasmodic attempts, little more successful, to bring about their harmonious and Christian fusion. The Spanish monarchy had once hoped (1501) that Europeans and Caribbean islanders would intermarry 'freely and without co-ercion'. Seventeenth-century French statesmen entertained similar ambitions for Canada, the VOC planned mixed marriages for the settlement of Sri Lanka and Indonesia and in the early 1700s the English Board of Trade was urging the merits of intermarriage for North America.

Such unions were not unknown, as in Portuguese Goa. The Virginian John Rolfe had his renowned and spirited Algonkian wife Pocahontas. Europeans in South Africa might buy the freedom of female slaves and marry them. French traders and hunters at Detroit married Illinois women. Affluent Europeans in India purchased and espoused converted (and white) Georgian, Iranian and Iraqi girls, or had Christianized Chinese or upper class females for their wives. In the Spanish Americas Europeans took converted ladies of rank and wealth as spouses, while poor whites married whoever would have them.[19] These unions were occasionally the outcome of affection, more often the result of hopes of wealth or property, and frequently the product of European policies designed to secure the speedy population of new territories with loyal subjects and the establishment of models of Christian domestic harmony for emulation by others. But it was everywhere well understood that the whiter the bride the better the match. Settlers in Dutch South Africa, who in the early years usually married Bengali women later favoured the fairer-skinned Cape Coloureds produced by miscegenation.[20]

But the mixing of peoples was opposed by the missions and interracial marriage in any case a minority taste. There was hardly, particularly in remote regions, the ecclesiastical machinery to enforce it, nor much hope of doing so in societies in which polygamy was endemic, indigenous women plentiful and, if dark-skinned, generally considered unworthy of any such formal relationship, especially by males who as likely as not had wives elsewhere. So there were sired progenies ranging from Luso-Japanese and South African Cape Coloureds to the offspring of North American fron-tiersmen and the squaws who served their sexual and other needs and who were the indispensable intermediaries in dealings with local tribes. Fornication with Indian women occurred even in godly New England, though far less frequently. There was, as in much of English North America, an almost hysterical concern not to be contaminated by association with the natives and religious precept taught that 'strange wives' were to be eschewed. There were, moreover, few Indian women, while white females were relatively plentiful and reared, unlike their indigenous sisters, in the farming skills vital to agricultural communities.

Very different were the Iberian empires. European women were scarce in Brazil, as in most of Portugal's colonies, through the influence of the country's Islamic past. Amerindian females, on the other hand, were abundant, naked, and as the missionaries disapprovingly observed, more than willing. In the Spanish Indies royal policy and a benign climate ensured that white women were soon present and flourishing in the major centres of settlement. Even so, colonists were far from impervious to the charms of local females, particularly in the years following the overthrow of the Aztec and Inca states when, as is commonly the case with such upheavals, traditional morality collapsed. Fornication with unmarried women was not considered a sin in contemporary Iberia. Some Indian girls were attracted to the tough and masterful victors, some were supplied to the conquerors by those seeking their goodwill, but most were considered, as by whites elsewhere – including many of the clergy – as simply there for their benefit. Already in the early 1500s it was alleged that young Spaniards were rotten with venereal diseases picked up from Indian mistresses and prostitutes. Travellers through Nicaragua bought or hired native women for their comfort.[21] Celebrated *conquistadores* had concubines galore, with whom some achieved prodigies of procreation, like that pioneer who fathered thirty children in three years, while obscurer and less energetic compatriots lived, at least for a time, in virtually monogamous relations with their native women. With the influx of European females and with the royal insistence on marriage, there developed on the whole no equivalent to the harem societies of Portuguese Brazil and Asia. The colourful exceptions were regions beyond government control, or where, as on the frontiers of Paraguay, conditions were such as to deter all but the most intrepid or desperate of European women. And here, too, among the Guarani where females were the workers, the more a man had the happier, in every sense, his lot.

Hence throughout the colonial world there was engendered a large and generally depressed class of so-called mongrels – 'half breeds', *mestizos*, *métis*, *mestiços* – whose numbers continued to grow as it proved impossible to segregate the races, as frontiers advanced (so opening new opportunities for sex) and, as in the Iberian empires in particular, offspring were produced by peoples of increasingly diverse ethnic origins. In some places, such as Portuguese Goa, those of mixed blood became a major, if not the numerically preponderant, element in the population, while by 1700 there were probably few American creole families entirely without Indian blood. But neither *mestizos* nor the members of other pejoratively defined racial groups can be counted with any precision. In the Spanish possessions people were known as Spaniard or Indian or free black according to where and how they lived, whether their parents were united in Catholic wedlock, whether they followed a European or an indigenous way of life, whether they looked Spanish or not, whether they dwelt in towns (where they were most likely to be accepted as fellow Spaniards) and above all whether their families had power and money, which could make blacks white and Indians Spanish.

So the successful and affluent were absorbed into those strata of colonial society below the dominant white oligarchy, while those formidable frontiersmen and warriors, the Paulistas of Brazil, sons of European fathers and Amerindian mothers, elicited respect if nothing else. But in Spanish America the dashing and ambitious young men sired by *conquistadores* from aristocratic Indian mistresses felt themselves so slighted as to plot revolt in Peru in 1567. The poor, the unsuccessful and the dark-skinned were worse off still. Colonial society was increasingly imbued with intense racial prejudice, and since marriage between white males and indigenous females was rare, mixed blood became synonymous with both inferiority and illegitimacy. In the Iberian empires those of such parentage were excluded from the religious Orders and, as in British India later, from public office. Some took up ranching, clearly finding it an existence whose freedom and excitement brought escape from grudging acceptance in more populous centres. In Spanish America the better off were equated, and in some degree fused with, the lower levels of white society, and where other candidates were lacking they could secure admission to the humbler ranks of Spanish guilds, the army and even the clergy. Some *castiza* girls (daughters of European males and *mestiza* mothers) found an acceptable niche as wives or concubines of surviving members of the native nobility. The great majority of *mestizos*, however, formed an intermarrying class – above Indians and blacks, but below whites – comprising servants, farmers, traders, clerks, labourers, minor officials, craftsmen and secular clergy. But if they took a black or indigenous spouse then they sank further down the social scale. True, where European settlement was sparse and where the native culture was destroyed or weakened, the most improbable candidates could pass as whites. But where indigenous peoples were unsubjugated, their cultures intact and Europeans few, those of mixed blood were, like the Canadian *métis*, usually engulfed by the maternal way of life. So, too, in English America, virulently hostile to 'inconstant aboriginal savages', half-breeds remained almost invariably Indian – though some became fur traders and intermediaries between whites and local tribes – and were commonly abandoned 'to be provided for at random by their mothers', making them amongst the colonists' most determined opponents.

Thus, as the result of conquest and settlement, through the ravages of the diseases they introduced, through their import of alien slaves and servants, by intercourse with local women and through their imperial policies, Europeans made their mark on the societies of the wider world. Some peoples were destroyed and the lives of others radically and brutally changed. Yet through much of the Iberian Americas there developed, beneath a white ruling class, an increasingly homogeneous, ethnically mixed population and here and there pockets of genuinely multiracial civilization evolved, as in the densely settled parts of Mexico, where Spanish-speaking Amerindian artisans worked alongside African, *mestizo* and Spanish colleagues. Almost everywhere, too, there were indigenous peoples who did well by collaborating with the intruders, including some who in the Spanish Indies even married European women. Throughout the colonial world there was widespread acceptance of anything from European forms of warfare to European agricultural techniques and styles of dress. In Spanish America native peoples were brought within the jurisdiction of Spanish courts, whose workings some came to understand so well as to be able to turn them to their own advantage, while many from the upper classes married, Spanish-style, in quasi-dynastic matches, carried on enterprises much like those of the Spaniards, and were fully conversant with the assumptions and conventions of Spanish life.[22] Nevertheless, other than in those regions where the indigenous population was destroyed or radically reduced – a relatively small proportion of the non-European world – the essential patterns of indigenous culture survived, and survived, moreover, notwithstanding the determined assaults of the Christian missions.

All mankind was not, as the Catholic pioneers had once euphorically expected, speedily brought within the fold of the church. Least time was devoted to black slaves who, despite occasional Christian qualms, remained unfree even if converted. Elsewhere the missions faced formidable obstacles. They had to contend with lethal climates, like those of Asia and Africa, or indigenous ways of life, such as those of the North American Indians, hard for whites to endure. They needed to master languages and dialects for the most part hitherto unknown to Europeans. In the East they faced ancient and distinguished civilizations commonly sustained by assumptions diametrically opposed to those allegedly embraced by Christianity, and employing tongues and scripts fundamentally different from anything known in the West. Their compatriots might, like the Portuguese in India, be dependent on the very peoples the missions were seeking to convert or expel. In Asia they clashed with Buddhism, one of the greatest expansionist and proselytizing creeds, and in Asia too, and in much of Africa, they were confronted by a vigorous and triumphant Islam, more likely to attract than to lose adherents. In many parts of the Americas and Africa they encountered societies unfamiliar with abstract ideas and without written languages. Such peoples, it was believed, were to be made sedentary, just as the naked were to be clothed, and all were to be brought to 'civility' (i.e. a European way of life) by engaging in that regular toil which would prepare them to receive the Christian message. But to potential acolytes this commonly meant no more than being subjected to a collection of vexatious restrictions which prohibited their customary polygamy, pre-marital sex and freedom of divorce, and endangered their traditional economy. To implement these grand ambitions the missions were undermanned, weakened by theological and political rivalries and opposed by fellow Europeans who saw their activities as a threat to the supply of black slaves or the quiescence of their native labour force.

Nevertheless by missionary endeavour of a scale unparalleled since the conversion of pagan Europe, pockets of Christianity, some of them to prove impressively tenacious, were implanted in Asia, Africa, the Pacific islands and the Americas. In some cases, notably in China and Japan, this was chiefly effected by argument and persuasion, as it was understood the Christian apostles had once triumphed with the Greeks and Romans. Elsewhere a variety of techniques, old and new, were tried. In India Francis Xavier expounded Catholic doctrine to local children 'in the fish market' of Cochin. One view in the Spanish Indies was that every means of communication – words, symbols – together with suitable adaptations of native rites and customs should be employed. In Canada it was hoped that important chiefs, impressed by the exemplary lives of the missionaries, would allow them a foothold, just as Isabella of Castile had once innocently believed that the 'good example' set by Spaniards would persuade Caribbean islanders to live in European Christian style and the Massachusetts Puritans had expected the local Indians would be similarly inspired by the spectacle of their 'pleasing experiments and useful inventions and practices'.

In many other instances the faith was spread by force, fraud or blandishments. In the Iberian Americas the missions, however noble their ideals and intentions, were not beyond using crude violence, as when in the mid 1500s over 4000 Yucatán Indians were put to torture. In Portuguese Asia indigenous orphans were rounded up to be raised as Christians and in Goa, so it was alleged, Hindus were forcibly defiled – their lips smeared with forbidden beef – so obliging them to accept conversion. Moreover, the appeal of the new religion was very often less what it offered in the next world than what it could provide in this. Members of impoverished and oppressed lower castes in Asia sought relief in Christianity and the Dutch agreed not to enslave indigenous debtors who became Christians. The Portuguese promised (1514) the ruler of Benin arms as soon as he should embrace Catholicism and the prospect of European skills, tools and aid eased its establishment in the Congo. Commercial advantages added to Christianity's attractions for the Japanese, while it was observed that the emperors of Muslim Iran and India accepted the missions in the hope that Christian merchants would follow in their tracks.[23]

For most of this period Christianity meant Catholicism, disseminated in particular by the religious Orders subject to the authority of the Iberian monarchs who had secured absolute authority over the churches of their empires.[24] The newly established Protestant creeds, other than that of John Calvin (1509–64), had no such skills in proselytization as Rome, no equivalents to its religious Orders – some with centuries-old traditions of such endeavour – and little to compare with the resources they deployed. Whatever energies remained from the struggle to survive and expand in Europe itself were largely devoted to theological debate and mutual persecution, while their assumptions, and particularly those of such of Calvin's disciples as the English Puritans, were not conducive to the conversion of non-European peoples. The New Englanders at first regarded the local Amerindians as yet another manifestation of the evil of the world and best left alone, though not without the hope that their observation of the 'good life and orderlie conversation' of the godly settlers might bring about their Christianization. To Dutch Calvinists it long appeared that energies devoted to evangelizing native peoples were dangerously diverted from the prime and pressing task of upholding the moral and theological standards of their compatriots overseas.

Nevertheless in the seventeenth century some Protestants came to take a livelier interest in spreading their beliefs. The English in North America, conscious of Catholic success, were spurred on by renewed fervour and a growing awareness of the advantages – long appreciated by settlers elsewhere – of dealing with docile Christian natives. The Virginia Company made ambitious but abortive plans to convert the indigenous survivors in its territory, including schemes to set up a college for their Christian education. There was some modest progress in Plymouth, while in the rest of New England, as settlement expanded, it was realized that a suitable and secure setting for colonization would be provided if the remaining Indians – those 'dregs and refuse of Adam's lost posterity' – were brought into 'subjugation to Jehovah'. To this end communities of 'praying Indians', feeble counterparts to the 'Congregations' of the Catholic Orders, were established in which the native converts lived in English fashion, engaged in English-style farming – avoiding, however, any pursuits which might compete with those of the colonists – and read the vernacular translation of the Bible provided for them. By 1700 the now expanding Anglican church was working among the Iroquois – dominant in the fur trade and exposed to Catholic missions from Canada – and there was some activity in Carolina. The Quakers attempted to convert the black slaves of Barbados, and were persecuted for their troubles, while in Asia the Portuguese alleged that following their acquisition of Bombay the English were spreading their 'false doctrine' among neighbouring Indian Christians, and by the end of the seventeenth century the East India Company was displaying an occasional concern for the souls of local peoples under its jurisdiction.

The outcome, however, was insignificant – a handful of Asian Protestants and a few Amerindian converts in New England, considered as disappointing as Christians as they were as military allies. In 1674 there were probably no more than a hundred indigenous communicants in Massachusetts, and as one disenchanted observer put it in familiar language, the missions were 'a plain cheat'. Meanwhile the Dutch accomplished little or nothing in the New Netherlands, enjoyed a transitory success in Taiwan – until, that is, the Chinese expelled them – and a modest but more enduring one in Batavia and some of Portugal's erstwhile Asian possessions. But quite apart from the limited effort and resources applied to the good work by a society in ardent pursuit of profit, the Protestant message was not the easiest to transmit, nor were its advocates as well placed as their Catholic brothers. They rarely enjoyed the prestige of belonging to a conquering power. As a rule their acolytes had to be able to read the Bible, which presumed a familiarity with written language that North American Indians did not possess, and required the provision of a vernacular text. Nor could New England ministers depart to labour among the natives, even if they had wished to do so, when Puritan belief insisted they should be on hand to tend the needs of their European flock. In Asia Dutch Calvinism was at a disadvantage in that its public expression lacked Catholicism's ritual, images and ceremonies, which closely resembled those of some major oriental religions. And it also lacked Catholicism's sacerdotal hierarchy and that respect for the sacramental aspects of the priesthood akin to the veneration accorded to their Hindu and Buddhist equivalents.

For Catholicism the results were very different, and nowhere more so, numerically at least, than in the Iberian Americas. Spain's overthrow of the native empires discredited their traditional cults and facilitated the imposition of Spanish will, which in the sixteenth century meant that of a devout ruling house influenced, and for a time guided by, the aspirations of the missionary Orders. These, whether dating from the Middle Ages, like the Franciscans and Dominicans, or new like the Jesuits – founded in 1534 by the redoubtable crippled Basque soldier Ignatius Loyola – reflected the energy, idealism and enthusiasm of a flourishing civilization imbued, as the result of Iberian triumphs the world over, with a sense of enjoying God's especial approval. The Jesuits in particular were highly educated, rigorously disciplined and prepared for martyrdom. All the missions, Portuguese and Spanish alike, initially attracted men of exceptional ability, many of whom had received an education powerfully influenced by the ideals of Renaissance Italy – with its admiration of all things classical - and those of the Christian humanism of the Netherlands. Some Spaniards, arguing the essential rationality of all mankind, believed that the Amerindians, once introduced 'by reason . . . love and industriousness' to Christianity would be freed from that inferiority to which they had been condemned by their ignorance of God's word. Others, accepting, as Antiquity taught, that there had been a Golden Age in the past, identified the Amerindians as survivors from that time of pristine bliss, who were to be protected from European decadence and brought by divine grace to their full potential. There were dreams, inspired by the traditions of European millenarianism, of creating in the Americas a replica of the Apostolic church, and indeed of converting the whole world before its imminently impending end. Throughout the

Iberian Americas schools were set up in which sons of chiefs in particular were educated in European ways. An Indian clergy was to be created, and in Mexico there were hopes, momentarily realized, that young Aztec nobles would be brought up as Christian gentlemen.

Much of the missions' success reflects their own devotion and determination. Barefooted friars, many of them subsequently martyred, set off unarmed into Indian lands, conquered and unconquered alike. But their task, onerous though it was in a huge continent of formidable natural barriers and a multiplicity of unknown languages, was less forbidding than that of their colleagues in Africa and Asia. They were not confronted by religions as ancient and complex as those of the Far East or as vigorous as Islam. They represented a conquering power which could use troops to round up the natives for conversion. The one-time subjects of the Incas and Aztecs were, moreover, as was widely and contemptuously remarked, meek and tractable. The Amerindians of Mexico were familiar, in their own religion, with penance, fasting and the idea of a second coming. Those of Peru were accustomed to convents, temples and an elaborate sacerdotal hierarchy. It was also their wont to abandon gods who failed them. Thus the leap to Christianity was, superficially at least, a relatively easy one.

For a time the missions enjoyed spectacular success. True, they had little impact in some parts of the Panama Isthmus among peoples alienated by Spanish slavers, and they had to overcome the resistance resulting from conversions effected by *conquistador* brutality – torture, burnings, hangings – and the subsequent despoliation by *encomenderos* in the guise of ensuring the spiritual well-being of those committed to their care. They made little progress among the more primitive tribes of the south of the modern USA, just as the Jesuits were in similar trouble in Canada. Even in Peru progress was slow. The terrain was particularly difficult, the military conquest a long drawn out struggle, and the predominantly Dominican mission demanded a more thorough preparation of neophytes than did the Franciscans who pioneered the conversion of Mexico. Nevertheless by the early 1700s a huge area of the Americas, twenty or more times the size of the mother country, had been made in some degree Catholic – as had the Philippines – and other varieties of Christianity had been excluded. Something the same was accomplished in parts of the immense Portuguese Brazil, and throughout the Iberian Americas the Catholic church was magnificently and munificently established, albeit chiefly for the benefit of whites. Amerindians innocent of an urbanized existence were brought together in great 'Congregations' in which, under the direction of the missions, they learned a Christian way of life and European skills, were tended in hospitals when sick, and protected from the attentions of the settlers. The most extensive were in Brazil and on the fringes of the Spanish empire, to which arduous regions the energies of the Jesuits, who arrived in the field later than the mendicant Orders, were particularly directed. Though in difficulties through the opposition of settlers in Portuguese Maranhão, they were able to enforce their will and ideals successfully in areas such as Spanish Paraguay, where secular government was fragile and colonial pressures weak, and where, by the early 1600s, they reputedly controlled 100,000 Indians.[25] In the one-time Inca and Aztec realms there were Indian churches, parishes and Spanish-style religious confraternities. Throughout the Iberian possessions incest, polygamy, nakedness and human sacrifice were less openly practised, pagan religious organization largely destroyed and even black slaves were introduced to, and maintained in, some form of Christianity.

But already by the mid 1500s there were growing doubts as to the genuineness of the conversions effected, and increasing signs of Amerindian incomprehension or resistance. A subversive millenarian movement emerged in Andean Peru in the 1560s and many Indians believed that the wars and diseases afflicting them were the revenge of offended deities. There were insufficient Catholic priests, and of these only a few fluent in the vernaculars abounding in what was despairingly described as 'this forest of languages', in which different and mutually unintelligible tongues were spoken by tribes living in close proximity. Services were conducted, European style, in the alien and incomprehensible Latin until it was decided in the early 1600s that Spanish was to be used, which the Indians were to learn to avoid misapprehension, though no adequate machinery of instruction was provided. Meanwhile missionary zeal and effectiveness dwindled. Part of the limited supply of able and dedicated men – and before 1600 no more than 5000 from all the Orders were sent to the Spanish Indies – was diverted into new, challenging and prestigious fields in Asia. The once confident and ebullient cultures of Iberia succumbed to self-doubt and introspection. The Orders in the Indies were at times shaken by bizarre heresies, quarelled among themselves, with the crown (which suspected them of theocratic leanings) and with their secular brethren. Disillusioned, they came to see their flocks as stupid and confused, or at best simple and childlike, capable of little of use, refusing or failing to learn Spanish, fleeing from their settlements or, as it was baldly put, dying 'through sadness' – not surprisingly, since they witnessed the spectacle of the widespread disregard by the white laity of every Christian precept and of the entire church strenuously engaged in making money, whether from silver mines or sugar plantations, which even the Inquisition possessed. The cossetted affluence of fortunate non-indigenous Christians – like those creole nuns with five servants apiece – was commonly synonymous with the oppression of their native fellows. Indians were used as forced labour by the clergy individually and corporately. They were obliged to build churches and monasteries and to toil on ecclesiastical estates, while their alleged spiritual mentors might well pass the piously accumulated funds of their confraternities to influential relatives, or, as in Jesuit Brazil, hand over 'Congregated' Indians to neighbouring planters. In return the native peoples were almost universally despised and humiliated. They were beaten and cheated. Their women were seized and seduced, not least by the clergy. They were excluded from the priesthood, until necessity secured their grudging admission at the end of the sixteenth century and they were treated, like the majority of converts, as a subspecies of the Christian community.

Conversion was accordingly often superficial and ephemeral, nor to many Spaniards did this matter. The native population was dying out, while that of mixed blood, generally eager to ape European ways, was increasing. Surviving Indians resisted the missions passively, as did their brothers in Canada, agreeing with whatever was put to them, but tenaciously pursuing their traditional ways. By the 1550s force was needed in most Mexican towns to get the indigenous population to church or to behave in what was considered a Christian fashion. At the end of the century there were Indians in the vicinity of the capital itself unable to make the sign of the cross, let alone comprehend the finer points of doctrine. Few Aztecs were Christian in the sense of having adopted a Christian view of life, and many converts, as happened elsewhere, desperately or prudently sought salvation in the simultaneous practice of the old and the new faiths. Even those who admitted the existence of a Christian God commonly considered he cared only for Europeans. Marriage according to the laws of the church was largely ignored, particularly in towns, with over 70 per cent of births among Indians and blacks in sixteenth- and seventeenth-century Lima illegitimate – for whites the rate was a scarcely more edifying 40 per cent. In Peru, Hispanized tribal chiefs, fearful of forfeiting popular support, encouraged or participated in native rituals. Indian spiritual leaders widely pursued their various callings, with those who fell into the hands of the authorities frequently, and significantly, men of considerable wealth. Sacrifices to the old gods continued in the Philippines, while indigenous ceremonies persisted in Central America and were openly performed in Mexico City itself in the seventeenth century. And when and where the Spaniards reacted, their harsh measures served to intensify an Indian sense of cultural unity.

Even when Christianity was professed – as it was in places with great fervour – it was often little more than a veneer under which ancient beliefs endured to produce, as in other parts of the world, a curious syncretic Catholicism. The Christian God joined the deities of the old order and Aztecs indulged in ferocious bouts of flagellation to induce rain or cure sickness. It was a confusion encouraged by some of the missions, mindful of the ancient precept that it is 'impossible to cut out everything at once from . . . stubborn minds'. Hence, as in the conversion of medieval Europe, churches were built on the sites of pagan shrines, and traditional usages were studied and where possible adapted, as when in Canada the Jesuits turned native dirges – 'hellish howlings' to the uninitiated – into Latin chants. And some of the fathers, accepting the juvenile qualities of their charges, were persuaded they needed a dramatic and colourful religion to attract and retain their attention. Indians were exempted from the jurisdiction of the Inquisition – though they remained enthralled spectators at its ceremonial burnings – and treated to a lavish assortment of processions, spectacles and festivals, enlivened with familiar music and drinking 'to remove the memory of the old idolatry'.

Another success, though short-lived and of a radically different nature, was that of the Portuguese in Japan. Here there was no European conquest, and no likelihood of one. Nevertheless for a time the missions enjoyed a measure of that secular support invaluable in ensuring large-scale conversions. It was, however, the support of local potentates, not of some European overlord, and as easily withdrawn as it had been offered. The Jesuits arrived in Japan in 1549, shortly after its accidental discovery by the Portuguese, and there Francis Xavier and his successors, to whose Order the Portuguese crown entrusted the conversion of the islands, encountered opportunities unparalleled elsewhere. The Japanese, proud and bellicose, yet courteous and affable, were treated with a respect rarely accorded by Europeans to other peoples. The Spartan code of their military caste was congenial to an Order pursuing an equally rigorous way of life, and Japanese concern with honour and reputation was entirely acceptable to Iberians who quickly identified them as 'the Castilians of the East'. The Jesuits, moreover, fortunately arrived at a time when there was widespread dissatisfaction with existing creeds in a country avidly eclectic in its approach to other cultures. It was, furthermore, a country in which dialectic skills – and in these few could outshine the highly trained and highly educated Jesuits – were admired. Nor was intellectual agility all the Portuguese could offer. They soon established themselves as middlemen in the trade to China from which the Japanese had been excluded by the imperial authorities as a result of their alleged piratical activities. Thus from the westerners the Japanese could receive not only a new faith but also Chinese gold, silk and other products, together with European weapons highly valued in a martial society. None were more appreciative of such benefits than the local feudal lords in whose hands effective power was concentrated at a time when central government was feeble. The Portuguese accordingly first directed their trade to the territories of magnates willing to admit the missions. Then Nagasaki became both the entrepôt for Luso-Japanese commerce and the headquarters of the Jesuits. The fathers established themselves as the agents of Japanese feudatories in the China trade, thus rendering themselves indispensable, and at the same time securing the resources needed for their work. Finally, friendship with the *shogun* Odo Nobunaga (1534–82), who was engaged in reasserting central authority, brought the Order what was in effect monarchical backing.

So the conversion of Japan went triumphantly forward. Great schemes were projected and by the end of the century there were 300,000 Christians

– the Jesuits claimed – in the islands out of a total population of about 20 million. How thoroughly the work had been done was shown when the tide turned. Other Europeans appeared, the Portuguese were driven out (1639) and eventually the only westerners allowed to trade, and under the closest supervision, were the Dutch. Christians, suspected of being the forerunners of foreign domination and of subverting the true ways of Japanese life, were persecuted, tortured and put to death. But despite the inevitable apostasies the faith, though outlawed in 1614, and with the missions expelled, survived for centuries.

Elsewhere much less was accomplished. In many cases Asians accepted Christianity at their peril – Christian widows and pregnant Christian girls could be enslaved in Hindu lands – and other than in Japan and China converts were generally treated with undisguised contempt by Europeans, and Eurasian Catholics were excluded, until the late 1600s, from the Orders and from high office in the secular church. To expound the Christian message of spiritual equality to societies (as in Hindu India) organized in rigidly defined castes was, if not impossible, difficult. Nor was it easy to overcome the revulsion of many adherents of major oriental religions – passive and stoic – from what they saw as the strident, volatile and tasteless behaviour of the apostles of Christianity. Moreover, in China only those learned in the writings of Confucius and his glossators were held fit to discuss the wisdom they enshrined, obliging the Jesuits to master the country's complex language and voluminous literature before they were taken seriously. They also found it expedient to accept ancient usages, whether ancestor worship in China or caste in India, though other Orders were less accommodating, engendering acrimonious controversy. Nowhere else did the missions find, as they did in Japan, a densely populated country whose remotest regions were easily accessible, and where a single language was universally understood. Nor did they enjoy anywhere else – other than briefly in the Congo – such secular support as in Japan and Spanish America. Europeans were not prestigious conquerors in Asia (nor in Brazil, Africa or North America) where, to the many endemic obstacles to success they soon managed to add others of their own making. The commercial operations of the missions, originally undertaken to finance their work, but before long conducted for the benefit of their members, were distasteful to peoples who held trade in contempt, besides arousing the jealousy and hostility of lay compatriots. Equally unhappily, in 1608 the papacy abrogated Portugal's exclusive right – deriving from the *Padroado Real* – to evangelize Asia, thereby intensifying friction between Portuguese and Spanish missions, notably with the arrival of Spanish fathers in Japan.[26] Then in 1622 Rome belatedly sought to bring all such endeavour under its control, leading to the despatch of French missions to Burma, India and elsewhere and provoking further disputes. Yet even as Portugal protested against the infringement of its ancient privileges, officers of the *Estado*, ever more conscious of the fragility of the imperial regime, were urging the need to placate wealthy indigenous merchants and neighbouring potentates by allowing the continuance of traditional rites and practices.

Nevertheless by 1600 there were about one million Christians – most of them Catholics – scattered throughout the East, with the missionary impact most profound in a number of minuscule territories in which, as a rule, there was some measure of European political control. The grasp of many neophytes on their new faith was, as elsewhere, often tenuous and short-lived. By the late 1600s, as subjects defected to enemies European and native alike, the Portuguese were convinced that their Catholicism was so fragile as likely to succumb at the sight of the junketings at Hindu festivals. Nor did the behaviour of others who continued in the faith inspire confidence, praying as many did to Hindu deities or removing their shoes on going to church as if entering a mosque or temple. To some Europeans such Catholicism seemed, then as now, more oriental than Christian, particularly when a Jesuit summoned to defend the conduct of his Order appeared clad in Brahminical robes, and when the host was distributed to Christians of the untouchable caste on the end of a stick. The opposition of the secular church and of other Orders eventually brought papal condemnation of such behaviour (1645), though the Jesuits characteristically continued as they had begun until the (momentary) suppression of their Order in the eighteenth century. Even so, the Spanish conquered Philippines became intransigently Catholic. In some Indonesian islands – Ambon especially – the Jesuits planted, as they did in Japan, a Christianity which was to endure for centuries. Around Goa the Franciscans and Jesuits between them secured, one way or another, large numbers of conversions to a faith still alive today, and there were some modest successes in China, Indo-China and Sri Lanka.

Least of all was accomplished in Africa, despite a promising Portuguese start in the Congo – where the converted indigenous potentate ruled as Dom Afonso I (1506–43) and where a royal Congolese bishop was enthroned – and despite the subsequent heroic efforts of Italian missions. There were the same difficulties as in the Americas with tribal societies, a galaxy of tongues and cultures unacquainted with written language. An even greater obstacle was that to most whites black Africans were fit only for enslavement. The attractions of the Christian message, initially heightened by the prospect of material aid, accordingly soon faded, not least since the church itself engaged in slaving. Hence few missionaries were attracted to lands where failure seemed inevitable, and of these only a handful survived the local climate and diseases. Meanwhile in the north and east of the continent the message of Islam was reinforced by the military power of Turkey and Morocco. Conversions there were, even in Muslim areas, but never on the scale originally achieved in the Congo. And as elsewhere strange heresies and syncretic faiths appeared while some converts, despised and humiliated, apostasized and turned on their former mentors, as did the early seventeenth century ruler of Malindi.

For the most part Christianity took root where, for any reason, the missions had secular backing. They did best in countries whose climates were agreeable to Europeans, in which a common language was spoken in a homogeneous society, or where more or less organized states existed. And success was more likely if they had respect for, or at least sympathy with, the peoples among whom they laboured. But after the triumphs of the sixteenth century the work of conversion, though never abandoned, was halted and indeed reversed. The missions were expelled from Japan, largely failed in Africa and lost their impetus in the Americas. To introduce a new faith, often by force, was one thing. To ensure its survival and spontaneous growth quite another. Indigenous disenchantment, resistance and hostility increased. Africans learned that baptism brought no release from slavery and Amerindians found that the new god gave them no protection against the white man's diseases. With the decline of Spain and Portugal, the pillars of Christianity's initial victories, enthusiasm cooled and there was a shortage of suitable clergy. Catholics quarrelled with Protestants and among themselves. Ideals preached by the churches were notoriously ignored by Europeans overseas, including the clergy themselves. Converts, other than from the high civilizations of the East, were expected to dress and behave according to European conventions and to break with traditional ways of life. And all for very little, since it was soon abundantly clear that whatever else Christianity conferred it did not confer equality with Europeans and provoked the ridicule or worse of compatriots.

On the balance of political power in the world Europe's expansion had an effect locally profound but generally insignificant. Outside the Americas there was no extension of Christian influence comparable to that achieved by Islam in Asia, Africa and indeed Europe itself. Nevertheless Ethiopia, Christian, even if of the wrong variety, was saved from the Ottomans by Portugal in the 1540s. It was similarly the Portuguese who, by briefly disrupting the westward flow of spices through the Red Sea, fatally weakened Mamluk Egypt – whose sultan drew much of his income from a monopoly of the trade – so contributing to its conquest by the Turks (1517). In Asia various minor potentates were dispossessed (as was the Sultan of Malacca by the Portuguese) or had their powers curbed (as by the Dutch in Indonesia). Yet it was European intervention in the East that ensured Muslim opposition, drew in the Ottomans and convinced the Japanese that, with China lost to the Manchus, their country alone stood as the 'land of the gods' against the barbarians.[27]

The arrival of the white man commonly aggravated indigenous rivalries as peoples struggled to monopolize the supply of those goods sought by Europeans and to become the sole recipients and redistributors of whatever they provided. Often enough the outcome was the radical modification of local political organization. In north-east America it was first the Huron (with French support) and then the Iroquois (aided by the Dutch and English) who secured control of the fur trade between the hunters of the interior and their white clients. In South Africa in the late 1600s the Khoikhoi chief known to the Dutch as Klaas rose to wealth and power as one of their agents in dealings with inland tribes.[28] Afonso I of the Congo and his successors, rich on slaving and the commerce in goods provided by their European allies, were, for a time, able to extend their authority. Portuguese purchases of gold in West Africa destroyed its ancient flow northwards across the Sahara from the upper Niger, so weakening powers such as Mali and Songhay which had formerly benefited from its passage, and enriching those like Cayor which were now its outlets. The trade was again drawn north with the rise of Sa'dian Morocco in the sixteenth century, but following its decline, and with the English, Dutch and others established on the Gold Coast by the mid 1600s, bullion once more moved westwards, strengthening the producing states of the interior, first Akwamu and then in the eighteenth century, Asante.[29]

More potent still was the impact of an insatiable European demand for slaves and an unshakable African addiction to the drink, weapons, cloth, tobacco and other commodities whites could provide. To acquire slaves West African potentates pressed more heavily on their subjects and attacked their neighbours. Such policies eventually brought about the disintegration of their authority, as villages and chiefs resisted and as erstwhile provinces went into the trade on their own, as did Sohio in the Congo, and were soon powerful enough to withstand their supposed sovereigns. Hence by the late 1600s, throughout much of Atlantic Central Africa, old states and societies, whose lords had lived on the agricultural tribute of their subjects, had been replaced by regimes sustained by the proceeds of slaving. The constant search for slaves drove peoples to flee inland for safety and the marauding of the Portuguese and their clients inspired attempts, like that of the Angolan Princess Nzinga at Matamba in the early 1600s, to create principalities beyond their reach. And as raiding, fighting and slaving penetrated deeper into Central Africa a new political pattern emerged, comprising a hinterland of warlords with a facade of small slave-broking powers along its Atlantic seaboard.[30]

Yet, notwithstanding such developments, the economy of the wider world as a whole was scarcely more affected by Europe's expansion than was its political organization. Colonial America and the Caribbean apart, ownership of land, agricultural production and industry were rarely significantly altered other than locally. Despite such notable casualties as the traffic in spices from Asia through the Levant – ultimately effectively stemmed by the arrival of the Dutch and English in the East – and despite some re-routing, most of the great and ancient trades survived. But clearly there were changes, and often remarkable ones. Formerly uninhabited islands like the Azores became of prime commercial and strategic importance.[31]

Obscure Caribbean islets such as Curaçao were transformed into vital entrepôts. Ports developed, as in the Americas, where there had previously been
none, or as at Macao and Bombay, in places hitherto insignificant. New
routes were established, some linking parts of the world either previously
only indirectly in contact, or totally isolated from one another. Portugal
discovered a direct sea passage from Europe to Asia. The Iberians opened
trades between Europe and black Africa, Europe and the Americas, Africa
and America. European products could now reach an almost global market,
while American silver circulated in Europe and Asia, African slaves were
shipped to Asia, Europe and the Americas, and American furs, fish, sugar
and tobacco sold in Europe. The Spanish entrepôt of Manila – handling in
its heyday American silver, Indian diamonds, Sri Lankan jewels, Persian
carpets and Chinese silks – linked Asia with the Americas and, through the
Americas, with Europe.

These trades, of increasing complexity with the passage of time, were
sustained by a multitude of others of shorter range, some new – like the
export of sugar and then of wines from Madeira and the Canaries – some
old, like the Asian country traffic now penetrated by Europeans. But it
was in the conquered Spanish Indies, and to a lesser extent in French and
Protestant North America, that new trading patterns were most apparent
and important. Some internal commerce there had been before the coming
of the white man, but it was quickly eclipsed by trades more extensive,
complex and substantial as specialized regional economies developed and
exchanged their particular products with one another and provided cargoes
for, or redistributed those supplied by, transoceanic shipping – Peru, for
example, received woollens from Mexico, grain from Chile, mules from
Argentina and horses from Nicaragua. New routes were pioneered through
the Spanish Indies, bringing the Andean settlements into contact with the
Atlantic, by land and river, via Buenos Aires. Goods were now less
frequently carried on native backs, but, in greater volume, by the ubiquitous
mule and in places by wheeled vehicles. New maritime routes were similarly
opened around the continent, none more important than that along the
Pacific coast which enabled Peru to send silver north, destined for the
Philippines or (through Panama) for Seville, and to receive in return black
slaves, European and American products and those oriental goods brought
in through Mexico from Manila. The English North American colonies did
business with one another by sea, as also with the neighbouring Caribbean
islands, Catholic and Protestant alike, providing them with anything from
food to furniture. At the same time, through such entrepôts as Jamaica,
they were in touch with the Spanish American mainland, and even, through
Curaçao, with Asia.

True, in some places Europeans disrupted, dislocated or occasionally
destroyed indigenous trades, just as their presence could ruin, distort or
damage indigenous economies, deflecting energies (in North America) from

agriculture to the acquisition of furs for the white man, or in East Africa from farming to supplying the gold and ivory he demanded.[32] European policies in Asia – attempted monopolies, the licencing and taxing of native shipping – forced the ancient spice trade into new channels. The presence of the Portuguese in East Africa damaged Arab commerce there, while their capture of such entrepôts as Hormuz and Malacca deprived them of their former importance. The Dutch VOC ruined the pepper ports of Sumatra and reduced one-time clove producers and exporters like Tidore to subsistence agriculture. Perhaps because of intense European activity in the waters of eastern Asia, Indian shipping found those of western Asia more attractive, and eventually, as a result of the doings of Europeans, many Indian merchants shifted their interest from seaborne to landborne commerce.[33]

But there was another side to the coin. Europeans brought new crops and unfamiliar livestock whose impact, if it could be devastating, could also, on occasion, be beneficial. They introduced tobacco to India, the Philippines and China, the banana to the tropical Americas – where it came to provide a basic subsistence – maize to India and China, the sweet potato to China, and maize and the sweet potato to Africa, where their cultivation rapidly spread. Both the latter crops were comparatively easy to grow, gave high yields, were resistant to drought and were suitable for storage. Hence they quickly came to supplement, and often to supersede, the staple African millet. Their dissemination increased the amount of food available, and on the west coast of the continent may have permitted population to grow sufficiently to compensate for the losses resulting from the slave trade.

In the East, moreover, indigenous merchants could often outmanoeuvre Europeans, or at least hold their own against them. The rich bought their way round obstacles erected by the intruders. The less affluent avoided areas of western commercial primacy – these very shifts sometimes bringing prosperity to ports and producers now handling additional business. With the advantage of local knowledge and lower costs, and willing as they were to accept lower profits, Indians could beat Europeans when the competition was purely economic, and remained dominant in the subcontinent's commerce. The European presence furthermore stimulated whole sectors of the region's economy, as it did to a lesser degree in parts of Africa and the Americas, handsomely rewarding enterprising or unscrupulous locals, just as slavers profited in Africa and amenable chiefs flourished in the Indies. Asian spice output perhaps doubled in the course of the sixteenth century to meet western demand, and by 1600 prices were rising partly as a result of competition among European buyers. Japanese silver and copper, readmitted by Portuguese initiative to such old markets as China, and finding new ones as well, were mined in greater quantities. Dutch and English trade enlarged the market for Indian opium in Malaysia and

Indonesia in the 1600s. Chinese textiles and ceramics found a new outlet in the Americas – with Drake's men amazed to encounter oriental crockery in Hispaniola in 1586 – and a growing one in Europe. Silk production apparently increased in south China, perhaps encroaching on the cultivation of rice, and by the early 1600s pieces specially designed to appeal to western tastes were being manufactured, while there was an even larger, almost global demand for Indian cotton textiles.[34]

More extensive markets, European imports of precious metals, and increased local purchasing power probably benefited merchants such as those of Hindustan and Gujarat in India. As a result of western trade bullion now circulated sufficiently freely in the East to become widely accepted as a medium of exchange and payment and to permit, particularly in India and China, the amassing of even greater amounts of superlative jewelry than hitherto. Its influx into western India, especially the enormous flow introduced by the Dutch in the seventeenth century, enabled more land revenue to be collected in silver and maybe aggravated that inflation known to have troubled the Mughal empire. Silver was of similarly increasing importance in Chinese imperial revenues from the late 1500s, possibly with the same inflationary effect, and such was its role in the empire's economy that when imports were reduced in the seventeenth century – the outcome of war, dwindling American exports and Spanish massacres of the Chinese in the Philippines – the repercussions were serious and extensive.[35]

Meanwhile ships were constructed for Europeans by indigenous builders, manned by indigenous crews, or leased to westerners by indigenous owners. Governments, companies and individual Europeans employed local capital and the skills of local entrepreneurs, who enjoyed, in exchange, an assortment of privileges. And European obstruction or oppression of merchants of one race or religion could well be to the advantage of those of another, with Coromandel Hindus profiting from the exclusion of Gujaratis, Bengalis and Arabs from Malacca by its new Portuguese overlords after 1511. Hence some orientals were handsomely rewarded, like that Hindu broker employed by the French at Surat in the seventeenth century, who in five years was said to have acquired 'three or four fine vessels which were always on voyages to the richest kingdoms in the East and brought him immense profits', some of them invested in 'splendid houses'.[36] Other like-minded Indians shipped cargoes in European craft – just as rich American creoles thought their goods safer in European rather than in colonial ships – operated vessels under the security of European flags, and conducted, in the wake of the intruders, trades reaching to the China Sea and the Philippines.

But Europe's most enduring legacy to the wider world was cultural. Around the globe there were scattered its unmistakable place names, customs, creeds, buildings and above all, languages – Portuguese which

survives in East and West Africa and flourishes in Brazil; the still spreading
Spanish of the Americas; French in Canada and the now ubiquitous English.
Where Europeans could impose their will and religion the most distinctive
native arts were usually destroyed. Elsewhere, however, there were varying
degrees of cultural interaction. On the whole the acceptance by Europeans
of the usages of other peoples was limited, not least by their conviction of
their own innate superiority. Even so, in East and West alike whites lived,
dressed, travelled and fought in ways affected by indigenous practice, just
as some learned local languages either for utilitarian reasons or in the hope
of preaching the Christian message more effectively. There were Dutch
farmers in South Africa who dwelt, like the Khoikhoi, in mat houses.
Tobacco was smoked and potatoes were eaten throughout the Americas –
both habits acquired from the Amerindians. Spaniards adopted Inca cotton-
quilted armour, Luso-Brazilians fought Indian-style, virtually naked, and
white North Americans learned from local allies and bitter experience how
to campaign in forests, how to take scalps, and how to travel by canoe,
toboggan or on snow shoes. In Asia, where already in 1632 employees of
the English East India Company at Agra lived 'after this Countrie manner',
Europeans ate rice, drank tea and arak, occasionally bathed, were introduced to the delights of massage, and sensibly employed ships of local
design – such as junks – in war and trade.[37]

But more was involved than convenience. From pragmatic tolerance and
from genuine friendship – the word itself appears in correspondence –
peoples joined in one another's pastimes and ceremonies. Amerindians and
Europeans joyfully danced together in early seventeenth-century North
America. Greenland 'savages' played football against Elizabethan seamen.
In Goa, to the disgust of the ecclesiastical authorities, Portuguese Catholics
lent jewelry to Hindu neighbours on special occasions and joined in the
celebrations marking the end of Muslim Ramadan, while Christian church
festivals were enlivened by the 'very indecent postures' of troops of local
dancing girls.[38]

The extent to which white overseas society was influenced by indigenous
cultures was largely determined by whether or not Europeans were
conquerors, whether or not they were present in strength, whether they
confronted ancient or vigorous civilizations, and especially whether or not
they were accompanied by women of their own race who, as spouses,
ensured any children were brought up as Europeans – as was the case in
most of the Spanish and English Americas. But in Portuguese Brazil, where,
through lack of Lusitanian females, men took local girls as their partners,
the mothers passed on their own customs to their offspring. So, too,
rank and file employees of the VOC, married to Indo-Portuguese women,
fathered children who were to all intents orientals. Where, moreover, European males were isolated among indigenous peoples they usually, of
necessity, spoke the local language (as in Paraguay), or some version of

their own modified by the vernacular into a patois like the Africanized Portuguese of the Cape Verdes. And, as was widely complained, they commonly 'turned completely native' as did the French pioneers in Brazil or the Portuguese *lançados* of Senegambia.

Non-Europeans were more willing to accept – or less able to resist – alien usages. True, among the conquered, whether in Spanish America or even Portuguese Goa, there was adamant opposition to learning the victors' language. Nevertheless there were plenty who could speak and write unfamiliar tongues. Congolese aristocrats were much admired in Renaissance Lisbon for their mastery of both Portuguese and classical Latin, a legacy of missionary endeavour. Survivors of the old imperial families in Spanish America and chiefs who supported the new regime ostentatiously paraded their loyalties and talked of having their children brought up 'civilized and Christian'.[39] Among those in regular and intimate contact with whites – indigenous mistresses, servants, slaves, merchants – fluency in European languages was, for obvious reasons, common, though rarely did they abandon their own vernaculars. Furthermore, where Europeans linked societies not previously in touch with one another, where they penetrated or dominated a network of commercial routes, or where they achieved any sort of supremacy over peoples of great ethnic diversity, their language could become the medium of communication, as did Portuguese in West Africa and large areas of maritime Asia. And many non-European tongues absorbed European words for unfamiliar objects and ideas, with Gulf Arabic, for example, assimilating an abundance of Portuguese nautical terms.

As often as not the white man's ways were imposed on non-Europeans, as on that multitude of the naked now obliged to dress. Others were taught 'civility' or emulated skills and behaviour they believed to be advantageous. Amerindians adopted trousers, shirts and hats. The Choctaw (from the south of the modern USA) gave up wearing durable but uncomfortable buckskin garments in favour of cottons, while brightly coloured English woollens were soon in great demand among the tribes of North America. New crops were accepted and unfamiliar commodities enthusiastically received. Smoking spread across continents and the white man's drink found insatiable takers the world over. Some of the peoples of Spanish America consumed, probably to their benefit, the flesh of acclimatized European livestock. They raised pigs, sheep, chickens, horses and cattle and now had the invaluable ass as a means of transport. The even more versatile horse was soon widely employed in societies to which it was previously unknown, spreading in the Americas (as did the sheep) to tribes far beyond the boundaries of white settlement, some of whom became, like the Khoikhoi in South Africa, 'very accomplished riders', as it was coolly put.

Regions as different as the Congo and the Spanish Indies accepted European-style buildings, and European skills of every kind were widely sought after. Indigenous craftsmen learned European techniques, with such success in Spanish America – where it was said they could pick up 'any trade that doth consist in arte' – that they were soon turning out familiar European commodities. The white man's tools, utensils and weapons were in almost universal demand. By the early 1600s some of the inhabitants of Andean America were using pickaxes, iron shovels and Spanish-style oxdrawn ploughs. Metals tools and pots eased the work and improved the cooking of North American Indians who, moreover, armed with iron arrow-heads, axes and knives, and subsequently with guns, could slaughter game, and one another, more effectively. Before long firearms were employed alike by Portugal's Brazilian auxiliaries, the troops of the Mughal emperors, the Africans of Guinea and the Indian opponents of the English pioneers in Virginia. European tactics were emulated by the Araucanians of southern America and translations of Iberian treatises on artillery appeared among the warlike peoples of Indonesia. The manufacture of guns was soon in full swing in Japan, to where they had been introduced by the Portuguese, and where their employment altered the whole nature of warfare. In the Arab Middle East and in western India European shipbuilding practice (with hulls fastened by nails as opposed to the lashings traditionally employed) was adopted, just as in Japan European rigs were modified for local vessels.

In the Spanish Indies writing rapidly took root in societies where such a form of communication was previously unknown, to the extent that already in the mid 1500s documents were being produced in a variety of Mexican languages.[40] Such borrowings went beyond simple utility. The growing willingness of some North American Indians to break ancient taboos – mentioning the dead by name, for example – was the fruit of their observation of English behaviour. More dramatically, French Jesuits introduced western science into China in the seventeenth century after the emperor himself and some of his major officials, having witnessed the accuracy of the missionaries' astronomical calculations, became eager to learn Euclidian geometry and other disciplines.

Occasionally there was a true fusion of cultures, sometimes by accident, as indigenous beliefs merged with Catholicism to give strange syncretic forms of Christianity, sometimes by design, as when in the post-conquest Spanish Indies peoples hitherto unacquainted with writing could set down their histories, songs and poetry in languages themselves strongly influenced by that of Spain. But most remarkable were the interactions which arose from the meetings of high civilizations, or when, for some reason, imperial masters were prepared to encourage indigenous cultures. Through Spanish missionary efforts to educate young Mexican aristocrats as Christian gentlemen there was produced in 1552 the *Badianus Herbal* in which Mexican plants were classified according to European tradition, but depicted in Indian style, with the vernacular explanation by one scholarly Indian put into Latin by another. Pleasingly, too, European designs might in some measure be executed in the local idiom, with Macao's Jesuit church planned by an Italian architect and gorgeously decorated by Chinese and Japanese craftsmen. Amerindian workmen added exotic ornament to Spanish buildings in the Indies and the seventeenth-century Catholic church in Arakan was embellished with oriental carpets. In lands visited, but unsubjugated by Europeans, local artists responded to new subjects and to unfamiliar styles and techniques. West African carvers depicted improbable-looking and curiously dressed whites. By the 1640s the Japanese were able to produce world-maps based on European cartographical knowledge. European motifs – among them the pope and the dignitaries of the Holy Roman Empire – appeared in Japanese paintings and on Chinese porcelains and Indian textiles. Influenced by exemplars (usually provided by the missions) artists in China, Japan and Mughal India experimented with realism and perspective, hitherto ignored. In Portuguese Asia Christian themes were charmingly handled in ways unmistakably oriental and Mughal painters in particular achieved a felicitous balance of eastern and European styles.

By the beginning of the eighteenth century Europeans were firmly established in the wider world, though more securely in the West - where huge amounts of land were coming under their control – than in Asia. The white populations of these western settlements remained tiny by European standards, but they were growing, and particularly rapidly in English America (at about 3 per cent a year), and by natural increase rather than as the result of emigration. Other than in relatively small areas their prosperity rested, to a far greater degree than that of Europe, on the labour of slaves or of a workforce of mixed or non-European blood, many of whose members were hardly better off than slaves, and to whom the only equivalents in the Old World were the serfs of eastern Europe and enslaved Africans of Iberia. Indeed, where cherished European ambitions were given free rein there emerged regimes which were almost parodies of those of the mother country. Iberian self-esteem and revulsion from the degradation of manual labour were nowhere more fully realized than in the slave-based societies of the Americas. The ideals of English Puritans found their fullest expression in the ruggedly independent and turbulent dissenting colonies of New England. But for the rest colonial society grew to be much like that of Europe. Its culture was overwhelmingly that of the Old World. Its members dwelt in, or among, buildings for the most part of obviously European inspiration. If in some degree conscious that they differed from the inhabitants of Europe they were even more conscious that they differed from the local populace, indigenous or African. They lived under familiar forms of political organization and the colonial economies, other than those of the Caribbean, developed the familiar divisions of labour and specialization of function. And notwithstanding considerable political friction the bonds between parent societies and their overseas offshoots grew closer. Rich colonials returned home to invest or flaunt their wealth. Churches, missions and the faithful abroad, whether Catholics or Quakers, were in touch with co-religionists at home. Colonial merchants dealt in European markets, acted as factors for, or were partners of, those of the mother country, and metropolitan resources and credit loomed large in colonial commerce.

European religion, like European political and social organization, was to some degree imposed on indigenous peoples, most notably in Spain's possessions. The ethnic balance of parts of the Americas was radically changed by the arrival of whites and their slaves, by the ravages of the diseases they introduced and by a luxuriant miscegenation. In many places they inflicted irreparable damage, which could extend beyond the bounds of their presence and authority. Nevertheless for some of the native population the European invasion brought the compensation of access to hitherto unknown foods and commodities, the chance to acquire new skills and eagerly accepted opportunities for advancement and enrichment. Yet much of the Americas remained unknown to Europeans and even in that part under Iberian rule for the survivors life, though modified by European custom and belief, remained essentially Indian.

In the Iberian Americas there emerged economies which allowed a minority an easy prosperity from the land's rich resources, the fruits of which were largely expended – or as some would say squandered – in ostentatious display, pious endowments and the accumulation of (very often unprofitable) land. Into the Caribbean Europeans introduced the monoculture plantation. The resultant regime – brutal slavery, a transient white population, dependence on external sources of food and labour, the disposal of profits abroad, the stifling of domestic agriculture – was to condemn the majority of the islands to the most wretched of futures. But if some colonies became in every sense dependencies (like the West Indies) of more advanced economies, others were soon capable of challenging those of metropolitan Europe. And none more so than British North America whose gross national product perhaps grew at 3.5 per cent a year in the century after 1650 – about seven times the rate of that of England itself – and whose inhabitants, particularly in New England, were impelled as much by their own convictions as by the lack of any such God-given riches as Spanish America enjoyed, into a host of energetically pursued enterprises.[41] The East was a different story. The European hold remained tenuous, and although westerners inflicted some devastating blows, redirected some ancient trades, accomplished some modest proselytization and established themselves in some established economies – and by no means to the detriment of Asians – they had yet to make their mark.

NOTES AND REFERENCES

1 *The Travels of the Abbé Carré*, ed. Fawcett and Burn, II, 358.
2 See pp. 46–8, 71.
3 See pp. 187–90.
4 See pp. 150, 153, 163.
5 Ian K. Steele, *The English Atlantic*, p.266; Louis B. Wright, *The Cultural Life of the American Colonies 1607–1763* (New York, 1957), p.107. In some French towns of the mid 1700s up to 90 per cent of lower middle class men could read and write, and over 50 per cent of the richer working class.
6 Ambrosini, *Paesi e Mari Ignoti*, pp. 262–3.
7 Steele, *op cit.*, p. 267.
8 See pp. 187–90.
9 See pp. 113–6.
10 Gillian T. Cell (ed.), *Newfoundland Discovered*, p. 297.
11 David W. Galenson, *Traders, Planters and Slaves*, pp. 12–13.
12 See pp. 117–9, 148, 184.
13 Gary B. Nash, *Red, White and Black*, p. 287.
14 See pp. 109–12.
15 See pp. 84–5, 148–9, 204–5.
16 Miles L. Wortman, *Central America, 1680–1840*, p. 74.
17 See p. 118.
18 Reports of the Royal Commission on Historical Manuscripts. *The Manuscripts of the House of Lords*. New Series, ix, no. 2793.
19 *The Travels of the Abbé Carré*, ed. Fawcett and Burn, III, 686; Richard Elphick and Hermann Giliomee (eds), *Shaping of South African Society*, p. 87.
20 Elphick and Giliomee, *op. cit.*, p. 129.
21 William L. Sherman, *Forced Native Labor in Sixteenth-Century Central America*, pp. 306–7.
22 See the essays of Woodrow Borah, Frances Kartunnen and James Lockhart in George A. Collier, Renato I. Rosaldo and Joseph D. Wirth (eds), *The Inca and Aztec States, 1400–1800. Anthropology and History* (New York, 1982).
23 See pp. 14, 47, 198.
24 See pp. 142, 146, 151.
25 See pp. 109, 147, 154.
26 The *Padroado Real* was the combination of rights, privileges and duties granted by the papacy to the Portuguese crown as the patron of the Roman Catholic missions and ecclesiastical establishments in vast regions of Africa, Asia and Brazil, by a series of privileges between 1456 and 1514. They were in effect limited only by those similar rights accorded to the crown of Castile by bulls between 1493 and 1512.
27 See the excellent discussion in R. P. Toby, *State and Diplomacy in Early Modern Japan* (Princeton, 1984)
28 Elphick and Giliomee, *Shaping of South African Society*, p. 16.
29 Roland Oliver and Anthony Atmore, *The African Middle Ages, 1400–1800* (Cambridge, 1981), p. 90.
30 David Birmingham, *Central Africa to 1870. Zambezia, Zaïre and the South Atlantic* (Cambridge, 1981), pp. 24ff, 60ff; Oliver and Atmore, *op. cit.*, pp. 158–9.
31 Scammell, 'The English in the Atlantic Islands'.
32 H. H. K. Bhila, *Trade and Politics in a Shona Kingdom. The Manyika and their Portuguese and African Neighbours 1575–1902* (1982), pp. 48, 252.
33 K. N. Chaudhuri, *Trade and Civilisation in the Indian Ocean. An Economic*

History from the Rise of Islam to 1750 (Cambridge, 1985), pp. 100–101.

34 See pp. 98, 103, 106.
35 William S. Atwell, 'International bullion flows and the Chinese economy *circa* 1530–1650', *Past and Present* **95** (1982), 68ff.
36 *The Travels of the Abbé Carré*, ed. Fawcett and Burn, I, 144–5.
37 *The Travels of Peter Mundy in Europe and Asia, 1608–1667*, ed. Sir Richard Carnac Temple and Lavinia Mary Anstey, 5 vols, Hakluyt Society (1907–35), II, 86–7.
38 *The Travels of the Abbé Carré*, 1, 135.
39 Steve J. Stern, *Peru's Indian Peoples and the Challenge of the Spanish Conquest*, p. 169.
40 The Maya, Mixtec and other Amerindian peoples traditionally kept records carved on stone and painted on paper.
41 John J. McCusker and Russell R. Menard, *The Economy of British America, 1607–1789* (Chapel Hill, 1985), p. 57.

7 The fruits of empire

The opening of new routes to the long-sought riches of Asia, the discovery of unknown continents and the overthrow of great empires gave Europeans an immense pride in their achievements. National epics were composed. Patriots urged the pre-eminence of their fellow countrymen in these astounding events. Idealists dreamed of the dawn of universal empire and the conversion of all mankind to Christianity. Such pride, however, slid easily into arrogance or worse, like the rabid intolerance of seventeenth-century Iberia, inflamed by the Catholic Counter Reformation and imperial commitments which brought prolonged conflict with pagans, infidels and heretics. Protagonists of overseas ventures might urge the merits of alien peoples to further their schemes, just as compatriots, obliged to seek indigenous assistance, might tacitly admit alien virtues. But Europeans, who saw themselves as at last equalling those heroes of Antiquity who had for so long overshadowed them, needed little convincing of the inferiority of the rest of mankind. True, there were some charitable opinions, chiefly among a handful of men of learning, and the Japanese and Chinese at least were treated more respectfully. But the general European view, expressed in a rich vocabulary of abuse and manifested in gratuitous insult and brutality, was one of disapproval and contempt.

Most of the peoples of the wider world, it was agreed, traded deceitfully, fought treacherously and were in any case usually cowards. They commonly differed in colour and appearance from Europeans and lived in unfamiliar and therefore unacceptable ways. They might be naked, pagan or infidel, polygamous or cannibal, and they frequently lacked those cities, which as Antiquity taught, were the prerequisites of a civilized existence. The inhabitants of the great Amerindian empires were dismissed as spineless and childlike. Those of the rest of the Americas were found to be 'brutish and deprived of reason' – like European peasants, dirty, ignorant and unstable. Black Africans were quickly cast in the enduring stereotype of the natural slave and the embodiment of every form of sexual licence and indulgence. And the more Europeans knew of their fellows the less on the whole they liked them. By 1700 the East was classed as stagnant, superstitious and despotic. Nor were whites born or living overseas much better. South American creoles, affected by 'climate and constellations' and tainted with

213

Indian blood, were seen as the degenerate and degenerating heirs of the *conquistadores*. North American colonists were 'tame Indians', and those of Jamaica – 'brutes' in the eyes of an English admiral in 1703 – allegedly too ignorant and vicious to be allowed office.[1]

The effects of Europe's expansion overseas, spreading as it did civilization and the word of God, seemed to many at the time entirely beneficial, as indeed it has appeared to many since. Europeans gained confidence in themselves. Speculation on their achievements allegedly freed their minds from the shackles of medieval superstition, just as the outlets and resources of the wider world conveniently rescued them from renewal of the 'feudal crisis' of internecine war which had plagued the fifteenth century. Equally dramatically, the 'capitalist economy' was supposedly born. Of potential stimuli, mental and material, there was certainly no shortage. Hitherto unknown peoples, together with commodities and products from the farthest parts of the world, became increasingly common in Europe. Japanese Christians visited Rome in the sixteenth century, there was a Chinese sage at Oxford in the 1600s, descendants of the Aztecs and Incas lived in Spain, and 'Negroes and Blackamoors' were so numerous in Elizabethan London that the queen ordered their expulsion.

European diet was enlarged and enriched. Monarchs like Philip IV of Spain could import Sri Lankan elephants and Cochin tigers 'as an ornament' to their courts. There was a massive influx of precious metals and precious stones and a substantial flow of oriental books, manuscripts, textiles, porcelain, artefacts, seeds, plants and archaeological fragments, together with treasures of every sort from the Americas. Natural history specimens, wonders and works of art were assiduously collected, like the magnificent Chinese library assembled for Louis XIV of France.

Exotic themes and topics proliferated in the arts. Palaces of *conquistador* families in Trujillo (Spain) were decorated with Amerindian detail. The library of the university of Coimbra (Portugal) has representations of the fauna of the imperial possessions painted on presses of wood from the respective regions. Exotic peoples, real or simulated, became features of fashionable gatherings and were depicted in the houses of the great, such as the Amsterdam residence of Johan Maurits, one-time governor of Dutch Brazil, or on monuments to sovereigns, like the statue of Queen Anne of England in St Pauls. In the late 1600s Chinese influences were reflected in European art, and reproductions of the works of the Dutch painters Frans Post (1612–80) and Albert Eckhout (c.1607–65), who had been in Brazil with Johan Maurits, were in wide and influential circulation. Poets and playwrights, William Shakespeare among them, found inspiration in subjects ranging from shipwreck in distant oceans to the fall of the Amerindian empires and the Manchu conquest of China, while the *Travels* (1614) of Fernão Mendes Pinto marks the first conscious attempt to capture the character and atmosphere of the Orient in words.

More important, Europeans were moved to depict strange lands and their inhabitants, endeavouring to convey some idea of unknown scents and colours and to describe the unfamiliar. Since the overseas world offered few prospects of the patronage vital to artists it was rarely visited by the most celebrated painters, though it attracted some lesser masters and provided subjects for some of the greatest at home. The Indians of northeast America were depicted by John White, who accompanied an English expedition in 1585, and those of Brazil – already shown in a Portuguese work of 1505 – by the protégés of Johan Maurits. Aztecs brought home by Cortés were meticulously drawn by Christoph Weiditz and in the following century Rembrandt made some powerful studies of Africans.

More numerous, and often of outstanding quality, were the written descriptions produced by that new race of Europeans familiar with lands and seas the world over. Much of what they wrote was based on personal knowledge, as opposed to that acquired from traditional authority, and marked by painstaking efforts to attain accuracy through the careful and critical handling of evidence. Unfamiliar plants and insects were observed, collected and described, as by the celebrated seventeenth-century English doctor, Hans Sloane, in Jamaica. The Portuguese historian Diogo do Couto (1543–1616), seeking to ascertain the setting and circumstances of his compatriots' feats in Asia, took not only the testimony of fellow countrymen but also questioned Sri Lankan princes, Mughal diplomats and learned Brahmins. And throughout this first imperial age there was a sustained output of careful and sometimes sympathetic investigations of the history and traditions of the high cultures of the Americas, and accounts and assessments of societies and civilizations ranging from the great empires of the East to the nomadic communities of the New World.

Thus in one way or another there was amassed a huge volume of assorted fact about the non-European world. By the early 1700s all its habitable continents and all its oceans, previously entirely or largely unknown, had been discovered. Other lands were thought to exist, notably in the South, and of those so far found the interiors, other than of Iberian Americas, were for the most part a mystery. Furthermore, following the voyages of the Portuguese and Spanish pioneers, some European seamen understood the pattern of winds in the Atlantic and in the seas between East Africa and Indonesia. And after Magellan's stupendous achievement they understood those of the globe from the Arctic Circle to about 40°S into the Atlantic, and from the northern shores of the Indian Ocean to about 15°S. After the mid 1500s they appreciated that the Pacific trades would carry a ship eastwards from the Philippines to America, and from the early 1600s that the 'roaring forties' gave a speedy if boisterous passage from southern Africa to the vicinity of Indonesia. Equally importantly it had already been found how to make the arduous voyage down the Pacific coast of the Americas, and how to clear the Caribbean through the Gulf of Florida.

This geographical and navigational information, familiar to many in the learned, mercantile and governmental circles of western Europe by word of mouth and personal contact, reached a wider audience with the publication – by a burgeoning and relatively new printing industry – of individual accounts and narratives. Then from the mid 1500s there appeared collections of voyages, travels and descriptions of distant lands such as those of Ramusio in Italy and Hakluyt (1589) in England, followed by editions and translations made available by their many successors throughout Europe. The potential impact of such materials – and popular selections, it should be remembered, were often unsympathetic to the new-found worlds – was strengthened as in the seventeenth century Dutch printers produced, unlike their Iberian counterparts, illustrated volumes, and as in this age of outstanding cartographic achievement there was a growing output of charts, maps and atlases. Many came initially from such ancient and celebrated centres of cartographical skill as Genoa and Venice. But primacy soon passed to Portugal, whose maps gave latitudes and longitudes (of sorts) in the sixteenth century and took notice of the difficult problem of compass variation. Ultimately pre-eminence shifted to the North, with the rise of distinguished schools in the Low Countries – where Gerhard Mercator (1512–94) showed how to project the globe realistically on to a flat surface – and England.

Among those who encountered and described non-Europeans, and among those who read, or knew of their experiences, was a minority anxious to understand their fellow men and an even smaller minority willing to admit their merits. There were, of course, Europeans who for a variety of reasons abandoned their own customs and beliefs and went to live among indigenous peoples, just as there were others who dwelt in amicable relations with those of different race, colour and creed.[2] But in Europe there were some whose views went beyond the purely pragmatic. Chairs were founded in Iberian universities for the study of indigenous languages, and grammars and dictionaries of exotic tongues were produced in Portugal and Spain and subsequently elsewhere. Admittedly the prime and indeed often the sole intention was commonly to facilitate the conversion or government of the peoples in question. Nevertheless their intrinsic merits might be accepted, and it might even be acknowledged that the ways in which they lived, unsupported by Christian truth, were more than expressions of folly or depravity. This was most readily conceded of those whose skins were white and whose government was 'well ordered' and most nearly approximated to European norms. China, whose wealth and grandeur had been rumoured since the days of Marco Polo, was regarded, in the earliest encounters, with an awe and enthusiasm somewhat cooled but never extinguished by closer acquaintance, while many were to admit that 'justice and rectitude' prevailed in Mughal India. So, too, the piety, wisdom and enlightenment of the Siamese were extolled in late seventeenth-century France, where it had earlier been allowed that the indigenous inhabitants of Canada were just as much humans as were Europeans, and even in some ways their superiors.

More fundamentally there were occasional pleas to 'let all nations enjoy their own customs' as a Portuguese writer put it in 1590. Such views received their most forceful and eloquent expression from the French poet Pierre de Ronsard (1525–85), who urged that Brazilian Amerindians should be left to themselves, and from his compatriot the essayist Michel de Montaigne (1533–92), who pleaded for the acceptance of the diversity of human custom. It was a sentiment foreshadowed in the opinion of one of the first visitors to Paraguay that its naked and delicately painted inhabitants were 'beautiful after their manner', and echoed by a Caribbean buccaneer of the late seventeenth century who bluntly remarked that although the customs of the local Indians were 'different from ours they ought not for that reason to appear ridiculous to us'.

But these were the views of a minority, and were long to remain so. They were largely eradicated from Counter Reformation Iberia and, pragmatists apart, were elsewhere confined to a handful of scholars. For most other Europeans the philosophical and ethical implications of the opening of the wider world were, like the impact of man's recent penetration of space, eclipsed by the many and pressing problems closer to hand – inflation, social unrest, poverty, the relentless advance of the Ottoman Turks, the religious strife and brutal and endemic wars of the sixteenth and seventeenth centuries. Accounts of distant lands were left unpublished, many remaining so to our own age. Investigations undertaken by zealous officers of the Spanish crown languished in the archives. Scholars in Iberia complained that their works went unread, not because of any policy of secrecy or security by the rulers of Spain and Portugal – whose subjects regularly defected with treasured information to the service of others – but since, as the historian Diogo do Couto bitterly remarked, there was a lack of curiosity. The first broadsheets and pamphlets to appear describing the achievements of Columbus and his successors were seemingly not thought worth preserving, just as the first collection of this material (1507) was left unrevised for nearly half a century. The death of Columbus himself in Valladolid passed unnoticed by the city chronicler. The Americas are ignored in the published memoirs of the Emperor Charles V, and scarcely find a mention in the voluminous writings of such influential figures as Erasmus (1466–1536) and Luther. The conquest of Mexico and Peru appears to have gone unrecorded in the official art of Spain as did the acquisition of Brazil in that of Portugal. Not until the 1630s did the Spanish crown commission any substantial works of art referring to its oceanic possessions, while the affairs of the flourishing English North American settlements in the seventeenth century were largely ignored by Venetian diplomats who considered that their fastidious patrician masters would have no interest in the doings of a nest of heretics set in lands whose natural qualities violated all the criteria of contemporary good taste.[3]

True, a great and increasing volume of books on the wider world was published in these centuries and an uncertain number of others circulated in manuscript. But together they never amounted to more than a modest and decreasing fraction of the growing total output of the presses, dominated by politics, religion, the classics and the nonsense of popular romance, ancient and modern. Of the books which appeared in Portugal between 1540 and 1600 little more than 10 per cent were concerned with Asia, the very heart of the empire. Nor, of course, was quantity synonymous with quality or a discriminating quest for enlightenment. Many collections of voyages and descriptions of exotic lands – that of Hakluyt, for example, in England – were intended to stir the interest of compatriots. Many in Catholic countries responded to the wish of the faithful to hear of the good work of the missions. Others were indiscriminate assortments of fact and fancy pandering to an insatiable thirst for the bizarre and wonderful. Cultured Venetians, however, favoured compact editions of colourful, undemanding and anecdotal material. Maps and charts were displayed as fashionable domestic decorations and travel literature was accumulated as the proper way for gentlemen 'to furnish out a library'. And commonly enough such volumes were read – like the enormously popular *Arabian Nights Entertainments*[4] or the various classics of piracy - to provide in their tales of daring, adventure and marvels that escape from reality every age craves.

Nor, moreover, were careful and dispassionate accounts of alien societies, or sympathetic attitudes towards them, necessarily indications of European dedication to the disinterested pursuit of truth and understanding. Government officials, notably those of Portugal and Spain in the early years of expansion, recorded, though not without much prompting, a mass of detail about the lands their sovereigns ruled or the peoples among whom their compatriots were established, to ascertain how they might best be exploited handled or controlled. Merchants and factors provided accurate information, as in the reports transmitted home from Asia by officers of the VOC, to allow commercial opportunities to be assessed and appropriate policies to be devised. The merits of non-Europeans could be urged simply to present them as a reproach to contemporary evil, as in the prolific literature – French especially – on virtuous Muslims and noble savages. Indigenous peoples could be favourably, not to say idealistically, depicted by those seeking to encourage colonization and well-disciplined states could be commended since they were potentially the most amenable to conversion. Necessity likewise fostered generosity. Portuguese officials in India in the hard days of the seventeenth century tolerated the practice of local rites and religions to placate neighbouring rulers and to prevent the loss of vital indigenous skills and capital. Caribbean buccaneers, probably as much from inclination as from need, found no fault with the way of life of the

Indians among whom they moved and whose supplies and assistance were of great value to them.

Naturally enough many of the opinions expressed on non-Europeans and many of the policies envisaged for their control and exploitation reflected long-established European views and usages. The employment of slaves was extended, justified and, in the sixteenth and seventeenth centuries occasionally and eloquently condemned, chiefly by Iberian members of the missionary Orders. Their condemnations, however, were rarely of slavery itself, but of the brutality and spiritual neglect it entailed. Spaniards were happy enough to use black Africans, accustomed as they were to slavery in the southern kingdoms of the peninsula and since blacks were provided by the Portuguese from regions outside Spanish jurisdiction. Not until the end of his life did Bartolomé de las Casas express the same concern for Africans he had long voiced for Amerindians. The forthright denunciation by the sixteenth-century Spaniard Bartolomé de Albornoz quickly became a bibliographical rarity and many defenders of the Amerindians were content they should be saved by the enslavement of blacks – used indeed by the church itself. The Protestant Dutch spoke in 1596 of freeing Africans into 'their natural liberty', but were soon slavers second to none, and only in the late 1600s did some English Quakers begin to doubt the ethics and justification of slavery.

The pattern was a familiar one. Mediterranean slavery flourished and was denounced in the late Middle Ages, and even as the Atlantic trade began its long history a scholar innocently proclaimed (1521) that since mankind were 'now nearly all brothers in Christ' slaves should not be kept. More- over, the great Castilian controversies on the Spanish treatment of the Amerindians in the early sixteenth century, culminating in the debate at Valladolid (1550–51) between de las Casas and Sepúlveda, were not about slavery as such but about the position of certain Amerindian peoples under Habsburg authority. It was an argument conducted in the ancient Iberian tradition of public debate among the religious, and of violent denunciation by the friars of all they disapproved of. It was conducted, furthermore, in terms deriving from the Middle Ages and Antiquity. The defence of the validity of Amerindian political organization by de las Casas stemmed from a venerable tradition holding that natural law justified the rule of heathen princes and prohibited its overthrow. His condemnation of forced conver- sions to Christianity – long practised by the church – had equally weighty support. Such behaviour had been rejected by Thomas Aquinas and oppo- sition to proceedings of this kind, as also to the seizure of non-Christian lands, had been voiced in the late Middle Ages, notably over the activities of the Portuguese in North Africa and of the Spaniards themselves in the Canary Islands. Natural law, however, could equally vindicate external intervention in defence of human rights, just as, according to another powerful tradition of the church, those resisting the Christian message, practising tyranny or living in 'sinful ways' could be enslaved and their societies destroyed. Again, if, as de las Casas maintained, the Amerindians were rational – and the papacy had ruled that they were 'true humans' in 1537 – then by Aristotelian reasoning their states were justified. But if, as others believed, they were irrational – supposedly demonstrated by anything from a lack of writing to an unselective diet – then by the same logic they were condemned to such restraints as would keep them from their wicked ways.

There was indeed very little for which the Middle Ages and Antiquity had no answer. Black Africans, as we have seen, were destined for slavery since their societies were not organized as the ancients prescribed, allegedly lacking, for example, cities and religion. They were said to be captured – as were 'unpacified' Indians – in wars designated as 'just' by some medieval thinkers since directed against peoples of evil behaviour resisting the Christian message. And by the tenets of Aristotle they had, as inferiors, to be subject to their superiors, just as, according to some theorists, had subhuman Indians and equally subhuman European peasants.

Catholics and Protestants alike established sovereignty over alien lands by age-old symbolic acts, such as the erection of cairns and crosses. Classical and medieval lore defined the nature and extent of the authority of discoverers and conquerors, even if some felt no need for this metaphysical support. In the early 1500s, when the philosophical debate on these very matters was at its height in Iberia, the king of Portugal crisply asserted the primacy of possession, while the rulers of Spain cited nothing more than their own will as authority for their actions.[5] Nevertheless it was usual to reinforce claims with any such conventional arguments as would serve. Some Catholic sovereigns, ignoring the denial by a succession of medieval thinkers of untrammelled authority to the papacy, subscribed to the age-old pretensions of the see of Rome to jurisdiction over pagan lands and to a plenitude of power. The kings of Portugal and Spain accepted that the popes could bestow title on them, parcel out the world between them, confer monopolies, define commercial privileges and empower them to enslave the non-Christian indigenous inhabitants of West Africa (as in a bull of 1455 for Portugal) and the Antilles (by a privilege of 1493 for Spain).[6] It was likewise papal grant that justified the demand intially made by the Spaniards of the peoples of the New World that they either accept the authority of the church and Castile or be reduced to servitude.

Nor were these the only weapons to hand. There were publicists in Habsburg service in the early 1500s who maintained that their master's world-wide authority derived from that universal lordship appertaining to the office – the most medieval of all – of Holy Roman Emperor, held by Charles V from 1519. Others urged that prior possession and the costs of exploration brought title and justified monopoly, with some Spaniards alleging that in the remote past their compatriots had not only reached

North Africa but America as well. Many of these arguments subsequently passed into Protestant use, as when an Elizabethan protagonist of empire claimed North America for the queen since in some distant age it had supposedly been discovered by the Welsh. There were familiar calls for, and opposition to, the forced conversion of the Indians, while the VOC defended its Asian monopoly, as the kings of Portugal had once justified their pretensions in West Africa, on the grounds of the expense incurred in establishing the trade.

Furthermore, many of those features of early modern civilization so attractive to posterity – rational curiosity, toleration, factual precision, a concern for the well-being of some indigenous peoples, argument by hypothesis rather than theological categorizing – stemmed from the same rich classical and medieval heritage, not from some intellectual revolution occasioned by the discovery of unknown lands. The art of the Middle Ages and the Renaissance was no stranger to realism. There had long been attempts to provide accurate descriptions of alien societies, as by an author writing on the Mongols in 1245 who reported, so he claimed, only what 'we ourselves have seen, or heard from others whom we believe to be worthy of credence'. Such attitudes reflect – among other things – in part the growing influence of the teachings of Antiquity, in part the outlook of an increasingly commercial society, in which merchants who hoped to prosper and seamen who aspired to sail again had of necessity to be capable of careful and accurate descriptions of markets and natural phenomena. A blend of similar influences underlay the sympathetic, tolerant and even enthusiastic views of non-European societies produced in the sixteenth and seventeenth centuries. Guided by classical teachings, Catholic theologians had long been prepared to allow that heathens possessed 'civil virtues'. Spasmodic unease at the treatment of indigenous peoples was expressed in a society some of whose members were much exercised by justice as a result of its social and economic difficulties and a new attention to law. The toleration of unfamiliar usages was encouraged by Antiquity's powerful legacy of rationalism and scepticism and the acceptance by some Greek and Roman thinkers of the effects of environment on human life. That new lands and their inhabitants should be carefully described reflects not only the desire of governments and investors to appreciate their potential, but the teachings of Antiquity, explicitly urging the merits of personal observation, and the classically inspired conviction of some scholars that writing was to be factual, accurate and of high moral purpose. So, too, the belief in a Golden Age in some distant past – yet another legacy from Antiquity – persuaded some learned Iberians, and more notably still Ronsard and Montaigne in France, to idealize the pre-conquest existence of the Amerindians. They were the survivors of this ancient bliss, living as God had intended man should before the fall – the precursors, in fact, of the Noble Savage. And Montaigne's eloquent plea for the acceptance of the diversity of human custom was strengthened by his revulsion from the cruelty and follies of half a century of religious wars in France.

Countries and centres where such influences – commercial precocity, classical and humanist learning – were strongest showed the liveliest interest in the non-European world and produced some of the most distinguished and illuminating accounts of it. News of the first voyages was eagerly sought in the Netherlands, in banking cities like Lyons and Nürnburg, and in Italy, the cultural and economic hub of Europe until the seventeenth century. Florentines provided perceptive reports on North America and western India in the early 1500s. Learned Italians were among the ablest and subtlest interpreters of the significance of the first voyages and keen collectors, in the country's well-established tradition, of botanical and zoological curiosities. In the sixteenth and seventeenth centuries there were few more acute and sympathetic observers of the major oriental civilizations than the Italian members of the Jesuit Order. But the most imposing achievement was that of Iberia, powerfully affected in the early 1500s by the Italian Renaissance, by the Christian humanism of Erasmus emanating from the Low Countries and by the vigorous intellectual life centred especially on the university of Salamanca. From the pens of missionaries, explorers, bureaucrats, scholars and soldiers there came a plethora of works on almost all the states and peoples so far encountered, among them the sensitive account of China by the Portuguese Gaspar da Cruz and the magisterial *Historia natural y moral de las Indias* of José de Acosta (1589), currently hailed as the precursor of modern ethnology. When, in the course of the seventeenth century, the cultural and economic vigour of Italy and Iberia dwindled it was the new centres of power and civilization – Holland, France, England – that provided a comparable output of writings on the societies of the wider world, such as those of the Stuart diplomat, Sir Thomas Roe, on Ottoman Turkey and Mughal India, or of the French imperial pioneer, Samuel de Champlain, on the Hurons of Canada.

Discovery, conquest and colonization raised new problems and stimulated debate on matters ranging from the echoes of ancient paganism detected in exotic cultures to the causes of unfamiliar ailments, the influence of oceanic currents on climate and the means whereby the indigenous inhabitants of the Americas had come to be there. The revelation of so much of which Antiquity was ignorant or misinformed shook the faith of some in its teachings. 'Had I Ptolemy, Strabo, Pliny or Solinus here . . .', proclaimed a Portuguese historian in 1531, 'I would put them to shame and confusion.' There were those who similarly felt the authority of the Bible and even of Christianity itself impugned. There was, as the Archbishop of Toledo admitted in 1556, no scriptural warrant for an American continent. It was, moreover, inhabited by people who could scarcely be descended from Adam and Eve, since their posterity, as was early pointed out, had 'by no means departed into out-of-the-way islands'. There was dangerous talk of 'another Adam', of insect-like spontaneous generation and of the diversity of mankind. In the diplomatic words of the Florentine historian Guicciardini (1483–1540), theologians had cause for 'some anxiety'. And by the late seventeenth century European suspicions that the Jewish-Christian revelation was not unique, and European awareness of other religions with comparable ethical and philosophical systems constituted another blow to a creed already facing criticism and hostility.

But this was far from being the end for either the Bible or the classics. Such was their influence that the wider world was commonly scrutinized for whatever would illuminate their teachings. And what was found was encompassed within the mental attitudes they engendered. Evidence was collected in the Middle East 'to justify', it was said, 'what is told us by the ancients'. Amerindians could be depicted as survivors from the Golden Age, were portrayed in art in the dignified poses familiar in classical sculpture, or alternatively seen as some species of the monsters and wild men of classical and medieval lore. A learned Iberian of the sixteenth century assumed Chinese political organization to have been lifted from the Romans and a compatriot took the ancients as his authority on Peru's aboriginal population.[7] The Americas, it was thought, could be part of that lost continent of which Plato spoke. Aristotle's views on the influence of climate on society served to explain what were identified as the sloth and conservatism of orientals. The huge variety of flora and fauna the world was found to possess vindicated the teachings of Antiquity and Christianity on the fullness and richness of creation.

Meanwhile Christian theology absorbed the revelation of new lands and peoples with an ease born of practice. The Bible, its influence enhanced with the advent of Protestantism, insisted that mankind was of one blood and one creation. Diversity must therefore have come about following expulsion from the Garden of Eden. The inhabitants of the newly discovered countries could accordingly be understood as the degenerate descendants of the primeval populace and the beliefs of non-Europeans as garbled recollections of the true faith. Hence black Africans looked as they did, while Amerindians, variously given Jewish or even Norwegian ancestry, were held to have crossed by some land-bridge to their present abodes, their culture sinking to its current lamentable state in the course of such wanderings. Men of learning scrutinized the beliefs and histories of exotic societies, as they did those of Antiquity, for signs of that original tradition of virtue God had communicated to Adam and his progeny. In the early 1600s an erudite Peruvian argued that the apostle Thomas had been in the Americas. At the end of the century a scholarly Dutchman laboured to prove that all the civilizations and religions then known shared some common basis in Judaism and early Christianity.[8]

So, by an large, European culture evolved with little benefit from acquaintance with the wider world. The unfamiliar was ignored, or seen through a haze of prejudice and incomprehension, or adapted to existing preconceptions. Indeed such knowledge and experience could equally well close as open the human mind, hardening old attitudes, reinforcing old prejudices, encouraging new ones. There was discovered the convenient and hitherto unknown tenet that migratory peoples had no title to their lands – thus made available to Europeans – with English Protestants justifying their occupation of North America from the Old Testament's description of how the patriarchs had 'removed from straiter places into more roomy where the land lay idle and none used it though there dwelt inhabitants in them'. Large-scale encounters with those whose skins were of a different colour brought the massive upsurge of racial prejudice among Europeans. The bigotry and intolerance that engulfed Iberia in the late 1500s were in part induced by the fruits and burdens of imperial rule. Seventeenth-century Venetians thought oceanic endeavours – from whose benefits they were largely excluded – futile.[9] Samuel Purchas deduced from the mass of information he published on so much of the world (1613, 1625) that Europe was the sole home of 'Arts and Inventions'. Slavery might be criticized, but its use spread and its legality, not to say desirability, were warmly defended. Countries like England and Holland, from which it had long since disappeared, became pre-eminent in the slave trade, and so whole-hearted was its acceptance in the Dutch Republic that even a converted African could draw a simple distinction between his fellows, descended from Ham and destined to servitude, and the Hollanders, God's 'chosen people', entitled to subject them to such usage.[10]

True, with the passage of time medieval discussions, however recondite, of universal justice or the unity of mankind gave way to debate on the freedom of the seas, the law of prize and the scope of commercial monopoly. But the great changes in European thought and culture, whether the emergence of Protestantism, the defence and criticism of absolute monarchy, the rise of and increasing faith in science, or the growth of rationalism and deism, were the outcome of forces generated within the continent itself. And it was precisely when in the early 1700s, as a reaction against the suffering inflicted by wars and religious bigotry, Europe became more tolerant and more swayed by reason, that the exotic world assumed a greater role in its culture. In the centuries of the first conquests and settlements, however, the arts, though they might absorb some alien detail, were essentially unaffected by such happenings. The revolution in cosmology that marked the age stemmed from the work of Copernicus (1473–1543), whose conclusion that the earth revolved round the sun was refined and substantiated by his successors, dethroning the planet and its inhabitants from their previous role as the centre of creation. The vital step towards the accurate cartographic representation of the world was not the voyages of Columbus or da Gama, but the recovery of Ptolemy's *Geography*, with its solution of the problem of projecting a spherical on to a two-dimensional surface. Some tentative new disciplines emerged in these centuries, like anthropology and ethnology, but their debt to Antiquity was substantial and they reflected, rather than redirected, the thought of the time. Other branches of learning – botany and zoology for example – could and did embrace evidence from non-European lands, but their basic assumptions came from the Middle Ages and the stimulus to their development was the desire to understand, emulate and eventually improve on Antiquity.

If, however, the fundamental tenets of the sciences were unaffected by the geographical discoveries, the skills of their practitioners were often enlarged by the needs of explorers and navigators. Improved trigonometry permitted attempts to construct charts in which the proportional relation of latitude to longitude was correct. But the development of methods of navigation allowing mariners to fix their position by observation of the heavens was basically the adaptation to the sea of techniques long familiar ashore.[11] In the process there were many substantial refinements. The ancient astrolabe was replaced for taking astronomical sights by the cross staff and eventually by the less cumbersome and more accurate sextant. Nevertheless, determining a vessel's position by observation of the Pole Star or the sun was a technique deriving from man's age-old study of the sky for pious and other purposes, not least to discover where he was. The well-attested skills of European scholars in such matters and in mathematical calculation were thus given new and wider application from the late fifteenth century, first by the Portuguese and subsequently in northern Europe. Hence in the mid 1500s the Englishman Leonard Digges eased the labours of navigators by showing them how to use the properties of similar triangles – long understood by academics – to work out the height of an object whose distance was known. But such navigational changes, impressive though they were, are not to be overestimated. The quality of charts was indeed enormously improved. Better instruments were produced. The behaviour of the magnetic compass was investigated. Nevertheless longitude could not be satisfactorily determined since it was impossible to make the reliable clock on which its calculation depended. And everywhere the acceptance of the new techniques was slow, in part from the innate conservatism of seamen, in part since, as one sixteenth-century Englishman put it, so many 'lacked the wit to understand them'. Hence the continued reliance on dead reckoning and hence the profusion of navigational errors, often fundamental and disastrous.

Nor did the opening of the oceans bring some dramatic change in the design, construction and capabilities of ships. Compared with their predecessors, they were by 1700 as a rule more effectively armed, more elaborately rigged, more easily handled (as a result of improved steering and the subdivision of the sail area), more economically manned and – especially for officers and affluent passengers – more comfortable. Their speed, however, showed on the whole no improvement on that of Columbus' craft and they continued to be in trouble with headwinds, like that British fleet trapped in the English Channel in 1718. Oceanic routes thus generally settled to those which allowed voyages to be made, as had been the case for centuries in home waters, with the greatest chance of a favourable wind. Changes there certainly were in response to the demands of distant seas. Some Portuguese carvels had adopted the square sail by the early 1500s. In the late sixteenth century the Spaniards built special vessels for the swift and safe carriage of bullion across the Atlantic. Oceanic privateering convinced contemporary Englishmen of the merits of heavily constructed, heavily manned and heavily armed craft. But these were modifications of existing types of ships. The fundamental changes in design and employment – the mounting of artillery in broadsides, the emergence of the specialized sail-powered fighting vessel – owed little to the challenge of newly opened oceans. And one of the most significant developments, the Dutch production c.1600 of an economically built and run carrier (the *fluit*) was in specific response to the needs of Holland's European trade.

Whatever else the first imperial age may or may not have done for Europe, it made some individuals prodigiously rich. There were those whose fortunes came from plunder, like Hernando Pizarro who returned from the Indies to build, from the loot acquired there, the elegant Palace of the Conquests in his native Trujillo, and to bequeath (1578) a staggering collection of precious objects, money and property. There were others raised to affluence by the opportunities of office, like that governor-general of the Dutch East Indies (1653–78), rumoured to be a millionaire, who, when reproached with corruption, replied that 'he had not come to India to eat hay'. And there was that multitude who profited from every form of acquisitive endeavour, whether smuggling home precious stones from Asia or enjoying returns of several hundred per cent on their investment, as did some of the participants in the early Portuguese ventures in the Far East.

Fortunately placed cities could do even better. By the early seventeenth century, Lisbon, seat of the Portuguese imperial government and of various royal commercial monopolies, was, with 165,000 inhabitants, the biggest city in Iberia and the third largest in Europe. It had developed industries like sugar refining, fed by colonial products. It drew in merchants, adventurers and peoples from far and wide, scotched the competition of those neighbouring ports which had figured so largely in the pioneering voyages, and enjoyed an opulence reflected in such magnificent buildings as the church of the Jerónimos. Seville, long the official centre of Spain's American trade, underwent a similar rapid and dramatic transformation, its population rising from 49,000 to over 100,000 between 1530 and 1594. It became another vast cosmopolitan city, celebrated for its handsome churches, elegant private dwellings and imposing public buildings, and notorious to moralists for its easy affluence, ubiquitous vice and frenetic pursuit of profit. It developed a new (and highly precarious) banking industry – in which Genoese financiers were much in evidence – largely geared to oceanic commerce. The wealth of its merchants was proverbial and even grandees were active in business.

Such benefits were not confined to Iberia. Antwerp, in the rich and troubled Low Countries inheritance which passed to Charles Habsburg, and already in the early 1500s northern Europe's greatest entrepôt, was swiftly transformed by oceanic trade and its master's imperial policies into the financial and business wonder of the times. It initially marketed Portuguese spice and provided Lisbon with copper (employed in West Africa) and silver (vital for dealings with the Orient) from Germany. When the spice staple was shifted to Lisbon (1549) it turned to furnishing Spain with the textiles (some made from Spanish wool) in demand for the Americas, to providing the Baltic naval stores and timber needed to build the ships to carry such cargoes, and to supplying (from German bankers) the money to sustain the government of Charles V. The exotic products it took in payment were redistributed in the north, and industries, notably sugar refining and dyeing, flourished on the processing of colonial raw materials. And the American silver which flowed in from Spain to balance the peninsula's trade deficit with the Low Countries helped to make Antwerp the continent's paramount financial centre. Its career ended when the bankruptcy of the Spanish monarchy (1557) rocked its money market and when, after a sequence of disasters, it surrendered to a Spanish army (1585) in the course of the Netherlands' revolt against their Habsburg rulers. It was now at the mercy of the nascent Dutch state which could blockade its seaborne commerce, and it was deprived of the skills and resources of many of its ablest citizens who, as Protestants or Jews, withdrew to the north, and in particular to the more tolerant Amsterdam.

Like Antwerp, the Dutch city emerged from an obscure past to buttress wealth and power deriving from its role in the European economy with that accruing from dealings with the wider world. Supreme in the Baltic trade by the mid 1500s, and able to call on the services of an imposing volume of shipping – some its own, the rest belonging to various north Netherlands ports – it could supply the embattled Iberian monarchies with the food, timber and naval stores they desperately needed. The Dutch, with Amsterdam pre-eminent, came to dominate the seaborne commerce and whole other areas of the economies of Spain and Portugal. As Antwerp had once done, Amsterdam imported and redistributed exotic products, together with that bullion with which the Iberians balanced their northern trade. When, in the late 1500s, during the Low Countries' revolt, Netherlands ships and merchants were excluded from Iberian ports, one Dutch response was to invade the colonial empires to obtain their products directly, and in the East and West India companies eventually set up to handle this commerce, Amsterdam's money and influence were potent. Oceanic trade did not make the city, but confirmed and reinforced an established supremacy. It fed such new industries as those for the processing of sugar and tobacco. It was a further stimulus to shipping – the more so since Dutch vessels carried so much of the long-distance trade of other nations – and by providing more commodities for re-export, it enhanced a business vital to the commercial prosperity of Holland in general and Amsterdam in particular. By the late 1600s, with a population of some 200,000, the city, tolerant and cosmopolitan, was the acknowledged focus of Europe's economy and the continent's greatest centre of banking and high finance. It was supreme in the collection and evaluation of business information from all over the globe and through its printing presses a major force for the dissemination of knowledge of the non-European world.

Eventually, under the combined pressures of internal change and the enmity of France and England, Holland was eclipsed by Britain, and Amsterdam by London. It was again the story of the rich becoming richer, since England's capital had long handled the lion's share of the country's overseas trade and in every way overshadowed the rest of the kingdom's towns and cities. It acquired new industries. From the seventeenth century Thames shipbuilders produced the large and expensive vessels required for such distant and hazardous voyages as those to the Far East, and London merchants effectively monopolized most of the new 'rich trades', like those to the Levant and Asia. They kept their hands on the bulk of tobacco shipments till c.1700 and were responsible for about 75 per cent of sugar imports before the mid 1700s, by which time, too, the capital was pre-eminent in banking and associated financial operations.

No more than at any other time, of course, was the wealth of individuals, companies or cities necessarily synonymous with the wealth of governments. Even so, in most states which had any contact with the wider world, rulers were – though maybe only briefly – enriched in one way or another. They might benefit from new revenues, from the profits generated by some monopoly, from the sale of privileges to individuals or companies, from taxes on richer subjects, or from the opportunity to tax new subjects and new commodities. The whole economy of the mother country might, in some measure, be stimulated, the revenues it produced increased and the government thus rendered, in the eyes of bankers, an attractive candidate for loans. In Portugal c.1500 the African slave trade – a commerce usually leased out – accounted for about 10 per cent of the royal income from taxes and monopolies, and was rumoured to be worth much more. West African gold doubled the income of John II (1481–95) and by the 1520s half that of John III came from trade with the East and Africa. This new-found wealth and an esteemed gold currency allowed Portugal to buy from abroad the grain she regularly needed and permitted the purchase of vital weapons, munitions and manufactures. The subsequent wealth of Brazil and the eventual discovery there of gold and diamonds revived the prosperity of Lusitanian ports eclipsed by Lisbon and rescued the mother country from the threat of renewed obscurity, Spanish domination and that economic stagnation which then engulfed much of southern Europe. The increased trades focused on Portugal as an entrepôt for colonial goods in its heyday brought the crown more revenues from customs, and so with their income enlarged, their credit improved and many of their most ambitious or potentially troublesome subjects engaged in strenuous imperial endeavour abroad, kings could rule untroubled and free from the need to summon the country's representative assembly to seek funds.

In Spain monarchs similarly enjoyed an income over which their authority was undisputed from the residue of the American revenues not consumed in the Indies, from the fifth levied on bullion and from leases of various monopolies. At best this never amounted to more than 20 per cent of disposable revenue. But it was an income in ready cash – foreign diplomats observing that the rhythm of court life at Madrid was determined by the movements of the treasure fleets – and one that could be augmented by seizures of private bullion imports. It was an excellent security for loans, and being rumoured to be far larger than in fact it was, conveniently bolstered Spain's reputation for wealth and power. So, too, in England revenues from sugar and tobacco were, by the late seventeenth century, sufficiently important to exercise the government as to their uninterrupted flow; and the yield from the customs, increased by the growing volume of oceanic commerce and re-exports, was a vital prop of the late Stuart monarchy. Taxes, like that secured by Charles II from Barbados and the Leeward Islands on the value of local sugar exported (4½ per cent in perpetuity), for one purpose (to meet the civil and military costs of the territories) could be diverted to others. Loans were extracted from affluent trading corporations, with the New East India Company advancing £2 million at 8 per cent for its charter in 1698 and the United Company £3 million at 5 per cent for incorporation in 1709. Then of course empire constituted a vast fund of patronage for all governments. Office, title, privileges and revenues could be sold or granted to those or their heirs and dependents whom it was necessary or expedient to reward or placate, and who might otherwise have been provided for from the resources of the metropolitan state itself.[12]

Other benefits of empire were more widely diffused. European food supplies were increased by the yields of new fisheries, such as that off Newfoundland, and the introduction of American crops like maize and the potato, which soon helped to sustain the poor. New drugs appeared, as did new foods (tomatoes, beans, pineapples and turkeys among them) and, less happily, new narcotics (Indian hemp). For the rich there were more spices, exotic textiles and precious stones, while luxuries such as chocolate (from Mexico), tea and coffee (from the East) and tobacco were introduced and rapidly achieved almost mass consumption. Fresh sources of supply were opened for hitherto scarce commodities. Sugar, once an expensive luxury from the Middle East, came to enjoy almost the same popularity as tobacco - both aided by legislation obliging colonial producers to sell in metropolitan markets. Alternative sources were found for many raw materials – among them the Azores for woad (the dye used in the manufacture of cloth) and Bengal for silk.

Imperial needs and products stimulated existing European industries and encouraged new ones. Portuguese demand for copper for the West African trade pushed European output to the point of overproduction in the early 1500s.[13] There was a great upsurge in shipbuilding in Iberia in the sixteenth century, followed, as Portuguese and Spanish yards were unable to cope with the pressure, by expansion in northern Europe. Output of Granada silk and Andalusian wine was stepped up during the reign of Charles V to meet colonial calls for the familiar products of home. The Spanish woollen textile industry grew to ensure that settlers and natives alike were suitably clad. Cities such as Toledo and Segovia flourished until Spanish cloth making was crippled later in the century by domestic troubles and competition from the textiles of France, Holland and England, now also penetrating new overseas markets in increasing amounts. For a time around 1500 the Portuguese took to manufacturing cheap, lightweight cloths for use in the purchase of slaves in West Africa, as did the English towards the end of the following century. The influx of Indian cottons into England encouraged imitations and so helped the country to develop a more diversified textile industry. English beer and cider sold in the Caribbean in the 1600s. French and Spanish wines were consumed anywhere from the West Indies to the Indian subcontinent. Sugar refineries sprang up alike in Iberia and in such northern cities as Amsterdam and London. Protected by the Navigation Acts English metallurgical goods found an excellent outlet in the country's new colonial markets. In Amsterdam there emerged a whole series of undertakings, said to give work to more than 4000 by 1706, engaged in processing tobacco or making beaver hats from American pelts which had been prepared in Russia. In France, England and Iberia the new oceanic fisheries were major employers of ships and men.

Imperial commerce was seen by governments to be of such importance as to need careful regulation. Closely defined monopolies were instituted. Discriminatory legislation sought to exclude aliens, to ensure undisputed markets for metropolitan products, ready access to colonial products for metropolitan merchants, and abundant colonial raw materials for metroplitan manufacturers. Yet commercial association with the wider world no more revolutionized Europe's economy than did experience of hitherto unknown civilizations its culture. The organization of agriculture, business and society, and the ways in which wealth was produced and distributed were, despite important shifts of prosperity within the continent, barely touched. True, Europe, linked by sea to Africa, Asia, the Americas and the Atlantic archipelagoes – they in turn brought into contact by European shipping – became the centre of the first tentative global economy. Its goods (notably textiles and metal wares) penetrated to the remotest corners of the world and the continent received in exchange the products of East and West alike, with much of whatever could be grown in or extracted from the Atlantic colonies (silver, tobacco, sugar) destined to meet its particular demands. It transmitted American bullion to Asia by the Cape route, through the Mediterranean and through the Baltic. Its currency, which meant Spanish gold doubloons and silver pieces of eight, was accepted everywhere – the Levant, Madeira, China, Indonesia, the Americas, Iran. But this did not entail the birth of what has been hailed as 'European capitalism'. Great corporations appeared, backed by substantial amounts of money – the Dutch East India Company in the seventeenth century, the English South Sea and United East India companies in the eighteenth. But large-scale enterprises, involving great sums of capital, personal or corporate, fixed and circulating, were well established long before Columbus set sail. Some were trading and financial associations, like those of the Italian and South German plutocrats of the late Middle Ages. Others were industrial undertakings, like the Venetian state arsenal, which built and maintained the Republic's impressive merchant and fighting fleets. That by 1700 such associations were more common and sometimes larger than their predecessors is true enough, though hardly evidence of fundamental change.

However, to urge that the wider world's impact on Europe's economy was limited is not to deny such an impact. The new transoceanic trades, whose importance was once overestimated, are now in danger of being underplayed. The tonnage employed between Spain and the Americas indeed amounted at its peak (according to the official record) to no more than 1 per cent of that engaged in Holland's commerce with the Baltic, while vessels of the English East India Company represented only 2 per cent of the country's total in the eighteenth century. Nevertheless long-distance traffic and the redistribution of exotic imports in home waters were between them a stimulus to the growth of merchant tonnage, and official statistics, imperfect as they are, suggest that in 1700 England, then the continent's leading maritime power, had as much as 20 per cent of its oceanic tonnage employed in commerce with the West Indies. Nor is this the whole story. Besides deep-water fishing fleets there were substantial numbers of vessels owned or based overseas.[14] There were many working in the oceanic trades of other states, with the Dutch prominent in the seventeenth century in the commerce between Portugal and Brazil and, before the Navigation Acts, in that between the English Atlantic settlements and Europe. In addition there were those engaged in the re-export of colonial produce from the parent continent (which accounted for 18 per cent of the value of Amsterdam's exports in 1667–8) and in smuggling, with the English of the opinion (1704) that such illicit dealings as those with Spanish America were far too valuable to be halted merely because their country was at war with Spain.

Government statistics similarly suggest that c.1700 imports into England from the wider world accounted for nearly a third of the value of the kingdom's trade and exports to the same markets for about 15 per cent of its value. As with Holland, where at Amsterdam non-European imports made up 25 per cent of the value of all imports in 1667–8, these are fractions, but far from negligible ones, of the commerce of the continent's two major maritime powers. And since fraud and smuggling were widespread and endemic – English trade was perhaps about 20 per cent undervalued in official returns – the true fraction was doubtless a more substantial one. Indeed for England at least the expansion in the nature and range of its entire commerce after 1650 was largely of oceanic inspiration, with the impetus coming from a surge in Asian and American imports and the simultaneous growth of a lively market in the Americas (North, South and Caribbean) for domestic exports and for re-exports.[15] According to one enthusiastic contemporary calculation 'the better half' of all goods brought into England from the colonies was re-shipped after paying 'considerable duties'. Besides which there were substantial earnings in France and England from transporting indentured servants, and in both England and Holland from the carriage of passengers and slaves, from inter-colonial commerce, from direct shipments of Atlantic produce to southern Europe and from the marine insurance and maritime loans required by these and other oceanic ventures.

The influx of American silver and Brazilian gold to Europe is another matter the importance of which has been urged or denied according to the fashion of the times. It arrived, as has already been noticed, in greater amounts and was more widely distributed than was officially recorded.[16] Vessels in the Spanish treasure fleets commonly carried twice their declared ladings. The French, English and Dutch obtained bullion through trades with Iberia which went on irrespective of wars and in which Spain and Portugal balanced their deficits with cash payments. Much was smuggled and much was taken by pirates and privateers so that already by the late sixteenth century there was 'great abundance' in London – linked by some to the inflation then troubling the country – and in the early 1600s England was minting gold coins. A century later vessels of the Royal Navy were among the most persistent smugglers of precious metals from Lisbon.

Yet this inflow, taxing the contemporary repertoire of metaphor and simile to describe it, did not end that shortage of money which allegedly had previously inhibited the continent's economic development. Much bullion stayed too briefly in Europe to have any effect before being passed on eastwards. Improvements in the machinery of credit, many already operative in the Middle Ages, speeded monetary circulation, and scarcity was spasmodically alleviated by the willingness of ruling houses to devalue their currencies. But a shortage of cash persisted all the same, both in the continent and in its colonies. Governments competed to secure what silver there was. Publicists debated how the situation was to be remedied. Tokens were widely employed instead of coins and even banks in Seville itself were short of liquid capital in the 1500s.

Nor did bullion imports determine, as was once thought, the course of Spain's foreign policy, supposedly bellicose when silver was abundant and conciliatory when it was scarce. For the most part monarchs were little swayed by such mundane considerations as the state of their finances, and Spain in any case was particularly aggressive in the early sixteenth century, when amounts of American silver were negligible, and much less so at the beginning of the seventeenth century, when the flow was substantial. Again, New World silver aggravated, but did not spark off – as some contemporaries believed – the inflation which affected Europe in the sixteenth century, but which was already in progress (probably through the pressure of an increasing population on limited food resources) in the early 1500s before treasure imports were seriously under way. Neither did Europe's economy breathe, as it was once graphically put, to a rhythm determined by the volume of American silver available, booming (as it certainly did) until the early 1600s, when supplies were abundant, in crisis thereafter as they dwindled. Unhappily, however, the many crises of the later seventeenth century, which coincided with some of the most prolonged and bloodthirsty of European wars, also coincided with a larger than ever influx of New World bullion.

Nevertheless, the import of treasure by the shipload made its mark, and not only in inspiring the efforts of pirates to seize it or of economists to understand it. The sudden arrival of large amounts of bullion either through trade (as in Seville) or through war (as in Elizabethan London) apparently encouraged high living and consequently high costs. Easy access to such resources sustained the messianic optimism of some Spaniards in the late sixteenth century that the necessary funds for any scheme, however grandiose, would be divinely provided from 'some new Indies, some new Potosí'. And indeed American silver underpinned the prodigious and almost global military effort of Habsburg Spain, with payments (however erratic) to the army fighting in the Low Countries until 1648 alone inducing the prolific minting of large silver coins. In the early 1700s Brazilian gold revived Portugal and permitted, as had that of Africa earlier, its integration into the European economy.

American silver did not determine Europe's ability to trade with Asia in a commerce in which, since western purchases in the East exceeded what the East could or would buy from the West, had to be balanced with cash. The trade had flourished (overland) for centuries without the blessings of American bullion. Nevertheless, though the deficit was reduced in the post da Gama era by European earnings from services and interport commerce in the Orient, it still remained, and the continuance of the trade was clearly eased by new resources. Portugal, it was early complained, was consuming 'the entire wealth' of the Americas in dealings with the Orient, and over the centuries with which we are concerned more than half of Europe's imports from Asia were paid for with precious metals. The pattern was much the same in another unbalanced trade, that – of far greater consequence – between western Europe and the Baltic lands which provided grain and, more important still, the naval stores and timber increasingly needed to build and maintain the growing volume of shipping required by Europe's maritime economy, fighting fleets and oceanic empires. The trade was again one which was centuries old before the Americas were discovered, and again one facilitated by new resources, with bullion closing a gap of some 30–50 per cent between the value of western imports into the area and western purchases there, and one element in Dutch commercial hegemony in the Baltic was the Republic's firm grip on supplies of American silver. Bullion fulfilled a similar role in other unbalanced trades, such as the acquisition of wine in the Atlantic islands, or central and west European purchases of livestock in Hungary and adjoining territories.[17]

Oceanic enterprise and commerce affected the accumulation and distribution of capital. Wealth acquired in one part of the world was invested in another. The depredations of pirates and privateers endowed Europe with gratuitous increments to its resources – Drake bringing home, after his exploits in 1587 alone, loot worth about 10 per cent of England's imports at the time. Plunder amassed overseas might be invested there (as in mining or planting) at no cost to, and to the ultimate benefit of, the mother country.[18] Court and landed money were, as under Elizabeth Tudor, used (and frequently lost) in colonizing and privateering ventures, with one magnate lamenting that he had 'throwne his land into ye sea'. But prudent and affluent London merchants, further enriched by similar undertakings, moved on into high finance in the early seventeenth century. For the wealthy there were more opportunities to become wealthier still. German and Genoese financiers in sixteenth-century Iberia soon had a finger in everything from voyages of exploration to slaving and the manufacture of sugar, while members of the merchant guild of Seville acquired the sole right to trade with Spanish America. A select band of London plutocrats dominated the monopoly companies to which England's commerce with West Africa, Asia and the eastern Mediterranean was entrusted in the sixteenth and seventeenth centuries. But their very concentration on these 'rich trades' left most of those across the Atlantic open to lesser lights – provincial merchants, shipmasters, squires - who by the mid 1600s had become sufficiently wealthy and influential to demand Navigation Acts to protect their interests.

New trades, new hazards and dealings alike with skilled merchants in the East and nomadic aboriginals in the West brought new problems and encouraged new business techniques – or at least attempts to apply familiar practices to unfamiliar situations. There was much experiment with the transmission of information, whether commercial or official. The Portuguese in Asia communicated with Europe both directly by sea and by the less precarious land and maritime route through the Middle East and the Mediterranean. At the beginning of the eighteenth century the English established a regular (but short-lived) packet-boat service to the West Indies. Shipping moving in convoy, as it had long done in some European trades, became common the world over, whether Spanish silver fleets in the Atlantic and Pacific, Indiamen working to and from Asia or those Portuguese flotillas which c.1700 were carrying home gold from Bahia, bullion and diamonds from Rio and sugar from Pernambuco.

Trade could now mean on the one hand an extension of the use of barter – as when in North America European manufactures were exchanged for Indian furs – or on the other transactions of an increasingly complex nature. Entrepôts emerged in northern Europe (Antwerp, Amsterdam, London) in which goods from practically the entire known world were collected, bought and sold all year round and not merely, in the old medieval style, at seasonal fairs. New multilateral trades developed, in which exports were exchanged not against imports, but against commodities to be resold elsewhere, with the English Royal African Company using in the late 1600s Baltic metals and oriental textiles (supplied by the East India Company) for the purchase of gold and slaves in West Africa. The conduct of business across thousands of kilometres of ocean brought innovation and refinement in technique. Commission trading, in which, for a fee, an agent in some distant market handled a merchant's goods and affairs, became widespread, curiously enough at a rate (around 3 per cent) Venetians had been accustomed to pay in the medieval Levant.[19] The north-European East India companies assembled their bullion through specialists and attempted to ensure that when their vessels arrived in the Orient there were no expensive delays, but that goods of the precise nature, quality and price demanded at home would be awaiting them. They learned, like their medieval predecessors in the Levant, how to handle indigenous authorities. To rationalize purchases they studied European re-export trades and searched their own records to detect patterns of past consumption in the hope of predicting those of the future. By bribes and gifts the influential were encouraged, as they are wont to be, to promote particular commodities and so boost sales, while the English East India Company ultimately ran what were tantamount to fashion shows.

The very prominence of these companies reflects experiment as to how commerce involving distances, risks, expenses and delays in return on investment of a hitherto unknown order was to be organized and conducted. One solution was to set up monopolies which were grander and more ambitious versions of those long used or enforced in many of Europe's great trades, whether that of the Venetians to the medieval Levant or of the Hanseatic League in the commerce of the Baltic in the Middle Ages. They might be operated directly by the crown or its agents, as was the case in Portugal's Asian and West African trades. Alternatively, as in Spain's dealings with the Americas, the monopoly might be established by the crown which was then no more than marginally involved in its business. Or yet again, as with the great Dutch companies and the English East India Company, the monopoly could be licenced by the state, financed by private money and conducted in the interests of the shareholders. Many of the companies founded from the mid sixteenth century onwards were joint-stock bodies, in which the risks for individual participants were lessened and which, by providing for passive investors, widened the area from which capital could be drawn.[20] They were larger than the great Italian associations of the Middle Ages – which rarely had more than twenty partners – often richer and longer lived, and in some cases (notably the VOC) enjoyed a more complete dominance within their particular field.

Companies, whatever their nature, were attractive to governments in that they paid for their charters, could be tapped for loans, and could be saddled with burdens and responsibilities states were unwilling to shoulder themselves. A monopoly corporation, conducting an important commerce through a recognized overseas entrepôt, could be a useful lever in dealings with the host country, while to the wealthy merchants who loomed so large in such businesses it brought recognition of their status and promised to safeguard their profits. Nineteen bodies of this nature were established in England alone before 1680, some purely for trade, like the East India Company, others for exploration or, like the Virginia Company (1606) and the Massachusetts Bay Company (1628) for colonization. Hopes of emulating Dutch success inspired a spate of companies throughout Europe on the model of the VOC and WIC, such as the French (1664), Ostend (1722) and Swedish (1731) East India companies and the Prussian Africa Company (1683) – many founded at the instigation, or with the assistance of disgruntled Netherlanders.

Setting up monopolies and companies was one thing, ensuring their successful operation quite another. Where, as in Spanish America, there was a rich and growing white population, the seasonal despatch from Europe of a limited number of ships was insufficient to meet the needs of colonists and a stimulus to their dealings with smugglers. The inability of the English Royal African Company to satisfy its customers' demand for slaves similarly encouraged a vast interloping commerce between West Africa and the English Caribbean. The fortunes of such corporations could, moreover, be at the mercy of non-commercial forces. Much of the capital of the Dutch and French West India companies came from public funds and was liable to sudden withdrawal with predictably disastrous consequences. Sometimes elaborate monopoly corporations, set up from an ill-matched assortment of political, strategic and economic objectives, had little prospect of commercial success. The Dutch West India Company was encumbered with impossibly grandiose responsibilities.[21] The English African Company was burdened with the upkeep of tropical posts while at the same time, like similar bodies, it had great difficulty in controlling its employees – who could well be running a rival commerce at its expense – and even greater difficulty in extracting payment from Caribbean planters whose gentlemanly reluctance to honour their debts had powerful backing both locally and at home. In trades like those across the Atlantic, in which the ventures of individual merchants or small partnerships flourished, companies were too cumbersome to respond swiftly to changing opportunities. Besides which there was a general and growing opposition to monopoly, muted in the case of the VOC by the fact that it was formed from the amalgamation of a number of existing local companies, acute in England where provincial ports clamoured against exclusive London privilege.

Nor were these the only problems of oceanic commerce. Its attempted regulation or restriction, whether by monopolies or navigation acts, was universally flouted or ignored. The astonishing prosperity of Pennsylvania in the late 1600s allegedly stemmed, for example, from its violation of the whole of England's commercial policies. The very expansion of the geographical area of trade brought the consequent widening of the field of action for the pirates who preyed on it. To those operating in home waters there were now added the buccaneers of the Caribbean and those formidable desperadoes who, at the end of the seventeenth century, were cruising in Asian seas and selling their loot alike in Bombay and North America. So, too, new trades, often in commodities of immense value, conducted over vast distances and supervised by rudimentary bureaucracies, encouraged fraud on an heroic scale. With office regarded as a form of property royal servants and company officials were tireless in the pursuit of their own enrichment, or, as it might now be more charitably put, in securing the maximum return on their investment. By the late 1600s assorted misdemeanours were reputedly depriving the English crown of two-thirds of its revenues on colonial tobacco. Dutch Curaçao and English Jamaica waxed rich on supposedly prohibited dealings with the Spanish Indies. Vessels working the monopoly routes to Asia and the Americas ludicrously undervalued the cargoes they were carrying when it was a question of paying dues. In 1633 an English Indiaman, with silk alone worth £58,000 on board, declared a lading of £800.

Such problems and developments were accompanied by intense and sometimes illuminating debate in Europe. The military might of sixteenth-century Spain, apparently sustained by New World silver, was enough to convince some of the merits of the classical view that money meant wealth and wealth meant power. But already in the mid 1500s there were suspicions, notably voiced by Martín de Azpilcueta Navarro in Spain and Jean Bodin in France, that the contemporary rise in prices was due to Spanish bullion imports. English publicists, who in the sixteenth century believed the non-European world might purchase their country's textiles, then lacking markets nearer home, were subsequently concerned that the American settlements were poaching business from the mother country and refusing to repatriate profits. Throughout the 1600s there were lively discussions in France as to the economic benefits to be derived from colonies, not least that by accepting unemployed artisans they would discourage the settlement of skilled men in neighbouring European states where they revealed the secrets of French industry to rivals and enemies.[22]

It was, however, trade with the Orient that provoked the most acrimonious exchanges. Portuguese pioneers in the East debated how best to raise the capital they desperately needed. Already in 1522 there were complaints from Germany of the folly of exporting the country's silver to pay for spices. For much of the seventeenth century there was erudite argument, especially in England, on the merits and disadvantages of such a commerce. It could be presented as either stimulating or destroying maritime strength, as killing off crews or as rendering them superlative seamen. To some it was pure madness, demanding the construction of huge, expensive and otherwise useless vessels and – most dangerously – the enervating drain of hard-earned bullion. But the debate sharpened wits as well as tempers, focusing attention on some of the basic principles of international commerce and bringing a clearer understanding of the mechanism of foreign exchanges.

A fundamental issue was the role that the products of colonies and the non-European world were to play in the economy of the parent state. For a time in Spain's American empire, with the mother country in no position, either economically or geographically, to provide the food, drink and clothing required by its New World subjects, industries such as the manufacture of textiles and the production of wines were encouraged in the Indies. But such was their success that from the late 1500s there were spasmodic attempts to prohibit or restrict them because of their competition with the ailing industries of the peninsula. The exceptions were those like shipbuilding and the production of arms which contributed to imperial defence, assisted in the carriage of vital colonial exports, and went some way – as did the continuing output of textiles – to meeting demands with which Spain herself was unable to cope.[23]

This was to be the general view. The ideal colony supplied precious metals, or, if not, staple crops which sold readily in Europe without competing with domestic agriculture. Failing these, it should provide raw materials more cheaply and reliably than could Europe. Industry, however, was the prerogative of the homeland. No sooner did substantial amounts of Persian, Indian and Chinese textiles commence to arrive in the West than there was outcry from local manufacturers of woollens and silks and widespread restriction or prohibition of such imports, as in France (1686) and England (1701, 1721). In the seventeenth century both states insisted that sugar was to be refined only in the mother country, while the Portuguese endeavoured to keep Brazilian brandy out of Africa to secure the market for their own product.

Meanwhile theorists like Hakluyt in England (1584) and Usselincx in Holland (1592) cast the North American settlements in the role of providers of raw materials to metropolitan industries, as convenient receptacles, Portuguese-style, for the undesirable or surplus population ('the offals of our people') of the mother country and as markets for its manufactures. Home industry would accordingly expand, bringing employment to a 'wonderfull multitude of poor subiectes' and consequently domestic peace like that enjoyed by the Iberians, together with an infinity of other benefits. In this spirit the Dutch West India Company forbade settlers in the New Netherlands to develop industries and by the end of the seventeenth century the English were much exercised to stifle those of their North American settlements, said to be causing the mother country great damage by 'furnishing themselves or others our colonies with what hath been usually supplied from England', and threatening the kingdom's industries with unemployment or worse. Their proper function was to provide those naval stores – hemp, pitch, tar, timber – whose traditional sources of supply were all too liable to sudden and arbitrary disruption by wars in or around the Baltic. And indeed with such materials subsidized by the mother country (1705) and with abundant opportunities for trade local and oceanic, the New Englanders themselves came to see commerce as more rewarding than industry.[24]

Another contentious matter was, once the first empires had been founded, the value and desirability of emigration. Precisely how many people left the continent to live either briefly or permanently overseas is uncertain. Many Europeans, the Portuguese in particular, served or settled in the possessions of powers other than their mother country. Ships regularly embarked more passengers than their quota – with a Spanish fleet in 1604 carrying 600 women instead of a supposed fifty – just as their crews regularly deserted in colonial ports. Such statistics as there are suggest emigration on an apparently modest scale, especially when compared with what was to happen in later centuries and even allowing for considerable under-registration. Between 1620 and 1640 England lost 60,000 emigrants to the New World. In the first half of the seventeenth century from 3000 to 4000 Spaniards left annually for the Indies, and in the late 1600s up to 2000

Portuguese departed every year for Brazil. In the course of the seventeenth and eighteenth centuries approximately one million people sailed from Holland for Asia. But these figures by no means tell the whole story. The departure of some 250,000 emigrants from Portugal in the sixteenth century (out of a total population of around 1½ million) was equivalent to the loss of the country's entire adult manpower in any one year and constituted an exodus of an order unequalled in any previous overseas emigration. It eclipsed that from Spain in the same period, which nevertheless amounted to about 8 per cent of the kingdom's male population. Emigrants, moreover, came from particular regions, which meant that their departure could have profound local repercussions. In Portugal most, other than deportees, were from the impoverished and inhospitable north. In Spain, until late in the seventeenth century, the majority were Castilians and more especially Andalusians. They were also from particular sectors of society. Many, as with those going from Portugal and Holland to Asia, were young, able-bodied, unmarried males, vital to any community at any time, and many others were, as the colonies developed, men trained in valuable skills and professions.[25]

As their achievements were to show, such emigrants included those of outstanding ability and enterprise, now for the most part lost to the mother country for good since there was little prospect of their return, even had they so wished, from regions like Asia. Of all those taken out by VOC ships before 1800 only a third ever saw Europe again. Already in the mid 1500s, as a result of such losses, and through ubiquitous and increasing demands for manpower – not least for interminable wars – the Iberian kingdoms were short of men. The position deteriorated further as their populations were decimated in the late sixteenth and early seventeenth centuries by plague and epidemics. And as the population of Europe as a whole shrank in the 1600s – for reasons other than emigration – colonies lost some of their appeal. Far from beneficially purging the continent of impurities (the unwanted and unemployable) they were sapping its strength. In 1597 the *Cortes* of Castile proposed that only clergy and bureaucrats should be allowed to go to the Americas. An academic argued shortly after that emigration was ruining Spain, with aristocrats forced to live on dwindling revenues because of a lack of tenants to work their lands. As England's American colonies flourished in the 1600s there was alarm that they were dangerously weakening a mother country now seriously under-populated by attracting labour, and at the beginning of the eighteenth century the Portuguese crown attempted to stem the exodus to the new El Dorado of Brazil since the north of the kingdom was said to have scarcely enough people left to till the soil.

To these problems, serious enough in themselves, were added those of imperial defence and of the provision and manning of the ships demanded by seaborne empire and oceanic commerce. From the mid 1500s Spanish trade with the Americas, like that of Portugal with Asia and West Africa was conducted by convoys, soon accompanied by armed escorts, and there were established, with varying degrees of permanence, naval forces responsible for the protection of particular waters. By 1600 Portugal, in addition to such men-of-war as she could muster in the Atlantic, had flotillas based in western India and operating anywhere from Indonesia to East Africa. Spain introduced the squadron of the Indian Guard into the Atlantic in 1570, built special fast and well-armed craft to carry New World bullion to Europe, and at the end of the sixteenth century, notwithstanding the losses in the Armada of 1588, had some seventy fighting ships in western waters. A defence force was eventually raised for the Caribbean in the 1640s, men-of-war (The South Sea Squadron) sailed the Pacific and an effective flotilla was stationed in the Low Countries in the early seventeenth century. At the same time elaborate and expensive fortifications were erected by the Spaniards in the Atlantic islands, the Americas and the Caribbean, and by the Portuguese throughout their empire, with the remains of huge strongholds like the seventeenth-century Fort Aguada (Goa) and Fort Jesus (Mombasa) testifying to the scale and cost of such undertakings. Ultimately, too, Spain established militias in Cuba and Mexico, and a standing army in Chile, while the Portuguese had a regular force in Brazil from 1625, but in Asia, after attempts to arrange something similar at Goa (1671), generally made do with slaves and indigenous allies and mercenaries.

Global warfare, the well-attested perils of the deep, disease and human folly and incompetence brought crippling losses of ships and men. Spain suffered a sequence of disasters, like the Armada and Heyn's capture of the Plate Fleet (1628), which cost her dear in vessels which could – at least for a time – be replaced, and in skilled hands, who could not. Between 1585 and 1604 English privateers alone took over a thousand Iberian craft, followed by a further thousand or so in the war of 1625–9, and the Dutch West India Company, in addition to all the other blows it inflicted, captured yet another 600 before 1636. Many of these losses could only be made good by the expensive purchase or hire of foreign tonnage, particularly since Spanish builders struggled to produce the large, powerful vessels required by the crown, but which were totally unsuitable for trade. By the 1630s Spanish freight rates were six times higher than those of the far from efficient English. Spanish-built ships succumbed to the competition of better and cheaper foreign and colonial craft. The Spanish merchant service, its crews taken and lost in royal employment, dwindled, as did Spanish shipbuilding, crippled by a lack of raw materials largely occasioned by ambitious royal projects. Naval control of the Atlantic and even the Caribbean collapsed, and throughout most of the seventeenth century there was no Spanish force of any consequence in the West Indies and no more than twenty Spanish fighting ships in the waters between Europe and America.

The maritime eclipse of Portugal was swifter still. So tiny a state was incapable of providing the men and vessels needed to carry the commerce and ensure the safety of world-wide possessions almost universally under attack. Already in the 1560s the English – mistakenly as they were to discover – considered the Portuguese too feeble to defend themselves, and half a century later the country had little more than 6000 seamen to meet its global commitments. Such ships as it possessed were hence commonly inadequately manned. With experienced officers in short supply they were frequently badly commanded, often poorly maintained and, since the country had for long no native metallurgical industry to provide artillery, usually feebly armed. As a result Portuguese fleets were defeated and Portuguese vessels lost at such a rate that by the early 1600s much of the empire's great and rich trades were handled by foreign craft.

But though imperial defences might be inadequate, they were none the less expensive. Shipboard disease, the sea and the endemic sicknesses of the tropics consumed men at a fearful rate, just as fortresses, armies and navies swallowed and demanded money in what appeared to metropolitan governments as staggering amounts. To meet such costs old taxes were increased and new ones introduced. By the early 1600s the levy on cargoes in the Spanish Indies fleets had soared to 35 per cent of their value. Spain laid more and more charges on an empire seen to be waxing rich as the mother country grew poorer. Merchants in the Manila trade, who had once only paid two taxes, faced a dozen by 1713. Defence costs, direct and indirect, became the single largest item of expenditure by colonial exchequers, and with wealthy Mexico and Peru further saddled with subsidizing the poorer provinces. Such burdens Spanish settlers, like the subjects of other colonial powers, bore reluctantly, if indeed at all, expressing their discontent in rebellion or threats of rebellion.

Portugal's experience was the same. The African possessions alone already cost the mother country roughly a sixth of her revenues in 1534 and the Asian empire was running at a loss by the mid 1500s. Worse was to come as European and indigenous attacks intensified. Apart from Angola, which in the mid seventeenth century was laying out nearly twice its annual income in the struggle against the Dutch, and Brazil, which was in effect fighting them for its own life, the overseas possessions, vociferous in their clamour for weapons, ships, men and money were rarely willing, even if able, to contribute to imperial defence. In the East in the seventeenth century, while individual posts fought long and hard, mustering, in the most unlikely circumstances, considerable resources in men and material and according one another financial assistance, the crown was reduced to auctioning offices in Goa, arming members of the religious Orders and soliciting, usually in vain, loans from all and sundry in its hopeless efforts to save the *Estado*.

Other European powers, though without the extensive commitments and possessions of the Iberian monarchies, faced similar problems. The financial difficulties of the VOC from the late 1600s stemmed in part from the cost of its wars in Indonesia. Conflict with Holland and France obliged the English to extend the scope of their naval operations in the course of the late seventeenth and early eighteenth centuries. Squadrons were detailed off 'for the care of the plantations and their trade', to protect the fisheries and to escort transatlantic shipping. In the West Indies visiting flotillas gave way to a permanent force working from regular local bases. Even so the government was exercised that its huge, growing and expensive navy – over 300 vessels in 1697 and chronically short of men – was barely able to look after the country's oceanic interests. At the same time it was harassed by merchants complaining of the losses inflicted by France on their seaborne trade – losses, it was alleged, the more readily incurred since the Navy weakened ships by pressing seamen from their crews.

In the Caribbean and North America Anglo-French rivalry inspired English measures for imperial defence and attempts, like those of the Iberians, to pass on to now notoriously wealthy colonies some of the responsibilities for, and costs of, the protection they demanded – with planters threatening, for example, to leave if naval assistance was not forthcoming. The outcome was much the same. Colonial refusal to pay official salaries was widespread. Forces sent out from home were regarded, not implausibly, as yet another enemy – the Navy, it was complained, heedlessly taking up men and consuming victuals. In the early 1700s it was reported to London that defences were frequently defective; that some colonies (like Massachusetts) were reluctant to contribute to their upkeep; that others (Connecticut and Rhode Island) were unwilling to raise men; and that Jamaica refused to house its garrison. Metropolitan generals, imbued with the new professionalism of the age of Marlborough, were as scathing on colonial military shortcomings as were peninsular Spaniards on the martial inadequacies of the heirs of the *conquistadores*. Urged to do their duty against the French in 1710, the inhabitants of the Leeward Islands rose and murdered their governor.

Oceanic empire and trade hastened the shift of economic power in Europe away from its age-old centre in the Mediterranean towards the Atlantic and towards the north of the continent. Sugar from the Iberian Atlantic islands early destroyed the old Mediterranean industry, just as in the sixeenth century American bullion ruined central European silver mining. After the mid 1500s bullion no longer flowed to Venice from southern and central Europe, but came from the Spanish Indies ostensibly to Seville, from where indeed large amounts passed into the Mediterranean. Soon after 1600 the ancient commercial routes to the Far East through the Levant had to all intents been sealed off by Dutch and English seapower in Asia. Oriental products were no longer redistributed by the great maritime republics of Venice and Genoa, who for centuries had disputed mastery of this most lucrative of all businesses, but who now instead received these very goods from the English and the Dutch. Venice withdrew to other interests – its intellectuals consoling themselves with bizarre speculation that their city was the sole seat of virtue and the true 'new world' – and Genoa dropped out of international finance in the early 1600s. Northern industries eclipsed those of the south. Commerce with the wider world came to be carried in French, Dutch, German and ultimately, above all, English ships. Along Europe's western littoral and adjoining coasts there emerged or re-emerged a whole series of ports – Glasgow, Liverpool, Bristol, London, Amsterdam, Hamburg, Nantes, La Rochelle, Seville, Lisbon among them – whose prosperity was wholly or largely generated by the new oceanic trades.

The control, defence and exploitation of the Americas drew economic power southwards and westwards in Spain in the late 1500s and early 1600s, a move further encouraged by enemy attacks on the trade of its northern provinces. The once flourishing commercial and financial city of Burgos declined and its merchants migrated south, as did many others from Biscay and Castile. Madrid replaced Valladolid as capital (1561), for a time there was talk of making Lisbon the centre of government of the united Hispano-Portuguese empire and Castile's supremacy within Spain, originating in the centuries of the reconquest from the Moors, was firmly and finally established. All this had its price, however. The influx of precious metals, whether into Spain from the Indies, or into Portugal from Africa and Brazil, enabled the Iberian powers to buy whatever they needed in Europe, thus sealing the decline of their own agriculture and industries. The scale of imperial success and the magnitude of the opportunities for the easy acquisition of great riches heightened that revulsion from menial toil and any supposedly degrading occupation, well-known in the peninsula since the years of the campaigns against Islam. The Iberian empires demanded, moreover, not peaceful and productive skills, but those of the soldier, administrator and missionary, strengthening the belief that Christian gentlemen should eschew any pursuit tainted by demeaning labour. And that such labour was both degrading and superfluous was further emphasized by the widespread employment of slaves, mostly Africans, in the peninsula, with some 100,000 introduced into southern Spain in the sixteenth century, while already in the 1550s they accounted for about 10 per cent of the population of Lisbon and of Portugal's southern provinces. There thus emerged, as was often remarked with varying degrees of literary venom, a widespread unwillingness 'to learn any skill', a devotion to peculation and an unquestioning worship of 'the lord money'. The economies of the Iberian imperial powers, fragile at the best and now further enfeebled by natural disasters and inept government policies, grew weaker. Portugal was in dire straits by the mid 1500s and Spain early in the following century. On these inadequate foundations there pressed the increasing burden and costs of populating, governing and protecting overseas possessions, combined, in the case of Spain, with the pursuit of ambitious schemes and the defence of almost limitless supposed interests in Europe. The outcome was royal bankruptcies (Portugal in 1560; Spain in 1557 and a further five times in the next ninety years) and the Iberian kingdoms reduced to dependence on the more advanced economies of northern Europe for most of their manufactures and much of their food. Empire, it now seemed, far from being – as royal panegyrists had once hailed it – God's especial reward to chosen nations, was the expression of his wrath against sinful peoples. Columbus and his crews were no more than the 'argonauts of syphilis'. Spain, the Count-duke of Olivares lamented in 1631, would have been better off without the Indies.[26]

Empire had further and far-reaching impact on the ordering of government and on the relationships between European states. It stimulated, sometimes momentarily, sometimes permanently, a general tightening of authority. Commanders by land and sea demanded, received or assumed powers of the most extensive order. 'The general', wrote the author of a memorandum for Sir Walter Raleigh, 'to Commaund absolutly.' As voyages by sea became longer and the responsibilities of those in charge consequently greater, the authority of the shipmaster – once rather like that of the chairman of a committee – became more extensive and the opportunities for imperious behaviour almost unlimited. It was complained of Francis Drake in 1587 that he decided everything 'without consultation'.

More important, empire enhanced royal prestige and offered monarchs prospects of increased power. Spain, it was urged in 1554, should govern Mexico Turkish-style, by direct military rule. Colonization, it was argued in countries like France and England, where empire got off to a poor start, was a matter for sovereigns alone. Among the advisers of the English monarchy in the late seventeenth and early eighteenth centuries were those advocating the ending of the regime of proprietary colonies. Authority over distant lands, the revenues they provided or were alleged to provide, the homage of their princes and the well-publicized story of the conversion of their inhabitants to Christianity added lustre to the reputation of a ruling house. The kings of Spain and Portugal claimed untrammelled authority over great tracts of the lands and seas of the globe together with the right to monopolize and regulate commerce within such regions. They secured control of the machinery of government established to deal with the affairs, spiritual and secular, of their new possessions. Though in Spain, the Indies and the homeland were idealized as two equal realms under a single sovereign, it was in the Americas that the absolutist aspirations of the crown received their fullest expression. The king reigned by virtue of conquest, had no duty, as in Europe, to swear to uphold traditional liberties, and had no elected assemblies to contend with. Colonies absorbed ambitious and unruly citizens, allowing imperial powers, it was noted in the sixteenth century, to enjoy internal peace – and significantly enough the most restive

of Spain's peninsular realms were those whose subjects were denied access
to the Americas. Imperial government entailed more offices, more officials
and accordingly more scope for patronage. Hence endowed with new
revenues, new titles and new subjects, the rulers of the Iberian empires in
their heyday appeared to many contemporaries as grander and more
powerful than their fellows without such possessions.

Developments in sixteenth-century Spain and Portugal were subsequently
echoed elsewhere. The two great Dutch chartered trading companies, branches in effect of the Netherlands state, enforced commercial monopolies of a
scale previously unknown, employed substantial bureaucracies, distributed
favours and controlled the Calvinist clergy who entered their preserves with
as firm a hand as any Iberian king. The French monarchy eventually kept
its colonies on the tightest of reins and sought to regulate their trade.
Charles II, and even more so, James II of England, whose dependence on
the financial generosity of Parliament was lessened by increased revenues
accruing from the country's New World settlements, entertained large plans
for extending their authority over them.[27]

There was, however, another side to the coin. As a result of their involvement in the lands and oceans of the wider world, Portugal and Spain, both
hitherto active in North Africa, abandoned, or were forced to abandon,
most of their interests there, so encouraging a spectacular proliferation of
pirate communities. Global commitments deflected the energies and
resources of the Spanish heirs of the Habsburg Emperor Charles V away
from Germany, accelerating its evolution into a collection of small states.
The outlay of men, money and materials by the Iberian monarchies in
attempts to defend and retain distant possessions, and to exclude rivals,
eroded that very authority empire had initially strengthened. Assets were
alienated, functions once undertaken by the crown were farmed out – as
were the Portuguese royal spice monopoly and the provision of naval forces
in Spain at the end of the sixteenth century – and colonies, with wills and
interests of their own, became increasingly difficult to control.

In non-imperial states publicists demonstrated the folly of imperial
ambition – witness impecunious Spain shouldering all the burdens while
the rest of Europe drew all the profits – and revealed how monarchs without
colonies were much better off, possessing within their own borders the
'true mines of the Indies'. The proper course of prudent statecraft was to
make the lands they had strong and prosperous. Others were not convinced
and seeing compatriots excluded from rich markets or threatened by the
advantages rivals drew from empire, urged that the balance be redressed. In
Elizabethan England Protestant squires like Humphrey Gilbert and Walter
Raleigh advocated the settlement of North America and London merchants
sought to open a direct maritime trade to Asia. Under Charles II a far more
powerful group, comprising blue-blooded men of action (like Prince Rupert
and the future James II), courtiers, planters and city magnates pressed for

the founding of colonies and the expansion oceanic commerce. Statesmen in seventeenth-century France were acutely aware of the prestige accruing from empire (as was Cardinal Richelieu) and the economic benefits it could generate (as was Louis XIV's influential minister, Jean-Baptiste Colbert).

Thus the first imperial age, far from freeing Europe from internecine strife by providing an outlet for aggressive energies, saw colonies, colonial trade and control of distant waters become yet further matters for conflict between the states of the continent. Disputes were briefly regulated by papal arbitration, as with the celebrated (or notorious) division of the world between Portugal and Spain in 1493. Thereafter they were settled by the well-tried ways of war and diplomacy, to the accompaniment of the evolution of a body of international law – derived by Spanish thinkers from medieval teachings – which received notable expression in the *De Jure Belli et Pacis* (1625) of the Dutch scholar Hugo Grotius. Relations in the non-European world were defined in a series of treaties commencing with those between Spain and Portugal (1479), France and Spain (1559), Spain and Holland (1648) and Spain and England (1670). For a time it was accepted, as in the Franco-Spanish agreement of 1559, that peace at home was no impediment to war abroad. So the English fought the Portuguese in Asia in the early 1600s during a period of supposed Anglo-Iberian concord in Europe, while in the West there was, in the celebrated phrase, 'no peace beyond the line' – eventually understood as the equator. But ultimately it was agreed that the same relations should prevail in the wider world as in Europe, with the English, for example, insisting from 1671 that their Atlantic colonies were not to engage in wars on their own initiative.

Of such wars there was no lack, even if at their bitterest and most extensive they remained ancillary to conflict in Europe, where generals like Marlborough had no time for such ventures. There was savage fighting between Spain and Portugal off West Africa in the fifteenth century, and between Spaniards, Dutch, French and English in the Caribbean in the sixteenth and seventeenth centuries. Holland's struggle against the Hispano-Portuguese empire in the 1600s involved engagements by land and sea the world over, with the Dutch invasion of Brazil and Sri Lanka the first attempt by one European power to deprive another of substantial colonial possessions. The ensuing Anglo-Dutch conflicts, though largely confined to home waters, where Holland's maritime and commercial resources were chiefly and most vulnerably concentrated, also involved actions in North America, the Caribbean and West Africa. But the end of the century brought, in the wars of 1689–97 and 1702–13, the renewal of large-scale colonial operations, as Louis XIV of France, opposed by an Anglo-Dutch alliance, sought to dominate western Europe and in effect, to annex Spain's New World possessions, whose wealth, as he himself put it (1705) was 'the main objective of the present war'.[28] The major campaigns were fought in Europe and at sea, with the English suffering badly from French commerce raiding. But there was much at stake in the West where a great deal of the campaigning was on the initiative of local colonial populations. France's possessions were open to English seapower, but the isolated English posts around Hudson Bay succumbed to the French before 1697 and the disunited North American settlements were threatened from Canada and Louisiana, some of whose officers were men of remarkable strategic vision. The valuable commerce of England's Atlantic colonies, the West Indian islands in particular, was in jeopardy, and it was from the Caribbean – from English Jamaica and Dutch Curaçao, now similarly at risk – that the allies had their easiest and quickest access to the rich markets of South America and to the silver of the Indies.

France attacked this clandestine trade and, as in the dashing raid by the celebrated privateer Duguay-Trouin on Rio de Janeiro (1711), the wealthy possessions of the alliance's feeblest member. The English several times took Spanish treasure ships, while in North America the French raided coastal settlements, those in Newfoundland especially, and the English and the English Americans attacked Quebec and Port Royal (Nova Scotia) in campaigns fought in association with Indian allies against better disciplined opponents similarly reinforced. For both sides the outcome was disappointing. French plans to conquer Carolina and Virginia were not implemented. Through lack of concerted endeavour the assault launched against Canada from New England came to grief, though the privateering base of Port Royal, 'that other Dunkirk', was taken. In the Caribbean, where both France and England had rich sugar colonies, the combatants were less concerned with territorial conquest than with ruining the enemy's industry and thereby forcing up sugar prices to their own advantage. Most islands were sacked at least once – the luckless St Kitts seven times – and plantations were destroyed to the accompaniment of a maritime war which cost England and her colonies dear. Their large volume of shipping, from a diversity of ports and working a diversity of routes, was reluctant to await convoy – which the Navy in any case found difficult to provide – and offered an attractive and ready target for French raiders. Eventually France's defeats in Europe and financial exhaustion, together with political squabbles in England, brought the war to an end, with the English able to consolidate their hold on North America and the West Indies.[29]

Conflict on a geographical scale hitherto unknown reflected and stimulated new strategies. To many of Spain's opponents in the sixteenth and seventeenth centuries it was clear that her strength could be diverted away from them at home – as from the Netherlands – by attacks on her overseas possessions. To ardent Protestants it became axiomatic that American silver was the very essence of Spanish military might, 'with which', according to the founding fathers of the Dutch West India Company, the country's evil rulers 'had so long battered the whole of Christianity'. If this transatlantic flow of bullion could be disrupted and diverted into Protestant hands

Spain would be ruined, the true religion saved and many deserving persons suitably rewarded. As Spanish power rapidly and ominously spread to so much of the known world the maritime strategies of her opponents became bolder and more ambitious. Isolated attacks on treasure ships in home waters gave way to schemes, such as that of the English in 1533, for concerted action against them. Then came daring plans to take the entire fleet in the Atlantic islands, vainly attempted by the French in 1570. Some thought the bullion might be intercepted in the Indies themselves, contemplated by France in 1555 and accomplished by Drake at Nombre de Dios in 1573. Others, notably John Hawkins in England, believed Spain could be cut off from the Indies by a standing naval blockade. There were projects for advance bases in the Atlantic and, as with the abortive French venture in Florida (1562–5) and that of the English in Virginia (1585–6), on the American mainland itself. In the seventeenth century the Dutch set up a company for this very purpose and England debated (1625) a similar move. The Caribbean was successfully tried and it was even urged by some of the backers of the Dutch West India Company that the mines of Peru could be taken by military assault from Brazil. Quite apart from their obvious and perennial appeal to impecunious predators such schemes never lost their allure. In the early 1600s they had the approval of Cardinal Richelieu in France, while there were those in both England and Holland who argued that peace with Spain was bad for business. And throughout the seventeenth and early eighteenth centuries the taking of plate fleet was repeatedly attempted by Dutch and English seamen, sometimes with spectacular success, as by Heyn (1628), Stayner (1656), Rooke (1702) and Wager (1708) and with operations now also directed against the treasure galleons in the Pacific.

Indeed there were some advocates of such strategies, particularly in England, who were convinced that a country's interests would be best served by concentrating on oceanic opportunities and avoiding continental entanglements. John Hawkins argued in 1587–9 that his compatriots should have 'as little to do in foreign countries as may be . . . for that breedeth great charge and no profit at all'.[30] The idea later appealed to Oliver Cromwell and was back in favour in the early 1700s among those opposed to England's massive military involvement in Europe.

The protagonists of such policies included the inescapable lunatic fringe, like the veteran Elizabethan seaman William Monson who contemplated his fellow-countrymen securing access to Saharan Timbuktu with the aid of African allies suitably prepared for the task by attendance at 'free schools' in England. This nonsense apart, however, there were now advocated, and in part implemented, for the first time since Antiquity, grand strategies embracing virtually the whole known world. True, Europe was by no means innocent of plans of a comparable order in the Middle Ages, when it was dreamed (c.1300) that Mamluk Egypt could be ruined by a blockade

of the Red Sea from the Indian Ocean, or that Muslim power in North
Africa could be encircled. But by the end of the sixteenth century English
opinion on how to handle Spain had evolved from simple schemes to seize
treasure ships to a rich variety of plans, worthy of Pitt himself, entailing
widely distributed attacks. Indian and slave revolts were to be provoked to
cripple Spain in America. Bases were to be established in Panama, Cuba or
Hispaniola. A settlement could be planted to command the Straits of
Magellan. The Atlantic was to be closed by a blockading force. The Azores
were to be occupied, a post set up in north-west Africa and Portugal
separated from Spain. Spain herself was to be harried by Anglo-Moroccan
and Anglo-Turkish attacks. She was to be denied Baltic naval stores and
her empire was to be simultaneously assaulted from Asia, the West Indies
and the colonies it was proposed to found in North America. In the early
1600s, while the English were now endeavouring to persuade the 'gentry
of Peru' to resist Spanish tyranny, the Dutch had dreams of overthrowing
Spanish rule in Chile with Indian assistance, of occupying the Straits of
Magellan and, most colourfully, of invading Peru from Brazil with a force
of Amerindians converted to Calvinism and taught to ride the better to
accomplish this godly task. The reality was even more impressive. The
VOC attacked the Iberian empires in Asia while at the same time the West
India Company launched campaigns in the Caribbean, Brazil and West
Africa.

Plans so bold raised many and often insuperable problems for metropolitan governments, as they were long to do. It was difficult, if not
impossible, to control fleets and forces operating far from home. Their
presence all too often exacerbated relations with settlers. There was argument as to where in the colonial world they were to be stationed, how they
were to be kept operational – as tropical diseases and climates thinned their
ranks – and not least how they were to be paid and supplied. Global
strategies, moreover, entailed great hazards and required naval forces on a
scale few European states were willing to risk, even if they could be
mustered. Oceanic warfare thus became largely synonymous with oceanic
privateering (private vessels supposedly operating under state licence), a
form of warfare also particularly attractive to those seeking swift redress
for losses inflicted by an enemy and to the many adventurers, often barely
distinguishable from pirates, hoping for instant riches.

Most of England's attacks on Spain and her colonies in 1585–1604 and
again in 1625–9 were the work of privateers. Zeeland privateering captains
were especially prominent in the Dutch onslaught on the Iberian empires
in the early 1600s, while in Asia there were even attempts to raise privateers
to defend the enfeebled *Estado*. Ships under Spanish colours took some
1500 English vessels in the Atlantic and the Mediterranean during the
Hispano-English war of 1655–60. In the prolonged Anglo-French conflicts
of the late seventeenth and early eighteenth centuries privateers from settle-

ments like Massachusetts, Jamaica and Martinique fought in the waters of
the New World, while France, with most of her resources committed to
land campaigns in Europe, and with her regular navy worsted at sea, loosed
a carefully planned and highly effective 'cruising war' against Anglo-Dutch
commerce. Craft belonging to private owners were reinforced by royal
men-of-war leased to them. Ventures mounted from such ports as Dunkirk,
St Malo, Nantes, Calais and Marseilles – commanding between them all of
England's major trade routes – were conducted on an impressive scale,
enjoyed some spectacular successes and involved many of the most illustrious names in France's maritime history, among them Jean Bart, Forbin
and Duguay-Trouin. The French worked in squadrons usually strong
enough to overwhelm enemy convoy escorts, but fast enough to escape
their heaviest fighting ships. Whalers were pursued off Greenland, Indiamen
ambushed off the Cape, Angola and Brazil were threatened and vessels
were taken anywhere from the Caribbean to home waters, with the English
– who together with their Atlantic colonies retaliated in kind as best they
could – losing over 3000 in 1702–13.

So had the wider world given a new dimension to the rivalries of European states. It had also added substantially to the drain of resources from
the continent and less substantially to its wealth. Europe's culture was
largely unaffected by the legacy of explorers and *conquistadores*, though
individual arts were enriched, a huge amount of new information was
assembled and circulated, and among a learned minority – predisposed in
any case to speculation of this kind – debate was stimulated by such
problems as the interpretation of what had been discovered. But the overwhelming forces for cultural change of every sort were generated within
the continent itself. Empire, whatever the power and glory it might bring,
came to be seen by some as a crippling and punitive burden, but in a
Europe which had accomplished so much, subjection of alien peoples and
experience of alien cultures fostered the conviction, soon widely held and
deeply rooted, that those unlike the inhabitants of the homeland were their
inferiors, and the darker their skins the greater their inferiority. The products of the wider world added variety to European diet and some new
pleasures and luxuries to European living. Transoceanic commerce increased
the value, volume and complexity of the continent's trade – even if it left
the nature of Europe's economy unchanged – and problems of its conduct
and organization stimulated economic thought and encouraged experiment
in commercial technique. The cultural and economic centre of Europe
shifted to the oceanic based powers and the continent was launched on its
way to global hegemony.

NOTES AND REFERENCES

1   Seville, Archivo General de Indias, Indiferente General 1624; Reports of the Royal Commission on Historical Manuscripts. *The Manuscripts of the House of Lords.* New Series, Vol. v, p. 500.
2   See pp. 169, 206.
3   Ambrosini, *Paesi e Mari Ignoti*, is of particular value.
4   First English edition in 1704.
5   See pp. 68, 142.
6   See pp. 24, 93.
7   Agustín de Zárate, *The Discovery and Conquest of Peru*, translated by J. M. Cohen (1968), pp. 23–4.
8   P. J. A. N. Rietbergen, 'Witsen's world: Nicholas Witsen (1641–1717), between the Dutch East India Company and the Republic of Letters', *Itinerario*, IX, 2 (1985), 121ff.
9   Ambrosini, *op.cit.*, p. 188.
10 See G. Groenhuis in *Kleio*, **21**, 7 (1980), 221–5.
11 See pp. 54–5.
12 See p. 95.
13 H. Van der Wee, 'World production and trade in gold, silver and copper in the Low Countries, 1450–1700', in Hermann Kellenbenz (ed.), *Precious Metals in the Age of Expansion* (Stuttgart, 1981).
14 See pp. 132, 135–6.
15 Maurice Aymard (ed.), *Dutch Capitalism and World Capitalism* (Cambridge, 1982), pp. 298–9; McCusker and Menard, *The Economy of British America*, p. 40.
16 See pp. 28, 34, 143–4.
17 Artur Attman, *The Bullion Flow between Europe and the East*, pp. 86, 126–7.
18 See pp. 30, 110, 128, 179.
19 Ashtor, *Levant Trade in the Later Middle Ages*, p. 403.
20 See pp. 101, 105.
21 See pp. 119–20.
22 F. Mauro, *L'Expansion Européenne, 1600–1870* (Paris, 1964), pp. 194–5.
23 See pp. 127, 134–8.
24 See pp. 43–4, 136–7.
25 See pp. 61, 62, 175–6, 178.
26 Treponematosis, a form of venereal syphilis, had, it would seem, long been present in Europe and elsewhere, but perhaps Columbus's men brought back a treponema organism that in European bodies evolved into a deadly venereal disease.
27 See pp. 158–63.
28 See pp. 34, 38–9, 44–5.
29 See pp. 39, 44–5.
30 Scammell, 'The English in the Atlantic Islands c. 1450–1650', 295ff.

Conclusion

At the beginning of the fifteenth century European knowledge of the rest of the world was scant and largely inaccurate, limited to some inkling of the greatness of Cathay and the riches of the East and to a better acquaintance with northern Africa and a handful of islands in the eastern Atlantic. By the early 1700s the Americas had been found, Europeans had penetrated to all the continents of the globe except Antarctica – a good deal of whose outlines they could now accurately map – and Europe itself was in turn occasionally visited by oriental seamen, Amerindian chiefs, Japanese aristocrats and Chinese sages. In the seventeenth century the Dutch Republic and the Iberians fought the world's first global war. Already by then a tentative global economy had been created. This did not mean that industry, agriculture and markets responded world-wide to some common prime-mover – though American silver could aggravate inflation in Europe and the East alike, and though the production of such crops as sugar and tobacco in the Americas was mainly governed by European demand. But it meant that there were now direct trades, handled by European ships, both between Europe and other continents, and between those continents themselves, of which only Africa and Asia were previously in contact. In a world thus for the first time in some measure united the balance of power was beginning to shift from the East, whose peoples – Arabs, Mongols, Turks – had for centuries threatened Europe, to the continent itself, a shift reinforced by the landward expansion of Russia into Asia which commenced in this same era.

The achievements of the first imperial age grew from medieval ambitions and antecedents. But whereas the Norse colonies in Greenland and North America, or the crusading kingdom of the Holy Land foundered, that cycle of expansion set in train by Portugal was eventually to have consequences of a magnitude eclipsing even the wildest fantasies of the panegyrists of its royal house of Aviz. Portuguese primacy in the beginnings of oceanic expansion and discovery, and the continuance of the initially unrewarding and apparently pointless pioneering expeditions, owed much to members of the same ruling dynasty. European enthusiasm for oceans and new lands was guaranteed once it was clear, as was rarely the case earlier, that they gave direct access to, and promised direct control of, riches of a dazzling order – and none more so than those revealed by Columbus and the *conquistadores*. European success was ensured by a relative unity and determination – whatever the factions and squabbles – in the face of victims unable or unwilling to unite against their opponents. There were, of course, many other important factors. Unlike the far better equipped Chinese, Europeans had the incentive to seek things – not least the riches of Asia – their homeland could not provide. There was the determined drive of the Catholic missions to spread their faith. There were the unparalleled openings for wealth and social advancement revealed, and the chance to live according to beliefs unacceptable in the parent state. There was the destruction and demoralization of indigenous populations by disease and the willingness, not to say eagerness, of some native peoples to collaborate with the intruders.

In the East, with little opportunity or incentive to embark on substantial territorial conquests, Europeans intervened, with locally disruptive consequences, in a long-established maritime economy, some considerable part of which they adapted to their benefit. In Central and South America they could, as victors in war, penetrate and settle inland, as opposed to their predominantly coastal presence in Brazil, Africa and North America. In this transatlantic setting they reproduced, in essence, the social structure of their mother countries, commonly enough revealing – whether in the fractious and turbulent existence of Puritan New England, or the way of life of Brazilian and Caribbean slave-owning magnates – the latent aspirations of the cultures from which they sprang. There emerged aristocracies of wealth whose metamorphosis into nobilities was, however, thwarted by metropolitan policies, their own failure to develop as martial castes, and the odium attaching to wealth both too recent and too nearly associated with trade. Despite the growth of a proletariate in the Spanish Indies and the continuing importance of family-worked enterprises in New England, the prosperity of Europeans in the New World was largely, though by no means exclusively, dependent on a slave or semi-slave work-force, white, indigenous or African. Like its counterparts in Asia and South Africa it was treated brutally and callously by peoples who in their homelands talked of peasants as subhuman imbeciles and who could, where labour was unfree, expect serfs to work up to seven days a week for their lords.

In the Iberian Americas buildings as grand as any in Europe were erected and by 1650 Potosí was a city as big as any in Christendom. But despite the demographic catastrophe that overwhelmed the Amerindians, whites remained a minority in the New World, and a tiny one compared with the population of the parent continent. The entire transatlantic settlements probably housed no more than two million of European origins *c.* 1700, when France had twenty million inhabitants and England between five and six million. It was, moreover, a population concentrated in a number of areas of relatively dense settlement, separated from one another by sea, or by great tracts of land either empty or occupied by native peoples.

In Europe, individuals, cities and for a time rulers, were enriched by empire, just as the reputation and powers of monarchs were enhanced. Colonies were brought under some measure of metropolitan control, most notably those belonging to the French and Iberian crowns. Clashes were common between parent states and their supposed dependencies, particularly when, as in Puritan New England, the monarchy attempted to impose its authority on those who had emigrated to avoid this very fate. But it was a friction blunted by distance, by colonial ability to temper metropolitan will and by colonial needs for the military assistance of the mother country. Nor had colonial ruling classes any desire to be divorced from the centres of fashion, reward and preferment or to be cut off from potential support against their fellows, free or slave.

Europeans exploited the opportunities they found in the wider world by every means from downright robbery to commercial policies of the sophistication of those of the Dutch East India Company. Where, in Asia, they encountered slavery, they gladly accepted it. Where labour was lacking they were prepared to employ their compatriots as virtual slaves. Where indigenous forced service was customary they adapted it to their own purposes and extended its scope. And once they could afford, they introduced the use of African slaves to most of the lands they had reached. Crops, whether native (like tobacco) or acclimatized (like sugar) were successfully produced on what, by contemporary standards, was a considerable scale. Portuguese country traders inserted themselves into the indigenous commerce of Asia with a skill and tenacity even their enemies admired. In the Spanish Indies there grew up specialized regional economies in vigorous contact with one another. Merchants waxed rich on comparatively effortless dealings in silver, while colonists in New England, less favoured by nature's munificence, generated wealth in a seaborne commerce of the greatest enterprise.

Thus many Europeans flourished in their new environment, as did some of the local peoples who for one reason or another collaborated with them. But for many the coming of the white man meant the coming of his diseases which wrought such havoc among those previously unexposed to them. The arrival of Europeans also meant the arrival of their religion, spread sometimes by persuasion but often with the aid of more strenuous measures. The work of the Catholic missions – Protestants had little time or organization for such undertakings – reached its peak in the sixteenth century, when it was of a scale and quality unequalled since the days of the conversion of pagan Europe. But then results became more disappointing – with many converts barely Christian even in name – and enthusiasm dwindled. Disenchantment was not defeat, however. Proselytization was never abandoned and now continued directed to a wider geographical area, a process hastened by the desire of the papacy to curb the powers formerly conceded to the

Iberian monarchies, with Italian missions appearing in Africa and those of the French in the Far East, including (1704–6), Tibet.

The attitudes of Europeans to the peoples they encountered, or among whom they settled, ranged – a few notable exceptions apart - across the whole spectrum or prejudice old and new. True, there might be occasional genuine friendships. The almost universal pursuit of local women by white males might also reflect more than sheer necessity. There could be relationships between white masters and non-white slaves, and more often between white masters and their non-white mistresses, based on mutual trust and affection. There was a pragmatic acceptance of the utility of indigenous skills and wealth in the East, and an equally pragmatic acceptance by a white minority of native ways of life in Africa and the Americas. Amerindians in particular aroused the compassion of a few and were the object of the stern paternalism of many more. But the general European view of non-whites was one of unbridled contempt.

Sustained by such convictions, and in search of wealth, land or freedom, Europeans powerfully affected the societies they subjugated or into which they intruded. And never more so than when they introduced blacks into lands where they were previously unknown, spread diseases which decimated or destroyed local populations, disrupted traditional economies and together with their slaves engendered peoples of mixed race. But against the background of the world's rich diversity of powerful states and civilizations, of its millions of inhabitants and of the huge continents and vaster oceans that cover its surface, the coming of the white man was more significant for what it foretold than for what it had effected. The impact of imperial experience on Europe was much the same. Economic thought was sharpened, strategic horizons were widened, European diet was enriched, more novelties and new luxuries became available. But this left little mark on Europe's slowly developing economy and rapidly changing culture. Yet the foundations had been laid, not least in the awakening of a general feeling of superiority to the rest of mankind, for what was to happen in the ensuing centuries of European imperial ambition.

Suggestions for further reading

This makes no claim to be a comprehensive bibliography of the subject. It includes books I have found particularly helpful, many of them up-to-date syntheses with exhaustive bibliographies of works in all the major European languages and guides to the immense periodical literature. This being so I have for the most part only included recent publications in the following paragraphs. A useful brief introduction is provided in Geoffrey Parker (ed.), *The Times. The World an Illustrated History* (1986). H. G. Koenigsberger, *Early Modern Europe, 1500–1789* (1987) gives the best short survey of the European background, outstandingly good on cultural matters. G. V. Scammell, *The World Encompassed. The First European Maritime Empires* c. 800–1650 (1981) relates the classic cycle of European expansion to earlier ventures and compares the way in which different peoples attempted to handle very similar problems. There is a mass of fact illuminated by stimulating hypotheses in Fernand Braudel's magisterial *The Perspective of the World*, English translation by Sîan Reynolds (1984), which is volume III of his *Civilization and Capitalism 15th–18th Century*. There are useful insights in Philip D. Curtin, *Cross-Cultural Trade in World History* (Cambridge, 1984) and an enthusiastic and ebullient evaluation of the migration of crops and livestock in Alfred W. Crosby, *Ecological Imperialism. The Biological Expansion of Europe 900–1900* (Cambridge, 1986).

There are many excellent surveys of the imperial and colonial activities of individual European states. Time has done little to dim the importance of C. R. Boxer's *The Dutch Seaborne Empire, 1600–1800* (1965) and *The Portuguese Seaborne Empire, 1415–1825* (1969). K. R. Andrews gives a perceptive and highly readable account of *Trade, Plunder and Settlement. Maritime Enterprise and the Genesis of the British Empire 1480–1630* (Cambridge, 1984). There is a good general survey by T. O. Lloyd, *The British Empire 1558–1983* (Oxford, 1984). Lyle N. McAlister, *Spain and Portugal in the New World 1492–1700* (Minneapolis, 1984) is comprehensive and judicious. Holden Furber, *Rival Empires of Trade in the Orient, 1600–1800* (Oxford, 1976) summarizes a lifetime of scholarship by one of the most eminent authorities in the field.

Roland Oliver and Anthony Atmore, *The African Middle Ages,*

1400–1800 (Cambridge, 1981) provide an admirable introduction to the continent's difficult history. Of the superabundance of regional studies I have made extensive use of David Birmingham, *Central Africa to 1870. Zambezia, Zaïre and the South Atlantic* (Cambridge, 1981) and H. H. K. Bhila, *Trade and Politics in a Shona Kingdom. The Manyika and their Portuguese and African Neighbours 1575–1902* (1982). Richard Elphick and Hermann Giliomee (eds), *The Shaping of South African Society, 1652–1820* (Cape Town, 1979) bring together important material not otherwise easily accessible. Robert Ross, *Cape of Torments. Slavery and Resistance in South Africa* (1983) is a penetrating and moving analysis, though chiefly concerned with the period after 1700.

A comprehensive guide to current views on the history of Latin America is available in the two volumes on *Colonial Latin America*, editor Leslie Bethell (Cambridge, 1984), which form part of *The Cambridge History of Latin America*. James Lockhart and Stuart B. Schwartz, *Early Latin America. A History of Colonial Spanish America and Brazil* (Cambridge, 1983) is wide-ranging, thoughtful and revisionist.

On the early history of the indigenous peoples of the Iberian Americas and their fortunes under European rule George A. Collier, Renato I Rosaldo and John D. Wirth (eds), *The Inca and Aztec States, 1400–1800. Anthropology and History* (New York, 1982) is a collection of important and often pioneering essays by various hands. J. V. Murra, *The Economic Organization of the Inka State* (Connecticut, 1980), in G. Dalton (ed.), *Research in Economic Anthropology* is a fundamental reassessment, making extensive and original use of early Spanish sources. David G. Sweet and Gary B. Nash (eds), *Struggle and Survival in Colonial America* (California, 1981) contains graphic and sympathetic studies of (for the most part) the underdogs, adding flesh to bare bones. E. Van den Boogaart (ed.), in collaboration with H. R. Hoetnik and P. J. P. Whitehead, *Johan Maurits van Nassau-Siegen 1604–1679. A Humanist Prince in Europe and Brazil* (The Hague, 1979) has an abundance of new material on indigenous Brazil and on European reactions to the land and its peoples. Colin M. MacLachlan and Jaime E. Rodriguez O, *The Forging of the Cosmic Race, A Reinterpretation of Colonial Mexico* (California, 1980) is lively and comprehensive, but a rather too flattering account of the origins and development of the country. Among the multitude of other local, regional and area studies are two splendid books by Nicholas P. Cushner SJ, *Spain in the Philippines from Conquest to Revolution* (Quezon City, 1971) and *Farm and Factory: The Jesuits and the Development of Agrarian Capitalism in Colonial Quito 1600–1767* (Albany, 1982). A rich collection of documentary evidence is analysed with a refreshing independence in William L. Sherman, *Forced Native Labor in Sixteenth-Century Central America* (Lincoln, Nebraska, 1979). A difficult and little-known region is illuminated by Miles L. Wortman. *Government and Society in Central America, 1680–1840* (New

York, 1982). Two model investigations of closely defined areas are John K. Chance, *Race and Class in Colonial Oaxaca* (Stanford, 1978) and Steve J. Stern, *Peru's Indian Peoples and the Challenge of the Spanish Conquest: Huamanga to 1640* (Wisconsin, 1982)

Current North American concern for the fate of the continent's indigenous peoples has brought a huge flow of scholarly investigations of their past. Bruce G. Trigger, *The Huron, Farmers of the North* (New York, 1978) is lucid and detailed, though stronger on anthropology than history. Robert F. Berkhofer Jnr. *The White Man's Indian* (New York, 1978) is stimulating as well as entertaining. An eloquent and persuasive exponent of the new-style ethnohistory (not to everybody's liking) is James Axtell, *The European and the Indian, Essays in the Ethnohistory of Colonial North America* (Oxford, 1981). Perceptive and immensely readable are Francis Jennings, *The Invasion of America, Indians, Colonialism and the Cant of Conquest* (Chapel Hill, 1975) and Gary B. Nash, *Red, White and Black: The Peoples of Early America* (New Jersey, 2nd edn, 1982). Patricia Dillon Woods details *French-Indian Relations on the Southern Frontier 1699–1762* (Ann Arbor, 1980). Neal Salisbury, *Manitou and Providence; Indians, Europeans and the Making of New England, 1500–1643* (Oxford, 1982) describes the forceful policies of the Puritan immigrants, who receive a less sympathetic treatment than is usual.

John J. McCusker and Russell R. Menard *The Economy of British America, 1607–1789* (Chapel Hill, 1985) is a vigorous and comprehensive synthesis of current work. There is much of value on all aspects of the evolution of European North America in Peter Marshall and Glyndwr Williams (eds.), *The British Atlantic Empire before the American Revolution* (1980). Ian K. Steele, *The English Atlantic 1675–1740. An Exploration of Communication and Community* (Oxford, 1986) is equally informative on trade, shipping and colonial culture.

There is an abundance of fact and many trenchant, if not always persuasive opinions, in Stephen Saunders Webb, *The Governor-General; The English Army and the Definition of the Empire, 1569–1681* (Chapel Hill, 1979). Richard R. Johnson, *Adjustment to Empire. The New England Colonies 1675–1715* (Leicester, 1981) handles a difficult theme dexterously and sensibly. J. M. Sosin, *English America and the Revolution of 1688* (Lincoln, Nebraska, 1982) gives a detailed and critical analysis of colonial politics and the political relations between England and the colonies. John G. Reid, *Acadia, Maine and New Scotland. Marginal Colonies in the Seventeenth Century* (Toronto, 1981) is a useful study of failure and Aubrey C. Land, *Colonial Maryland, A History* (New York, 1981) an exemplary piece of regional history.

The best introduction to the affairs of the Caribbean in these centuries is Kenneth R. Andrews, *The Spanish Caribbean: Trade and Plunder 1530–1630* (1978). Particularly illuminating of the patterns of life of the various social strata is Richard S. Dunn, *Sugar and Slaves. The Rise of the Planter Class in the English West Indies 1624–1713* (1973). There is much information, significant as well as curious in C. A. Banbuck, *Histoire Politique, Économique et Sociale de la Martinique sous l'Ancien Règime 1635–1789* (Martinique, 1972). Paul Butel, *Les Caraïbes au Temps des Flibustiers* (Paris, 1982) is a fine survey of colonization, trade and piracy, to which should be added the various works on slavery and servitude mentioned below. Nicholas Canny and Anthony Pagden (eds), *Colonial Identity in the Atlantic World 1500–1800* (Princeton, 1987) contains, in addition to the theme with which it is primarily concerned, important discussions of the social structure, intellectual life and political assumptions of Europe's western colonies, French, English and Iberian.

James A. Rawley. *The Transatlantic Slave Trade. A History* (New York, 1981) is a careful and dispassionate treatment of a subject which has generated, hardly surprisingly, a huge and often emotive literature. There are valuable reflections on the theme in David W. Galenson, *Traders, Planters and Slaves. Market Behavior in early English America* (Cambridge, 1986), though the mathematical economic analysis may not be to all tastes. There are devastating accounts of slave diseases and conditions in Richard B. Sheridan, *Doctors and Slaves. A Medical and Demographic History of Slavery in the British West Indies, 1680–1834* (Cambridge, 1985). On white indentured servitude there is a model study by David W. Galenson, *White Servitude in Colonial America. An Economic Analysis* (Cambridge, 1981).

Mark Elvin, *The Pattern of the Chinese Past* (1973) is a concise and elegant introduction to a vast theme. *The Cambridge Economic History of India* Vol. 1 c.1200–c.1750, ed. Tapan Raychaudhuri and Irfan Habib (Cambridge, 1982) is a magisterial survey, now amplified and reinforced by K. N. Chaudhuri, *Trade and Civilisation in the Indian Ocean. An Economic History from the Rise of Islam to 1750* (Cambridge, 1985); Sinnappah Arasaratnam, *Merchants, Companies and Commerce on the Coromandel Coast 1650–1740* (Delhi, 1986) and Ashin Das Gupta and M. N. Pearson (eds), *India and the Indian Ocean, 1500–1800* (Calcutta, 1987). M. C. Ricklefs, *A History of Modern Indonesia c.1300 to the Present* (1981) is a brief but valuable survey.

An extensive and often repetitive body of learning has been generated by the examination of the significance in European culture of experience of the wider world. Anthony Pagden, *The Fall of Natural Man. The American Indian and the Origins of Comparative Ethnology* (2nd edn, Cambridge, 1987) is a close and immensely erudite investigation of the intellectual attitudes of a small group of sixteenth-century Spanish thinkers. The subject is pursued further in E. van den Boogaart, H. R. Hoetnik and P. J. P. Whitehead (eds), *Johan Maurits van Nassau-Siegen* and in the especially valuable study of Federica Ambrosini, *Paesi e Mari Ignoti: America e Colonialismo Europeo nella Cultura Veneziana (secoli XVI-XVII)* (Venice,

1982). A wider perspective is suggested in G. V. Scammell, *The World Encompassed* and there is an excellent discussion in P. J. Marshall and Glyndwr Williams, *The Great Map of Mankind: British Perceptions of the World in the Age of Enlightenment* (1982) which covers a great deal more than its title indicates.

Colonial warfare, naval developments and British, French and Dutch privateering are all treated with great skill and learning in J. S. Bromley, *Corsairs and Navies 1660–1760* (1987).

Some more detailed studies are cited in the notes to individual sections.

Index

joint-stock finance, 101, 236
junk (ship), 11, 87, 206

Khoikhoi, 48, 79–80, 202, 206–7
Kilwa, 14
King Philip's War, 42

Labrador, 24
Lake Malawi, 48
lançados, 46, 66, 207
La Rochelle, 113, 244
las Casas, Bartolomé de, 26, 60, 219–20
latitude, astronomical determination of, 55, 225
leather, 36
Leeward Islands, 44, 162, 229, 243
lepers, 52, 65
Levant, the, 51, 78, 231, 243
Libya, 56
Lima, 26, 32, 77, 143, 172, 176–7, 182, 185, 197
Linschoten, Jan Huyghen van, *Itinerary* of,
Lisbon, 20, 28, 37, 58, 96, 151, 153, 226–7, 229, 232, 244
Liverpool, 244
livestock, 36, 234
llama, 76
Loango, 47
logwood, 127
London, 166, 178, 228, 235, 244; blacks in, 214; bullion in, 232–3; merchants of, 20, 64, 228, 234, 246; and the sugar industry, 131, 230
longitude, determination of, 55, 225
Louis XIV, King of France, 2, 34, 67, 158, 186, 214, 247
Louisiana, 39, 93, 113, 172, 248
Luanda, 47, 169
Luther, Martin, 3, 217
Lyons, 222

Macao, 14, 61, 67–8, 79, 100, 108, 135, 170, 203, 209
Macassar, 67, 100
mace, 12
mackerel, 132
Madagascar, 17, 108, 136
Madeira, 11–12, 46, 58, 66, 117, 231; wines of, 46, 203
Madras: the English at, 19, 82, 85, 106–7, 169; Hindu aldermen of, 167
Madrid, 229, 244
Magellan, Ferdinand, 16, 49
Magellan, Straits of, 24, 250
Maine, 38, 41, 161
maize, 5–6, 27, 74, 88, 130, 204, 229
Malabar, 21, 81, 87, 98
Malacca, 13–15, 79, 84, 152, 170; Dutch conquest of, 21; Portugal and, 14, 67,

86, 97, 99–100, 201, 204–5; Spain and, 16, 67
malaria, 75, 176, 182
Mali, 4–5, 202
Malindi, 13, 15, 201
Mamluks, 4, 15, 201, 249
Manáus, 36
Mandeville, Sir John, 57–8
Manila, 14, 17, 21, 28, 31, 99, 103, 144, 149, 170, 173, 203, 242; Chinese in, 180; galleons of, 67, 135
Manuel I, King of Portugal, 58, 88
Manyika, 48
Maracaibo, 29
Maranhão, 36, 75, 109, 153, 196
Marathas, 16, 87
Mardijkers, 156–7
Marlborough, Duke of, 243, 247
marriage: emigration and, 61; and imperial stability, 143; indigenous converts and, 191, 197; interracial, 122, 170–1, 183, 186–8, 191
Marseilles, 251
Martinique, 39, 65, 158; African slaves in, 116, 184–5; Jews of, 178; miscegenation in, 186; poverty in, 177; privateers from, 251; revolts in, 116; shipowning in, 135
Maryland, 41, 43, 66, 161, 163–4; economy and society of, 171, 177; servitude and slavery in, 114–16
Mascat, 15–16, 82, 100
Massachusetts, 41–2, 61, 66, 161, 163–4; and Amerindians, 112, 193; defences of, 243; economy of, 126, 136; and England, 93, 162–3; fisheries of, 132; government of, 42, 162; immigration to, 61–2; landed magnates in, 179; political life of, 43, 161, 165–6; privateeers from, 251; theological dispute in, 66
Massachusetts Bay Company, 236
Matamba, 202
Mataram, 86, 94
Mauritania, 13, 119
Maya Indians, 5, 75
measles, 182
Mecca, 5, 71, 106
Mediterranean Sea, 8, 12, 18, 22, 58, 243
Mendes Pinto, Fernão, *Travels* of, 214
Mercator, Gerhard, 216
merchants: European, 64, 177–8; colonial, 99–100, 177–8; Indian, 9, 84–5, 99; Jewish, 99; Parsee, 99
mercury, 31, 134
Mesopotamia, 14
mestiços, 152, 156, 189
mestizas, 176, 190
mestizos, 66–7, 124, 126, 134, 157, 173, 187, 189–90, 199